Representing Calcu

Representing Calcutta: Modernity, nationalism, and the colonial uncanny is a spatial history of the colonial city, and addresses the question of modernity that haunts our perception of Calcutta. The book responds to two inter-related concerns about the city. First is the image of Calcutta as the worst case scenario of a Third World city – the proverbial "city of dreadful nights." Second is the changing nature of the city's public spaces – the demise of certain forms of urban sociality that has been mourned in recent literature as the passing of Bengali modernity. By examining architecture, city plans, paintings, literature, and official reports through the lens of postcolonial, feminist, and spatial theory, the book explores the conditions of colonialism and anti-colonial nationalism that produced the city as a modern artifact. At the center of this exploration resides the problem of "representing" the city, representation understood as description and narration, as well as political representation. In doing so Chattopadhyay questions the very idea of colonial cities as creations of the colonizers, and the model of colonial cities as dual cities, split in black and white areas, in favor of a more complicated view of the topography.

Swati Chattopadhyay is an associate professor in the Department of History of Art and Architecture at the University of California, Santa Barbara. She is an architect and architectural historian, and specializes in modern architecture, the cultural landscape of British colonialism, and post-colonial theory.

Asia's Transformations

Edited by Mark Selden
Binghamton and Cornell Universities, USA

The books in this series explore the political, social, economic and cultural consequences of Asia's transformations in the twentieth and twenty-first centuries. The series emphasizes the tumultuous interplay of local, national, regional and global forces as Asia bids to become the hub of the world economy. While focusing on the contemporary, it also looks back to analyze the antecedents of Asia's contested rise. This series comprises several strands:

Asia's Transformations aims to address the needs of students and teachers, and the titles will be published in hardback and paperback. Titles include:

Asia's Great Cities

Each volume aims to capture the heartbeat of the contemporary city from multiple perspectives emblematic of the authors' own deep familiarity with the distinctive faces of the city, its history, society, culture, politics and economics, and its evolving position in national, regional and global frameworks. While most volumes emphasize urban developments since the Second World War, some pay close attention to the legacy of the longue durée in shaping the contemporary. Thematic and comparative volumes address such themes as urbanization, economic and financial linkages, architecture and space, wealth and power, gendered relationships, planning and anarchy, and ethnographies in national and regional perspective. Titles include:

Representing Calcutta
Modernity, nationalism, and the colonial uncanny
Swati Chattopadhyay

Hong Kong
Global city
Stephen Chiu and Tai-Lok Lui

Shanghai
Global city
Jeff Wasserstrom

Singapore
Carl Trocki

Beijing in the Modern World
David Strand and Madeline Yue Dong

Bangkok
Place, practice and representation
Marc Askew

Asia.com is a series which focuses on the ways in which new information and communication technologies are influencing politics, society and culture in Asia. Titles include:

The Internet in Indonesia's New Democracy
David T. Hill and Krishna Sen

Asia.com
Asia encounters the Internet
Edited by K. C. Ho, Randolph Kluver and Kenneth C. C. Yang

Japanese Cybercultures
Edited by Mark McLelland and Nanette Gottlieb

Literature and Society is a series that seeks to demonstrate the ways in which Asian literature is influenced by the politics, society and culture in which it is produced. Titles include:

Chinese Women Writers and the Feminist Imagination (1905–1945)
Haiping Yan

The Body in Postwar Japanese Fiction
Edited by Douglas N. Slaymaker

Representing Calcutta

Modernity, nationalism, and the colonial uncanny

Swati Chattopadhyay

Routledge
Taylor & Francis Group

LONDON AND NEW YORK

First published 2006 by Routledge
2 Park Square, Milton Park, Abingdon, Oxon OX14 4RN

Simultaneously published in the USA and Canada
by Routledge
270 Madison Ave, New York, NY 10016

Routledge is an imprint of the Taylor & Francis Group

Typeset in Baskerville by
Florence Production Ltd, Stoodleigh, Devon
Printed and bound in Great Britain by
TJ International Ltd, Padstow, Cornwall

British Library Cataloguing in Publication Data
A catalogue record for this book is available from the
British Library

Library of Congress Cataloging in Publication Data
A catalog record for this book has been requested

ISBN 0–415–39216–0

Printed and bound in Great Britain by
Antony Rowe Ltd, Eastbourne

To my mother
And to the memory of my father

Contents

Illustrations

Acknowledgments

Fred Matter, Denis Doxtater, and the late Ken Clark gave me an affectionate and encouraging environment at the University of Arizona, Tucson. At Berkeley, Dell Upton, Nezar AlSayyad, and Tom Metcalf shepherded this project through the dissertation stage, and have remained a source of support. Many of the early ideas in this work were shaped in discussions with Burton Benedict, Russ Ellis, Jamie Horwitz, Amos Rapoport, and the late James Deetz. Dianne Harris, Zeynep Kezer, and Bill Littman of the "Dissertators/Dessert-eaters Anonymous Club" shared their views on doing architectural history and much more in our long, pleasurable conversations. Greg Castillo, Preeti Chopra, Renee Chow, Kathy Edwards, Will Glover, Marta Gutman, Hosagrahar Jyoti, Elaine Jackson-Retondo, Kathleen James-Chakraborty, Neema Kudva, Faranak Miraftab, Suki Mwendwa, Arijit Sen, Jessica Sewell, Vaishali Vagh, and Sibel Zandi-Sayek gave me intellectual sustenance and friendship. Christie and Dave McCarthy, Lois Ito Koch, and Tracy Farbstein made me feel at home in Berkeley. Arijit Sen and Jessica Sewell carefully read through an early draft. Kumkum Bhavnani, Alison Fraunhar, Roger Friedland, Mary Hancock, Nuha Khoury, Rainer Mack, Sylvester Ogbechie, Bhaskar Sarkar, and Moira West have provided me with a conversational community at Santa Barbara. Gautam Bhadra, Partha Chatterjee, Keya Dasgupta, Anjan Ghosh, Alison Fraunhar, Nuha Khoury, Arun Nag, and Dell Upton read through parts or whole of the final draft and provided valuable criticism. I have greatly benefited from conversations with them, even if I have not been able to incorporate all their suggestions. Tony King and an anonymous reader provided useful comments. Rick Asher and Zeynep Çelik have supported this project for a long time. My grateful thanks to all of them.

This project has been funded by a Junior Fellowship of the American Institute of Indian Studies, a National Science Foundation Dissertation Improvement Grant, a J. Paul Getty Post-doctoral Fellowship, and research grants from the University of California at Berkeley, and the University of California at Santa Barbara. For their help and courtesy, I wish to thank the staff of the National Archives in New Delhi; the British Museum Library, the Oriental and India Office Collection, the British Library, and the Victoria and Albert Museum in London; and the following institutions in Calcutta – now Kolkata – the National Library, the West Bengal State Archives, the Federation Hall Society, the Center for Studies in Social Sciences, the Bangiya Sahitya Parishad Library, the Calcutta High Court, the Calcutta Municipal Corporation, Mackintosh Burn Pvt. Ltd, Martin Burn Pvt. Ltd, and the Rabindra Bharati Society. I am grateful to the staff of the Environmental Design Library at the University of California at Berkeley, and the Arts Library at the University of California at Santa Barbara, for looking up unusual requests.

The architectural documentation that went into this project would not have been possible without the assistance of Aditi Sen of the American Institute of Indian Studies, Calcutta; Ashim Barman, Debashish Som, and Anindya Karforma of the Calcutta Municipal Corporation; Sadhan Kumar Neogi, Ashim Datta, Nilmani Dhar, Gora Chakrabarty, Saibal Gupta, and Subhash Bose of Mackintosh Burn Pvt. Ltd; K. N. Fatehpuria and Aditi Mitra of Martin Burn Pvt. Ltd; and Prabhash Kumar and Santosh Ghosh of the Center for Built Environment in Calcutta. I am especially grateful to Prabhash Kumar for taking the time to introduce me to many of the residents and neighborhoods in the northern part of the city in the early stages of this project. My heartfelt thanks to the Deb family of Sobhabazaar, especially to Prabal Deb, Malobika Deb, and Sunitendra Deb; to Aurobindo Dasgupta and members of the Dasgupta family; and to Pritin Roy and members of the Roy family of Jorasanko Rajbati, for their hospitality, for sharing family histories, and providing permission to document their houses. Ratnabali Chatterjee, Prabir Mitra, P. T. Nair, Somendra Chandra Nandi, R. Sivakumar, Sovon Som, Shyamasree and Sumitendranath Tagore, and the late Siddhartha Ghosh have provided me with the benefit of conversation. My thanks to Debashish Basu, Gautam Bhadra, Shivashish Bose, Keya Dasgupta, Indranath Majumdar, Prabir Mukhopadhyay, and Arun Nag for helping me access difficult-to-find sources.

My friends in Calcutta – Suparna Bhattacharya, Sharmila Ghosal, Arup Ghosh, Chaitali Ghosh, Ratna Ghosh, Subrata Ghosh, and Sabyasachi Mitra – helped me measure-draw many of the buildings for this project, and kept me in good humor. Boni Banerjee provided hours of patient notetaking. It is a privilege to have such friends.

I would like to express my appreciation for a number of extremely capable research assistants at Santa Barbara – Jill Voss, Alexa Schloh, Krista Clarke, and Mahlon Chute – for keeping me organized.

I have been very fortunate to have Mark Selden as the series editor. His support, fine reading and suggestions on the manuscript, and infectious enthusiasm have made a meaningful difference to the final product. I thank Craig Fowlie, Stephanie Rogers, Laura Sacha, and Zöe Botterill at Routledge for editorial stewardship.

Chapter 2 is a long version of the article, "Blurring Boundaries: The Limits of White Town," originally published in the *Journal of the Society of Architectural Historians* 59: 2, (June 2000). I am grateful to the Society of

Architectural Historians for providing permission to reproduce the content of that article here. Dr. Oliver Impey, Keya Dasgupta, the Oriental and India Office Collection, British Library (special thanks to Jennifer Howes), the National Gallery, and the Victoria and Albert Museum in London, the Victoria Memorial Hall, the Rabindra Bharati Society in Calcutta, and the Peabody Essex Museum, Salem, Massachusetts have kindly provided permission to reproduce images from their collections. Many of the architectural drawings in this book are based on drawings in the collection of Mackintosh Burn Pvt. Ltd, and the Calcutta Municipal Corporation. I am grateful to them for copies of the original drawings.

Last but not least, I thank my family in India and the US for enduring the prolonged gestation of this book. Jerry White has accompanied me in this project from the very beginning – traveling with me, helping me with measure-drawings, and reading just about every draft of the chapters. His critical feedback, intellectual support, and love in everyday life hold these pages together. Shaoni has given me pleasurable distraction and a new sense of perspective. Dipankar Chattopadhyay helped me navigate the civil engineering world in Calcutta; Pinaki Das sought out and mailed me books long-distance whenever I requested; Basudha Chattopadhyay and Jayasri Basu have accommodated me in New Delhi and Calcutta as only siblings would. My biggest debt is to my mother, Pusparenu Chattopadhyay, for providing me a home in Calcutta, for stories, good food, love, views, and willingness to listen. I could never have embarked on this project without her help. It is my great regret that neither my father, nor my father-in-law lived to see this book.

Santa Barbara, July 12, 2004

Illustration credits

Unless otherwise mentioned all drawings and photographs are by the author.

Figure 1.1   Reproduced by permission of the National Gallery, London
Figures 1.2, 1.6–1.11, 1.13–1.21, 2.5, 2.23, 2.25, 2.26, 3.5   Reproduced by permission of the British Library
Figure 1.3   Reproduced by permission of the Victoria Memorial Hall, Calcutta
Figure 1.12   Private Collection
Figure 2.3   Courtesy of Keya Dasgupta
Figure 2.23   Courtesy of Dr. Oliver Impey
Figure 2.24   Courtesy of R. H. N. Dashwood
Figure 3.6   Courtesy of Prakash Bhavan, Calcutta
Figure 3.7   Courtesy of Rabindra Bharati Society, Calcutta
Figure 4.11   Reproduced by permission of the Peabody Essex Museum, Salem, Massachusetts
Figures 5.1–5.4   Reproduced by permission of the Victoria and Albert Museum, London

Introduction
The city in historical imagination

> Yet throughout this time (of decolonization) Rabat retained its – there is no other word for it – charm. . . . Nor . . . did Rabat become a seething, noisy and poverty-stricken "Calcutta."
>
> Janet Abu-Lughod[1]

Representing modernity and nationalism

Fourteen years ago, when I first began to study the contemporary image of Calcutta and the cultural and political processes that have contributed to it, I noticed a remarkable consistency in the representations of Calcutta.[2] Novelists and historians, travelers and administrators all seemed to agree that with its poor location on a swamp, the city was doomed from the very beginning. Contemporary authors discussing the entrenched poverty of the city cite 200 years of writing and painting as evidence to remind us that it has always been so. Plagued by poverty, politics, disease, and disorder, British attempts to build a city went awry.

What makes Calcutta shocking to visitors is that the abject poverty is undisguised – revealed in the disintegrating brickwork of stained walls, in the exposed life of street and slum dwellers, in the stench of rotting garbage on the sidewalks. Witnessing Calcutta's "primitive" problems, one anthropologist writing recently agreed with Rudyard Kipling that "the city is above pretense."[3] In other words, the poverty is so debilitating that there is no possibility that it might be left behind ghetto walls, the privacy of homes, or modern institutions such as prisons, poor houses, or disguised through a patina of modernity. After all, the project of becoming modern has been less about eradicating poverty than about classifying it, and designating for it well bounded spaces so that it might not contaminate the dignity of representable civic life. In the case of Calcutta, the poverty spills in the streets wiping out the distinctions between public and private spaces, colonizing your vision, and infecting the air you breathe. The dirt and stench confirm the existence of lives and spaces that apparently have escaped the scopic regime of modernity. Is this what early nineteenth-century European cities were like before they had been thoroughly refashioned into modern metropolises? Or is Calcutta a vision of "Third World" futures and their unfulfilled modernity? Calcutta, defined by lacks and absences, in its impossibility of becoming modern, then, most would agree, is what a city ought not to be, and definitely not what a modern city is like. A by-word for under-development, Calcutta has also become a convenient case for demonstrating that some Third World ex-colonial cities avoided its unsightly fate.

As the epigram to this introduction indicates, in her fine study of the Moroccan dual city of Rabat-Salé, Janet Abu-Lughod noted that despite the urban apartheid of apportioning modern amenities unequally between the native city and the new French city, and notwithstanding the economic problems faced by Rabat in the aftermath of decolonization, Rabat did not become "Calcutta." The comment was made almost in passing (there is no other reference to Calcutta in the book), but the comparison was based on the strength of the popularly shared image of twentieth-century Calcutta. Here, "Calcutta," set in quotation marks, stands for the worst possibility of urbanism, obviating any sustained comparison between the two ex-colonial capital cities. Her remark made in the context of discussing Rabat's "dependent urbanization," however, had a hint of unease and an important suggestion embedded in it. Her reference to Calcutta was about the *idea* of Calcutta, a perception of its physical attributes rather than the attributes themselves, and Rabat, she suggested, perceptually performed differently, more positively. Here, a historical narrative based on population and trade statistics, urbanization rate, and problems of developmental planning, capitulated to a different way of describing the city – a description that aimed to convey the "charm" of Rabat. Conscious of resonating an "Orientalist" way of looking at picturesque native cities, Abu-Lughod clarified that "there is no other word for it," before proceeding to assure the reader that the

> [P]hysical site remained outrageously beautiful. . . . The failure of the port, while disastrous from an economic point of view, cleared the waterway for small boats, swimmers, and fishermen, and the lack of heavy industries kept the air clean. An agreeable climate graced the city . . . The city remained remarkably clean, even in the worst *bidonvilles*, and the people retained their quiet dignity and discipline, making passage through even the most crowded *suqs* a pleasant experience.[4]

The language of this description is essentially modernist even as it underscores the aesthetic pleasure of underdevelopment. In moving us between the beautiful natural landscape of Rabat and the pleasant experience of the *suqs* and its disciplined populace, Abu-Lughod did not suggest that we abandon evaluating the city through a modernist lens, but provided us with the aesthetic counterpart of that vision. The quiet, orderly city (even when economic and social modernization remained unfulfilled) is worth our approbation and admiration. In Rabat the socio-economic deferment of a colonial modernity does not betray itself as visual–perceptual contradiction. Economic problems and poverty in such a city can be analyzed/gazed upon by the researcher/tourist safely, close-up, without any sense of revulsion.

The obvious lesson here for students of colonial urbanism is that not all colonial cities suffered Calcutta's fate, because colonial modernization did not operate everywhere similarly, and the absence of modernist apartheid à la Rabat (namely in terms of physical planning) had an even more adverse impact on Calcutta. What troubles Calcutta, then, we are led to infer, is not its un-modernity, but its modernity gone astray. Calcutta, subjected to modernization efforts by the British, and failing to live up to not just the economic promise but the architectural and perceptual promise as well, proved that something was different, even exceptional.

In this book I want to take up the question of modernity that haunts our perception of Calcutta and prevents us from exploring the historical process by which Calcutta came so readily to serve as a metaphor of urban disaster. I begin addressing this question by studying the British attitudes that produced the dominant image of a problem-ridden city in the nineteenth century, and then proceed to explore other ways of envisioning the city, emphasizing modes of Bengali spatial imagination, specifically the Bengali understanding of "public space." The crafting of a nationalist identity was central to modern Bengali spatial imagination and was animated by the conflictual response to city life as Bengali residents struggled to accommodate the colonial city within their idea of the nation.

My alternate descriptions do not attempt to displace one set of representations with another, more "favorable" set. Nor am I attempting to represent the city itself. Rather, my goal is to problematize the idea of representing the city – both colonialist and nationalist – and explore the structures of power and knowledge that underlie different representations of the city. Through these descriptions I am suggesting a model of modernity that cannot simply be described as the unfulfilled promise of a Western (and therefore assumed to be universal) idea, or one possible configuration of that universal idea. It was contingent on the "translations" inherent to the process of colonial encounter and formed in accommodation and conflict with Western ideals of individuality, progress, and public and private life. The city was rendered uncanny in both colonialist and nationalist imagination by repressing and resurrecting traces of an unreasoning modernity. I will have opportunities to elaborate on the idea of unreasoning modernity in Chapters 3 and 4. Suffice here to say that unreason does not refer to a lack of reason, but to the realm of memory, myth, and those aspects of experience that are not easily amenable to discourse or representation.

The modernity I am speaking of was particular to nineteenth- and early twentieth-century Calcutta, and was no less or more provincial, and as a process no more or less contradictory, than that of the urbanism of nineteenth-century Paris or Vienna, which are routinely suggested as birthplaces of nineteenth-century modernity. The "authenticity" and "originality" of the modernity of Paris and Vienna are understood, for the most part, to be the result of internal cultural and political dynamics.[5] Such cultural insularity is not granted to colonial cities of the last two centuries. An economic and cultural process of European domination is presumed to have provided these far away locales with the material for development, as well as the scaffolding of ideas necessary for a modern culture to come alive. For example, in Marshall Berman's imaginative mapping of the genealogy of modernism, there is a particular time and place allocated to Paris, New York, and Brasilia – each city is seen to come to its best/worst at a particular creative moment along a linear chain of progress/regress.[6] Everywhere except in Europe and the United States (of course by the logic of such history the thread of progress has to find its way to the twentieth-century US) the effects of modernism are distorted; modern cultural forms appear as caricatures or as fantasy – "shrill, uncouth, and inchoate."[7] Berman argued that the "modernism of underdevelopment," exemplified by eighteenth- and nineteenth-century Petersburg, is caused by the failure to institute economic, social, and technological modernization through a fully formed capitalist system.[8] And yet he claimed that modernity "cuts across all boundaries of geography and ethnicity, class and nationality, of religion and ideology" to "unite all mankind."[9] As Paul Gilroy has appropriately pointed out, Berman's Eurocentric position and desire for generalization did not allow him to conceptualize historically specific experiences of black–white, male–female, lord–bondsman within such a framework.[10] Difference in Berman's united world could only manifest itself through aberrations in the Third World, where First World experiences are produced vicariously, demonstrating in their incompleteness the originality of the European idea/product that came first.

Despite Berman's deeply flawed model of modernism, I find two ideas that form the very precept of his work to be useful for thinking through Calcutta's modernity. Of these, first is the idea of contradiction, and second is the desire to note the life on the street and the material culture of modern cities. Berman noted:

> To be modern is to live a life of paradox and contradiction . . . it is to be both revolutionary and conservative: alive to new possibilities for experience and adventure, frightened by the nihilistic depths to which so many modern adventures lead . . . to be fully modern is to be anti-modern.[11]

If we are to take this paradox to heart then the idea of modern life as a sudden break with the past loses potency and allows us to question the sources of ambivalence that resonate through the writing, performance, and politics of the people who find themselves to be modern. It also helps us stray from the misinformed idea of a European modernity slapped onto Calcutta by the colonizers to view modernity as a set of negotiations between individuals, communities, and the state, between ideational space and physical space, in which norms of private and public lives are worked out, and through which modern subjects are produced. While this dynamic of modernity breaks down the insularity of black/white, male/female, lord/bondsman dyads, it anxiously constructs these "differences" on a new topos of the nation. The emergence of such a topos in nineteenth-century Calcutta forms the basis of the present work.

The first half of the twentieth century witnessed a number of important spatial and cultural changes in Calcutta that led to the formation of a significant and identifiable body of Bengali literature, paintings, plays, films, as well as literary and art criticism that dealt with various notions of nationalism and modern Bengali identity and claimed the city as its own. Such a cultural space was in turn made possible by the proliferation of a number of public places for getting together – theaters, cinemas, cafés, and parks – which, from the 1920s, often borrowed European Modernist and Art Deco architectural forms to announce their novelty. In the southern part of the city the penchant for formal attributes of Art Deco gave entire blocks a formal coherence that would continue until the early 1960s. In other words, many of the spatial transformations between 1920 and 1960 can be read as Modern because of their expressive relationship (even when selective in its application) to Western Modernist aesthetics. What I study in this book, however, are mainly the events, symptoms, and spatial configurations that led up to the creation of such a cultural space. An understanding of the nineteenth- and early twentieth-century structural transformation is necessary to locate the later events in appropriate registers.

Long before the explicitly "political" domain became an arena of nationalist performance, Bengali literary imagination and spatial practice began the painstaking and paradoxical task of negotiating the dominance of the colonial city.[12] The paradox resided in the refusal to explicitly acknowledge one's creative location in the city. In nineteenth-century Bengali literary imagination, the city is rarely privileged as the space of creativity and "originality." Predominantly portrayed as an imposition, a constraint, the city seems to be made bearable by imagining a blissful countryside that performs as the ideal home. Such idyllic imaginings of the home-as-village life was a peculiarly urban discourse.[13] If such nationalist longings elicited a refusal to accept the dictates of Western modernity, such "anti-modernity" was itself a process of becoming modern. One of the tasks I take up in this book is to demonstrate how the city was shaped and used as a site of modern literary and artistic intervention even when this was often not explicitly acknowledged in the literature. City imagination and the casting of a moral topography were not absent in nineteenth-century Bengali discourse; it was figured differently than one would expect in

Paris or London. What distinguishes Bengali modernity and the nationalist construction of identity is the emplacement of the self in the troubled
relation between city and country.

I have been highly selective in choosing themes that help us in understanding the "structure of attitudes and references" that produced this
colonial modernity – *not* a colonizer's modernity – leaving out much that
can be considered in an urban history.[14] I use Edward Said's phrase,
however, in a broader scope than Said perhaps intended. The structure I
study was not unified or singular. Instead of a stable scaffolding, the structure of attitudes – both British and Bengali – consisted of a changing matrix
within which relations were reconfigured and realigned over time. The
scope of imperialism was not all-encompassing, and it would be inaccurate
to imagine that every aspect of urban experience can be understood by
relating it to the structure of imperial attitudes; but colonial contestation
did produce images of Calcutta that would have a significant impact on
pre- and post-independence cultural discourse. What I call Calcutta's
modernity was a product of both the modern forms and techniques of
governance instituted by colonial authority, as well as the nationalist –
literary, artistic, spatial – ambitions cultivated by the Bengali community.

I emphasize the particular and contingent in this study not as a plea
for either "cultural relativism" or a simple-minded "cultural difference."
Rather, I wish to move up-front the specific questions we may ask about
the physical landscape of Calcutta through a careful investigation of the
historical record, as a mode of addressing the issue of representation that
is at the center of my query. What is significant here are not simply
the diverse representations of Calcutta, but what Walter Mignolo calls,
"the politics of enacting and constructing loci of enunciation."[15] In other
words, I am trying to construct the links between the ideational space of
image, imagination, and production of subjectivity with the physical space
of urban form, claim, and territoriality, as a response to the specific problems of Calcutta's urban historiography. And yet I expect this work to
extend beyond a case study. Many of the issues I explore in this book
remain relevant for understanding the experience of modernity in most
parts of the world. Calcutta's historiography enables me to challenge the
assumptions of Western modernist discourse, in fact, by allowing me
positions that would not be available to someone studying "Western"
cities, positions that were made possible by Bengali literary and spatial
imagination.

Received histories

The key problem of Calcutta's urban literature is the uncritical acceptance of British sources and the resultant re-circulation of the colonizers'
ideas about the Indian landscape. Twentieth-century urban historians
of Calcutta have relied heavily upon European sources, particularly on

eighteenth- and nineteenth-century accounts of British administrators.[16] Not surprisingly, these accounts emphasized the writer's own interests and purposes of trade, mapping, surveying, revenue, and judicial administration, and only those issues of the Indian political and cultural landscape that were directly relevant to these interests, or those interpretations that suited such enterprise, found their way into these accounts. Despite three decades of inquiry into "Orientalism" by scholars across the globe, Calcutta's urban historians have been particularly resistant to such critiques and methods of analysis. In most of the pertinent urban literature, the categories of black/white, colonizer/colonized remain uncontested and, more problematically, the colonial sources are not interrogated for their motivation and point of view. This encourages the reproduction of Kipling-esque images, leading to the conclusion that the "city of palaces" was doomed to fail because of inherent problems that had little to do with the colonial construction of horrific images. Although Kipling's biases do not go unrecognized, historians attempt to see his work merely as an exaggeration of reality, corroborating his subjective representations with objective documents, such as government reports.[17] The nineteenth-century documents, particularly government reports on Calcutta are read in narrowly functional terms, detached from the larger imperial context, implying that if a particular representation is not explicitly related to any political agenda it is faithful in its correspondence to reality and unaffected by political aims. Such readings, more importantly, fail to distinguish between application of apparently similar ideas in the metropolitan and colonial contexts.[18] For example, such a reading presumes that the methods of sanitation adopted in London and Calcutta were directed towards the same goals, and that nineteenth-century sanitation reports can be read through the same lens of medical thinking. In contrast, the planning measures undertaken in Calcutta can only be understood when placed in the crossfire of differing opinions harbored by different groups inhabiting the city.

In a nutshell, the body of knowledge we have inherited and dub the "urban history of Calcutta" is an imperial history. It is a narrative of heroic British efforts to build a city in the marshes of Bengal, in the face of native hostility, amid festering jungles and tropical heat. The traditional treatment of the city's beginning is symptomatic of the manner in which its later historiography has taken shape. Two claims about this early history – that the first act in Calcutta's history was the founding by Job Charnock, and that British finance built Calcutta – sustained the myth of a British city, a notion called on time and again in the last decades of the nineteenth century to attest to the sole right of British residents to administer the city. In relating the story of Charnock, colonial historians disregarded the existence of settlement in the area and its importance for trade prior to British arrival.

In the seventeenth century, the British were one of several groups of foreign merchants given the right to trade in Bengal. They shared the mercantile fortunes with Dutch, French, Portuguese, Armenian, and Indian merchants. Bengal, as one of the most productive regions of the Mughal empire, boasted a strong agricultural base, a high skill level among artisans, and a financial and communications network supported by a fairly stable administrative structure, making it an important site of international trade. By the mid-seventeenth century, the volume of traffic in money had reached sufficient proportions to integrate the markets in the long distance commodities, such as silk. By the mid-eighteenth century Bengal had regional specializations of cash crops, textiles, and grain surpluses. There were large wholesale markets such as Bhagwangola and Narayanganj, numerous local markets called *ganjs*, and small-scale transactions in village *haats* (weekly markets). Dhaka and Murshidabad were established centers of Mughal royalty, and Krishnanagar, Burdwan, and Rajshahi were dominated by powerful *zamindars* (landlords).[19] The directors of the European companies stationed company servants in their factories to facilitate trade. In Bengal these factories stood on the west bank of the Hooghly, and by the mid-eighteenth century, these factory sites had been expanded into towns. In the lower reaches of the Hooghly, textile manufacturers inhabited populous villages, near where Charnock decided to restart the Company's enterprise after two failed attempts. The site was on the east side of the river, relatively free of inundation, and more secure from attack by competing powers, as potential enemies had to risk the breadth of the river to claim Calcutta.[20]

The nature of commerce in seventeenth- and eighteenth-century Bengal meant that Indian merchants were deeply involved with Europeans. Both the Dutch and British East India Companies, as well as private merchants trading under the Companies' protection, borrowed heavily from Indian bankers. Just as the European settlements provided large markets advantageous to Indian artisans and merchants, the Europeans needed the assistance of the native mercantile class to succeed.[21]

The idea that British capital built Calcutta is based on a peculiarly British colonial notion of what constituted the city itself. Calcutta's historians spun the story by choosing discrete events such as the founding act of Job Charnock, the Battle of Plassey in 1757 when the East India Company's forces defeated the Nawab of Bengal, Siraj-ud-daulah, and the granting of the *Diwani* to the East India Company in 1765, seamlessly tying these events together in a narrative of continuous development.[22]

The story rarely revealed contradictions and disruptions integral to the historical experience, and in so doing left out anything that did not fit the chaos-leads-to-order narrative. Furthermore, historians emphasized political events, with little spatial understanding of the city's history. The spatial extensions and appropriations seemed to happen naturally as a result of political events, relieving narrators of the necessity of delving into the complicated transactions involved in claiming territory. This standard urban history cited buildings and monuments such as the new Court House,

Government House, and Holwell's Black Hole memorial as facts corroborating the weight of political events. A few selected buildings became markers of an imperial domain and an imperial history, illustrating the inevitable growth of Calcutta as a British city. When the urban experience was described, such description presumed a European point of view.

Any serious attention to the historical evidence of late seventeenth- and eighteenth-century Bengal cannot fail to illustrate the precarious situation of the British East India Company during this time. Far from being able to predict future British control, the uncertainty of British enterprise was evident to British authorities, the same authorities whose deeds would be constructed into a story of uninterrupted success. The contributors to this story were historians as well as administrators who were involved in the conflicts, writing after British control had been somewhat consolidated.[23] Not only were the complex choices and decisions made by the British and Indians simplified into a British winning strategy, the enormous contribution and resistance of the native population during the entire duration of colonial rule is effectively subdued as part of the city's history. We are led to believe that although initially tainted by greedy mercantilism, the British made Calcutta a city worth living in. Consequently, it was no wonder the city slipped into a morass of "third-worldness" when the colonial yoke was lifted. The tale of the "black" and "white" towns encapsulates the nature and power of the simplistic and ritualistic metaphors used to convey this image.

Historians tell us that during the eighteenth century a "white" town developed in and around Fort William, characterized by sparsely distributed neo-classical and Georgian buildings and surrounded by a "black" native town of densely packed houses and shanties organized along caste and occupational lines.[24] Such an understanding of the center and the periphery indicates the vantage points from which these historians represented Calcutta. The story was told, and is recounted even today, from the point of view of the European standing within the safe confines of the white town.

An unqualified assumption of Calcutta as a British creation begets narratives in which the colonizers are the only active agents in the scene, relegating the colonized population to the role of passive inhabitants or, at best, resistors of domination. This issue is not at all peculiar to Calcutta, but common to the study of colonial cities. Two attitudes towards urban studies lead to such assumptions: an inordinate emphasis in architectural and planning scholarship on first acts and initial designs;[25] and the inclination to examine colonial cities as caught in the web of global capitalism, with the native culture seen as merely "impacted" by capitalist domination and Western intellectual and artistic ideas.[26] In the case of Calcutta, this notion derived support from the assumption of classical Orientalism that claimed that authentic India resided in the villages, in the country's cultural antiquity and defective theocracy.

Thinking spatially

By emphasizing the duality of the "black" and "white" towns one misses the idea that the critical aspects of colonial cities lie not in the clarity of this duality, but in the tension of blurring boundaries between the two. These settlements were far from autonomous black and white landscapes. In fact, the economic, political, and social conditions of colonial culture penetrated the insularity of both the black and white towns, although at different levels and to different degrees. In addition, *both* landscapes, not merely the "black" town, were fractured along lines of occupation, class, and ethnicity. Considering that the history of Calcutta was written from the point of view of a European residing in the white town, in this work I attempt to understand the impact of such a point of view and to excavate other vantage points from which the city was experienced.

Although Indian historians have partially relied on Bengali literature for depicting Bengali life in the nineteenth century, only a few have taken the first steps in presenting competing images. The most compelling analyses of the culture of nineteenth- and early twentieth-century Calcutta have been produced by scholars working in different areas of cultural history. With few exceptions, however, these works depend on literary analysis and lack a spatial dimension. Here I am making an important distinction between literary space of locution and physical space of inhabitation and production, and suggesting the need to recognize the nature of connection between these spaces. Analyses that only interrogate rhetorical positions without attending to the connection between rhetoric and the everyday practice and experience of space produce distorted pictures of historical and cultural processes. Cities and landscapes cannot be effectively studied simply as texts; they must be examined in terms of cultural *practice.*[27] W. J. T. Mitchell has argued for a critical reading of landscapes to recognize their role as instruments of power; but I am suggesting that we need to do more than "read" landscapes and cities as systems of representation. This is not to deny the power of representation; in fact I argue throughout this work in favor of its immense capacity to frame visions and prospects of the city. Nevertheless, the city is not limited to the sum of its representations. It is also the space where individuals and groups challenge, ignore, depart from, or accommodate the rhetorical and ideational level. By grounding the rhetorical in the material experiences of a city we can appreciate the extent and limit of the power of representation. The complex multi-layered landscape of colonial Calcutta demands a multi-centered approach. Instead of a fixed-point perspective from historian to artifact we need to adopt a mobile perspective that describes the heterogeneous topography of power. Such a mobile perspective would help us recognize the historicity and ideological underpinnings of the knowledge we have inherited about the city, and the stories we perpetuate.

Written and visual depictions produced by visitors and the city's inhabitants, official documents, and the extant urban fabric are the building blocks of this story. In the process of conducting research I have documented 215 buildings of which I present 15 as part of my analysis. Accounts of monuments and prominent buildings as self-contained facts are not the primary concern of this investigation. Rather, their embeddedness in a larger urban fabric, including mundane traces of social attitudes and ideology, is more significant. These ideological traces may be found in commentaries on household servants, in the prescriptions of appropriate decor for Bengali households, as well as in discussions of sanitation in municipal documents. The diversity of sources provides the opportunity for generating affiliations across texts and between text and space. In piecing these disparate sources together I have, however, been careful not to collapse them to form one continuous historical fabric. Many were fleeting descriptions of the city; to pin down these ephemeral impressions with other substantial evidence would add depth not otherwise there. Instead of treating them as several pieces of a jigsaw puzzle, I treat these sources as if they were several layers of experience separated by context. Collating these would not generate a composite picture, rather it would highlight the difference between individual portrayals of a city experienced from varying levels of intimacy and contested from divergent perspectives.

In order to unravel the complexity that contributed to the production of the nineteenth-century image and experience of Calcutta, I have adopted three inter-related analytic strategies. The first strategy is to analyze the social roles and vantages of the writers, journalists, and administrators. This approach is intended to explicate the positions from which British administrators, visitors, and the city's Indian population created their dialogue and the issues and images that they responded to. For example, in the case of European authors, I try to see how their individual narratives of Calcutta incorporated larger issues of imperialism. The versatility of the structure of imperialism resided in its flexibility and in its ability to accommodate a wide range of interests and points of view, even conflicting in many regards, within certain predefined parameters of the white man's burden. Men and women from diverse professions and pursuits found their own piece of ground in the diverse, large, and changing scope of imperialism. Thus, all of the evidence may not show up as a singularly defined imperial strategy, and far from being monolithic, imperial ideology contained the vagaries of particularity and expressive context. Calcutta was portrayed much more negatively than Bombay, although the planning problems of the two cities were similar in many respects. This suggests that attitudes, in fact, had little to do with physical realities, or that they cannot be interpreted as a uniform reading of the "native." Calcutta's negative impression had much to do with the Bengalis, who were considered disagreeable and politically dangerous, while the Parsis in Bombay were seen as allies of British interests.[28]

The second strategy addresses the narrative itself – exploring the rhetorical devices used to communicate cultural attributes and socio-political distinctions. For example, in colonial documents, whether they are government reports or travelogues, representations of the city and its people are fashioned in a characteristic colonial rhetoric. These hinge on essentializations that help to naturalize socio-spatial relations. The rhetoric of morality and benevolence was used to justify British intervention in the lives and spaces of Indians, and the notion of "historical advantages" deployed to explain the progress of imperialism as an inevitable process by which less developed regions submit to the sovereignty of developed nations. By the logic of this argument the "native" city needed to submit to the demands of progress to become a disciplined modern city along European lines. The basic tenet of this argument has been repeated numerous times since the nineteenth century. Since there is nothing natural about any of these processes, they required emphasis as essential features of history – a history in the making – a tale in which the historian simply stated facts, relating an action already performed, thus obscuring the process by which selected elements were organized to lead the narrative along a prefigured path. As Paul Carter explains in a different context, the purpose of such a narrative is not to understand or interpret, but to legitimate.[29]

If the rhetoric of natural superiority, Christian benevolence, and scientific objectivity was effectively used by the British to mask the economic and political gains of the colonization process and to exclude certain "problematic" groups from the normalizing discourse, such masking can be recognized where it reveals itself through slippage. Slippage occurs at moments when the discussion touches the internal contradictions of the colonial project. During the entire duration of colonial rule, the vastly outnumbered British residents could only provisionally trust the Indian population. To transform such a besieged position to one of command and control required "the arrogance" based on myths of racial, intellectual, and moral superiority. On the other side of this arrogance, however, resided a deep paranoia that was only thinly veiled by derogatory remarks about natives.[30] Beneath the rhetoric of unquestionable British superiority quivered unspoken fears and unspeakable desires.

The naturalization of socio-spatial relations took a different turn in Bengali imagination. Some of the most important literary figures of the nineteenth-century city, Bankimchandra Chattopadhyay, Rameshchandra Dutta, and Amritalal Basu felt obliged to respond to the British idea of Calcutta and Bengal by cultivating a different logic of spatial mastery. For Bankim, the naturalization of one's spatial claim would be performed by an appeal to history and the availability of a modern historical consciousness that could trace the moral contours of Sanskrit epic literature in the contemporary landscape of Bengal. For the first time a Bengali "landscape" was inaugurated, where the village community became naturalized as the locus of national regeneration, not as an autonomous unit, but by being set in a dialectical relation to the colonial city. The city was accommodated in nationalist imagination by contemplating mobility – by fashioning passages between the city and country, between the sacred and the profane.

In studying pictorial representations of Calcutta I am confronted with two distinct sets of images – one British and the other Bengali. The former demonstrates an attempt to legitimize British claim to the city through a characteristic pattern of visual framing, pictorial arrangement, and choice of generic elements to construct a scene. But the meaning of the pictorial elements and the rationale for selective inclusions and exclusions can only be understood in relation to contemporary written commentaries. These paintings and prints did not exist in a social vacuum; their authors relied on the prevailing rhetoric and symbolic repertoire used to represent colonial India. The striking aspect of nineteenth-century Bengali paintings – popular prints – is that the city is not presented as a landscape. The city, even when it acts as a site of narration, does not appear as a continuous ground or backdrop, as in British paintings. It is produced in fragments by the gestures of the figures, as well as the artifacts that surround them – chairs, lamps, musical instruments, smoking pipes – that work metonymically to construct the city as a space of intrigue.

My attempt here is neither to dismiss the literary writings, paintings, and government reports as inaccurate depictions nor to accept them at face value. Rather, I try to recognize the signs, myths, and metaphors consistently used to represent Calcutta and to analyze the reasons why they were used, the issues and positions underlying these external representations, the ways in which the colonized and the colonizer were inscribed in these myths, and the authors and audience of this myth-making process.

The third strategy explicitly seeks out the relations between the image-making process and the experience and transformation of the landscape, while keeping in mind the interwoven nature of verbal, visual, and built landscapes, including the sense of sound, smell, and tactility.[31] Many aspects of the landscape were shaped by alliances and fractures among different groups inhabiting the city, none of which grasped a clear understanding of, nor an unequivocal claim to, the entire city. With the evidence gleaned from visual depictions of Calcutta, urban plans, and written evidence from journals, novels, and newspapers, I aim to understand how distinct forms of urban space were produced out of the contradictions of colonialism and the deep ambivalence about being modern. The speeches and writings of Bengali nationalists were marked by a hegemonic desire to overcome the fractures along lines of caste, class, as well as religion. The conceptual apparatus mobilized for such wished-for hegemony was drawn from the idea of an "extended family" of the *palli* and *para* (neighborhood), and imaginatively inserted within a framework of Western public discourse. Municipal debates became platforms for contesting the British right to represent the city. At the same time the municipal documents were not innocuous commentaries that merely provide us with pictures of a distant colonial conflict; these were blueprints for the physical transformation of the city's urban fabric.

Public space

The emergence of a Bengali middle class with political ambition was, itself, a complicated process of migration, and economic and socio-spatial restructuring that occurred in the second half of the nineteenth century. It resulted in the acute awareness among middle-class men and women that they were living in a "modern" age; they were becoming "modern." Three aspects of this Bengali modernity are important for understanding the nineteenth-century city: the establishment of modern institutions and the generation of public spaces and public spheres, the concept of domesticity that was worked out in relation to the above, and a new-found aesthetics that permeated the discussion and production of public, private, and personal spaces.

While the colonial state introduced certain modern institutions that were directly linked to the process of capitalist expansion – the army, the colonial bureaucracy, the judicial system, and the university, many of the modern cultural institutions were created, managed, and patronized by Bengalis. As Partha Chatterjee has noted, the Bengali elite, keen to develop Bengali as a modern language, generated "an entire institutional network of printing presses, publishing houses, newspapers, magazines, and literary societies ... outside the purview of the state and European missionaries."[32] Two public arenas where the importance of modern Bengali found legitimation were the urban Bengali public theater and the "national" campaign for establishing primary and secondary schools in every part of the province, both under Bengali leadership. But it was also the arenas designated as belonging to the state and/or the colonizer by the stamp of colonial authority – the municipal office, the courthouse, the colleges supported (at least partially) by the colonial government, and the Town Hall – that came to be appropriated by the elite Bengalis in the process of claiming these public spaces as their own. Of these, the municipal office and the Town Hall did not strictly belong to the state, as neither did the colleges, but the peculiarity of colonial civil life in nineteenth-century Calcutta meant that these public venues were seen as products of colonial authority and therefore dominated by Anglo-Indian residents. Consequently, these became sites of contestation between the colonial state and the Bengali middle class. I use the term "arena" here to describe these public spaces to emphasize their role as theatrical stages for shaping public identities. These "players" were extremely self-conscious about performing to an audience and about their own role in shaping public attitude. But who constituted the public?

It should not surprise anyone that this public was understood to be male. Educated Bengali men, mostly from the upper castes of Hindu society, who made their presence known in the Town Hall and municipal committee meetings, often worked against the structure of a colonial state that bestowed subjecthood without citizenship. For the majority of British residents of the city the only public that mattered was the European community. If British residents in Calcutta, as elsewhere in India, formed a civil society, it was, however, not based on a strict separation from the colonial state. Rather than bracketing status and professional affiliation as was expected in the *ideal* bourgeois public sphere in western Europe,[33] one's social status, measured in terms of location in the hierarchy of colonial service, was the dominant premise for structuring social relations in this domain. The physical spaces constructed to house these civil gatherings – clubs, *gymkhanas*, literary societies, were explicitly segregated to privilege middle- to upper-class whites; Indians and lower-class Europeans could only perform the role of servants, and even European women were only allowed provisionally. Consequently, Bengali men in addition to appropriating the Town Hall and committee rooms of the Calcutta Municipality, created alternate spaces for getting together – a range of voluntary associations, literary and theater groups – mostly for their own benefit, that did not exclude European men, as much as they wished to exclude the lower classes and women. Rajat Sanyal notes that between 1815 and 1876 at least 200 formal voluntary associations were created and played an important role in structuring political relations of the Bengali community.[34] These voluntary associations, with their individual membership, constitution, recording of minutes, and publication of proceedings, were modern forms and differed from the *dal* (group), the predominant formal mode of getting together among Bengali men in the first half of the nineteenth century. The *dal* was, itself, a product of the urban culture of Calcutta, and many of the *dals* indeed had formal memberships and newsletters, but their concern was the internal socio-religious dynamics of the immediate community determined largely, but not exclusively, by kin and country relations.

The men who formed the public in such a public sphere presumed to speak for the rest of the Bengali community – Hindus and, often, Muslims as well. That is, they claimed themselves to be representative of the public per se. If the public sphere in nineteenth-century Calcutta was necessarily fractured, harboring different notions of the legitimate and qualified public, and incorporated a range of public spaces – exclusive on different bases and degrees, there was certainly no simple co-relation between public spheres and public spaces, that is the physical spaces for people to get together. It is this complex relationship between public *sphere* and public *space* that has been insufficiently theorized.

Several scholars writing in the last decade have made a point to articulate the difference between the Bengali nineteenth-century ideas of publicness and the Habermasian notion of the ideal bourgeois public sphere. Both Partha Chatterjee and Dipesh Chakrabarty have persuasively argued that Bengali conceptions of privacy and publicness (and their effects on the experience of modernity) were not grounded in the notion of a bourgeois self, but necessarily incorporated the structure of the Bengali extended family and larger community that performed as the site of nationalist imaginings. According to Chatterjee, "anti-colonial nationalism creates its own domain of sovereignty within colonial society well before it begins the political battle with imperial power."[35] The originality of Bengali nationalism was to divide the world into two domains – the material and the spiritual.[36] He argues that it is in the domain of the inner/spiritual that nationalism launched its most powerful project of defining a modern nationalist consciousness. It quickly becomes clear that this spiritual/material distinction did not take up the contours of not only the bourgeois private/public split after the Western European model, but it was also not coterminous with the distinction between private and public *space*.

Habermas's explanation of the relation between public sphere and public space is not without its own problems. His notion of the public sphere is rooted in a strict distinction between state and society along the public/private divide, and based on two key ideas: that the modern bourgeois self originated within domestic space, and that the process of rational-critical debate gave birth to the "authentic" public. The "authentic" bourgeois public sphere was located in the private realm constituted of private people. The latter was again divided between the public sphere in the political realm that arose from the world of letters, and civil society in the narrow sense of commodity exchange and social labor within which was embedded the conjugal family and its intimate sphere. The generation of a successful bourgeois public sphere was contingent on the development of a domestic sphere – a privateness that was oriented towards the public. In other words, it was in the physical space of the bourgeois family, that included both the intimate sphere of the family (the site for developing a sense of bourgeois individuality) and the social sphere of the salon (the site where these individuals came to discuss politics and social norms, and argue about arts and literature) that the bourgeoisie learned to become modern selves. While Habermas noted the critical overlap of public and private spheres within domestic space – "the line between private and public sphere extended right through the home"[37] – his understanding of the role of space, and also his articulation of the boundaries of public space and its relation to the bourgeois public sphere are less convincing. Discussing twentieth-century social-structural transformation of the bourgeois public sphere, he suggested that the

> [H]ollowing out of the family's intimate sphere received its architectural expression in the layout of cities. The closedness of the private home, clearly indicated to the outside by front yard and fence and

made possible on the inside by the individualized and manifold struc-turing of rooms, is no longer the norm today, just as conversely, its openness to the social intercourse of a public sphere was endangered by the disappearance of the salon and of rooms for the reception of visitors in general.[38]

Even without getting into the accuracy of this sweeping architectural generalization, it is fair to say that he recognized the importance of phys-ical space to the birth and life of the public sphere (although his main concern was with the world of letters – letter writing, journals, and the free press), but his static understanding and limited attention to space warps his theory of the public sphere. Also, in reading space as a fixed representation of social order, one tends to underestimate the dynamic possibilities of spatial interaction – that people necessarily do not follow a spatial script, but improvise and challenge socio-spatial norms. Production of space is a continuous *process*.

Habermas's misreading of space is also linked to his static conception of the production of the self. According to Habermas, individuals with their bourgeois identity fully formed (in the intimate sphere) emerged in the public spaces to take part in rational-critical debate. He did not entertain the idea that, perhaps, these identities were not acquired before the fact – perhaps they were acquired in the process of relating to others within the socio-spatial dynamics of these public spaces. What drew people to these public spaces was the conviviality of public eating and drinking. Other "irra-tional" modes of conversing and arguing were a part of the culture of public spaces with their propensity to be raucous and even carnivalesque. Kevin Hetherington has correctly argued that a bourgeois identity that placed a strong emphasis on rational-critical debate was formed in the process of engaging and negating its raucous Other.[39] This ambivalent space of the Other was not only present at the birth of the public sphere, but performed as a critical element in its formation. What allowed the public spaces of the taverns and coffee houses (and here Habermas privileges only some interior public spaces) to be "cutting edge" was not their literary insularity, but their situatedness in a larger network of outdoor public spaces. As Nancy Fraser has noted, one of the primary uses of the public sphere – and I will add, public space – was the creation of social identity – the conviviality and debate was a mode of social performance.[40]

One of the more attractive propositions of Habermas's theory of the public sphere is the idea that the freedom of the bourgeois individual was mediated by access to public space. And, as he recognized, this free-dom was only limited to the propertied men of the world of letters. Published 30 years ago, before feminist and civil rights movements inserted the problematics of race and gender into the question of the public, Habermas's theorization did not adequately incorporate women and people of color, except, along with the working class, as a source of degeneration of the public sphere.[41] A critical examination of the history of eighteenth- and nineteenth-century European (as well as American) cities demonstrates the practical difficulties of supporting a philosophy of equal access given the race, class, and gender segregations and hierarchies that dominated the use of public space. Access to public space was severely restricted in planned and unplanned ways. Blacks, women, and the poor found their way into privileged public spaces, but with an awareness of the limits placed on their presence, and the difficulties and violence that invited perceived intrusion.[42] The problem of being "at home" in public for those left out of the imagination of the bourgeois public sphere has been a long drawn out process that continues into the present century.

The point I wish to emphasize is that access to public sphere and access to public space are related in discrepant ways for different people. It was possible for women to be part of the public sphere of letters, even when they were denied physical access to public space. Consequently for them social performance in modernity took on a different *spatial* strategy that only enabled to expose the myth of a single homogeneous public sphere.

The maleness (as well as class bias) of the discourse on publicness, nationalism, and modernity also finds a troubled presence in some excellent works on Bengali cultural history published in the last decade. Partha Chatterjee's *The Nation and its Fragments* and Dipesh Chakrabarty's *Provincializing Europe* demonstrate the authors' concern with the subjectivity accorded to women in Bengali nationalist culture. Their imaginative reading of the literary archive of Bengal immensely facilitates discussion of the "women's question" in the city's history.[43] In this work I extend their argument to the analysis of spatial relations to locate the role of the middle class in the production of urban space, other than the negative citation for Calcutta's urban problem. And in doing so I wish to suggest that we must note both the dangers of conflating the ideas of public sphere and public space and, correspondingly, the blurring of differences between private sphere and private/domestic space. In addition we must pay attention to the slipperiness between these conceptual categories as they are worked out in practice. However, in foregrounding a spatial understanding I am also reconsidering their reading of the location of women in the patriarchy of Bengali modernity.

In discussing nineteenth-century Bengali identity I take up two important issues: Chatterjee's argument that the "real history of the women's question" is to be found at home, and Chakrabarty's interest in examining the "creative" side of Bengali patriarchy.[44] If we proceed with the assumption that the domestic realm was the principal site of women's struggle, we risk the normalization of women's exclusion from public space. Could it be possible to write a history of nationalism and the Bengali public sphere by beginning with women in public space? What would that mean in terms of Chakrabarty's suggestion that we *not* confine ourselves to a "reactive" model of Bengali modernist discourse which assumes that

Bengali men had to construct a compensatory sovereign space at home because colonial authority left them no such space in public?

While excavating the "creative" side and site of this patriarchy, Chakrabarty has gone to great lengths to remind his readers that he does not "defend" what he seeks to "understand."[45] This insistence that his effort not be construed as supportive of women's oppression is based on the nagging recognition that such life worlds were grossly inequitable. Summarizing his discussion of *adda* as a modern male social gathering Chakrabarty suggests that the proliferating public spaces of colleges, coffee-houses, and bookshops in the early twentieth century helped to "extend, deepen, and modernize" the homosocial space of the *adda*, while allow-ing limited participation of women in it, "leaving the heterosexual men involved in literary endeavor with a sense of . . . 'phallic solitude'."[46]

I do not wish to get into the intricacies of his argument about *adda* here but it would be sufficient to say for the moment that Chakrabarty notes that he has taken Henri Lefebvre's phrase "phallic solitude" out of context and applied it with more irony than Lefebvre intended. Lefebvre invoked "phallic solitude" in the context of the advent of abstract modernist space in Europe and America in the early decades of the twentieth century – in art, architecture, urban planning – its virulent masculinity and violence (particularly towards women).[47] Without implying that the abstraction of space and the attendant pulverization of the body took an identical turn in Bengali modernity, I would like to suggest that we re-insert the idea that lurks behind the reign of "phallic solitude," and learn to read the violence inherent in such a metaphor in the spaces of Bengali modernity. A plural history of nationalism and modernity would require rethinking home as the real site of women's struggles. While we point out the immense significance of the desire to reconstitute the Bengali home as a site of nationalist struggle, we also need to consider the location of this idea of "home" within the imagination of public space. The dyads of inside-outside, spiritual–material, female–male themselves have to be pried open, even when these are entrenched in the rhetoric of Bengali nationalism. One of the ways I propose to unglue these binaries is by examining how communal memory was created and mobilized in the process of aug-menting a public sphere. This is related to the problem with which I began this introduction: how we remember and characterize Calcutta as a modern cultural space and physical artifact.

Plan of this book

It is a commonplace in Indian urban history that the decision to move the capital of British India from Calcutta to New Delhi in 1911 was a result of the political climate of Calcutta. The 1905 partition of Bengal is considered the "cause," and the Raj in New Delhi the "effect." Calcutta became difficult, and since the permanence of British India depended on the maintenance of administrative control, the choice of a new capital, far from political insurgence, recreating the grandeur of the late Mughal empire, was a logical choice. But my reading of Calcutta's history suggests that the political problem did not begin in the early twentieth century, nor even in the late nineteenth century. Rather, we must trace the story to an earlier era when Calcutta became populated by a growing Bengali middle class. But any discussion of Calcutta's urban plan and sanitation must consider the early nineteenth-century recommendations to improve the "health" of Calcutta. While it is difficult to put a finger on any firm beginning date in the first three decades of the nineteenth century, the Lottery Committee Report of 1817 is as convenient a beginning date as any. When it comes to graphic evidence, the date must go further back, as it is difficult to understand the work of early nineteenth-century artists who painted Calcutta without discussing the work of Thomas and William Daniell, who first came to Calcutta in 1786 and saw a city in which the British had established a considerable settlement. Therefore, my investigation begins roughly in the third quarter of the eighteenth century and concludes in the first quarter of the twentieth century. These dates, however, are tenuous historical mileposts, and only make sense in a vortex of happenings before and after – the dates are only guides for an equally tenuous memory. I have made no attempt to chronologically chart all urban transformations since the eighteenth century. The chapters, instead, are thematically based, and attempt to address some of the conceptual and methodological questions I have raised. Needless to say, this treatment is far from exhaustive.

1   The colonial uncanny

For the British, the palimpsest side of Calcutta is its real fascination, however melancholy: the pleasure of ruins. Here once there were riches unimaginable. Here were high fashions, pomp – and some kind of orderliness. Calcutta is quite different from other British inventions like Simla, Ooty or even New Delhi. Ideally you should arrive at Calcutta having read your William Hickey, Macaulay's letters, Emily Eden or Fanny Parks, and be familiar with the aquatints or watercolours by the Daniells or Charles D'Oyly.

Raleigh Trevelyan, 1982

Eye of a European

In 1827 Elisabeth Campbell traveled to Calcutta with her husband, and in her journal she recorded the eagerness with which she embarked upon a new life.[1] When the ship entered the Bay of Bengal and the coast came into view, she was charmed by the novelty of the countryside:

> With what eager interests you watch the first objects which denote your arrival on new soil, from the moment you see the Island of Sagur like a small cloud in the horizon! then you perceive it thick with mighty forests, you distinguish separate trees, and their luxuriant foliage is so refreshing to your eyes. Presently you are surrounded with bamboo boats filled with natives, presenting fish and fruit all equally strange. My gratification was quite childish; I sat hour after hour in the stern window, with a beautiful child belonging to a soldier . . . and my delight was not less than his in watching the dandies cooking their curry![2]

Elizabeth Campbell, later to become Mrs. Fenton, conveyed in great detail the variety of trees that grew on the riverbanks and their manifold uses. She noted how the banks of the river, although quite flat, contained "luxuriant vegetation and the variety of tropical productions" all of which interested "the eye of a European."[3]

Mrs. Fenton used the second person to bestow on the reader her own privileged vantage, immersed in the exotic. After all, seeing was believing.[4]

She related her gratification in observing this land with an infant delighted by the most mundane surroundings. Every aspect was novel. As a nineteenth-century British woman visiting a strange land, she was careful to restrain her vantage within prescribed roles of femininity. In sharing her position with a child, she relied on a familiar gender role, an assurance necessary to speak as a woman about the colonial landscape.[5] Claiming the innocent vision of a child, she simultaneously complied with the notion of a unique untainted European vision prevalent in eighteenth- and early nineteenth-century colonial descriptions of India.[6] It was the latter that gave her narrative authority.

This European eye, as formulated by two centuries of colonial encounter, was not just any point of view. It was a scientific understanding of the experiential world that could be deployed with superior advantage when traveling through a strange country.[7] Above all it was inquisitive. The predisposition to be curious was supposedly the single most important feature distinguishing the European vision from the "superstitious" vision of native Indians.[8] The Indian view of the world, as summed up by Hegel in his celebrated discussion of Asia, was a "Universal Pantheism of the Imagination, not Thought," leading Indians to revere as Gods everything from the Ganges to beasts.[9] Because of this, Hegel argued, in India history was non-existent, "for History requires Understanding – the power of looking at an object in an independent objective light, and comprehending it in its rational connection with other objects."[10] A convenient corollary of this lack of true understanding among Indians was that, "a relation to the rest of History in their case could only exist in their being sought out, and their character investigated by others."[11] Since Indians could not see with any accuracy or objectivity, the seeing and recording had to be done by others.

The obsessive articulation of difference between "natives" and Europeans, a mainstay of the colonizer's discourse, does not need elaboration here. In this chapter I wish to examine the language of those representative strategies that chose to accentuate only certain types of differences, and the anxieties and desires underwritten in such ways of describing the land and its people. My objective is to focus on a selection of pictorial and written documents produced by British residents, medical authorities, and missionaries. Rather than granting the painters an imperial innocence I attempt to understand the ways in which colonial authority assumed the power of narration in the depiction of Calcutta. These written and visual depictions were part of a loosely aggregated body of knowledge that became important referents in a larger discourse of British imperialism in India.

By using the terms narration and depiction interchangeably, I am suggesting that these descriptions of Calcutta went beyond the function of recording interesting facts and peculiar features of the land. They entered the realm of narration. The empirical was meant to take on the burden of narrating empire by being engaged in a pre-determined set of spatial relationships, expected to be static and coded in terms of material progress. At a very basic level, color coding – black, white, and the troubling in-between – functioned to establish the requisite cultural signifiers of a narrative of imperial progress. Such color coding, most saliently presented in the paintings of the black and white towns, were produced between 1786 and 1819, and this colored imagery was reinforced in health maps of the city produced between 1880 and 1899. Through these two forms of visual description, the idea of Calcutta as a pathological space was firmly grafted in British imagination. The tropes that were consistently used in these depictions – disease, darkness, and wild nature – made a lasting impression on generations of Britons and Indians alike. While these tropes of empire may be found in colonial texts in other parts of the world as well, I am interested in their particular import in the case of Calcutta. In the later part of the century, when colonial rule had been challenged by Indians, these tropes were magnified by British residents and administrators to justify their view of the city and its people. Such justifications operated in a self-referential ideational space formed by a century of travel writings, administrative reports, and paintings. The textual and visual representations created a space of British authority that claimed to be the geographical space of Calcutta, with all its attendant suggestions of fidelity and accuracy.

By analyzing affiliations between written texts, paintings, and health maps I am arguing that the connections between these disparate forms and descriptive domains have been largely overlooked. Perusing the British topographical paintings of the city and the limited artistic skill displayed in the large majority of them, it is difficult to imagine their significance unless we insert them in the material culture of the colonizers. The recurrence of analogously coded spatial relationships in visual and textual representations indicates their complementary function that served to magnify the power of suggestion. The urge to create a purely visual mastery of the city was, nevertheless, both necessary and inadequate from the British colonial point of view. Visual framing that attempted to settle the chaotic land and bring it within colonial order, suppressed the multi-sensory experience of the environment only provisionally. The disagreeable heat, sounds, and smells that assailed vision could be retrieved when it became necessary to suggest the difficulties of making the city habitable for Europeans.

British response to Calcutta was complex – a result of unfamiliar landscape, climate, and cultural practices, as well as racism and the economics of imperialism. The authors attempted to create a safe and familiar sphere in this alien land, a vantage of authority from which one could explore and explain the city. The unfamiliarity of the colonial city could on occasion even pass as novelty. What irked the colonizers most was *not* the unfamiliarity, but the suggestion of certain familiar practices in unexpected places. Such uncanny presence threatened to destabilize colonial narratives of savagery in need of civilization.

The process of asserting authority over space worked at several levels. But before sovereignty could be claimed, a domain had to be defined. That is why European visitors so often appealed to the logic of novel encounter and to the inherent difference between Europeans and Indians to structure their narratives. To justify one's claim and expertise, a space had to be invented both intellectually and materially. Seen through the filter of British eyes and organized through British expertise the land was transformed into "landscape." Although what made the landscape memorable was its pictorial depiction, the analytic structure set up by language preceded the ocular. The sovereign eye of the European was, in fact, the sovereignty of language.

The idyllic scenery that inspired Mrs. Fenton to convey the sense of entering an enchanted land, also had its darker side that could not escape the European eye. This strange land consisted of half-savage people inhabiting a dark and uncontrolled natural world. Mrs. Fenton's initial response was echoed by several others who came to India before and after her. In 1805 Mary Sherwood landed in Madras, and relying on the same "innocent" vision, wrote:

> Never shall I forget the yells of the boatmen when preparing to meet the fury of a wave. Amidst the wild howlings of the men, all of whom were almost naked, the roar of the surf, and the agitation of the whole fabric of the boat, there was no time to analyse a single feeling. All appeared to me to be one wild scene of terror and confusion . . .
>
> Were it in my power to recall even to my own mind the feelings of that moment, I should still find it impossible to describe the feeling to another person. . . . As an infant opening its eyes in a new world is unable to distinguish one thing from another, or to comprehend any object it sees, so in a similar degree my first views of India seem strangely confused in my recollections.[12]

Perhaps women were more prone to concede their own confusion in attempting to convey the novelty of their experience, but the utter strangeness of the new world was a consistent theme in both men's and women's travelogues, enabling them to emphasize the "pioneering" nature of their travels.[13] However, Mrs. Sherwood does not seem to be in control at the moment of landing – agitated by the waves and howling naked men. When the colonizer symbolically takes possession of the land – at that moment of landing – an inversion occurs. Mrs. Sherwood is not the surveyor as she disembarks; nature embodied by naked natives takes possession of her, dispossessing her of innate rationality. Such inversions in colonial travel narratives, always declared to be momentary, were necessary to highlight and reassure the norm of objective colonial control. The momentary indisposition is followed by a recoupment that allows the narrative to continue. Immediately after conceding her inability to describe the new land where nothing was familiar, Mrs. Sherwood proceeded to display the facility with which she could decipher objects and customs. She noted English-looking carriages and "natives dressed in muslin, looking at a distance like an assembly of ladies," the latter leaving no doubt in her mind (and those of other lady passengers) that she was in a new land, for these were a description of persons until then represented to "her fancy only in the Arabian and Persian tales."[14] And when they were about to ponder the "grade of society" to which these natives belonged, the latter soon settled her opinion "by the profound salutation which they bestowed upon the ship's officers and other gentlemen, by bending their bodies very low, touching the deck with the back of the hand and their foreheads three times." She immediately concluded: "these persons were, in fact, nothing more than stewards or head servants."[15] She not only knew what to expect but, immediately upon arrival, she had been able to decipher the hierarchy of this supposedly alien society. Using a framework of comparison in which everything Indian was matched against a European idea or artifact, she was able to "translate" the Indian landscape in an English idiom, thereby generating a familiar space of comprehension. Here, the "explanatory power of writing," in Stephen Greenblatt's words, "tames the opacity of the eye's objects by rendering them transparent signs."[16] And whatever sense of disorientation remained, she knew that this strange scene would make itself more legible over time, as it had resolved itself for Mr. Sherwood, once he became accustomed over the years "to a tropical climate and tropical scenery, and the sight of half-savage people, and people of other countries and other habits."[17] At one level this may be read as Mrs. Sherwood's deferring to her husband's knowledge. At another level, it illustrates the process through which knowledge of India was to be accumulated – when the initial sense of horror and enchantment had passed, experience of this land and people would help organize these numerous features into an ordered vocabulary.[18] The initial multi-sensory perception of the environment that confounded reason would ultimately gain the power of pure analytic vision.

At the outset, European travelers such as Mrs. Fenton and Mrs. Sherwood would have their readers believe that the European eye was unprepared to encounter this utterly strange land. The unknown features blended into a scene of confusion rather than a recognizable order. This new land required learning a new vocabulary and the imposition of a new ordering principle; otherwise the strange topography, objects, and people failed to resolve themselves into a coherent pattern. This claim implied that such fresh vision came with clear advantages – it was preconceptually uncontaminated. The anxiety of the unfamiliar was quelled by the certainty that this strange land would be ordered and made familiar, just as an infant's vision, over the years, manages to bestow order and make sense of the world. A lack of visual clarity in the Indian landscape demonstrated the native's inability to order the landscape productively. Native agency had failed (and would continue to fail) to usefully reap the wealth of a plentiful country like India, making European intervention necessary to fulfill this incomplete project. Such a point of view also made Mrs. Fenton's meticulous attention to the productive capacity of the land transform it beyond picturesque scenery, all the while appearing motivated by nothing more than conveying privileged information. Sovereignty of vision was used as a powerful rhetoric to efface the compromised conditions and sources of this presumed superiority of European knowledge.

The professed innocence of vision belied the predetermined impressions that Mrs. Fenton and Mrs. Sherwood carried with them to India. Descriptions of the Bay of Bengal and Calcutta were grounded in firmly held preconceptions of a subject race, the natural supremacy of Christianity over heathenism, and a good landscape – ideas that in a loose fashion had come to constitute the parcel of common knowledge every European visitor took to India. It was not a coincidence that for over a century visitors saw glimpses of the Arabian tales and biblical stories in India. Echoing Mrs. Sherwood, Mrs. Fenton indicated how her European eye had been tutored in the lores of the Orient by the "wild magnificence of the Persian tales."[19] For some, the patterns of trees and pagodas seen in imported china came to life in India with all their oriental splendor, and for others the tropical plants tended in hothouses by the wealthy appeared in accessible profusion. Despite the rhetoric of uncontaminated vision, the European eye was necessarily constituted by a European framework of judging and attributing a land, which they used to understand and describe this distant corner of empire. This framework appears in the remarkable similarity among travelers' descriptions of the country as their ships entered the Bay of Bengal, with Calcutta finally. "bursting into the scene." The narratives are so consistent as to be formulaic. Consider this long description of the approach to Calcutta by Maria Graham, written in 1812:

> Nothing can be more desolate than the entrance to the Hooghly. To the west, frightful breakers extend as far as the eye can reach, you are surrounded by sharks and crocodiles; but on the east is a more horrible object, the black island of Saugor. The very appearance of the dark jungle that covers it is terrific. You see it must be a nest of serpents, and a den of tigers; but it is worse, it is the yearly scenes of human sacrifice, which not all the vigilance of the British government can prevent. The temple is ruined, but the infatuated votaries of Kali plunge into the waves that separate the island from the continent, in the spot where the blood-stained fane once stood, and crowned with flowers and robed in scarlet, singing hymns to the goddess, they devote themselves to destruction; . . . Possessed by this frenzy of superstition, mothers have thrown their infants into the jaws of the sea-monster, and furnished scenes too horrible for description; but the yearly assembly at Saugor

is now attended by troops, in order to prevent these horrid practices, so that I believe there are *now* but few involuntary victims. As we advanced up the river, the breakers disappeared, the jungle grew higher and lighter, and we saw a pagoda, or a village between the trees. The river was covered with boats of every shape, villas adorned the banks, the scene became enchanting, all cultivated, all busy, and we felt we were approaching a great capital.[20]

The frightful natural features of Sagar Island were made even more terrifying by reminders of a heathen culture, irredeemably steeped in super-stition. For Bishop Reginald Heber "it required no great stretch of fancy to picture feverish exhalations rising from every part of it."[21] This region, crowded with tigers and crocodiles, infected with miasma and blood-stained idolatry, reminded Europeans of wicked deeds and violence – "the dark corners of the world" that awaited the redemptive touch of Christianity.[22] British visitors reported in great detail the sacrifices committed by the superstitious local people in the name of religion. Until recently, they noted, human sacrifices were performed in these islands. Thus, the "black-ness" of the island became a figure of native atrocity in several senses: in its appearance as an impenetrable surface, in its association with the dark races, and in its suggestion of heathen practices. Mrs. Graham obviously had no personal experience of the Sagar Island atrocities. Indeed, it would have been considered terribly inappropriate for a European woman to witness such savagery. Either she relied on stories she had heard or read before coming to India, or she had been informed of these horrid deeds by the ship's crew. But what made her narration credible to her readers was that she had seen this dark landscape with her own eyes, even if from a distance, and there had been no doubt in her mind that such dark impenetrable jungles harbored such atrocities. She could imagine jungles full of wild animals – "it must be," given their remote appearance, but more importantly she was certain "it *is* the scene of human sacrifice." Her narrative imperceptibly slipped from first-hand experience to second-hand knowledge, obliterating the source of this knowledge. Instead, what emerged conspicuously was the "very appearance" of an impervious land-scape symbolic of uncivilized natives. Her tale could not proceed beyond suggesting "scenes too horrible for description," but her narrative did not stop at the point of indescribability.

Where language stopped, British surveillance took over. Even the dark, seemingly impenetrable landscape could not escape the scrutiny of colonial authority. Stopping short of a long catalog of atrocities, she urged her reader to imagine what that surveying eye saw. To impress the full measure of atrocity that the Sagar Island represented she had to claim human sacri-fice as a practice that continued despite the "vigilance of the British government," only to repeal it a few sentences later. She "believed" that there were "now" few involuntary victims because the presence of British troops must have ensured so. And yet that could not be allowed to erase the horror. Even when success was only partial in the daunting task of civilizing, British presence had to be introduced into the picture of darkness to enable its inclusion within an imperial history. But this darkness was not the awe-inspiring darkness of the sublime; this darkness repulsed.

William Hunter in his *Statistical Account of Bengal,* published in 1875, deployed a similar rhetoric to describe the dark, "uninhabited," jungles of the Sunderbans. For Hunter, conveying the experience of "surveying" the Sunderbans required an emotive rhetoric in excess of statistical account.[23] The Sunderbans were meant to serve as a contrast to the civilized phenomenon of white Calcutta, while reminding the British residents of the closeness of feral and fearful nature. Preparing the document six decades after Maria Graham penned her description of the Sagar Island, Hunter was in effect extending the impression of the Sagar Island to the Sunderbans, thereby lending administrative authority of a "natural scientist" to a popular British perception.

The narratives of visitors and resident-administrators alike oscillated between unreadability and voluminous catalogs of fact, only to affirm that in the nineteenth century, unreadability, that is a Burkean untranslatability, could not be acknowledged, lest one confronted one's own fear and anxiety.[24] The unreadable space had to be transformed into a spectacle of horror, like the Sagar Island or the native town of Calcutta, or had to be aesthetically ignored, like the Bengal countryside.

Drawing boundaries

Following the thread of British intervention in the Sagar Island, the reader was led into Calcutta where the effects of British civilization could be most clearly appreciated. Mrs. Graham could anticipate the closeness of Calcutta because the monotony of the desolate landscape had given way to variety, arrayed in a predictable order – first the jungles disappeared, then she glimpsed a "pagoda" or a village, the river became busy with shipping, then villas appeared on the banks. These were clear signs of civilization, and she could no longer doubt she was approaching the capital of the eastern empire. That most visitors used the frightful specter of the Sagar Island to anchor their account of arrival in Calcutta is not surprising. To narrate one's first view of Calcutta in an edifying manner one had to construct the savage landscape as a polarity against which to examine the wholesome imprints of British occupation. The Island provided a convenient starting point for a lesson in imperial history. Playing a well-rehearsed role in the performance of empire, Mrs. Graham was astonished on her "first" view of the city. As her vision expanded and gained in experience she could see the chaos naturally resolving into order and magnificence.

Even when most European visitors found fault with the neo-classical pretensions of the buildings, no one questioned the use of neo-classical vocabulary in the early nineteenth century. For Britons, neo-classicism was more than fashionable. It represented the imperial legacy of Greece and Rome.[25] The British Empire was projected as the heir to the Roman Empire, albeit nobler and with a more defined sense of moral purpose. It was this relationship that was proudly invoked in discussing neo-classical architecture as representative of British power in India. The distinctive European vocabulary enabled one to recognize the space occupied by colonizers, setting out in observable material terms distinctions between the rulers and the ruled. Even when it strayed from "the rules of art" it produced a sense of loftiness and grandeur, prompting visitors to agree upon the splendor of the buildings of Calcutta and the ennobling effect they produced.[26] For Britons this enchanted city was a British invention, and the large white houses in the city were a physical manifestation of British industry. Several authors reminded their readers of the founding act of Job Charnock and the Black Hole incident, attributing to the events a significance approaching mythical proportions. But the city they took pride in was white Calcutta; the black town was treated as a sprawling appendage that only survived because of the white town and remained the great defect in this capital of empire.

Although most advocated the clear drawing of race lines, there were a few who found an absence of sympathy between the different classes of Europeans, and between Europeans and natives, a detriment to colonization. A London missionary visiting Calcutta in 1848 considered such race-bound identity to be a deterrent to missionary activity. He studied the view around Calcutta and the European edifices attempting to bestow the scene with vertical features of interest, and noted that the absence of Christian sympathy had left its imprints as well. He was chagrined at the absence of a "true" landscape:

> The most defective point of the whole scene, however, cannot easily be kept out of mind by a person accustomed to countries of a more varied aspect. All that is seen is a mere margin. There are no vistas of any kind, giving a peep here and there into the country, . . . You may look at, and count the houses, the gardens, and the trees, standing on the banks of the river, and admire them as much as you please; but there is no landscape. It is a place admirably adapted for near sighted people.[27]

He argued that if one had good eyes and a desire to see farther than the row of gardens and trees, one could allow one's imagination to fill up this void with visions of fine parkland, but "the real fact" is that these fine houses only occupied the immediate bank of the river, and beyond lay a "dull extent of fertile districts of rice fields, swamps, and useful, though uninteresting flats."[28] In leaving this testimony the anonymous missionary perhaps left the most critical British aesthetic reading of Calcutta and its

[handwritten: no landscape but British]

surrounding environs at mid-century. Comparing the Bengal countryside with the varied aspects of Europe – specifically the English countryside – he confirmed the aesthetic feelings of British travelers on landing in Bengal. In his unequivocal rejection of the existence of a landscape beyond the confines of European occupation, he captured the most troubling aspect of the British view of Calcutta.

The problem of Calcutta's lack of landscape, according to the missionary, was a matter both of discernible visual form as well as the moral implication of such absent formality. Where he expected "vistas" to channel his vision, he was confronted with a "margin" – there was nothing that would enable him to access the territory beyond and lead him to explore the country. The visual margin of Calcutta represented an inadequacy of aesthetic intervention – where he sought parkland, he found dull rice fields. For him the distinction between the rice fields and parkland was critical. The former signified commerce and the latter a moral comprehension of nature.

The missionary's expectations of the colonial city were planted in eighteenth- and early nineteenth-century ideals of English landscaping and an appreciation of the English picturesque. By the time of his visit, the English elite as well as the middle classes had learned to discern the necessity of a foreground, middleground, and background in a scenery and the usefulness of side screens to frame a landscape. The merit of scenery was deemed to reside in its topographic variety. The missionary's desire for "parkland" indicated that his notion of the ideal landscape originated not with nature in its "unimproved" condition but with the artifice of the house itself. From the house the enclosed parkland stretched out to negotiate cultivated fields and the countryside. Mid-eighteenth-century landscape designs by Lancelot "Capability" Brown and Humphry Repton had introduced a new informality into English garden design. Just as the "real" nature in the countryside increasingly came to be enclosed and marked by signs of agro-capitalism, the garden became a site for the "natural."[29] The controlled geometry of French formal gardens was abandoned in favor of immense rolling parks dotted with clumps of trees and providing select vistas of the cultivated land beyond the park. All disagreeable features of the countryside were removed – sometimes entire villages – to make space for the conspicuous consumption of nature. Favorite glimpses of the countryside – a peep here and there – included church spires or fine meadows. Only those views that worked in harmony with the form of the garden were allowed to be disclosed. Despite such selectivity, the concealed boundaries between park and cultivated fields ensured a visual continuity, thereby emphasizing a natural connectedness between these artifacts. While such park design spoke of the endeavor to improve nature on its own lines, it also demonstrated the proprietor's ability to command the initial capital and labor necessary to redress nature's lack in an unimproved state.

Late eighteenth- and early nineteenth-century critiques of Brown's and Repton's landscape designs faulted them for being too artificial, and alluded to the social dangers of such ostentatious practice. Nevertheless, such disagreements were about the appropriateness of form – the vocabulary they chose to embrace and its power to signify – but not what ought to be signified.[30] They concurred on the English landscape's moral capacity to represent ennobling ideas, to work as a repository of healthy values.

Landscape design, taking its cue from painterly compositions, was meant to generate visual frames that highlighted moral relations in a carefully annotated nature. A "goodly prospect" was one that elicited sweet sensations, triggered pleasant memories, and inspired noble thoughts. What might appear a pleasant prospect on first glance could easily become horrifying should it reveal danger or an unpleasant populace.[31] To ensure a pleasant and healthy vision, laborers were made to wear happy faces in English landscape paintings, and even in their poverty appear orderly, healthy, and content.[32] But it was not simply the lack of vistas and the flatness of the land, that is, the mismatch between the Bengal landscape and formal criteria of a good landscape that was aesthetically dissatisfying. The aesthetic sensibilities European visitors brought to Bengal did not agree with the new land because Bengal departed from the idea of a healthy landscape. Bengal was, after all, the archetype of the tropics, with its hostile climate and the capacity to harbor in its hot, humid air the disease-generating miasma.[33]

Implicit in the descriptions of Calcutta's fine buildings was the very location of the city: the notorious swamps of lower Bengal. The landscape on entering the Bay of Bengal set the stage for this unwholesome topography. The flat landscape became associated with physical discomfort and ailments peculiarly tropical. Even though productive, these flats were just land to be cultivated; they had no ennobling quality to transform them into "landscape." Significantly, the missionary's description revealed a countryside that only hinted at the existence of people; the cultivated rice fields signified the presence of natives. And yet the land unmarred by native presence was not enough to provide satisfaction as the European eye had nothing significant to rest on – no church spires, ruins of antiquity, or hills to punctuate the "sameness" of the topography. The absence of elevated vantage points from which to survey the land suggested a difficulty of mastering the territory through visual means. In Bengal, only if the land was marked by signs of European occupation could it please the eye. If Britons could project their social fantasies of a stable and happy rural populace, and could attribute high moral and aesthetic values to construct the ideal landscape in England, such imagination could not be transferred to Bengal because it would contradict the role played by the natives of Bengal in the British colonial narrative. The anonymous London missionary was assured "by those who know" that the lack of varied aspects was not to be bemoaned, as there was nothing to see beyond the line of European houses and gardens. Perhaps it is not surprising that Bengali nationalist writers felt obliged to extol the virtues of the same land in both its productive and aesthetic capacities. For British visitors, defining the boundaries of European occupation was a critical first step in describing their own experience – it was necessary to block out these unseemly aspects that emerged on closer inspection. But such bounded-ness also produced problems for the sovereign imagination. No matter how enthusiastically Britons enumerated their material possessions, they amounted to nothing more than a catalog of imperial collection. From the missionary's standpoint this was the result of Britain's shortsightedness, its failed evangelical mission. For him the absence of landscape signified the British failure to impress on the surroundings a superior understand-ing of beauty and religion. A deliberate articulation of difference as the fundamental criteria of existence in an alien land had, in fact, worked against the objectives of establishing authority over the land. The signify-ing power of an absence, a lack – of beauty, morality, colonial control – became the most pervasive theme in the British perception of Calcutta and its surroundings.

Even such pleasant views as European houses surrounded by "oriental gardens" were marred by reminders of the very character of the land and climate. Mrs. Fenton felt a sense of morbidity on seeing the effect of climate on the buildings:

> The rains have such a destructive influence on everything . . . an effect more ruinous than one neglected for centuries will do. The Venetian windows rot and fall out, the white or yellow walls become blackened and seem like houses destroyed by fire – the resting-place for birds and beasts of prey. The fearful familiarity of the former almost startles you.[34]

A reflection that was initiated by the strangeness of climatic effects turned fearful, not through its alienness but, paradoxically, from the famili-arity that such otherness invoked. The effect of weather-stained build-ings in and around Calcutta would seem to be the reverse of the "disturbing unfamiliarity of the evidently familiar."[35] However, in the context of Calcutta and its approach marked by the Sagar Island, the terror of the sublime was normalized, made familiar through repetitive writing, repeated recollections. Seen against this normative savagery, the colonial architec-ture of Calcutta was meant to be a surprise British achievement. Instead, the unexpectedness of neo-classical architecture in the swamps of Calcutta appeared frighteningly familiar to visitors such as Mrs. Fenton. It gener-ated a feeling of the uncanny. Such startling revelations about the char-acter of colonial enterprise – the colonial uncanny – refused to confer upon the British resident a secure vantage from within which one could articulate a landscape of difference. The comforting neo-classical façade that was meant to remain "secure and clear of superstition" became re-appropriated.[36] The "familiar" architecture harbored a dreadful secret – the impending death of the inhabitant.

In his discussion of the uncanny as an aesthetic and psychological phenomenon Anthony Vidler has noted that:

> its effects were guaranteed by an original authenticity, a first burial, and made all the more potent by virtue of a return that, in civilization, was in a real sense out of place ... revisited by a power that was thought long dead.[37]

Women such as Mrs. Fenton, who had embarked on the voyage to India with expectations of riches and oriental picturesqueness, recognized their journey as a passage to a new life in which the unwanted associations of England could be left behind. Yet, her desire to translate the Indian landscape into an English idiom ricocheted back in unexpected ways. Her innocent, expectant vision that dominated her entry into the new land, was interrupted by her gaze when it turned inwards. While appreciating the picturesqueness of Indian ruins and natural scenery upcountry, she came upon abandoned English gravestones.[38] Such experience left her to contemplate a lonely death in India – the English picturesque applied to India literally seemed "out of place."

The use of the aesthetic category of the picturesque in descriptions of Calcutta (and to a large extent of colonial India as well) bears the trace of a barely concealed tropical anxiety. Such anxiety appears at the moment of slippage between desire and experience, between representational mastery and inadequacy of the representative strategy, and takes the form of the uncanny. And it is this sense of uncanny, not as an aesthetic strategy, but as an unexpected outcome of the *process of representation*, that marks the passage from picturesque paintings to health maps. It is useful here to recall Freud's definition of the uncanny as "something which is familiar and old-established in the mind and which had become alienated from it only through a *process of repression*" (my emphasis).[39] In suggesting that the process of representation produces the effect of the uncanny, I am also attending to a critical function of colonial representation: the repression of likeness, familiarity that may not be acknowledged. The colonial uncanny is a product of the unexpected effect of the process of repression of the self-as-native. Central in this task of representation was "managing" the troubling figure of the Indian – in the form of the multi-valent native body, and the desire to rationalize the heterogeneity of the colonial landscape.

Scientific accuracy and the picturesque

Although Calcutta, with its flat terrain, did not easily comply with picturesque standards, art historians tell us that since Thomas and William

Daniell's arrival in India in 1786, several artists attempted to paint Calcutta by incorporating it within the English picturesque tradition. The artists, on their part, claimed they bore the responsibility of conveying an accurate topographical description of the city. These late eighteenth- and early nineteenth-century paintings, however, were not innocuous portrayals of a city in which the artists recorded historical facts with fidelity. Nor were they straightforward translations of the English notion of the picturesque into an exotic Indian vocabulary. In mediating the need for scientific accuracy and the aesthetic burden of the English picturesque, the artists constructed a way of looking at Calcutta that played a key role in forming ideas about the "white" and "black" towns.

Artists and art historians alike have applied the idea of the picturesque to British paintings of India so unproblematically that they invariably tend to obscure more than they illuminate.[40] Some of this confusion is attributable to the fashionable use of the term "picturesque" by the artists themselves. But scholars have paid little attention to the reasons the artists used this term, often flippantly, to describe a variety of elements and characteristics of the Indian landscape. Fewer have analyzed these paintings in the context of contemporary colonial discourse. There was a pattern, quite predictable in fact, in the choice of the picturesque referents that made these paintings appealing to the British audience. Although the notion of the picturesque was tied to the currency of ideas in Britain at that time, the artists gave visuality to a new vocabulary linked to the ideological function of representing empire.

When Thomas Daniell, a little-known British artist, and his nephew William Daniell, requested the East India Company's permission to travel to India, British presidency towns such as Calcutta and Madras already enjoyed small but well-established British populations.[41] Artists found eager reception not only among British residents but also among wealthy Indian patrons.[42] Oil paintings depicting either the Indian landscape or family portraits were in demand for enlivening the stark rooms of the large villas in presidency towns. The Daniells were attracted by the possibility of making a fortune if they could take advantage of this growing interest.[43] In contrast, the art market in England was a difficult one for an unknown artist. India provided a wonderful opportunity to explore subjects that were new and exotic to the British, and thus would not only be challenging from the artistic point of view, but could also bring recognition for charting new territory.[44] The Daniells recognized from William Hodges's experience as draftsman for Captain Cook in the South Seas that documenting the Indian landscape and architecture would be of interest to British authorities, not just as reminders of service in a distant land, but as tangible symbols of increasing authority and knowledge.[45] Hodges himself emphasized the need for recording the Indian landscape and articulated the role British artists were to play in the great cause of empire:

The intimate connexion which has so long subsisted between this country and the continent of India, naturally renders every Englishman deeply interested in all that relates to a quarter of the globe which has been the theater of scenes highly important to his country; and . . . may be the residence or the grave of some of his dearest friends.

It is only matter of surprise, that, . . . so little should be known. . . . of the face of the country, of its arts, and natural productions.[46]

At the outset, Hodges described history in pictorial terms – as a progression of scenes– so that India could be likened to a stage set where British history happened. The artist's role was to capture, through drawing, this history already in progress, and to explicate colonization in terms of natural history and material culture, areas he claimed had not received the attention of the orientalist scholars. The abstract idea of India found in English translation of religious texts, Hindu jurisprudence, and Sanskrit literature was to be made real by the artist unveiling the "face" of the country – by revealing native corporeality. Seen from his point of view, the difference between natural history paintings, archaeological drawings, portraiture, and history paintings dissolved, and the distinct genres acted together as material culture to perform the heroism of empire in front of a British audience. But Hodges also recognized the need for a written commentary to accompany these drawings, which was to be: "a few plain observations, noted down upon the spot, in the simple garb of truth."[47] Hodges was not the first to claim absolute fidelity. This claim to truth in drawings and narratives was important but not new to the European artistic tradition. Artists like Hodges and the Daniells, however, claimed a special role for art in colonial exploration. In this role art made the unseen visible, bringing to light that which inhabitants of an ancient land had until now jealously kept hidden. Art became an indispensable tool for enabling Britain's civilizing mission.[48]

In the introduction of *A Picturesque Voyage to India by the way of China*, Thomas Daniell refashioned in his own words precisely the same idea that Hodges wanted to impress on his audience:

> From the earliest era of history the attention of Europe had been drawn to the east; whose fastidious people, . . . have been implicated in the fate of distant nations, and compelled to endure their unwelcome alliance, or to embrace their suspicious friendship. . . . Curiosity has penetrated the veil of mystery that so long enveloped their civil and religious systems; . . . their venerable laws and institutions. . . .
>
> It was an honorable feature in the late century, that passion for discovery, . . . was exalted to a higher and nobler aim than commercial speculations. . . . [T]he shores of Asia have been invaded by a race of students with no rapacity but for lettered relics . . . ambitious only for the extirpation of error, and the diffusion of truth. It remains for the artist to claim his part in these guiltless spoliations, . . . delineation

is the only medium by which a faithful description can be given of sensible images: the pencil is narrative to the eye.[49]

The Daniells were careful to distinguish their Indian adventure from that of earlier British merchant-adventurers, although their primary objective also was profit. The telos of empire accommodated both initial greed and the noble occupation of acquiring knowledge. This distinction within a rhetoric of continuity, sustained an imperial innocence. The tropes of spoil, sacrilege, rape, were recoded with the positive filter of Enlightenment values. By such logic the exposure of India to the "sacrilegious scrutiny of strangers" became a necessity for engendering a new "humanity."

To ensure the distinction between greed and knowledge they relied on a rhetoric of artistic disinterestedness that aligned them with the eighteenth-century stalwarts of oriental scholarship, such as Nathaniel Halhed, Robert Orme, and William Jones. Like Hodges, the Daniells alluded to the works of these men by referring to the concealed knowledge of India and the necessity of unlocking such knowledge for larger goals of administrative control.[50] William Jones's concern, for example, was to legitimize British rule in an Indian idiom, a sentiment evoked in the works of the Daniells. However, there was a critical difference of medium between Hodges and the Daniells and Jones and Halhed. Although Jones realized the importance of illustrating his translations, the Daniells' goal was obviously to demonstrate the central role of artists in this endeavor of securing accurate information about India.[51] About the same time the Daniells were traveling in India, John Zoffany depicted the artist's central role in the project of empire by painting himself in the center of a composition, accompanied by his friends in high places of the eighteenth-century colonial administration.[52]

When the Daniells arrived, if India still remained an exotic world to be explored and from which exciting careers could be launched, the terms of engagement were certainly different from those of the previous century, and were to change even more in the next hundred years. Most importantly, there was already an acknowledged vocabulary of painterly elements considered essentially Indian and suitable for depiction of the Indian domain developed by artists who preceded them. The picturesque in the Indian context was a vehicle through which the already rehearsed, "true" nature of the Indian landscape and people was to be revealed.

It is important to remember here that although the term picturesque was in circulation in England before the Daniells embarked for India, the picturesque as an aesthetic category became codified only in the last two years of the Daniells' visit. In 1792 William Gilpin published *Three Essays: On Picturesque Beauty, On Picturesque Travel, and on Sketching Landscape*, and the first edition of Uvedale Price's essay *On the Picturesque* was published in 1794. Thomas and William Daniells' first publication of the *Oriental Scenery* in 1795 coincided with this codification.[53] The Daniells used the term picturesque in the text of *Oriental Scenery* to align themselves with contemporary artistic discourse, even when their artistic practice suggested a different concern with pictorial content. Much of their argument in favor of their own representations of India was based on a critique of Hodges's delineation of picturesque India that emphasized sharp black tonal contrasts and a blending of the architecture with the natural landscape. In mapping out their travel route in India they closely replicated Hodges's journey, and indeed expanded upon his trail. This replication was intended to ascertain the accuracy of Hodges's representations of Indian monuments and landscape. It was against the standard set by Hodges that they argued for the authenticity of their own work. Their rendering of the Indian landscape, which drew upon a European tradition of topographical drawing, was supposed to be more accurate, undistorted by fancy. But the Daniells did not discount the artistic value of their drawings. By associating their artistic project with that of scientific discovery – imbuing it with Enlightenment values – they proposed a Romanticism that was not opposed to reason.[54] Rather, this notion of Romanticism, already prevalent in colonial India, was necessary for colonialism and was one of the most important inventions of the colonizers. The Daniells' contribution to this colonial scientific-aesthetic worldview was the proposal of the Indian picturesque as a set of pictorial codes that made the presence of the colonizer in India natural and necessary, without the need to inscribe the colonizer's body in the paintings. Here, the drawings worked as maps – by evoking knowledge and mastery of geographical space without acknowledging the incompleteness and difficulty of such mastery.[55] The continued positive reception of the Daniells' work in the nineteenth and twentieth centuries may be attributed to their success in deploying the colonial codes effectively. There are two critical aspects in the Daniells' claim to veracity that bear relevance to the views of Calcutta. One involves the representation of the figure of the Indian as the repository of unchanged Indian tradition, and the other was the manner of organizing the visual field in depicting landscapes.

Between Spiridione Roma's depiction of the East offering its riches to Britannia and the paintings of the death of Tipu Sultan, the parameters of representing the figure of an Indian became defined in British imagination. In Roma's 1778 painting (Figure 1.1), which adorned the ceiling of the Revenue Committee Room in East India House, London, a kneeling, bare-breasted, dark woman representing India offers a casket of jewels to a white-complexioned woman who is representing Britain and is seated on a high perch. To the left a river god representing the Thames pours water at Britannia's feet, while to the right Mercury is directing the performance of the offering by the Eastern nations which include China with tea and porcelain, and Persia with silk. In the space between Britannia and India the viewer can catch a glimpse of an East Indiaman, the conveyance that makes this exchange possible. The superiority of British

Figure 1.1 The East offering its riches to Britannia, by Spiridione Roma. Ceiling painting from the East India House, London, 1778, from C. A. Bayly (ed.), *The Raj* (London, 1990)

trade and power is made obvious and is acknowledged by the East's voluntary gift of wealth. Inferiority and impending subjecthood are suggested by the gestures of the figures signifying India, China, and Persia, as well as by the space they occupy in the painting. Such depiction of authority was repeated in the next hundred years until the differential positionality of Britain and the East became naturalized to the eye.[56]

One of the most telling depictions of Britain's increased authority is a portrait of John Zephaniah Holwell (Figure 1.2). In 1756 Holwell surrendered to the troops of Siraj-ud-daulah, the Nawab of Bengal, and was among those who spent the night of June 20 in the infamous Black Hole, eventually retiring to England to write his tale of the incident.[57] The painting, finished in 1760 and attributed to Joshua Reynolds, depicts Holwell showing a drawing of the Black Hole monument to an Indian mason, presumably dictating how it is to be assembled. Behind the two figures the monument is under construction, and in the distance a British flag is flying over the Old Fort. Holwell stands well lit in a commanding pose, while the native stooping over a basket – a mass of blackness, the color and gesture denoting his race and degenerate condition – looks back apprehensively at Holwell, as if guilty of a mistake for which he may be punished. The picture commemorates Holwell's heroic survival and his contribution to the history of the Black Hole. Here, Holwell's construction of that incident is being retold with a rejoinder – the natives have to atone for their villainous crime by physically building this monument. It also encapsulates the premise of race relationships on which British artists invented the idea of Calcutta as a "British" city.

Figure 1.2 John Zephania Holwell, Governor of Bengal, attributed to Joshua Reynolds, 1760, from Jeremy Losty, *Calcutta* (London, 1990)

The use of native figures to denote the act of possession became a common representational technique in portrait paintings. For example, the portrait of Mr. and Mrs. Hastings by John Zoffany (1783–4) expressed their identity through a setting that highlighted their role as propertied consumers in a colonial domain (Figure 1.3). In a manner similar to Thomas Gainsborough's painting of Mr. and Mrs. Andrews, Zoffany conveyed the message of the status of the Governor General and his wife through the images of what they owned and controlled.[58] Mr. and Mrs. Hastings stand underneath a jackfruit tree, while their neo-classical house in the expansive grounds of their estate in Alipore, Calcutta sets the tone of the painting. The landscape in the background is animated by other native figures, a palanquin, and an elephant. In addition, a native maid, standing close-by, obligingly holds Mrs. Hastings's hat.

The presence of European neo-classical architecture in the painting, marking British superiority, locates British presence in this native landscape and transforms the land into a colonized domain. Between the maid and the estate the source of the sitters' authority is clearly defined. The figure of the native woman in fine clothing is crucial in making the desired statement about the Hastings's privileged status in India, as is the depiction of the estate grounds and the house. Similar uses of native figures abound in colonial portraiture and conversation pieces of that time.[59] These figures are not afterthoughts or entourage, they are the vehicles through which authority over the landscape is demonstrated.

Figure 1.3 Mr. and Mrs. Hastings by John Zoffany, Calcutta, 1783–7. Collection of the Victoria Memorial Hall, Calcutta

British landscape paintings of India were, in turn, commentary on the Indian people and society, and were infused with the desire to create order out of what was seen as chaos. The norms of landscape painting that applied to other colonial contexts were insufficient for the purpose of India.[60] Unlike Australia, India could not be claimed as a newly discovered, "uninhabited" territory. But it could be invented in ways that admirably substituted the spirit of discovering "untrodden" land. The rhetoric of empty lands here had to be given a different turn to serve the claims of occupancy and intervention. Seen anew through British eyes, many parts "mapped" for the first time, India could be claimed through the power of representation. The paintings suggested that there was a hidden order in the disparate, exotic, and savage elements of Indian life that could be deciphered and pictorially organized.

Many British artists, including the Daniells, used the camera obscura in sketching the scenes.[61] The camera obscura consisted of a dark box with a small aperture fitted with a lens. Light entered through the aperture to cast an image of the external object on the opposite surface. The instrument was meant to ensure an accurate recording of the landscape, unadulterated by fancy or the artist's emotional reaction to the scene. In a post-Copernican world, in which the all-seeing eye had vanished, and the landscape or the city revealed itself from multiple vantage points, the camera obscura became the metaphor for the most rational possibilities of a perceiver within the increasingly dynamic disorder of the world. Its proponents claimed it presented the information in pure form, free from the intrusion of other senses, unifying the data received.[62] However, the ideal of such a pure vision was inadequate both for the purpose of representing empire, and for the painting to become a work of art. One nineteenth-century critic wrote:

> It must be remembered that the result [using a camera obscura] was merely an outline, a sort of tracing, and far from being a work of art. The younger Daniell could well make drawings in a Camera Obscura, and his uncle, with all his observation and stored knowledge, could readily work over a drawing of this nature, inserting figures and incident, and putting in the shadow washes which would give it a pictorial form.[63]

The form of the land could itself be captured by tracing the outlines of the camera's image, but the meaning of the landscape – the art – evidently did not reside in the form's verisimilitude. It resided in the events, figures, and shadow washes. Elements in the landscape needed to be given value recognizable through a consistent use of visual language. "Pure" vision was insufficient to create the redundancy necessary for that language to become familiar, and the paintings depended on written accounts to create the multi-sensory world of meaning that enlivened the placid drawings.

In other words, the ideals of the camera obscura were being down-played in favor of knowledge gained through experience and introspection. The camera's mediation between artist and object was, in fact, considered detrimental to producing a work of art. Nevertheless, once re-worked into art the painting and accompanying text still could be touted as empirically precise thanks to its origination from the camera's lens. What was important in representing the scenes accurately was the ability to judge the value of the elements that were to be inserted in the field, so they could be assigned suitable roles and significance. And that was only possible if one had previous knowledge of what one was supposed to be seeing through the lens. It needed an acquaintance with the vocabulary of Indian elements and Indian history. Meaning was to be imparted through the act of organizing, by the creation of a visual field in which Indians and Britons took up predictable roles of subjection and authority. Ordered through a particular way of seeing, India could be "settled," so to speak. The Daniells, as prolific and enterprising as they were, contributed actively to constructing this vision of India.

Mildred Archer, in recalling the Daniells' tour in *Early Views of India*, conveyed the spirit of this construction. One aim of her book was to examine the extent to which the Daniells' paintings were accurate depictions of the Indian landscape. She explained in the introduction:

> The illustrations have been arranged for the first time in the order of the Daniells' journeys, rather than in the order of publications of the aquatints. This arrangement helps to emphasize the pioneer character of the artists' travels, which were frequently through little-known areas. It may also encourage readers to visit India and themselves follow in the footsteps of the Daniells – something which with modern transport is perfectly feasible.[64]

Archer was quite correct in identifying the Daniells' paintings as a guided tour of picturesque India: the Daniells intended them as such. In a sense they were like colonial maps of the Indian terrain. And yet in ignoring the colonial ideology of the paintings, in extolling their accuracy, and re-presenting them as guides for the neo-colonial traveler to India, Archer unwittingly explained their purchase for the nineteenth-century viewer. The paintings were as much representations of empire as pictorial guides for Britons to develop a colonial aesthetic. The paintings purported not only to establish the vantage points from which India could be correctly observed, but also to suggest by the selection of sites and elements what or how one was to see, indeed how one was to feel about the landscape. Thus, the selection of sites and landscapes is instructive.

The Daniells' choice of sites resulted in the image of a country consisting of crumbling ruins signifying lost glory (Figure 1.4). Here India lies, inhabited by a people who have no sense of history, and who are incapable of

Figure 1.4 Ruins of the Ancient City of Gour formerly on the Banks of the River Ganges, by T. and W. Daniell, *Oriental Scenery,* 1795–1801

recognizing the value of these ancient monuments. Although they have an innate sense of art, they are unable to explicate their ideas, and therefore it is incumbent upon the British to take on the responsibility of revealing India. When the paintings did not depict ruins, they described "singular" topographical features of the Indian landscape that had no parallels in Europe. These singular elements were made sensational by the symbolic reminders of a heathen culture (Figure 1.5).

A cursory look at many of these paintings fails to indicate the emotions they could invoke through the power of association based on the "knowledge" created by the early history of India and popular knowledge gathered from travelogues.[65] The positioning of native bodies, rather than landscape or architecture, assured that a nexus of colonial values would be "correctly" articulated across the space of the paintings to generate an aesthetic alliance between the artist's conception of India and the particularities of the viewer's experience of India. Those travelers who followed in the footsteps of the Daniells and retraced their journey were not disappointed. Ignoring James Mill's stricture of objective distancing,[66] travelers such as Mrs. Fenton refashioned the Indian sites with their own expectations and emotions, and made the images potent in their aesthetic content.

There was a careful balance between the savagery of the primitive people, which suited eighteenth- and early nineteenth-century tastes for

Figure 1.5 Waterfall at Papanassum, by T. and W. Daniell, *Oriental Scenery*,
1795–1801

the horrific, and the viewing of these primitives as picturesque elements
of the landscape. In the Indian context the picturesque became, in both
writing and drawing, a process of making accessible that which was not
within grasp. It was a manner of dispensing with the British anxiety of
comprehending India as the sublime, and deferring the feeling of the
uncanny. Unlike Edmund Burke, the artists maintained that India could
be comprehended and accurately represented.

Hodges's narrative did not fail to mention the importance of native
figures who supplied the picturesqueness to the scenes.[67] This depiction
of the Indian people as bearers of unchanged traditions possessing an
untutored gift to form picturesque compositions portrayed them as
"naturally" picturesque, a wishful image that continued to flourish into
the twentieth century. For example, Richard Temple, while charting a
grand tour of India for his British audience in *A Bird's Eye View of Picturesque
India*, created a fantasy land of obliging primitive people, in which British
travelers could feel their authority and cultural superiority as they moved
through the land:

> As a rule, [the people] are by nature artistic, following art almost
> unconsciously. . . . They cannot describe their feelings for, nor define
> their ideas of art; but they are ever showing it in all their ways
> and deeds. . . . When any person of authority, approaches a town or
> village, the natives come out to meet him with innate courtesy, bearing

not presents of any value but offerings of fruit and the like, investing the little scene with a picturesqueness peculiar to the country.[68]

Surely it was not lost on his nineteenth-century readers that the "person of authority" was a European. The violence of coercion is masked by the preposterous suggestion that natives bring out food and "offerings" as if they had recognized the natural superiority of the British. The native could be subjugated in the colonial imagination by being constructed merely as part of a picturesque composition. The Indians' presumed inability to convey feelings to define their art made British intervention and interpretation necessary for India's history to be inaugurated. It also followed that natives could only perform the role of objects in the British enunciation of the Indian landscape.

However, the written narratives of picturesquely savage people were just as liberally sprinkled with attempts to associate certain parts of the Indian landscape with the familiar landscape of England.[69] Such associations were comforting reminders that this land would not remain completely alien; it could be appropriated with relative ease. The sites that evoked fond memories of home were safe havens from which to observe the exoticness. And in this tension between homeyness and exoticness lies a critical aspect of these descriptions – the contrast enabled the audience to see the two opposite characteristics of the landscape in a clearer light within the framework of the same narrative. Rather than erasing the emotive content of the English picturesque, the colonial picturesque in India bracketed the emotive content of the English countryside to foreground a colonial aesthetic and emotion.[70] This parenthetical connection between metropolitan and colonial space, English aesthetics and colonial aesthetics was important in developing a unique British colonial subjectivity. As the title of Richard Temple's book suggested, the position occupied by the author/colonial administrator (and one that could be shared by his British reading public) allowed him to conceptualize the space of India with godlike omniscience, and with unimpeded mobility. Transferred to the colonial context, the picturesque as a mode of travel was coupled with the image of the British colonizer's elevated position. Even when the flat topography of the Indian plains physically denied such a vantage, such a position was already available to the colonizer in the form of the machinery of colonial knowledge. This territorial mastery, attributed to natural/racial and cultural superiority, was the ground on which a colonial subjectivity was to be mobilized. It demanded not just the definition of a space, but the repeated rehearsals of placing Indians and Britons in appropriate roles and locations to ensure a stable and fixed reading of colonial dominance. The notorious fluidity of the concept of the picturesque allowed the British imagination to locate on the native body a series of meanings that contributed to the "othering" – antique figures that represented a civilization temporally separated from England, sexualized bodies, primitives, captives of a barbarous theocracy, immoral and diseased bodies. The multi-valent native body, although useful in colonial discourse, would come back to haunt the space of British imagination, as would the desire to move the colonizer's body away from the ground plane.

Just as the savage land was interspersed with depictions of civilized prospects, the Daniells' paintings did not simply involve the rural Indian landscape. They were interspersed with depictions of the presidency towns, drawn in a manner that celebrated the pride of their British inhabitants.[71] The buildings of Calcutta were not drawn because they were picturesque; they were carefully recorded to illustrate the city as material possession. In such a rendition, the picturesque elements of the Indian landscape were used to highlight the difference between the degenerate state of the inhabitants and the civilized nature of British intervention.

Depicting Calcutta

The earliest views of Calcutta in the early eighteenth century are all depictions of the port and fort of Calcutta, two symbols of emerging British dominance in Bengal. Shocked by Maratha attacks on the new city limits, the British launched proposals to fortify the palisade around the town as early as 1747. A plan was drawn indicating the area for the "Christian and European" population of Calcutta (Figure 1.6). The drawing of the palisade in the plan marked an early effort to distinguish between the Christian white domain, and the threatening heathen native country that lay outside it. The plan specifies the important Company buildings and churches comprising this territory. Inserted in the drawing is the riverside elevation of that part of town. The view from the river was the one that most visitors enjoyed on arrival, and it was drawn several times during the next hundred years.

In 1757, after British troops recaptured Calcutta from the Nawab of Bengal, the fort became indefensible, and most of the native town around it was ruined by the attack. To secure the fort, the surviving houses around it were cleared to form a firing field or the esplanade, that came to be called the *maidan*. Not only did this move bring about changes in the form of the city, giving it a new physical definition, but the artist's field of vision was also expanded – the vast expanse of the *maidan*, which would remain uncluttered until the late nineteenth century, provided an opportunity to obtain an enlarged prospect of Calcutta. One could survey the fast-growing town from different points along the edge of this vast field, not just from the river. The important British public buildings were located near this edge, and the artists used this open field as a formal device to generate a series of panoramic views that defined all that was important to these painters and their audience.

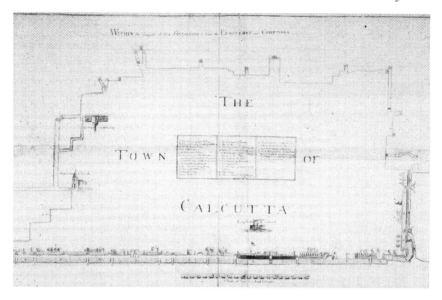

Figure 1.6 Map of Calcutta, Anonymous, 1747, British Library, K Top cxv. 41 2,
    from Jeremy Losty, *Calcutta* (London, 1990)

Among the first 12 views that the Daniells drew of Calcutta, only two
were of the native town, the rest were of the white town.[72] The views of
the white town were of prominent buildings along the main streets –
Esplanade Row and Chowringhee Street drawn from the *maidan*, and the
streets and buildings around Tank Square. The drawings documented key
public edifices – the courts, town hall, churches, fort, wharf, the Governor's
palace, and the residences of important British inhabitants – structures
that proclaimed Company supremacy by displaying the seats of administration. The buildings were drawn with care, bringing out the important
characteristics of the architecture: the tall, gleaming white colonnaded
verandahs, windows with venetian blinds, spacious arched porticoes, open
terraces, and each building with ample space around it for free circulation of air, arranged in neat rows. The neo-classical buildings conveyed a
clear sense of prosperity. These same streets and views would be drawn
by future artists, sometimes from slightly different angles. William Hickey,
who was residing in Calcutta while the Daniells produced these drawings,
redrew exactly the same views with his camera obscura and annotated
them in detail in 1789.[73] William Baillie also used the same vantage points
to generate his drawings of the city. Thus, the Daniells' drawings were
used in a manner equivalent to a city map informing visitors of the key
elements of the Calcutta landscape. What was missing in Hickey's as well
as Baillie's drawings were the human figures, and their absence makes
even clearer the importance of their inclusion in the Daniells' prints.

Numerous figures populate the Daniells' paintings of Calcutta. There
are few Europeans in the crowd; mostly it is comprised of native servants
and attendants waiting on their employers or local people plying their
trade or taking part in processions. These figures may be seen as an attempt
to depict the variety of conveyance and people, an aspect of city life evident
in many written commentaries. But their other purpose was to supply
the picturesque that could not be expressed through the architecture. In
England, the category of the picturesque was not considered appropriate
for application in cities. Connected to rural values and land politics, it was
essentially a construct for the English countryside. In the colonies, however,
the picturesque performed an important role in depicting city life. Yet,
the object of the paintings of Calcutta was not ancient ruins, but the newly
built edifices of a proud mercantile empire on its ascent. These buildings
were composed as orthogonally as possible, without any temptation to
introduce a taste for the irregular. Such adoption of contemporary architectural fashion in this far corner of empire would have been imprudent.
It was bad enough that the architectural vocabulary often failed to satisfy
dogmatic classical taste, but presidency towns were certainly no place for
expressing formal asymmetry or whimsical composition. Such a mistake
would fly in the face of all that the British inhabitants relied on to distinguish the white town from the black town. The adoption of a formal
classical vocabulary was convenient for other purposes as well.

The allusion to classical Rome was part of a long tradition in British
imperial discourse.[74] Those who had taken the Grand Tour in the late
eighteenth century, or British artists, such as the Daniells, were trained to
see classical architecture through the lens of Giobattista Piranesi. Convinced of the antiquity of Rome over Greece, Piranesi adopted a series of
devices of the traditional Italian *vedute* to glorify the ruins of antiquity.
He exaggerated perspective depths, diminished the size of human figures
and secondary buildings to enhance the main monument, stripped later
additions to create his ideal Roman ruins, and, in the later prints, scattered
the compositions generously with ragamuffins, beggars, and stevedores.[75]
His use of deep shadows and ruinous elements pleased the British eye for
the picturesque, and the Daniells transferred them faithfully to Indian architecture and the Indian people. But depicting the architecture of the *new*
empire required a vocabulary that looked forward, rather than backwards;
in fact, it needed to be as little encumbered with ruinous effect as possible.
By using native elements as the part constituting the picturesque, they could
sharply express the fine regularity of the buildings through the element of
contrast. The ordered placemaking that proclaimed authority in a foreign
land was juxtaposed with native scenes of ruins and chaos.

There is something quite distinctive about the choice of station point
in these drawings. The raised eye level affords a commanding vantage, a
method that was often repeated by other artists. Also, in all the Daniells'

sketches the foreground is extended to create a large space for introducing a tableau of native life.[76] In the views of the Old Court House and Writers' Building (Figure 1.7), Old Court House Street (Figure 1.8), and the east side of the Old Fort (Figure 1.9), the elevated station point places the focus on the street rather than on the buildings. In the drawing of the Old Court House, the building itself is not even completely included. The Court House and the long plain façade of Writers' Building form a wall that contains the street space and leads the eye from the right of the picture to Holwell's Black Hole Monument in the distant left. In the view of Old Court House Street the buildings are carefully delineated, but the viewer's eyes are led from the foreground, along the street and into the distant *maidan* and the horizon. Similarly, in the painting showing the east side of the Old Fort, it is difficult to figure out which structure is of particular interest to the artist. The Old Fort, Holwell's Monument, and the Theater were important buildings for the British residents of the city, but since none of them specifically draws attention to itself, the space created by the enclosure of the buildings becomes the stage which invites attention.

On this stage the artists inserted aspects of Indian life that were considered typical. Only in three of the Daniells' views is the activity specifically related to the setting. One view is that of St. John's Church, clearly

Figure 1.7 North side of Tank Square showing Old Court House and Writers'
• Building, by T. and W. Daniell, *Views of Calcutta*, 1786, from Jeremy
Losty, *Calcutta* (London, 1990)

Figure 1.8 Old Court House Street, by T. and W. Daniell, *Views of Calcutta*, 1786, from Jeremy Losty, *Calcutta* (London, 1990)

Figure 1.9 Old Fort from the East, by T. and W. Daniell, *Views of Calcutta*, 1786, from Jeremy Losty, *Calcutta* (London, 1990)

Figure 1.10 St. John's Church, by T. and W. Daniell, *Views of Calcutta*, 1786, from
Jeremy Losty, *Calcutta* (London, 1990)

concentrated on one building (Figure 1.10). It shows a wide flight of stairs
leading to the front portico of the church, supported by Ionic columns.
The roof is flat, creating an open terrace crowned with a handsome spire.
A curved path leads to the door of the church, while a procession of
natives animates this path. A European gentleman is being carried in a
palanquin, and other native servants wait on the portico and church
grounds for their employers. The church grounds may very well be
imagined to have been busy with people during services, but the moment
chosen for the depiction of the church was neither a time when there were
few worshippers present, nor does it show a ground flocked with European
men and women going to or coming out of church. The British worshippers are implied by their conspicuous absence, and their presence and
authority are demonstrated through the body of the servants. The natives
either wait on their masters obligingly or lower themselves to a *salaam* at
the passing of a European. The native figures not only supply the drawing
with picturesque elements but provide the contrast against which to admire
the noble edifice of the church, a symbol of the civilizing mission in a
heathen land. The church, as well as the other public buildings included
in the Daniells' drawings, such as the Court House, the Fort, and the
Council House, are physical manifestations of colonial authority, while
the natives constitute the domain over which such authority is extended.
If the former is the symbol of an advanced civilization, the latter consists

of that which needs civilizing. Seen as repositories of Indian antiquity, these figures were interchangeable with other aspects of Indian culture, including native buildings.

The native figures were not drawn on site. They were inserted in each picture by the artists from their own vocabulary of the "typical" Indian (Figure 1.11). The Daniells traveled with a large retinue of servants and it was from these people that they derived their models of Indians.[77] They made several sketches of these attendants, but none of these delineations were about the individuals who acted as models. These natives were cast into types depending on the job they performed, and each occupation had a corresponding sign that was carefully rendered. This was in keeping with written narratives of India by British residents and travelers who meticulously noted the number of servants that were "essential" in India, their job descriptions, and how to identify them.[78] For example, the *chubdar* was drawn with his silver staff, and other attendants indicated by their clothes and accessories. The occurrence of servants as "typical" Indians in drawings reinforces the idea that the main role of the native population was to serve Europeans, and it is through the recognition of this relationship that European authority is validated.

James Baillie Fraser's drawings of Calcutta in 1819 used similar techniques.[79] James Fraser went to India as a merchant while his brother William was in the Company's service in the Delhi Territory. Both collected paintings of Indian artists on topics of Indian village and clan life. In November 1819, James triumphantly wrote to his father:

> I have just received from William, a Portfolio of native Drawings, some old and valuable as being illustrative of native costume and feature; groups of Goorkhas, Sikhs, Patans, and Affghans, Bhuttess, Mewattees, Jats, and Googers. Now these will illustrate anything I may have to show of these countries; and how valuable are these to me, as studies of costume, from which to fill in figures in my drawings.[80]

James Fraser's interest in these drawings was confined to their use as sources for deciphering native "types." These formed a catalog of objective illustrations of tribes and clans, and he was not interested in conveying the delicately rendered expressions and realism of these paintings (Figure 1.12). The remarkable difference between the drawings Fraser collected and those he drew was not simply a matter of style or skill, but an indifference to the order that the Indian paintings depicted. In his Calcutta drawings we see little use even of the costumes and features. Instead, the native figures that populate his paintings are as formulaic and devoid of individual content as the broken pot shards, rocks, and weeds strewn about the foreground. There are some critical differences between the Daniells' and Fraser's prints. While the Daniells' aquatints were reproduced with

Figure 1.11 Patna Bearer, sketch with annotations, by T. Daniell, Oriental and India Office Collection, British Library, WD3124

light, muted colors and little tonal contrast, with much of the delineation dependent on line drawings, Fraser's prints relied on a stronger color contrast and the application of deep shades and shadows. The main focus of each drawing, always in the background, in case of a building in the white part of town, was shown glimmering in the sunlight, with touches of gray marking the shadows cast by tall columns and deep porches. The deep shade was carefully added to enhance the main focus of the composition. The foreground and the middle ground were filled with native figures whose dark bodies provided the necessary contrast to the white buildings.

In Fraser's view of the Scotch Church from the Gate of Tank Square, it is easy to recognize the focal point of the drawing – the white-painted church with its neo-classical façade and tall spire (Figure 1.13). But it is placed in the background, and the regularity of its architecture and whiteness are set off against the colored confusion of the extended foreground. Earthen pots, natives filling their vessels with water, and cows and horses give life to this contrast. In his view of the newly constructed Government House (1803), not yet built in the Daniells' time, there is a new dominant element in the Calcutta landscape, conveying the increasing power of the British in India (Figure 1.14). In this drawing the main object is, again, set in sunlight. The gate of Government House acts as a triumphal arch with its imposing architectural vocabulary and, in conjunction with

Figure 1.12 Five Tribesmen, Delhi, Anonymous Indian painter, *c.*1816–20, Private Collection

Figure 1.13 A View of Scotch Church from the Gate of Tank Square, by James Baillie Fraser, "Views of Calcutta and its Environs," 1819, from Jeremy Losty, *Calcutta* (London, 1990)

Figure 1.14 A View of Government House from the Eastward, by James Baillie Fraser, "Views of Calcutta and its Environs," 1819, from Jeremy Losty, *Calcutta* (London, 1990)

Figure 1.15 St. John's Church, by James Baillie Fraser, "Views of Calcutta and its Environs," 1819, from Jeremy Losty, *Calcutta* (London, 1990)

the neatly delineated fence, boldly marks the territory defining the Governor's domain from the rest of the town. In front of the house, a handsome horse-drawn carriage carries its European passengers, while native servants run alongside. Predictably, a group of natives are placed in the right-hand foreground, in the shadow of another building. Keeping a respectable distance from the gate, palanquin bearers wait for customers, while the natives in the foreground stare in awe at the power expressed by the material wealth of their British rulers.

Fraser also drew the St. John's Church depicted two decades previously by the Daniells, but from a reverse angle (Figure 1.15). The idea conveyed in the Daniells' depiction comes out with more emphasis in Fraser's drawing. Not only do his natives make the white church shine in all its glory by the juxtaposition of their own bodies, but he also enlarged the proportion of space taken up by the natives to enhance the contrast. The same manner of depiction may be noted in Charles D'Oyly's drawings of the Sudder Diwani Adalat and Esplanade.[81] It is difficult to recognize from the "Sudder Diwani Adalat" drawing (Figure 1.16) that D'Oyly's view concerns the building in the background rather than the large figures in the foreground. Fraser made the figures appear much more slovenly than did the Daniells, who drew the natives in the same style as they drew the few Europeans appearing in the paintings. The difference between the Daniells' Europeans and Indians lay in gestures and clothing. But in Fraser's view of Government House the small European figures in the carriage are drawn with more refinement than the much larger native figures in the foreground, who are painted as a mass of blackness wrapped in scanty robes, with no visible expression on their faces – their color and posture dictate their position and role in the painting. This technique of representation is most evident in Fraser's oil painting *Old Court House Street* (Figure 1.17). The huddled masses in the shadow and the brilliant tall buildings in the light mirror the relationship between blacks and whites encapsulated in Holwell's portrait. The messy foreground shared by storks, crows, and dogs fighting over rubbish and natives squatting on the street or collecting water from the aqueducts were symbolic of native lifestyle with its abject failure to recognize order from disorder. It was this characteristic that was emphasized in the few depictions of the native town.

Although the Daniells' view of the native town indicates the juxtaposition of huts, temples, and brick residences, and the street is animated by typical Daniell figures, the chaos is not as obvious as in Fraser's drawing of the Chitpore Road (Figures 1.18 and 1.19). Interestingly, William Hickey, in his annotation of the Daniells' drawings, remarked that the temple was "built by a native of great fortune, but never completed," and added that "part of it had fallen." As Jeremy Losty points out, it is unclear from the drawing which fallen part he is referring to,[82] but such a suggestion in the brief description indicates the need to invoke the idea of ruins in delineating the black town. Following the Daniells' depiction of the Hindu temple, Baltazard Solvyn, Charles D'Oyly, and Francis White drew views of native

Figure 1.16 Office of the Sudder Diwani Adalat (Revenue Board) from Kyd Street, by Charles D'Oyly, *Views of Calcutta and its Environs*, 1835. Oriental and India Office Collection, British Library, WD 4305 f19

Figure 1.17 Old Court House Street, by James Baillie Fraser, *c.*1819, Oriental and India Office Collection, British Library, WD4035, from Jeremy Losty, *Calcutta* (London, 1990)

Figure 1.18 A view of the bazaar leading to Chitpore Road, by James Baillie Fraser, "Views of Calcutta and its Environs," 1819, from Jeremy Losty, *Calcutta* (London, 1990)

Figure 1.19 Govindaram Mitter's Black Pagoda on the Chitpore Road, by T. and W. Daniell, *Views of Calcutta*, 1786, from Jeremy Losty, *Calcutta* (London, 1990)

temples. The only other type of representation of the native city was a generic view, typically showing a bazaar. Looking at the decrepit bazaars and temples it is difficult to imagine that the large bazaars of Calcutta were not only important centers for retail trade but also major centers of wholesale trade linking the upcountry traders with the outgoing sea-trade.[83] They formed the nucleus of Indian residential neighborhoods and the center of activity of the city's numerous artisans. These views contained street scenes that were extensions of the foreground idiom of the white town drawings, the buildings being as chaotic as the natives. The structures in which some attention had been given to front façades were distorted by bad maintenance and the addition of huts. The native town seemed to lack the type of order sought after in the streets inhabited by Europeans.

Unlike the views of the white town, the artists picturing the native town did not specify which buildings the views were meant to illustrate. Hickey put it bluntly in an annotation: "description of this view must be short as it represents a part of the town entirely inhabited by natives."[84] He thus summarized the reason for paying so little attention to the physical fabric of the native town: there was nothing important in it deserving careful consideration.

These early nineteenth-century drawings of Fraser, D'Oyly, and others, not only went a step further than the Daniells in establishing the relationship between the British and Indians, they also successfully crystallized the idea of the white and black towns of Calcutta. The same views, drawn from the same vantage points, and depicting a similar relationship between blacks and whites, were drawn over and over again, and each time the artist claimed the absolute correctness of such rendition. The patriarchal condescension towards simple obliging natives of the eighteenth century, exemplified by the work of the Daniells, had shifted to a nineteenth-century caricature of slovenly natives, and was a critical aspect of the image formation of the black and white towns. What had remained under the surface in the Daniells' drawings, was explicitly articulated in bodily images of the native.

The advent of photography in the mid-nineteenth century did little to induce a new perspective. In fact, nineteenth-century photographers assumed the same vantage points in seeing the city as their artist predecessors, including the use of native figures in photographs to illustrate the authority of "British" elements in the landscape (Figure 1.20).[85] Fredric Feibig colored the native figures in a photograph of a European house to drive home the point. The larger part of the native city was never adequately explored visually except as a foil for the white town.

The impact of such a way of seeing was far reaching. While it asserted Calcutta as a British creation and possession in which the importance of

Figure 1.20 European house with Indian Servants, Calcutta, by Frederick Feibig, *c.*1851, Oriental and India Office Collection, British Library, Photo 247/1 46.3

the white town was paramount, the few stereotypical images of the black town claimed the insignificant contribution of this part of the city towards its prosperity. These later images were products of a fundamental change in British attitudes towards Indian culture, empowered by a strong current of evangelicalism and utilitarianism characterized by the work of Charles Grant, James Mill, and Thomas Macaulay, who failed to see any redeemable quality in Indian culture and society. But, perhaps more importantly, the sparseness of images of the native town and their lack of specificity gave room for the colonial imagination to project horrific attributes on this blank visual space. By ignoring the complex physical characteristics of the native town and many of its fine buildings, British artists and photographers paved the way for an even more rigid attitude towards the native city in late nineteenth-century colonial discourse.

Looking back, the huddled masses in Fraser and D'Oyly's drawings were more than mere conquered props. From the very early days of empire, the exuberance of the British inhabitants of imperial Calcutta was tempered by what they considered the inherent problems of the landscape – its humidity, extreme heat and lack of proper drainage. Not a few visitors questioned the wisdom of making Calcutta the capital of British India. The weather was conducive to rot and one had to be constantly vigilant to prevent the gathering of dirt. Most of the streets in the early days were unpaved and lined with open drains and ditches prone to collect refuse. And the natives on the street who supplied the picturesque could as easily become the focus of irritated attention. Visions of the city's streets and public spaces littered with native bodies, as in Fraser's drawings, could be read as a threat to the colonial order in which they were designed to act as fixed signs. The sharp contrasts and messiness of the foreground idiom in Fraser's drawings of the white town, as well as colonial representations of the native town, suggested a tactility in excess of vision – a concern with filth, heat, and dust. This tactility threatened to destabilize the visual mastery of the colonial picturesque; visuality seemed inadequate to illustrate the colonizer's experience of the tropics. Thus Fraser's renditions paralleled the structural ambivalence of Mrs. Fenton's narrative. The emphasis on the native's lack of morality, the lack of a hospitable climate and public order designed to reiterate the wholesome grandeur of colonial architecture, created a vision of precarious plenitude. The aesthetic pleasures of colonialism were always provisional, haunted by the colonial uncanny.

These nineteenth-century drawings brought out in clear terms the nascent discomfort with Calcutta – its inhospitable climate and the danger of dirt and disease physically embodied by the natives and their disorderly lifestyle. Described in the eighteenth and early nineteenth centuries as Calcutta's topographical problem, burdened as it was with its location on a swamp and unflattering climate, the delineation of this problem would reach its climax in the clinical description of health maps. And with the urging of medical authorities such as James Ranald Martin and F. P. Strong, Calcutta's imperfections would be characterized as a problem with its native inhabitants.

Pathological space

James Ranald Martin's authoritative work, *Notes on the Medical Topography of Calcutta*, published in 1836, made a lasting contribution to the image of Calcutta. *The Medical Topography* was the key sanitary appraisal of Calcutta in the early nineteenth century and became a model for later evaluations.

In the late eighteenth and early nineteenth centuries European medical thought was still based on the humoral understanding of disease. Disease was caused by disorders in the blood, bile, and other bodily fluids, which found expression in fluxes and fevers. Although the effect of a hot climate on Europeans was already under investigation in the eighteenth century, the early nineteenth-century European medical practitioners in India claimed with certainty that disease developed along foreign principles in the tropics, and that tropical disease affected Europeans differently than it affected native inhabitants. Consequently, they insisted on clinical observation to acquire first-hand knowledge of the progress of diseases in tropical countries, which was supposed to be complicated by changes in temperature, wind direction, and topographical differences. Noxious exhalations, caused by the effects of the sun on defective features such as decaying vegetation, marshes, and sandy soil, and trapped by the hot humid air, were the principle causes of sickness. An intimate knowledge of these local conditions was necessary to prescribe remedies. By emphasizing the effect of topography on disease, medical authorities made themselves indispensable to the colonial project of surveying, mapping, exploring, and controlling space. To underscore the economic advantage of disease prevention they frequently drew comparisons between different colonies and attempted to explain how hard physical labor in the colonies had to be performed by the natives, even if that meant forced labor.[86] The intimate connection between medicine and economics was acknowledged in the East India Company's decision to employ medical practitioners to survey its territories. These surveys and medical topographies, beginning in the 1820s, were attempts to understand the nature of the possessions and how they could serve the Company's economic interests. In 1807, Francis Buchanan, a surgeon, was employed by the Company to produce a survey of eastern India in which he reported on the physical condition of the people, their diet, and the diseases prevalent among them, as well as the topography, land tenure, natural resources, commerce, religion, and customs of the inhabitants. Medical doctrines, as David Arnold notes, became the master narrative of all the empirical sciences in India.[87] Given the environmentalist paradigm of disease and the climatic difference of

Disease

biopower

India and Europe, disease became central in understanding the Indian environment, and one of the most frequently used tropes for describing Indian culture. Districts were mapped and relative health of sites determined. In 1813 James Johnson, a surgeon, argued that in Bengal proliferating nature produced an "inexplicable something"[88] that gave rise to peculiarly tropical diseases. Such diseases, although impervious to European medical explanation, could yet be followed and its trajectory mapped on the diseased body. The hot season swelled the exterior of the body, and the cold season deterred sufficient discharge, the suppression causing "abdominal and cerebral engorgement."[89] Fever was caused by an imbalance in the blood circulation, certain organs retaining more blood than others. On the surface of the body this was indicated by the bounding pulse, fever-flushed cheek, and throbbing temples. To restore balance in such cases, Johnson recommended vigorous bloodletting to relieve these organs of excess blood. Given the rapidity and violence of disease, "heroic measures" were required. The lancet, he claimed, "dispelled the mists of prejudice and the phantoms of debility and putrescency."[90] The same principles of opening up the body could be applied to the treatment of defective topography. He believed that noxious exhalation was "capable of concentration . . . when it is detained among woods and jungles . . . especially during the rainy seasons when there are no regular breezes to dissipate it, and when the beams of the sun are obscured except at intervals, by dense clouds, it becomes exceedingly powerful as the annual mortality too plainly proves."[91] Nature left unimproved acted with fatal consequences on humans. It was through the act of colonial conquest – felling trees, draining marshes, clearing river channels, and ploughing the earth to "open it up" to the rays of the sun – that "vanquished nature yields its empire to man who thus creates a country for himself."[92]

What distinguished the early works of James Lind and James Johnson from their successors was the growing concern with not just the topography and climate but the habits of the native people in determining the causes of diseases. Mark Harrison has argued that prior to 1830 European medical men in India had a "Burkean" ethos and did not dismiss indigenous medical approaches because their practices were epistemologically similar to that of Indian practitioners.[93] While Indian and European medicines were not granted the same privileges, it was believed that survival in the tropics required adoption of some native conventions of living. By the 1830s such an approach had become a thing of the past.

James Ranald Martin, in his *Medical Topography of Calcutta*, re-emphasized the unhealthy location of Calcutta and adopted an antagonistic stance towards native lifestyle.[94] Although he retained the environmentalist paradigm of disease, natives became an inextricable part of this environment. It is interesting to note that the diseased body analyzed by Johnson was not the native body. In contrast, for Martin, the native body was inherently diseased. Disease, he and his contemporaries maintained, was only partially due to climate, and largely due to the moral and social conditions of the people. Thus, the surrounding suburbs and the native town were as dangerous as the swamps and jungles for contracting jungle or bilious fever. What was needed was the "constant efforts of industry," the relaxation of which caused disease to spread its seeds.[95] To make the town inhabitable the irregular terrain had to be leveled and drained in the salt lakes to the east. But much more than leveling and draining was necessary. One had to understand the natural disposition of the inhabitants.[96] He had no doubt that only European knowledge and sanitary measures executed under European direction could improve the health of Calcutta. Reminding his readers of the axiom of medical topography: "a slothful squalid-looking population invariably characterizes an unhealthy country," Martin went on to chronicle the defects of native living, including a vegetarian diet, the inadequacy of native clothing, child marriage, and polygamy.[97] These customs prescribed by a superstitious religion were prejudicial to public health. The role of Europeans became all the more crucial in Calcutta because the Indian residents had no sense of public virtue and did nothing for the benefit of the town or towards improving the social condition of its inhabitants. The Indian spent his money on pious contributions and on women, and "in his dress and table there is little devoted either to the purposes of elegance or magnificence, unless the insipid *nautches,* marriage and religious festivals deserve that name."[98] Their money, he agreed with the missionary William Ward, disappeared in show, noise, and smoke. To prove their lack of public virtue he reported that although Bengalis were loquacious, they were never seen "assembled in groups, like all European people, to discuss matters of public interest."[99] Responding to the claim that the physical and moral condition of natives could not be automatically dangerous to Europeans new to the land, Martin argued to the contrary. He linked physical, moral, and material progress to argue that the Indian landscape would invariably affect Europeans for the worse, if steps were not taken to improve the topography, that is.

Although Martin seemed to recognize the inextricable relation between the European and native habitations, he believed the native town needed to be described separately, as there were "few points of resemblance."[100] The native town was characterized by densely built brick buildings that did not have sufficient provision for letting in air and light, and contained the defects to be found in all Indian cities. He found the building habits of Calcutta's natives worse than many "primitive" cultures which raised their houses from the ground to reduce the effect of noxious exhalations. The narrow lanes of the native town were saturated with "villainous smells that offended the nostril."[101] The natives' reluctance to fight the natural conditions were indicative of a deeper problem; such an acceptance of the vileness of nature reflected a degenerate civilization constituted of corrupt bodies and corrupt morals:

[T]he natives have yet to learn, in a public and private sense, that the sweet sensations connected with cleanly habits, and pure air, are some of the precious gifts of civilization, and a taste of them tends to give a distaste to degrading and groveling gratifications.[102]

By situating the problem of sanitation in the realm of improving native morality, he nicely complemented missionaries who found the customs and religious practices of the natives appalling. Nineteenth-century British visitors would have had no difficulty understanding this line of argument. In their worldview the climate and people's abilities were inextricably connected, and good morals were equated with physical and material well-being. The Reverend James Long regretted the inevitability of the negative impression created on arriving at Calcutta via the Bay of Bengal – "the unfavorable views regarding the Indian climate, the Indian people and Indian scenery formed by Englishmen making Calcutta their first place of debarkation in India," and added that "the weakly looking natives, their filthy habitation and the low swampy ground of Bengal is looked upon as the standard of India."[103]

Martin's language was heavily borrowed from James Mill, and he bolstered his claims by providing statistical information. Martin was the first in India to introduce medical statistics on a systematic basis to convey information on disease, temperature, and mortality. He also successfully persuaded the Governor General, Lord Metcalfe, to establish a scheme of preparing sanitary reports for each town and cantonment.[104]

If early medical doctrines relied on detailed descriptions of diseases on the surface of the body and on inference drawn from the action of climate on the surface of the soil, Martin and his colleagues regarded this knowledge to be inadequate for combating the virulence and unpredictability of tropical ailments. They argued that if the individual knowledge of the medical practitioners was to be useful in the goal of empire, it needed to be systematized by the use of a uniform nomenclature and descriptive statistics. The logistics of colonialism necessitated that the describing eye move from the surface of the individual patient's diseased body to the larger body of city, region, and territory. Doctors were urged to cultivate a "habit of observation" that would help them produce numerical accounts of diseases.[105] An environmentalist paradigm made that move convenient. With little hope for cure, statistical descriptions exuded a belief that somehow diseases could be contained if their pattern could be mapped on a grid of race, religion, caste, and season. Abstracted from the diseased body, the statistical description as a form of knowledge could come back with renewed power to address the diseased body. Statistics could be used to compare mortality in various parts of the globe. Such a wide field of comparison, it was explained, provided a necessary idea of how climate affected longevity in particular races of men.[106] Perhaps, foremost in the mind of these doctors was the usefulness of these statistics in demonstrating their own success. Martin claimed that although

Calcutta had become healthier through the intervention of medical practitioners, in the absence of numerical data it was difficult to make such an assertion. These statistical descriptions and medical topographies became powerful manifestations of the neutral grid of knowledge that James Mill might have applauded. More significantly, they formed the bases on which Calcutta's sanitary requirements were formulated. Linking race, religion, and social customs with topography and disease, Martin provided the structure of argument for his successors. He gave scientific credence to the idea of the native city as a pathological space contrary to the European town.

Descriptions of the native town by British visitors echoed Martin's sentiments of the danger of moral and physical disorder. Accompanied by her English friends, Mrs. Fenton visited the houses of two wealthy Indians on the occasion of a religious festival and was "cured for ever of all curiosity respecting native entertainments:"

> Well! after driving furiously to different houses all lit up in the same style, as fast as horses could take us on, the glare of lamps, the rapid motion of the multitudes moving round us almost bewildered my brain.[107]

Mrs. Fenton's description is propelled by a sense of irreconcilable racial and cultural difference. In a space outside the hierarchical dictates of colonial authority, she cannot find a secure, stable position from which to observe and analyze. Without that stability picturesque India disintegrated into unceasing chaos – blurring boundaries of private and public spaces, between races. In concluding that her visit provided "little to please the European eye" she acknowledged the conceptual and physical space necessary to generate a distance between herself and the object of her gaze. On a rare trip to the Burrabazaar without her European friends, she expressed her colonial anxiety through the conflictual economies of disgust and desire:

> [T]he lanes are dark, narrow and filthy, filled with the effluvia issuing from the dens (for I cannot call them houses) of the natives, and they too look barbarous, half-naked, and as if on the watch to take hold of you. There is a kind of market-place covered over and divided into separate stands; they are perfectly wonderful to a European. There are heaped on one board all sorts of shoes, slippers, sandals to suit the native taste . . . wonderful specimens of boxes, lacquered work, playthings . . . flowers, china, silks, chintz.[108]

Mrs. Fenton's reaction was fairly typical of British visitors, few of whom took more than a casual interest in the native town. From their point of view, the native town lying beyond the "front-line" of elegant houses was a troublesome territory inhabited by a people whose habits made social intercourse with them impossible. The spare exoticism, although carefully enumerated, was heavily underscored by the spatial and sensory barriers that lay between someone like Mrs. Fenton and the native town. Vast fortunes existed next to squalor, apparently with no desire to differentiate between the two. British visitors were unable to read the effect of the conspicuous wealth of Indians in the geography of the native town. Expectations of an oriental city crowned with minarets and mosques were disappointed in Calcutta.[109] Those who paid attention to architectural style considered the inclusion of classical elements in Indian houses an indication of poor taste. Such hybrid architecture was not born of genuine conviction in classical architecture, but was a sign of blind and inept mimicry of Western fashion. The lack of an authentic architectural vocabulary was, itself, an indicator of the absent rationality of the native mind.

The density of experience that disoriented Mrs. Fenton took on a different urgency for missionaries who found a more compelling interest in native life. For them the disorder spoke urgently of a need to reform Bengali society on Christian principles. In 1818 William Ward, an English missionary living in Serampore, published a scathing commentary on the life and customs of the Hindus.[110] According to Ward the Bengali house was a hovel built in an irregular manner with no objective in mind other than to create a place for the idol and to imprison the women of the house. What bothered Ward was not simply the irregularity of the streets or the materials used in the construction of the houses or their sparse furnishing, but a lack of what he perceived as a rational system of ordering the street, fence, compound, and house: a visually transparent sequence that was easily decipherable. He was appalled by the lack of attention paid to the front façade of the house, which was often "a high wall with a door in the center," and the absence of a low fence and pleasing frontage to the street. Ward's account was not an exception. The visual opacity implied in these descriptions reinforced the frustration of being unable to clearly read the layers between the public and the private domains. Given the propensity of Indians to use open public spaces for a variety of functions, including sleeping and urinating, the difference between public and private spaces seemed blurred to an uncomfortable degree in the eyes of Europeans. The visibility of the "private" functions seemed particularly contradictory to the various manners of shielding the interior of houses from the outsider's view. It was not difficult for Europeans to imagine that "privacy" was compromised in these invisible chambers, just as the public domain was violated by private activities.

Ward and other Europeans found the seemingly arbitrary signs denoting private and public domains alarming. Elements of built form, such as walls, fenestration, rooms, and streets, seemed to convey a range of meanings, many of which disturbed elite British sensibility. Civilized existence was equated with objects acting as fixed signs.[111] To understand building practices in India required an appreciation of plural spatial meanings and a different conception of interiority. But many of the disagreeable traits of native Calcutta, such as the claiming of public spaces for multiple, private uses, were found in contemporary European towns as well. Descriptions of the contemporary East End of London expressed a similar sense of moral and physical danger.[112] The difference in description was, to a great extent, a product of the racialized language of colonialism that strove to enforce distinctions on the bases of color and religion. Plurality, interpreted as arbitrary and antithetical to progressive classificatory ideals, when cross-hatched with the concept of "race," became an obstacle to European understanding of the culture of native cities such as Calcutta. The landscape of native Calcutta could never be visually articulate to British authorities. This unreadability, as in the description of the Sagar Island, was translated as an absence of morality among natives. Ward claimed that this lack of rational ordering produced the "notorious" unchastity among native women.[113]

(margin handwritten note: multi use space → inarticulate → amoral)

Ward was obviously prompted by an overzealous missionary spirit, but the implication was clear. A rational ordering of space, as found in the white part of town, was superior because it was visually transparent and actually diffused the threat of "mixed company," while a spatial order that used opaque barriers to shield its women was easily turned on itself to subvert the very purpose it was intended for. The development of European ideas, the building of wide roads, a transparent landscape, Ward and Martin would argue, was not only necessary for the emancipation of natives, but was needed to shield Europeans in a land contaminated by noxious air, dangerous bodies, and corrupt minds. Surviving in such a land required a discriminating European eye to decipher rational choices from irrational ones and the incessant striving to uphold European ideas to stave off native contagion. The resilience of the environmentalist paradigm of disease in colonial India, long after it had been abandoned in the metropole, indicated the usefulness of such metaphors to characterize India, and in particular its capital city. The environmental metaphors were successfully used to define Calcutta as a pathological space that deviated from normalcy and to attribute to the Bengali all that was unnatural in a colonized population.

From picturesque paintings to health maps

The Resolution on the 1889–90 Calcutta Municipality Administration Report concluded that despite sanitary improvements the "Metropolis of British India" remained highly insalubrious and noted that the "cholera map of Calcutta is still simply a map in which the whole native town appears a mass of red dots indicating cholera deaths."[114] The map the author was referring to was one in a series of maps prepared for presentation with the Annual Report of the Health Officer of Calcutta (Figure 1.21). These reports tabulated mortality rates, causes of death, and the race and religion of the deceased. Inclusion of cholera maps with sanitary reports of the presidencies was suggested in 1868, noting that the

> study of cholera is so important, and easy reference to its seat and progress so valuable . . . that to the (sanitary) abstract of each presidency

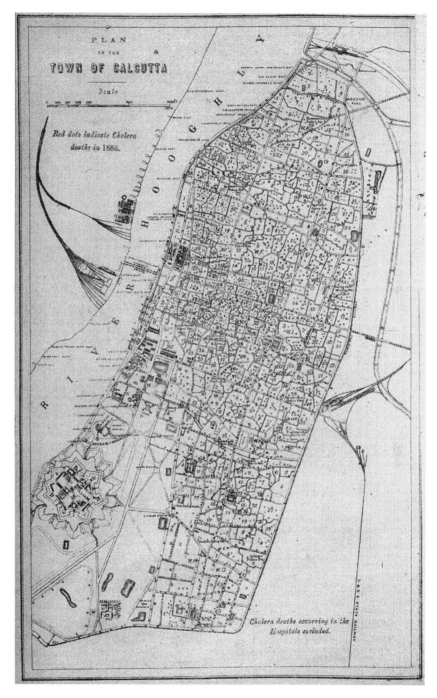

Figure 1.21 Map of Calcutta showing cholera deaths in the year 1886, Oriental and India Office Collection, British Library V/24/2873

should be appended an outline map which will tell at a glance the cholera history of the year under report.[115]

Since 1880 the numerical data was translated into the graphic format of health maps, while the accompanying report elucidated the conditions under which disease flourished. The format of a map provided a critical *spatial* component to the reading of statistical data. It allowed a stark reading of the spatial vector of the disease within approved limits of scientific inquiry, seemingly unadulterated by political motives. However, one had to study the map in conjunction with the Report or be fully acquainted with the history of cholera in the city to comprehend the meaning of the map. The increased concentration of red dots indicated the most frequent occurrence of disease, but if one did not know that the spaces occupied by the red dots were also the more populous localities, there would be little basis to judge mortality rates. If one did not know the connection Europeans made between native lifestyle and cholera there would be little opportunity to recognize that the concentration of red dots implied the black town. The understanding of the map was predicated on a previous knowledge of the black and white towns. The Resolution was clearly not speaking of a single year, but drawing the reader's attention to the history of a problem. The map, Health Officer Dr. Simpson, argued, was illustrating the problem of persistent cholera in Calcutta and its virulence in the native city. The map was Dr. Simpson's opinion of the sanitary condition of the city, and was meant as a severe criticism of the Indian commissioners of the Municipality, who took no interest in the welfare of the city.

In the second half of the nineteenth century no significant British drawings of Calcutta were produced. Instead, British authorities preferred statistical descriptions to convey information about the city. Produced at a time when scientific and administrative endeavors were coming together in the cause of empire, the health maps of Calcutta were irrefutable depictions of the state of the city. There was apparently no room for fanciful rendition, an aspect that every artist who painted Calcutta had to address. The move from qualitative to quantitative descriptions silenced the need for further visual exploration of the city. The city had already been convincingly rendered in terms of disease.

The power of health maps resided in the scientific illustration of the "native" problem. Such reliance on numerical measures in medicine was not isolated from a qualitative exploration of India. For a long time qualitative and quantitative descriptions were used side by side to bolster arguments for particular methods of sanitation and disease control. The comparative method exemplified by the neutral grid was also used in the obsessive cataloging of Indian "types" in ethnographic surveys and in anthropometric studies. Indians were photographed against the Lamprey grid to measure physical features considered accurate indications of racial characteristics. From the nineteenth-century point of view physiognomy expressed racial

racial

characteristics, and provided scientific evidence for determining a person's abilities, intelligence, and moral characteristics. The use of a gridded plane to produce perspectival representations had, of course, been in use since the European Renaissance. But in the anthropological use of such a system of mapping the body, features were given value by linking surface features with innate disposition. By bringing the power of numbers to work in spatial terms, the health maps were operating on similar principles.

No other disease captured the horrified imaginations of Europeans more than cholera. The quickness with which it struck, the frightful symptoms, the lack of therapeutics, and the absence of a predictable pattern made it the most feared disease and the most salient among administrative concerns.[116] The disease was considered endemic to Lower Bengal and linked to the disorderly habits of the natives. It became the disease of poverty and racial weakness. The discovery of a connection between cholera and Hindu pilgrimage sites confirmed the European perception of the disease as peculiarly Indian.[117] The mass bathings at the pilgrimage sites and the sipping of water for ritual purification increased the possibility of contracting the water-borne disease. This coincidence bolstered the missionary argument that even that which the Hindus considered highly sanctified and pure was a cause of death and disease.[118] It mattered less that the pilgrims died, but what concerned them more was that heathenism slayed "thousands of the most talented and beautiful" in Vienna, London, and Washington.[119] The administrative reports of the Calcutta Municipality incessantly reminded the readers of the main incentive for making Calcutta healthy – to provide a salubrious environment for Britons to conduct trade and rule the country.

In the nineteenth century, the first major outbreak of cholera occurred in 1817 when the epidemic ravaged Northern India. From that time on the disease came increasingly under the scrutiny of British medical authorities. Not surprisingly cholera mortality became the standard for measuring the healthiness of Calcutta, and prominently shaped the image of the city.[120] The disease was believed to be caused by the effluvia arising from a damp ground impregnated with filth as well as by the consumption of filthy food and water. The native town, in particular the *bustee* or "native village," was considered its breeding ground. But the idea of the *bustee* as a specific site of disease, representing the worst attributes of the native population, arrived relatively late. Shortly after Ranald Martin's *Medical Topography* was published, the Fever Hospital Committee was set up at the request of Indian and British residents for a comprehensive understanding of the city's sanitary needs and in particular to evaluate the sanitary condition of the native town.[121] The Report of the Fever Hospital Committee was published in 1840 and its evaluation incorporated many of Martin's ideas of black and white towns and the superiority of European ideas and morals. The problem they found in the native town was related not only to climate but to local conditions defective in ventilation and drainage.[122]

The close clustering of houses prevented free circulation of air, and the numerous tanks, very few of which were kept clean, became receptacles of ordure and stank like "a corrupted corpse."[123] There could be little doubt that they harbored disease. But neither of these documents made a clear differentiation between the *bustees* inhabited by the poorest classes and the habitations of the upper and middle classes. The appellation of the "*bustee*" for designating slums appeared only in the mid-nineteenth-century reports of the health officers. The *bustee* population had a higher mortality rate than their better-off neighbors, and in 1862 the Justices of Peace had already been vested with the power to deal with the problem.[124] But little was done for want of funds. So health officers took up the cause thereafter and made cholera in *bustees* the central theme of sanitation. Writing in 1872, Arthur J. Payne, the Health Officer of the Calcutta Municipality, reiterated what he had said four years ago regarding the *bustees*, and provided a description that would be used by his successors to impress on the public the danger of the situation:

> A bustee or native village generally consists of a mass of huts constructed without any plan or arrangement, without roads, without drains, ill-ventilated, and never cleaned. Most of these villages are the abodes of misery, vice, and filth, and the nurseries of sickness and disease. In these bustees are found green and slimy stagnant ponds, full of putrid vegetable and animal matter in a state of decomposition and whose bubbling surfaces exhale, under a tropical sun, noxious gases, poisoning the atmosphere and spreading disease and death. These ponds supply the natives with water for domestic purposes and are often the receptacles of filth. . . . The entrance to these bustees are many, but not easily discoverable, whilst the paths are so narrow and tortuous that it is difficult for a stranger to find his way through them. The huts are huddled together in masses and pushed to the very edge of the ponds, . . . the intervening spaces, . . . are converted into necessaries and used by both sexes in common.[125]

Payne's descriptive language continued Ranald Martin's legacy of portraying an inherently defective landscape and a people untutored in the science of sanitation. Although Payne, like Martin, stuck to a miasmatic theory of disease, the responsibility of such insanitary conditions belonged entirely to the native community. The condition of the *bustees*, Payne claimed, was as much due to the habits of the poor tenants as to the apathy and negligence of the proprietors, who profited from the rents but cared little for public welfare. The native population certainly paid the largest share of the taxes, but since they were indifferent to death and disease, and did not recognize the relation between cleanliness and health, it was up to the Municipality to teach them sanitary lessons. He went on to remind his readers of the danger of leaving some portions of the city unimproved:

"It is a well known fact that many of the epidemics that have visited Calcutta have first made their appearance in the northern division of the town."[126] The monsoon winds carried the germs from the northern division to the southern division of the town. Consequently, when an epidemic occurred in the *bustees*, it rapidly "invaded" the southern portion.[127] Demolishing *bustee* huts was the only solution to prevent the periodic returns of cholera, fever, and dysentery. *Bustee* improvement in Payne's terms meant the preparation of a "correct plan of each bustee, showing its exact boundary, the situation of tanks or ponds, and distinguishing the high from the low lands."[128] The *bustee* was to be adequately provided with drains and roads for efficient conservancy, was to have a large tank to provide wholesome water, and separate public privies for men and women. Private privies attached to huts were not to be allowed unless a family had too many children and aged women. Finally, the *bustee* would have to be well lit to help the police prevent crimes. In Payne's desire for well-bounded, easy-to-survey spaces it is not difficult to read the ideas espoused by preceding medical authorities and missionaries. Control of disease was unapologetically aligned with social and economic control. Like the medical statistics, the idea of the "model" bustee evoked a desperate belief that disease could be contained once the boundaries and rules of surveillance were in place.

When Payne made his recommendation he had the most recent of the many cholera epidemics in mind. He reminded his readers that the International Sanitary Conference had implicated Bengal, and partially Calcutta, as the originating point of the epidemic that had devastated Europe. Payne was writing at a time when the origins and nature of transmission of cholera were furiously debated. Long after its water-borne nature had been recognized in Europe, following the work of John Snow in 1847, European medical practitioners in India continued to support the environmentalist theory of disease for explicating cholera.[129] Even those who recognized the improvement in mortality following the increased supply of pure drinking water in the city maintained the miasmatic theory.[130] "As long as these bustees are allowed to remain in their present stage," Payne suggested in 1872, the European community was "sitting on a volcano, ready to burst at the slightest atmospheric perturbation."[131] Under the threat of international quarantine regulations, the anti-contagionists, including the Sanitary Commissioner of the Government of India, J. M. Cunningham, claimed that cholera was not communicated from one person to another. His statistical officer, Dr. J. Bryden, argued, in the vein of Arthur Payne, that the prevailing winds carried the effluvia from infected spots.[132] If the Indian Government accepted Snow's water-borne theory, they would be required to radically improve the city's water supply. It would not only mean a large capital investment, but international quarantine regulation would mean loss of revenue. There was significant pressure on the part of the British mercantile community to resist quarantines. For the Anglo-Indian residents quarantine would mean acknowledging that social status and racial difference inherently did not make one susceptible to disease. Because British authorities could not draw physical boundaries for the fear of loss of revenue, the discussion of cholera in the city became charged with racial overtones.

The designation of *bustees* as hotbeds of cholera flourished in the 1870s and continued into the 1890s with the approval of the Bengal Government and the Army Sanitary Commission.[133] The overwhelming concern became the removal of the *bustees* from the white town. Such propositions were premised on the idea of separate white and black towns and different needs of blacks and whites.[134] The Bengal Government recommended a radical reform of the *bustees* by making their destruction and reconstruction a top priority, reminding the municipal commissioners of the adverse effect of cholera on trade and consequent prosperity of the city.[135] Thus, the "Resolution on the Calcutta Municipality Administration Report of 1889–90" did not simply draw the public's attention to the native town, it highlighted a threat posed to the white community as well. The spatial continuity between white and black towns implied by the scattered dots was distressing to a colonial imagination relying on a rhetoric of difference to constitute the colonizer and the colonized. Cholera did not respect such boundaries. The resulting anxiety necessitated that blame be laid at the doorstep of the native population, ensuring that cholera become the dividing line between Europeans and Indians in colonial discourse.

If Indian society was perceived as lacking a rational structure, and if the very essence of Indian-ness rested in the incapability of Indians for order, these features demonstrating British superiority were also those that constantly threatened British efforts to order and control this chaotic landscape. The wishful configuration of the map of 1747 that neatly demarcated the white town was no longer inviolate. The desire to separate the black and white towns was contradictory to everyday experience in which the separation between black and white populations was only provisional. As in the early nineteenth-century paintings of Calcutta, the native figures in their numerousness loomed large and sought to disrupt the creation of a homogeneous space controlled by whites.

The European part of the city was less affected by disease, but by no means immune from it. While on the one hand the maps seemed to challenge the idea of the white town and the black town as distinct entities, on the other hand they fed off, and indeed cemented, the characteristics of the native and white population, particularly when they were read in conjunction with the written commentaries. These maps illustrated the complicated problem at hand. While the obliging native figures in the paintings had become infected bodies in the health maps, they also pointed out the difficulty of removing these infected bodies to a different enclave. The large native presence that had been, at times, reason for imperial pride and at other moments cause for dismay was now dangerous. Those who perused these maps were already fortified with horrific images of the black town and could quickly estimate the danger of contagion that native habitations posed to the salubrity of an imperial city.

Discussing the two dominant cultural facts of the nineteenth century, landscape and imperialism, W. J. T. Mitchell has observed that "empires have a habit of coming to an end, leaving behind their landscapes as relics and ruins."[136] In the Indian context, British artists and administrators, travelers and scientists, created a way of seeing that tried to link together distinct aspects of the landscape by encompassing them within the same imperial narrative. In this imperial scheme, the different genres of landscape, portraiture, and history paintings shared symbols and modes of appropriation to such a degree that to understand one it is necessary to explore the others. In a sense they were all about landscapes. The early depictions of the Daniells were not mere aesthetic projects, nor were the health maps disinterested presentations of statistical information. They were both ways of representing the landscape in a manner that reflected the desires and fears of their authors and audience. After all, Calcutta was neither the only nineteenth-century city with sanitation and infrastructure problems, nor the only one built on a swamp. Obviously much more than topography and climate was involved.

The paintings of Calcutta, with their vocabulary of picturesque natives positioned against the brilliant material prosperity of British neo-classical architecture, suggested the key elements of the cityscape and devised a way of seeing the city through imperial eyes. But at least these early depictions demonstrated a lively interest in the native population, if not the native city, an interest later severed by the growing antagonism between the British and Indian inhabitants. The health maps were symbolic of this climate of distrust, and in the end came to justify the idea of Calcutta as a dreadful city. Health maps were used in many cities around the world, but the particularities of the context of nineteenth-century Calcutta endowed them with added significance. The shift in depiction from qualitative renditions to health maps and statistical descriptions, which were considered more accurate than the former, representationally effaced the three-dimensional space of the native town. Perhaps more significant was their circulation as objective documents in the higher echelons of the Indian Government and the British Parliament, confirming the notion of Calcutta as a nightmare of ill health for which the native inhabitants were to blame. Thus, until recently, Calcutta has been seen from the vantage point assumed by the Daniells and other early artists, its prospect evaluated from the reified perspective of colonial need and desire for appropriation. The power of these imperial relics manifests when they are used uncritically by twentieth-century historians as evidence to construct Calcutta's urban history. We are supplied with examples of the Daniells and D'Oyly, Martin and Mill, and expected to acknowledge that the British were those who made Calcutta anything worth living in. Calcutta, an imperial history would claim, could not do without the British.

2 The limits of "white" town

Topographic palimpsest

One of the enduring assumptions about colonial cities of the modern era is that they worked on the basis of separation – they were "dual cities" divided into "black" and "white" towns.[1] Obviously, the degree of separation between black and white inhabitants varied according to the particularities of the context.[2] In the case of Calcutta, the idea of black and white towns is seemingly based on the perception that European residents of the town inhabited an area that in terms of layout, density, architecture, and everyday life was fundamentally different and divorced from that of the native inhabitants. Scholars have emphasized the distinctiveness of the architecture of the white town – the European neo-classicism brought by the colonizers. From such a perspective, the emergence of a neo-classical vocabulary in eighteenth- and nineteenth-century India is seen as a rather straightforward transplantation of English ideas on Indian soil, attenuated/disfigured (depending on one's point of view) by vagaries of local labor and availability of building materials.[3] In this chapter I examine the so-called white town to argue that such racial divisions were neither complete nor static. The black and white towns were far from being autonomous entities; the economic, political, and social conditions of colonial culture penetrated the insularity of both towns, although at different levels and to varying degrees. As an examination of the residential pattern of the white town will demonstrate, the story is more complicated.[4] One of the factors that contributed to this complication was the discrepancy between the norm of residential living that British visitors to the city expected to find, and the ones that they met with. As the unfamiliar spatial rules reconfigured them as subjects, they found it necessary to articulate their subjectivity in a new vocabulary.

The description of colonial Calcutta as a city divided into black and white rests on scant evidence, on a static reading of urban plans (a reluctance to move between the city scale and the architectural scale), and on a lack of critical attention in reading the change in density over time.[5] The notion that these building ideas were completely imported from England, for example, is based on the neo-classical "looks" of the buildings, with no attempt to document and examine plans and sections. Also, there has been little concern with everyday use of space. In other words, the existing scholarship is remarkably non-spatial. It is this lacuna I address in this chapter by explaining the organization of house plans as a means to supply a speculative market in which functions of buildings changed frequently and residences were used for non-residential purposes and vice versa. The blurring of boundaries lies in the heterogeneous use as well as the heterogeneous population who inhabited the buildings. If the terms *black town* and *white town* were used frequently in the nineteenth century, we need to understand why they were used and the nature of the inclusions and exclusions they implied in order to sustain an imperial narrative of difference and European superiority.

English visitors to late eighteenth-century and nineteenth-century Calcutta did assert that there was a white town and a black town.[6] The former was represented by the fine rows of houses surrounding the *maidan*, while its counterpart, the black town, was seemingly situated somewhere beyond. But while most agreed about the existence of these entities, few could concur on the boundaries between the two domains (Figure 2.1). The population distribution of ethnic groups in the various localities undoubtedly shifted between the eighteenth and nineteenth centuries, but any strict demarcation between the black and white town was arbitrary. Such boundaries were fluid, and at no time did the white town form a homogeneous space of European inhabitants. In addition, the urban fabric in the so-called white town did not follow the same pattern throughout. Historians have frequently pointed out that the most significant distinguishing feature of these two "towns" was the density of the urban fabric – sparsely distributed buildings of the white town as opposed to the close-knit fabric of the black town. This characterization, however, does not withstand close scrutiny. The area of sparsely distributed single detached dwellings on Chowringhee, typically seen as representative of the white town, was an exception, not the rule. Much of the "white town" had a higher density and a closely-knit urban fabric that embraced the street. In fact, well into the 1830s the area around Tank Square was regarded as the fashionable European district and Chowringhee was considered a suburb.[7] Chowringhee became the most desirable locale for the wealthy who wished to have the ambiance of country living and yet be close enough to the heart of administration and European shopping. For those who could afford a garden estate, the suburbs of Russapugla, Ballygunge, the area near Circular Road, and Entally offered plenty of choices for large plots of land. Yet many preferred to live near Tank Square, next to the shops, taverns, and smaller houses occupied by the less privileged. When both Chowringhee Road and Park Street became prime locales for commercial real estate in the mid-nineteenth century, the wealthy residential area retreated further inwards and to the south around Alipore.

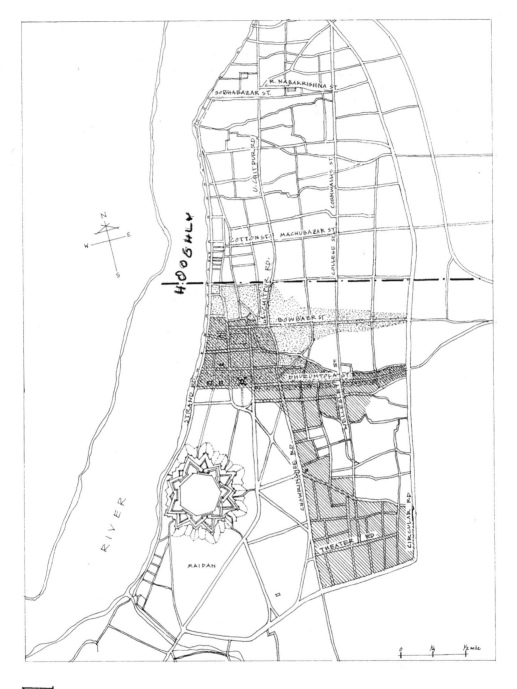

Figure 2.1 Map of Calcutta showing boundaries of "white" town

Boundaries as indicated by William Baillie, 1792

Boundaries as indicated by Leopold von Orlich and Edward Thornton

Boundaries as indicated by Lieutenant R. G. Wallace

The landscape of colonial Calcutta was far too complex to be usefully described in terms of the duality of black and white towns. The city consisted of overlapping geographies and conceptions of space and territory, both indigenous and foreign, that were constantly negotiated. Not surprisingly, the line of demarcation between the white and black towns shifted depending on the context and the perception of the observer. In the absence of clearly defined separation the colonizers created discrete containments for both public and private sociability. The spatial choices oscillated between a theatrical display of open plans and a proliferation of confining elements – elaborate compound walls and railings that spoke a calculated language of exclusion.

Much of the insistence on strict demarcation was an imperial impulse for racial distinctions, a vestigial desire from the days of early settlement when the walled city cordoned off the world of Christian inhabitants, banishing the heathens from the privileged Eden. In 1756 the settlement of Calcutta was destroyed by the Nawab of Bengal's forces. After the British regained Calcutta, the Company abandoned the idea of a walled city. The fort that replaced the old form of defense generated a fundamentally different city pattern. The 99 cannons of the fort commanded a vast open field, called the esplanade or the *maidan*. This was not meant to be a place of gathering, but a *glacis* to protect the fort. Such an open plan was predicated as much by advances in military technology as by a renewed confidence on the part of the British, who could now afford to have an open plan. This grand gesture was pregnant with possibilities of imperial display. The intersection of military objectives and commercial interests, however, produced an urban pattern that demanded that the colonizers rethink their boundaries. The commerce that the fort was meant to protect thwarted the full possibilities of an imperial city design. The British merchants who flourished in the protection of the Company did not consider it worthwhile to forego their rights to private property for "public" imperial projects.

Maps from the late eighteenth and nineteenth centuries offer clues to the process of drawing boundaries that began with the city scale. In 1794 the Governor General issued a proclamation fixing the limits of the town between the Hooghly River to the west and the inner side of the Mahratta Ditch to the east, and between Dihee Birjee to the south and the Chitpur *nullah* (creek) to the north.[8] Even before such boundaries were drawn, wealthy landowners, both Indian and European, bought large chunks of land and built on them, anticipating a wide range of uses and renters. They invested in bazaars, warehouses, residential buildings, shops, *bustees* (slums), godowns (storage spaces), and garden houses. Entrepreneurs like Dewan Kashinath sought permission from the Company to set up bazaars and "people" them with shopkeepers.[9] The population estimates of the time are not reliable, but the commercial and administrative activity in the city had attracted approximately 200,000 inhabitants by 1820.[10]

Landed property became a lucrative business. Building costs were high, as basic building materials like brick, stone, and durable wood had to be imported from outside the city. Consequently, rents were exorbitant and *pucka* (masonry) buildings could be fruitful investments. Only a few wealthy inhabitants could afford the luxury of a large house in a spacious garden; many more settled for smaller apartments and cheaper dwellings. The majority lived in single-room dwellings and huts. Property changed hands frequently, and it was common for Indians to rent property to Europeans and vice versa.[11] In the early days of colonial rule, it mattered little with whom the owners were dealing, as long as there was money to be made. For example, an 1803 advertisement in the *Calcutta Gazette* announced the private sale of a four-*beegah* property in Taltola-bazaar containing a pucka-built house that could be "made very comfortable for a trifling expense," and was "suitable for any gentleman about to leave India, who may be solicitous to provide for an Hindustanee Female Friend." The advertisement also mentioned that the ground "may be rendered productive by letting it out in small parcels to native tenants."[12]

Although wills and probate inventories provide a narrow glimpse of a person's financial dealings, the wills of some of the wealthy Indian residents of Calcutta in the early nineteenth century show an extraordinary investment in landed property. Many of them had earned handsome commissions as *banians*, but they also traded independently in cotton, opium, and salt. Sobharam Basak, a merchant who died in 1780, owned 37 houses in Burrabazaar alone. The 1819 will of Joykissen Singh, a *banian*, shows that he owned Rs. 740,430 of landed property in Calcutta, some of the most expensive of which were in Baranussy Ghose's Street, Harrington Street, Chowringhee Road, and Clive Street.[13] Even those of middling income considered landed property a worthwhile investment. It was common practice to have a few rented premises in addition to one's own dwelling house. In fact, the very sign of Bengali middle-class well-being was ownership of landed property.

Nineteenth-century Bengali texts were rife with anxious commentaries on money as a social leveler in an urban milieu prone to discarding traditional modes of socio-spatial order.[14] The ability to pay, however, was not the only determinant of spatial use or social power. As in any other city, social and political power was manipulated by the inhabitants to determine in whose image the landscape was to be shaped. It is this tension between the tendency to homogenize space as commodity and the desire for control over local territory that we need to keep in mind when we study the maps and plans of colonial Calcutta.

The late eighteenth-century mapmakers of Calcutta, keen to record the growing city, found ways to impress the stamp of the colonizers on the maps, thus unabashedly projecting their biases. The primary impulse behind surveying and mapping in colonial India was to fix boundaries and territories, and to locate people and objects in fixed space. This was seen as necessary both so that the colonial state could assess revenues, and for military and policing needs.

In 1780 the East India Company appointed the Commissioners of Police for the administration of the city, expecting the Commissioners to produce a registry of lands, houses, and estates, and to suggest suitable names for all streets and lanes. The Commissioners in turn appointed Edward Tiretta, the Company's architect, for the purpose, but by 1784 no maps had been produced.[15] Consequently, they turned to Captain Mark Wood who completed a survey and produced the maps at a scale of 200 feet to an inch. Since the production of such a large-scale map was too expensive, Wood, Chief Engineer in 1791, hired William Baillie to reproduce the map at a smaller scale, but with the addition of the changes that had taken place in the meanwhile. Hoping the map would be useful for the Police, the government agreed to buy 150 copies at 20 rupees each. Wood was, however, disappointed with the map Baillie produced, and subsequently the government refused to pay the remaining two-thirds of the balance to Baillie:

> Had Mr. Baillie only taken the trouble to have made a correct copy of the Plan on a reduced scale ... the Engraver would have found no difficulty in executing the work, in place he has merely traced the streets and Lanes ... and filled in the intermediate space with black lines, which renders the plan of no sort of value.[16]

Baillie's advertisement claimed that he had waited many months for the streets in the native city to receive new names. Considering such paucity, the plan was an accurate copy of the one in possession of the Police Commissioners, and showed all "ghauts," streets, lanes, and public buildings.[17] In other words, Baillie's plan diagrammed the streets, but chose only to emphasize a few selective elements of the European landscape. Predictably, this included a cluster of spatial markers around Tank Square, defined by the clean edge of Government House and Council House along Esplanade Row that perpendicularly intersected the sparse landscape of single detached houses along Chowringhee. It left out not just the entire "native" city, but many common European residences as well. Baillie's map, in privileging the elite European landscape, projected the elite British residents' and visitors' notion of what was important in the city, but his strategic silence in dealing with the rest of the town posed a problem for the administrators. What irked colonial administrators like Wood and the Police Commissioners was that such lack of knowledge of the town's physical geography, and particularly that of the native town, was not conducive to commercial interests or to policing. Although their concern was oriented differently from the anonymous missionary who bemoaned the lack of landscape in and around Calcutta (see Chapter 1), each in their own way was reacting to the lack of rigor in claiming authority. Unlike Baillie, the Police Commissioners recognized that cartographic opacity could easily work against the colonizer's desire to control the city.

elusive
transparency

In the nineteenth century this desire for control led to the creation of new
cartographic representations that sought to generate an elusive transparency. The most noteworthy among these was an elaborate survey of the
city undertaken between 1887 and 1892 under R. B. Smart that resulted in
a series of maps at 1:50 scale, showing not just every street and building,
but trees, lampposts, and other fixtures of the cityscape in great detail. The
transparency and authority of Smart's maps, however, foregrounded the
paradox of such representative strategies – transparency in this case also
implied recognition of the "other." What is, then, important in understanding the shifting experience of the city between the late eighteenth and
late nineteenth centuries is the manner in which scale, nomenclature, and
grids in maps encouraged colonial visions consistent with this increased
desire for control, as well as the limits to such desire.

In October 1791, Aaron Upjohn, Baillie's printer, started another survey.
This map, published in 1794, was also "incomplete," but it mapped the
parcels of property and paid more careful attention to what was considered the European town. Three spatial features are apparent from Upjohn's
plan. These are the ribbon development along the main arteries, the *ghats*
(stepped landings) along the edge of the Hooghly river, and the formation
of the administrative center between Esplanade Row and the Old Fort
(Figure 2.2). The narrow rectangular plots carved out along Bowbazaar
Street and Dhurumtola Street indicated the importance of having street-
front property on these east–west commercial arteries that intersected the
old channel of the Chitpur Road, connecting the "vast network of bazaars"
with the numerous *ghats*.[18] Such a network testified to the city's overwhelming commercial character. The purpose of *ghats*, however, was not
solely commercial. Trade as well as social and religious factors proved a
compelling combination prompting several wealthy Indians to build *ghats*,
thus inscribing their family names on the landscape. *Ghats* were built for
bathing, cremation, transporting people as well as cargo, and for dumping
night soil.[19] The river was the primary commercial transport route until
the construction of the railways, and the wholesale bazaars owned by
Indian merchants were set up in convenient proximity to the *ghats*. In the
course of the nineteenth century many more east–west arteries were created
to connect the wholesale markets with the retail outlets located in the city's
interior. The three-tiered commercial network of import-export, wholesale
bazaars, and retail outlets created a mutually supportive geography.

The administrative center of the city was defined by the Mint, the
Customs House, and warehouses along the river's edge; the Writers'
Building on the north, and Government House, Council House, and the
Supreme Court on the south (*maidan*) edge. Because of the proximity to
the port and the offices of the colonial government, this area became a
sought-after locale for European entrepreneurs. Large auction houses and
taverns commanded substantial spaces and chose prime spots on the main
thoroughfares to attract customers with the latest arrivals of "Europe

Figure 2.2 Portion of the Map of Calcutta, by A. Upjohn, 1792, showing the ribbon development, *ghats*, and the administrative center

goods." At the turn of the nineteenth century the north-east and south-east corners of Tank Square were claimed by the large auction houses, Lawtie & Gould and Ord & Knox. Facilities such as the "London Tavern" and the "Harmonic" on Lal Bazaar Street vied with each other to provide the inhabitants with the best food and wine and generous rooms for lodgers. They boasted spaces large enough to accommodate 500 people for a ball, and constituted venues for public meetings.[20]

There were few public places of entertainment. The couple of theaters that engaged amateur actors had a difficult time surviving. Consequently, until the mid-nineteenth century, the taverns and auction houses were the only public buildings where the European inhabitants could socialize. In 1805, I. H. T. Roberdeau was charmed by the amenities of the auction houses and the regularity and silence in which they conducted their business.[21]

In a city where "gentlemen" did not walk, the taverns and auction houses created self-contained worlds, protected from the weather and the humming city. The London Tavern at one time even offered "large and extensive rooms fitted up in a Rural Style" embellished with "rural walks" within its confines.[22] Here the desire for sociability conveniently met the needs of the merchants to inspire conspicuous consumption. And yet, the entertainment at the Taverns was considered unfashionable by the Company's elite, who cherished a pronounced difference among themselves, the non-commissioned servants of the Company, and the tradespeople.[23] The preferred elite alternative was gathering at private residences where the same pleasures could just as well be obtained within more controlled confines.

The large commercial enterprises were interspersed with petty shops and dwellings of various sizes occupied by Indians and Europeans alike.[24] From streets bearing names of distinctly indigenous origin, such as Cossitola Street (derived from *kasai-tola* or butchers' neighborhood) and Nuncoo Jemadar's Lane, European wigmakers, milliners, carriage-makers, and undertakers offered the best services money could buy. In 1784 an advertisement sought "a good Dwelling House, in a centrical situation of the Town, more agreeable if it was to be on the southward of the Great Tank."[25] Such a location would place the renter within two to three blocks of every kind of service, including those of cabinet and carriage makers, wax and tallow chandlers, watchmakers, butcher shops, livery stables, fashionable assembly rooms, warehouses, and three bazaars.[26] While many of the entrepreneurs lived above the shops, smaller entrepreneurs, like oyster-sellers and hairdressers, worked from their own houses. European business spilled from this area eastward along Dhurumtola Street and Bowbazaar Street and northwards into Chitpur Road, Clive Street, Chuttawallah Gully, and Moorgehatta Street, the last locality considered notorious by the elite for its low taverns and gambling houses.

The intricate mixed use that characterized the area around Tank Square was similar to the bazaars that crowded the river's edge. Most of these bazaars were wholesale markets specializing in particular commodities, and provided a nucleus for the gradual accretion of wholesale dealers, retailers, and entrepreneurs around them. Some of the bazaars were indicated in Upjohn's map, but the precise rendering of the surrounding physical environment in the northern part of the city was sacrificed. Consequently, we have to rely on documents of a later date to get a clearer picture of the accommodation of wholesale and retail business. A map of Calcutta, accompanied by a Bengali directory, was published by Ramanath Das in 1884, to provide Bengali visitors and temporary residents a better orientation in the city.[27] The map provided a wealth of information about institutions, professionals, offices, and markets (Figure 2.3). His map illustrated the specialized nature of the bazaars, such as cotton in Burrabazaar, books and stationary in Radhabazaar, and spices in Raja Sukhomoy's Posta. In all he noted 40 bazaars within the Calcutta municipal limits.

Bazaars not only served the city, but a larger region beyond. Just as European entrepreneurs sent consumer items from Calcutta to upcountry towns, every major social occasion in middle- and upper-class Bengali households necessitated a trip to Calcutta.[28] In providing shopping locales Das indicated markets as well as commercial streets containing contiguous shops dealing with specialized commodities. Durmahatta Street, for example, contained three bazaars and three large warehouses with concentrations of grain, linseed, timber, and jute merchants, interspersed with residences and petty shops. The major arteries such as Durmahatta Street, Chitpur Road, College Street, Machuabazaar Street, and Sobhabazaar Street, formed a series of superblocks. The streets that formed the outside edges of the superblocks developed mixed use with a preponderance of commercial activities, while the areas in the interior of the blocks became primarily residential. Das's 1884 map was, of course, produced a hundred years later than Upjohn's map, and showed a city that had tripled in size. But the network of bazaars he presented was a pattern that was set in the previous century.

Although these markets formed the lifeblood of the inhabitants, they were also the sites that most clearly blurred the lines among classes, ethnic groups, and races, contradicting the fundamental basis of a colonial culture. Both Bengali and English commentaries noted the cosmopolitan nature of the main bazaars. Not surprisingly these were the same sites that threatened the imagination of both British and Bengalis in their mutually exclusive effort to create a sovereign domain. To address such problems, nineteenth-century colonial planners emphasized efficient channels of trade on the one hand, and ridding the urban fabric of undesirable elements on the other.

As early as 1803, Lord Wellesley realized the need for a more comprehensive approach to creating an ordered city and set up a Town Improvement Committee. The objects of efficiency, sanitation, surveillance, and beautification were brought together to create a more controlled urban fabric:

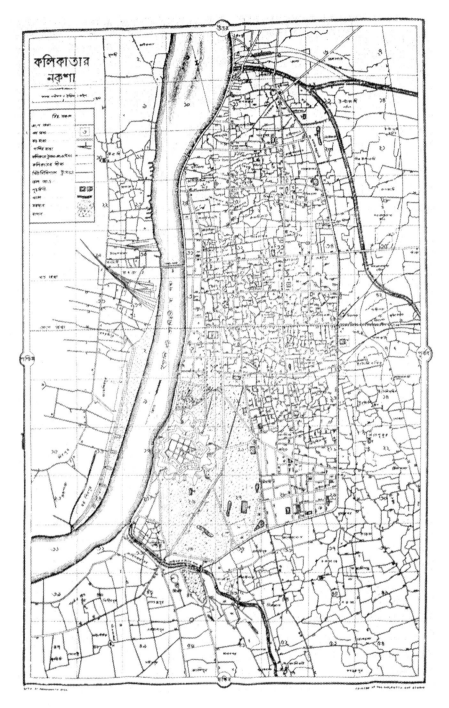

Figure 2.3 Map of Calcutta, by Ramanath Das, 1884, Collection of Keya Dasgupta

It is a primary duty of the Government to provide for the health, safety and convenience of its inhabitants of this great town, by establishing a comprehensive system for the improvement of the roads, streets ... and by fixing permanent rules for the construction and distribution of the houses and public edifices. ...

The appearance and beauty of the town ... and every improvement which shall introduce a greater degree of order, symmetry, and magnificence in the streets, ... will tend to ameliorate the climate and to promote and secure every object of a just and salutary system of Police.[29]

Wellesley proposed an aesthetic that in the early modern British imagination was connected to ideas of health and therefore civic virtue. A beautiful city was also one that was well policed. An efficient administration and policing of the city, according to him, required orderly, symmetrical, and magnificent streets and buildings, exactly contrary to his perception of the generic native town. Civic or public virtue would not only be reflected but fostered in appropriately policed public spaces. The significance of his aesthetic vision with its connection between efficiency and beauty, however, was not appreciated by many British administrators.

Subsequently, the responsibility of town improvement was handed over to the Lottery Commissioners, who were responsible for raising funds for municipal improvement by holding a series of public lotteries. The success of the lotteries prompted the government to appoint a Lottery Committee in 1817 to investigate the city's needs. The Committee debates considered a host of issues for improving the health of the city and the convenience of its inhabitants, including drainage, building roads, excavating new tanks and filling old ones, constructing aqueducts, bridges, and *ghats*.[30] Much of the lottery money went into beautifying the area around Chowringhee and the *maidan*. G. I. Gordon, one of the members of the committee, however, urged that efficiency should be the prime concern, with comfort and beautification secondary.[31] In keeping with Gordon's objectives, the two major goals were leveling the land to improve drainage and the creation of additional roads. The main purpose of driving roads into the native town was to create air-passages that were supposed to dilute the miasma rising from dense habitations. After all, unhealthy habitation in the vicinity was detrimental to the entire town. No one, however, lost sight of the additional advantages of these roads, namely, improved connection among markets and easier policing. The committee intentionally chose road improvement routes through the *bustees*, the cheapest yet the most densely populated areas, evicting the impoverished residents. The compensation for such appropriation of property went to the landlords and not to the tenants. The residual land increased in value "affording the speculator in building an opportunity of obtaining portions of grounds suitable to his purposes."[32] This scheme, the Committee argued, would create more agreeable neighborhoods.

The Committee's proposals resulted in an artery, parallel to Chitpur Road, that traveled from Chowringhee to the heart of the native town bearing the names of the colonizers: Cornwallis Street, College Street, Wellesley Street, Wood Street. By 1826, several other streets had been created including Elliot Road, Strand Road, Wellington Street, Hastings Street, Moira Street, Louden Street, Amherst Street, and Hare Street, and still others had been widened and straightened.[33] The Strand Road was the first decisive step in ordering the river's edge between Prinsep Ghat and Hatkhola, providing a direct vehicular route between the commercial establishments, *ghats*, warehouses, and colonial administration.

The Lottery Committee, however, had higher aspirations. They briefly considered the possibility of nine 70-foot-wide parallel streets at equal distances between Bowbazaar Street and the northern edge of the city. The objective was to create a grid with cross streets of similar width. These blocks were to be further divided by avenues at distances of 150 to 200 feet, in a desire to reorganize the landscape of north Calcutta. This scheme did not mirror the pattern of Chowringhee, where the city blocks ranged from 300 to 600 feet in depth and at least 1,200 feet in length, and formed a pattern of back-to-back lots that would remain largely unchanged until the turn of the twentieth century. The Committee's plan would also have fractured the tight linear configuration of businesses that thrived on mutual adjacency. Such a closely spaced grid plan seems less likely to have resulted from aesthetic prerogatives, than from concerns about producing a transparent landscape convenient for surveillance. The Lottery Committee's ambitions were, however, curbed owing to the limited capital in the hands of the Committee and the predictable resistance from the native community that would ensue from such an overhaul. Some of these new roads could facilitate the movement of goods for both European and native merchants, but Indians were shaping the landscape by a different agenda of power and social relations and would not be easily persuaded, despite the financial benefit they could reap as landlords from some of these measures.[34]

Nineteenth-century maps, despite their biases, provided other readings of the landscape. Both Upjohn's and Schalch's maps presented a landscape that was delineated not only by *ghats*, markets, and administrative institutions, but by the indigenous pattern of *paras* as well. It is worth noting that in Bengali parlance there was no equivalent of the white town/black town duality. From the Bengali point of view, the city was divided into a host of *paras*, *tolas*, and *tulis*, all terms used to distinguish localities. The *paras* covered an area approximately ¼ mile by ½ mile, a space that was within easy walking distance. Cognitively, the space constituted a territory, and derived a sense of identity from a physical feature, which could be a *bagan* (garden), *pukur* (pond), or a bazaar (invariably implying the presence of a wealthy family who owned the bazaar). Localities such as Banstola, Champatola, Chorebagan, and Jhamapukur can be seen clearly delineated in Simms' 1854 map (Figure 2.4). Although the localities did not have

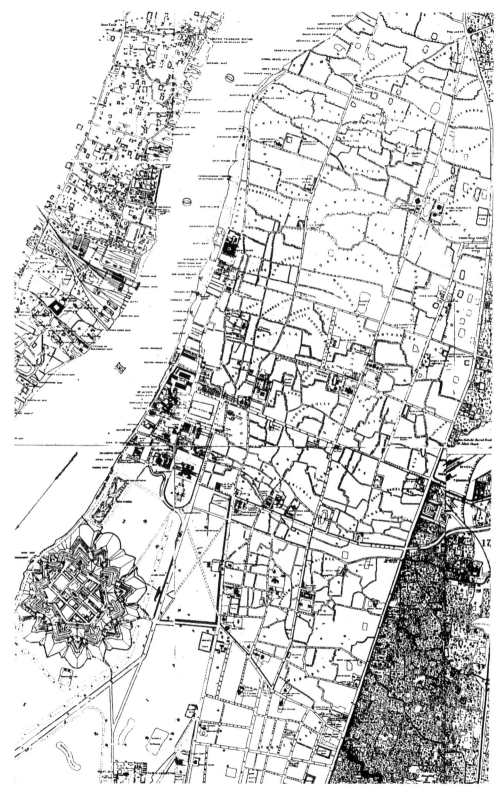

Figure 2.4 Plan of Calcutta showing the *paras*, by W. Simms, 1852

fixed boundaries (the name of the locality was simply scrawled across a large space), they were mostly contained by four streets, that is, they formed a block that its residents could identify with.[35] The area between Chowringhee Road, Park Street, Theater Road, and Wood Street, with its preponderance of well-off European residents, was known popularly as *sahib-para*, one among the 18 *paras* that constituted nineteenth-century Calcutta. This recognition of the city in terms of *paras* was reflected in the 1785 designation of *thanas* for policing purposes. The city was divided into 31 *thanas* roughly corresponding to the *paras*. In 1852 the *thanas* were replaced by wards for administrative purposes. The wards encompassed larger areas, with the ward boundaries corresponding to the major arteries, paying little attention to the notion of *paras*. The problem of using the *paras* for administrative purposes was that their boundaries were unclear – either those limits had to be defined or a different system had to be superimposed. The municipal authorities eventually chose the latter as more convenient. Since the *paras* and adjacency to important landmarks and not street numbers continued to be the means of locating a place, for a person unfamiliar with the city in the latter part of the nineteenth century, the process could be difficult. Ramanath Das, however, found an ingenious way of conveying information about the city by overlaying a grid on the *paras*, a technique not used in the contemporary government maps of Calcutta.[36] The numbered square or rectangular grids provided an abstract base within which to locate places without either relying on the street numbers as guides or fixing the boundaries of the *paras*. This allowed Das to generate several layers of descriptions in a single map. Such layering of information was a way of dealing with the city's complex identities, a method that would disappear from government maps at the turn of the twentieth century. The mid-nineteenth-century ward maps produced by the Municipality erased the notion of the *para* to generate a singular reading of the geography of the city. Late nineteenth- and early twentieth-century topographical maps relied on a similar limited description. The cognition of the *para*, however, remained in Bengali language and everyday practice.

A significant difference between Upjohn's 1794 and Schalch's 1826 plans was the morphological change of the area around Tank Square. In the late eighteenth century the buildings stood on fairly large plots of land, even when the houses themselves were small. By the third decade of the nineteenth century the smaller lots on Esplanade Row had been agglomerated to create larger parcels for siting the main administrative institutions, and the individual lots on the other streets had been more densely built up to maximize rental space.[37] In the Schalch plan we notice the new Government House and its gardens interrupting Esplanade Row, while the new Town Hall claimed a piece of the *maidan*. After the fort, Government House was the single most salient feature of the plan. The other important change was the reordering of the *maidan* to create, a race course, a spacious drive, and the Respondentia walk. A radial network of roads emerging from Fort

William linked the military stronghold with other institutional anchors of the expanding imperial landscape. The first three roads established the connection between the fort and the commercial and administrative heart, including Government House, the banks, and courts; the fourth road joined Park Street to connect the fort with the Asiatic Society, the Survey Offices, and the most exclusive residential locality; the fifth road linked the fort with the hospital and jail; while the last one facilitated the connection with the suburbs of Kidderpore and Garden Reach. The quasi-baroqueness of these vistas was largely symbolic. They certainly represented a desire for spatial control but, except on the south, the axes halted beyond the *maidan*, confronting the already set urban pattern. The authorities could not completely overhaul the areas around Tank Square and Chowringhee unless such reshaping was directly beneficial to the large companies and agency houses that had come to dominate the area. Under Wellesley's aegis the Company attempted to buy the houses between the Writers' Building and Government House, but owners quoted prices that were too high.[38] In the minds of the owners, most of them Europeans, profit and the right of private property obviously superseded the need for imperial gestures.

Instead, the focus of symbolic power turned from the urban fabric beyond the eastern and northern faces of the *maidan* to the *maidan* itself. The *maidan* was planted with trees under the auspices of Lord Auckland; the firing field became the field for displaying imperial leisure and splendor. The *maidan* formed an extension of the Government House, providing space for ceremonial grandeur. Special celebrations at the Governor's mansion would conclude with fireworks in the *maidan* which the guests could witness from the several porticoes, apartments, and balconies that opened on to it. A drive in the Course, in the perennial search for cooling sea-breeze and appropriate society, was a byword for genteel leisure. A necessary part of gentility consisted of grooms and an entourage of servants accompanying their masters. Such places of outdoor leisure – the drive, the race course, and the walks – were highly defined paths of movement contained by their geometry and regulations that favored the rights of Europeans. Significantly, these pieces retained their isolated identities. No attempt was made to integrate these different elements within a singular formal arrangement. Although Indian gentlemen crowded the Course like their British counterparts, in 1821 the Course and the Respondentia Walk were made a European preserve between five and eight o'clock in the evening and morning.[39] Such exclusionary measures were considered necessary to prevent "natives" from disfiguring a valued social event.

The desire for strict boundaries was rooted in an eighteenth-century British obsession with classification, division, and separation, exaggerated in the colonial context by the need to distinguish between black and white. Such proclivities gained impetus through incidents such as the Black Hole reminding the British residents of the constant native threat to their existence in the city. In their zeal to protect islands of sociability and symbols of imperialism, the colonizers resorted to building elaborate artifices of delimitation – wrought-iron railings, masonry walls, and gates – often designed after European pattern books. Since the buildings in the large lots were situated far away from the road, the architecture of the boundary wall and gate, as an extension of the architecture of the building, displayed to the outside world the quality of the artifact thus delimited. They functioned as preparatory devices for what was to be found inside. The boundaries became symbols of the ruling class, as was amply illustrated by the drawing of the gate of Government House on the frontispiece of Charles D'Oyly's *Views of Calcutta and Its Environs* (Figure 2.5).[40] The gate itself was a representation of imperial power. As territorial markers these protective devices that secluded the world of British inhabitants, also worked to create a fractured public space that could never be gathered within a single imperial gesture. If the symbols and spaces of imperialism had to be carefully bounded to prevent native intrusion, it also meant that the native threat had to be placed at the center of colonial life, disfiguring and delimiting the colonizers' desire for unbounded and unpeopled territory.

Wherever we look, the city was heterogeneous. Exclusionary measures, intended to organize this heterogeneity, were defeated by the inherent contradictions of colonial life. Even within the colonizers' own domain the realization of a homogeneous enclave proved difficult.

Built for speculation

If the touch of neo-classicism introduced to simulate a sense of grandeur rendered the buildings in the white town a note of familiarity from the outside, for British residents the familiarity disappeared on the inside. On closer inspection the interior of the houses functioned according to different rules. Mrs. Fenton observed in 1821 that even within the walls of these large houses she felt exposed to curious eyes:

> Your idea of a bedroom – and it was mine also – is that of retirement, a sanctuary where none can or will intrude! ... "who could sleep in a room where four doors and four windows all stand open?"[41]

There were no locks or bolts in the doors, indicating too plainly that Indian doors were not supposed to be shut. Without the possibility of closing off rooms, the boundary between the house and the outside world became ineffective. This blurring of boundaries, and the consequent lack of interiority, became one of the more disturbing aspects of colonial life, reminding the colonizers that the locus of a hybrid culture was in their midst.

Most British residents disapproved of the way the houses were built. Among them was the surgeon and medical topographer Ranald Martin, who noted in 1836 that the buildings were raised by "natives and other speculators on their own plans at the cheapest rates and for the mere

Figure 2.5 The South-East Gate of Government House, Calcutta, by Charles D'Oyly, 1835, Title page of *Views of Calcutta and its Environs* from Jeremy Lostly, *Calcutta* (London, 1990)

purpose of letting to the highest profit."[42] Indeed, Indians as well as Europeans invested in building for speculation in the white town, and deftly combined local planning practices with ideas from European pattern books to generate designs that were unique.

From the Schalch plan of 1826 we know that several lots in the area around Park Street, Chowringhee, and Wood Street were owned by Indians.[43] However, since many lots were unnamed we cannot be certain of the exact distribution (Figure 2.6). Only the names of those who were considered prominent were included. The lots were exceptionally large, and a few individuals owned several lots in the area. In 1801 William

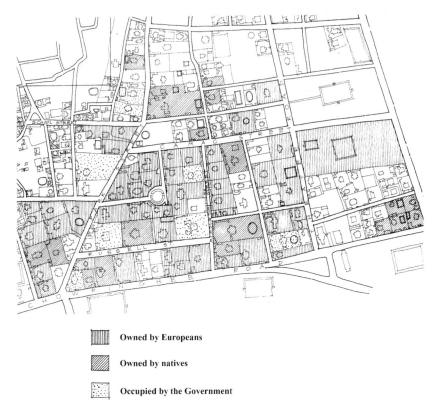

|||||| Owned by Europeans

////// Owned by natives

:::::: Occupied by the Government

Figure 2.6 Ownership of land in the Chowringhee area

Camac put up for sale five such houses and a bazaar worth 131,500 *sicca* rupees.[44] Property value depended largely on the location and the "room-iness" of the house. The buildings, with rare exceptions, were oriented with their long axes running north–south, allowing for carriage ports to the north and verandahs on their south sides to catch the summer breeze. Inside, the layouts differed, depending on the total area of the house, but typically they consisted of three sets of rooms – one set on axis with the carriage-port and the south verandah, and two sets of rooms on either side, thus creating a three-bay pattern. In the late eighteenth century it was customary to have the ground floor devoted to storage and services, as it was considered contaminated by rising miasma. If not adequately damp-proofed, the ground floor could be unlivable. There were many substantial single-story houses that differed from that pattern, however, obliging their owners to emphasize that such accommodations were dry and perfectly habitable. When Aaron Upjohn's "villa" in Sealdah was put up for sale in 1800, Dring and Company's advertisement noted that the lower-story house was "well-raised," "flued throughout, and perfectly dry at all seasons." The house consisted of seven rooms, two halls, and an open verandah to the east, west, and south; it was located on a garden "well stocked with choice fruit trees, exotics," and was a mere 20 minutes' ride to the Black Hole Monument.[45]

Advertisements at the turn of the nineteenth century emphasized the size and beauty of the "compound" over descriptions of the house, and sought to entice renters and buyers by intimating the nearness of the property to respectable houses and estates.[46] An advertisement for a new upper-roomed masonry house on Burial Ground Road (later renamed Park Street), to be rented in May 1803, noted its proximity to Captain Anthony Greene's house and its commanding view of the Salt Water Lake and the country for several miles from the third floor. The house consisted of "four rooms, a hall, and three verandahs below, the same above stairs, with two verandahs, and a large room over the hall in the third story, with front, and a large winding back stairs," and suitable outhouses.[47] Advertisements suggested the pleasures of country living – rooms with generous dimensions, orchards, and well-stocked ponds, as well as the possibility of using the fertile land for agricultural purposes.[48] Except for the extensiveness of the adjoining grounds, the description of rural property did not differ significantly from descriptions of those located in the city.

The hall was the principal entrance and gathering space in the "Anglo-Indian" house, and typically was of the largest dimensions. The rooms surrounding the hall were seldom differentiated by function and were often referred to as bedrooms or chambers, irrespective of their actual use. House plans, however, sometimes designated a billiards room, which was considered a necessary amenity in wealthy households, and less frequently a drawing room was featured in the advertisements. Bathrooms and closets (sometimes called "necessities") were situated in close proximity to sleeping rooms. The most fashionable houses, like the Belvedere House, had marble-lined hot and cold baths.[49] In 1793 Dring, Cleland and Co. announced the sale of a prominently located house on Old Court House Street:

> (T)hat commodious, elegant, and well built upper-roomed house with extensive premises, at present rented for Sicca Rupees 500 per month by the Marquis of Cornwallis for the residence of His Lordship's Aide-de-camps, situated immediately to the northward of Sir William Jones on the great road leading from the old Court House to the Esplanade, consisting above stairs of a large hall, and a room to the southward, a drawing-room, and a bed-room to the westward, with a private staircase, to the east, and the same number of rooms, &c., below, with a verandah to the north. The lower storey is raised upon arches, the rooms under appropriated to Abdarkhannahs, godowns, &c., &c.
> There are two coach-houses, stabling for ten horses, a cook-room, a bottlekhanna, a palankeen house, and a well, &c. and upon the same premises to the westward a small upper-roomed house consisting

of a room eighteen feet square, venetianed, &c., the whole standing on one biggha and 10 cottahs of ground.[50]

Such a conveniently located building with extensive outhouses formed the high end of the market, and yet we are not sure that all the outhouses were of masonry construction. If they were, the advertisers usually did not fail to point that out. Outhouses or the servants' wings were built as separate structures; beyond that there was little distinction between service and served spaces. In houses of more than one story, the "private stair," sometimes the only stair, provided access for both servants and masters.

The city dwellings, despite their smaller lots (small compared to the suburbs, but large by today's urban standards), commanded significantly higher rents. A two-story house consisting of two bedrooms, a hall and a verandah on each floor, with cook rooms, bathrooms, and storage in Moorgyhatta, yielded 150 *sicca* rupees in rent in 1784.[51] Larger establishments were predictably more expensive, and if advantageously located could earn between 500 to 900 *sicca* rupees per month.[52]

If we compare these with a 1789 advertisement for a large country house in England that was to be sold by lottery among the residents of Calcutta, we find some clear points of distinction. The house, located in Walton upon Thames, boasted extensive farm houses and a formal garden, "seven bed chambers, drawing room, dining and breakfast parlours, a hall, wainscotted, and neatly fitted up with marble chimney pieces and convenient closets; two staircases, a passage, and large China closet," and a distinctly articulated array of servant spaces including "five servant's bed rooms, a most convenient kitchen, scullery, Butler's pantry, larder, dairy, brew-house, tool house, and commodious cellars, with a variety of connected offices, a detached laundry, Fruit-room, Coach-house, stabling for four horses, with loft over, and various useful buildings."[53]

This description conveys the image of a reasonably elaborate late eighteenth-century English country house. In contrast with the Calcutta houses, the functions of the rooms are clearly stated. The unspecificity of the rooms in Calcutta was not related to the spaces being multipurpose (although nothing would prevent such use); rather, it was a method of responding to a changing market, in which there was no assurance that the building would continue in its present use.

In 1799 proprietors of the Calcutta Exchange, unable to meet their debt for the construction of the building, wished to sell it. In their advertisement they noted that it would be ideal for public offices, shops, or an assembly house.[54] The Theater, which in the late eighteenth century served the amateur dramatic interests of the Europeans and their penchant for lavish balls, was transformed into an auction house by Mr. Roworth, and in 1808 was bought by Gopi Mohun Tagore, who converted it into the New China Bazaar, after he persuaded the shopkeepers of the old China

Bazaar to move to the new venue.[55] The transformation of a theater into a bazaar was drastic, but, because of the arrangement and dimensions of rooms, most of the houses were admirably suited to various uses. Additional profit from the premises was seen as appropriate in country estates as well as urban houses, which often contained large godowns and attached shops.[56] Residences were frequently transformed into offices, boarding houses, retail shopping space, and clubhouses, with little or no major remodeling. In other words, the building stock was designed for a speculative market in which needs changed frequently. This flexibility came with certain advantages and disadvantages for those who made these buildings their homes. On the one hand, few other patterns could accommodate the public nature of display and sociability that became a mode of life for the colonizers. On the other hand, the residents could never aspire to the type of privacy that they – the elite, at any rate – had come to expect in houses in England.

Visiting Calcutta in the mid-nineteenth century, Colesworthy Grant observed the remarkable similarity of internal arrangement in the houses in Calcutta.[57] The main difference was between upper- and lower-roomed houses, the former enjoying a cooler breeze. In the typical lower-roomed house you entered directly into the hall from a verandah or a door that was always kept open. The hall opened on to four rooms that answered the purpose of "parlour, dining, drawing and sitting rooms, – titles, not generally – the first never – heard in these latitudes."[58] The bathrooms, one for the master and one for the mistress, were located on opposite ends of the house. All of these rooms opened directly on to the grounds. In other words, they could be entered from outside, necessitating that "the premises be enclosed."[59] The terrace or rooftop accessed by a stair from within and without, he noted, was "the greatest extent of ground trodden, in a way of exercise, by the European foot."[60] Upper-roomed houses would contain at least two halls, one used for dining and the other for breakfast. The large Chowringhee mansions sometimes contained 16 or 20 apartments for the convenience of friends and visitors. The residents were not lacking in hospitality "in a land where inhabitants seem to shift with the monthly steamers and passenger ships."[61] Clearly, Grant was struck by the novelty of the arrangement. Few of these late eighteenth- and early nineteenth-century houses survive, but by reading the surviving plans in conjunction with the urban plans, we learn much about the spatial arrangement that suited changing market needs of Calcutta while contradicting contemporary practices in England.

In his discussion of European residential design, Robin Evans persuasively argued that house plans embody social relations; they highlight the desirable kinds of interaction within the household and exclude undesirable possibilities.[62] In such a view, passages, the arrangement of rooms, and the location of doors and windows appear as poignant clues to social relations. They set the parameters of interpretative possibilities for using the space. Studying the plans of nineteenth-century colonial houses in Calcutta one could not be more aware of how different these houses are from their European counterparts.

The three buildings I am about to examine at length were constructed between 1800 and 1832.[63] Two of these were ordinary buildings located in different areas of the white town and the third was *the* grand mansion of the presidency – Government House – the residence of the Governor General (later the Viceroy) of British India. By examining the structural changes made in the blueprints, I attempt to trace the genealogy of house form. Then, to understand the logic of their spatial organization, I compare the house plans in terms of their site emplacement, the dimensional arrangement of rooms, the types of access between spaces, and the location of primary spaces in relation to service spaces.

In the mid-nineteenth century, traveling along Old Court House Street from Esplanade Row, one could find on the left a narrow city block between Waterloo Street and Ranee Moody Gully that had the rare advantage of having two streets opening to the lots. The third lot from the other end of the block (that is from Cossitola Street, renamed Bentinck Street) was 180 feet deep and 96 feet wide on the Ranee Moody Gully side and 86 feet on the Waterloo Street side. It had an additional advantage of abutting Crooked Lane on the west. Despite the narrow streets and lanes – Waterloo Street was only 25 feet wide with 7- to 8-feet-wide sidewalks on either side, and Ranee Moody Gully was 16 feet wide – the blocks between Cossitola Street and Old Court House Street were the prime locale for fashionable shops and prestigious offices. Consequently, many residential buildings in this area were transformed to suit such needs or, put another way, the building stock was amenable to both residential and nonresidential uses. The house on 23/24 Waterloo Street was ideal for such a changing market (Figure 2.7a).[64]

Initially, the front of the house faced Ranee Moody Gully. The front edge of the site was defined by the carriage house and servants' quarters. A couple of steps led to an 11-foot-deep portico, with a pair of symmetrical double columns giving it a sense of formal dignity. Six more steps at the entrance door led to a square entrance hall with a small chamber to the left that could be used as a cloakroom. The entrance hall opened on to a 30-foot-deep and 19 foot 4 inches-wide central room, the largest room in the house, which in turn was directly connected to two sets of rooms on either side, each measuring 16 feet by 19 feet 4 inches and symmetrically arranged. The central hall and the two rooms on the south led directly to a 14-foot-wide south-facing verandah. A circular private staircase on the north face of the building connected an identical set of rooms on the second floor. In addition to the stair, the north face contained the other service spaces typically included within the house at that time – bathroom and storage (*bottlekhanna*). The winding staircase continued to the terrace above the second floor. At a later time, probably within a couple of decades, a larger

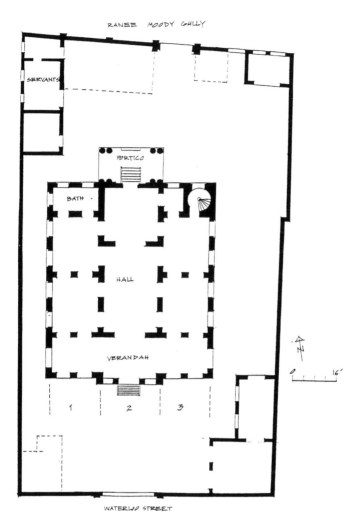

Figure 2.7a House on 23/24 Waterloo Street, original ground floor plan.
Based on drawing in the collection of Mackintosh Burn Pvt. Ltd

staircase was built in the south-east corner of the verandah to provide independent access to the second floor (Figure 2.7b). The 1862 Street Directory
indicated that the house was being used as the Adelphi Hotel. Consequently,
the proprietor must have felt the necessity to add a more public stairway.
The positioning of the public stairway in the verandah was obviously
designed to cause minimum changes to the building, but it also opened up
the potential for interpreting the house as having two "fronts." Still later, a
third floor and extra bathrooms on the south-east and south-west corners
of the second floor were added, serviced by narrow balconies (Figure 2.7c).

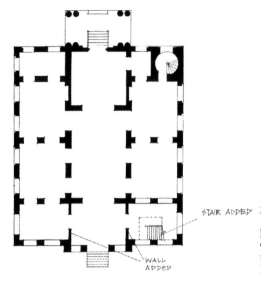

Figure 2.7b House on 23/24 Waterloo Street, ground floor plan showing first set of changes. Based on drawing in the collection of Mackintosh Burn Pvt. Ltd

The large staircase on the south-east was not extended to the third floor. Instead, at a later time the ground on the south was enclosed, creating three large interconnected spaces, which could be defined as more public spaces, considering their proximity to the street and their relative dimensions (Figure 2.7d). A third staircase (in the fashion of a grand stair but with smaller dimensions) was built on the central axis, connecting the public spaces directly with the upper floors. The central axis on the south side on the second floor was extended and enclosed to accommodate the stairs from the shop. Two 10-inch walls were extended southward along the central axis to separate the two staircases and create a room on the south-west side, maintaining the symmetry of the plan. At the same time, perhaps, the east edge of the lot was built up to provide extra outhouse and storage space. The 1892 Street Directory indicated that the building was still being used as a hotel but had changed hands. It is not hard to imagine the manner in which the large spaces on the south and the formal central stair would be advantageous to the needs of a hotel.

Smart's plan, from the turn of the century, indicated the shops and the adjacent outbuildings, while the municipal drawing of 1911 showed another set of changes taking place (Figures 2.7e and 2.7f). The formal stair on the south was eliminated and a separate channel of access was created to the south-east staircase. Some of the walls in the house were replaced by iron columns and beams to create more generous space between the bays. The north portico was eliminated, presumably to create unimpeded access to the godowns now formed by dismantling the interior walls of the outhouses on the east. In addition, several entrances now opened directly on to Crooked Lane. The first two floors were used as office

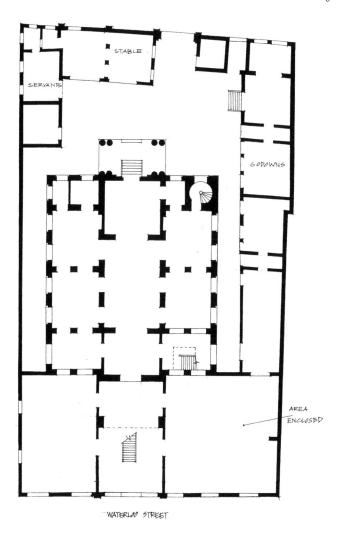

STABLE

SERVANTS

GODOWNS

AREA
ENCLOSED

WATERLOO STREET

Figure 2.7c House on 23/24 Waterloo Street, ground floor plan showing second
set of changes. Based on drawing in the collection of Mackintosh
Burn Pvt. Ltd

spaces, the third floor was used for lodging, and the large spaces on the
Waterloo Street side were converted to three independent shops, which
received a newly articulated elevation. Thus the proprietor, Cawnpoor
Woollen Mills, was using the site for at least four purposes – shops, offices,
godowns, and lodging – each of which could be rented independently.
With the property given over to multiple uses in an attempt to maximize
rental space, there was hardly any open space left in the premises. The
south-facing verandahs, supposed to welcome the refreshing evening breeze

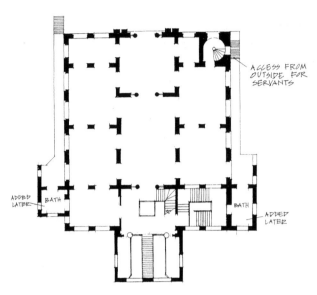

Figure 2.7d House on 23/24 Waterloo Street, upper floor plan showing second
set of changes. Based on drawing in the collection of Mackintosh
Burn Pvt. Ltd

had become a secondary concern. By this time, the front of the house had
turned away from Ranee Moody Gully (by this time renamed British
Indian Street) and definitely belonged to Waterloo Street.

The changing configurations of the house on Waterloo Street demonstrate the principles on which houses were built and transformed in the
course of the nineteenth century. The dimension of the rooms in the initial
ground floor plan was determined by the comfortable span of 20 feet,
constructed with 10-inch-deep timber beams spaced approximately 24
inches apart. The width of the rooms could obviously be increased with
the additional expense of increased beam depth and close spacing of beams.
In the largest houses in the city, it was not uncommon to find rooms
30 or even 40 feet wide.[65] This was the basic structural principle that
determined the pattern of house plans until iron columns and beams
became the vogue. That, however, explains little of house planning and
use. The generous dimensions and the multiple openings between rooms,
which created an ideal pattern for uses that were more public than private,
raise some issues about the social life of the residents.

Let us consider another house, one on 3 Camac Street, that had quite
a few points of similarity with the Waterloo Street house. This one, built
in the early nineteenth century, was located far from the bustling crowd
of Old Court House Street, in the then quiet grandeur of the suburbs of
Chowringhee.[66] As far as the street directories indicate, the house was
not used for purposes other than residential and was occupied by one

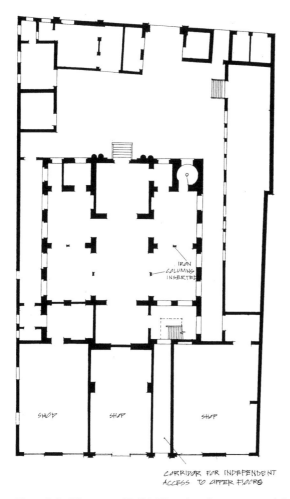

Figure 2.7e House on 23/24 Waterloo Street, ground floor plan showing third
set of changes. Based on drawing in the collection of Mackintosh
Burn Pvt. Ltd

or two families, unlike the Waterloo Street house.[67] This was exceptional,
considering that most residences in the latter part of the nineteenth century
in the Chowringhee area, rather than being single-family dwellings, were
either shared by several families or used as boarding houses. This trend
of shared occupancy was already in place by the 1850s. In the area bounded
by Chowringhee Street, Wood Street, Park Street, and Theater Road,
there were 12 boarding houses in 1858, 18 in 1872, with one less in
1892, but the number of houses with shared occupancy increased sharply
from 26 in 1858 to 56 in 1892.[68] The sparseness of the single detached
dwellings in the maps belies the occupant density of so many of these

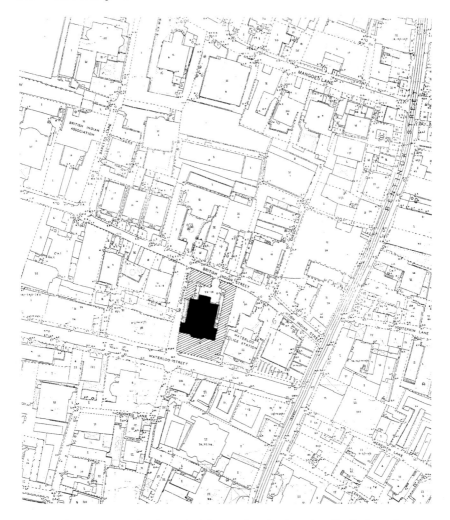

Figure 2.7f House on 23/24 Waterloo Street, site plan based on R. B. Smart's
        Survey of Calcutta, 1887–1909

houses, which could have, on average, 15 boarders as well as numerous
servants.

The single-family house at the crossing of Middleton and Camac Streets
stood on a large lot 240 feet wide and 285 feet deep (Figure 2.8a). The house
was built 150 feet away from the entry on Middleton Street. The entrance
portico, however, did not face Middleton Street. In keeping with the norm
of having the carriage port to the north, the path that led from the Middleton
Street entrance went around the house to the back of the site where the
formal entrance was located. This was the standard practice in all south-
facing lots on east–west streets such as Harrington Street and Theater Road.

The intention was to create a distance from the street, yet to leave the southern aspect open for verandahs, gardens, and informal living. The street edge was, as usual, defined by the carriage house and servants' accommodation, while the cook rooms and storage were located on the northern end, close to the main house but separate. By 1856 an entrance to Camac Street had been created, thus reorienting the approach to the house.[69] This was a privilege arising from the corner site location, one that other houses on the same street did not possess, and it invariably suggested other readings of the site, for example, building another house near the Middleton Street edge. In fact, the site was carved into four separate lots in the early twentieth century.[70]

The entry sequence, the position of the service spaces, and the system of three sets of rooms on axis were reminiscent of the Waterloo Street house (Figure 2.8b). The entrance hall led to five rooms nestled in between the service spaces that claimed the corners of the building. On the second floor, the room deployment was similar except in the southern room where, instead of two walls creating two smaller adjoining service rooms, two pairs of columns on each end were used to define a larger space. Two

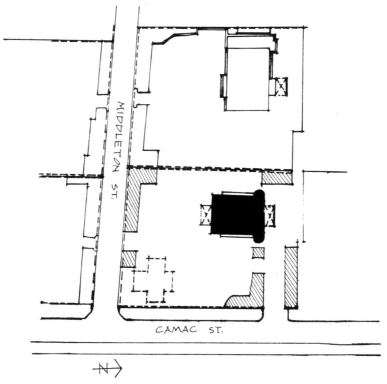

Figure 2.8a House on 3 Camac Street, site plan. Based on drawing in the collection of Mackintosh Burn Pvt. Ltd

major differences from the house on Waterloo Street were the location of
the main stairs, which defined the stair-hall as an integral part of the
design, and the north–south instead of east–west spanning of the rooms.
Although the stair faced away from the entrance door, it created the
possibility of a defined path of circulation, a suggestion taken up at a later
date with the addition of a 15-inch wall to create a central vestibule
through which movement could be controlled. Challenging this path of
axial movement was the spanning of the rooms in the opposite direction.
Although two or more doors from each room led to an adjoining room,
creating the familiar permeable pattern, the spanning suggested the direction in which spaces could be expanded or contracted. It also created the
possibility of articulating zones of privacy (from more public to private)
perpendicular to the central axis of movement.

A 1905 plan of the house attempted to create two porticoes instead of
one and return the house to its former interior configuration by eliminating
the bathrooms added on the east and west and the storage space on the
south (Figure 2.8c). In the process it also eliminated the two walls on
the southern side of the ground floor, integrating the space of the smaller
rooms on the sides with the larger room to form a spacious hall. The
15-inch wall articulating the central axis was also removed, demonstrating
the ease with which the spaces could be modified on the east–west axis,
depending on individual needs.

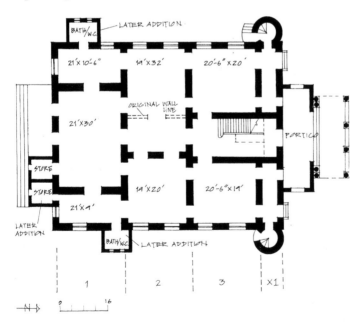

Figure 2.8b House on 3 Camac Street, ground floor plan showing nineteenth-
        century additions. Based on drawing in the collection of
        Mackintosh Burn Pvt. Ltd

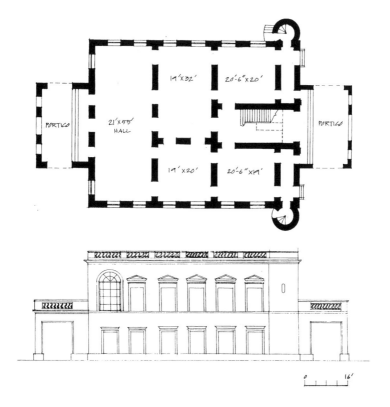

Figure 2.8c House on 3 Camac Street, ground floor plan and elevation after modification, 1905. Based on drawing in the collection of Mackintosh Burn Pvt. Ltd

The three-bays-of-rooms principle was adhered to in houses where lot size permitted. An extra bay was sometimes added, parallel to the entrance axis, to accommodate service spaces, verandahs, and even an extra set of rooms. Extra bays were used innovatively to suit specific needs of site and function. A house on no. 17 Chowringhee Road, constructed in the first half of the nineteenth century, ensured the presence of the verandah on the south, as well as providing the three-bay-and-one arrangement to be approached from a central hall, by switching the axis perpendicular to the verandah, which doubled as a side entrance (Figure 2.9).[71] On the ground floor, the shops engaged the street, while the servants' quarters and storage were moved to the back of the lot. The shop space on the right was a post-1856 addition. Chowringhee Road north of Lindsay Street was mostly commercial, as opposed to Chowringhee Road to the south of Lindsay Street, which contained residences set back from the street. The arrangement of no. 17 was predicated on using the commercial potential of the site.

A house located on the east of Free School Street, used a strategy similar to the one on Chowringhee Road (Figures 2.10a–c).[72] Free School Street, a north–south street, became skewed near the site. The builders, instead of aligning the house with the street, chose to retain a north–south orientation, creating a triangular wedge of front space. A house that was intended to be 54 feet deep with a projecting south-facing verandah 14 feet deep could not contain a separate carriage port on a 100-feet-wide lot without getting too close to the compound wall. The solution was for the southern verandah to double as an entry porch. An extra bay was used to accommodate a verandah (and two extra service rooms) on the west so as not to impinge on the integrity of the rooms of the three-bay system.

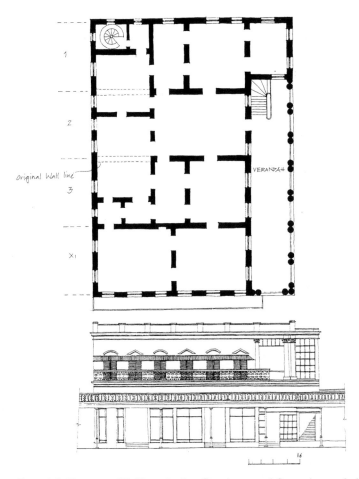

Figure 2.9 House on 17 Chowringhee Road, ground floor plan and elevation. Based on drawing in the collection of the Calcutta Municipal Corporation

The wrap-around verandah was used in many houses to provide a convenient transition space that answered several purposes. An early nineteenth-century building on Little Russell Street (the building occupying the eastern part of the site) displayed the utility of the wrap-around verandah (see Figure 2.20).[73] The building was at one time being used by several boarders, and the large central space could be interpreted as drawing room, dining hall, and billiard room as the proprietor chose. The verandah in this context not only provided an extension of living space where one could enjoy the cool breeze or a delightful view, it could double as ancillary service space in which servants could work in close proximity to the main rooms. In fact, the service spaces and the verandah formed complementary parts of the same spatial envelope.

Out of England?

Despite the classical garb of the buildings, the plans bear little resemblance to Palladian villas or neo-classical English country or town houses. Comparing the colonial houses with the examples in James Gibbs's *Book of Architecture* published in 1739, we find some critical points of difference.[74] In Gibbs's plans, modeled after Palladian villas, the private spaces were located near the wing ends, which were in turn connected to the service wings by a careful deployment of stairs and passages (Figure 2.11). In European mansions of the late seventeenth and early eighteenth centuries, the axis of honor was located perpendicular to the entrance axis, with the

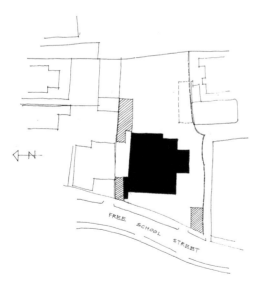

Figure 2.10a House on 54 Free School Street, site plan. Based on drawing in the collection of Mackintosh Burn Pvt. Ltd

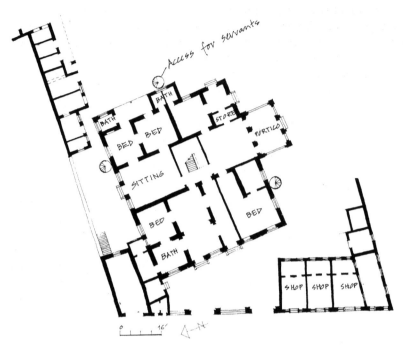

Figure 2.10b House on 54 Free School Street, ground floor plan as shown in 1914. Based on drawing in the collection of Mackintosh Burn Pvt. Ltd

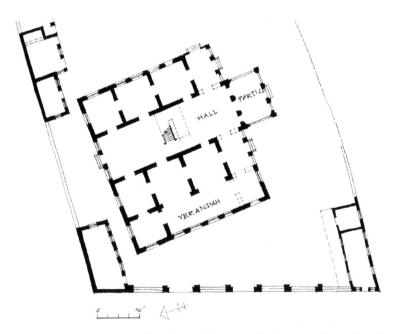

Figure 2.10c House on 54 Free School Street, original ground floor plan. Based on drawing in the collection of Mackintosh Burn Pvt. Ltd

"best" room situated farthest away from the central public spaces.[75] The second point of difference is their axial orientation. The long axis in Calcutta's houses was not engineered to produce an elongated frontal presence as in Gibbs's examples; it typically ran north–south, suggesting a formal movement through a sequence of rooms from a more public entrance porch to a more private verandah on the south. The narrow face to the street and the sense of increased privacy as one moves further into the house along its long axis can be interpreted as an urban response, similar to Victorian town houses, and dictated as much by narrow lots as by the bustle of city life. But the narrow configuration in Calcutta's houses did not arise from lot constraints. One glimpse of the urban plans of Chowringhee makes it amply clear that very few houses had an elongated façade, even when they had the lot size to indulge in such elaboration.

An important exception was, of course, Government House in the Esplanade, which projected the English country house idea when it was completed in 1803. Government House was the residence of the Governor General and his family and also accommodated his offices. Charles Wyatt, the architect of Government House, supposedly borrowed from the vocabulary of James Paine's plan for Kedleston Hall in Derbyshire, built in 1761.

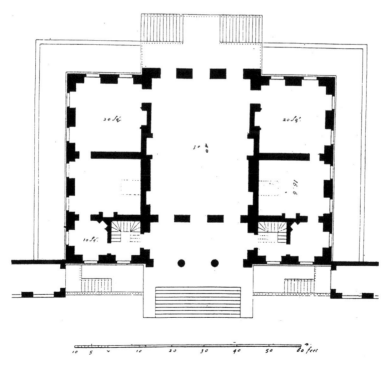

Figure 2.11 Plan of Residence (plate 59), James Gibbs, *Book of Architecture*, 1739

Historians have considered Government House an ostentatious yet poor copy of Kedleston, pointing out the "slackened" rhythm of the former and the difference in the façade and roof configuration.[76] The difference is not simply in the articulation of the elevation and in the proportion and rhythm of the columns, but in the spatial arrangement itself. The supposedly "borrowed" vocabulary differs so fundamentally from Kedleston Hall that their similarity is limited to their outlines (Figures 2.12 and 2.13).

The state apartments of Government House were approached by a grand stair on the north which led to a transverse hall on the first floor. The ground floor was entered by a portico underneath the grand stair. The stair was large enough for an elaborate retinue of servants and for soldiers to present arms at the side. During official functions the north stair was used by the public and the south stair by special guests.[77] The north transverse hall, used as the breakfast room, could be entered through five doorways, although the central one was distinguished from the other four. From there the processional route continued into the large colonnaded central marble hall or the *durbar* hall (audience hall) used as the grand dining room, and then into another transverse hall called the throne room, which finally opened on to an apsidal portico. The marble hall had a coffered ceiling, but in contrast to Kedleston Hall all the rooms were lit from the side. The second floor was laid out similarly, with the central hall, sporting a polished teak floor, being used as the main ballroom. The transverse hall above the throne room was the public drawing room and the one over the breakfast room, the small ballroom. The ground floor

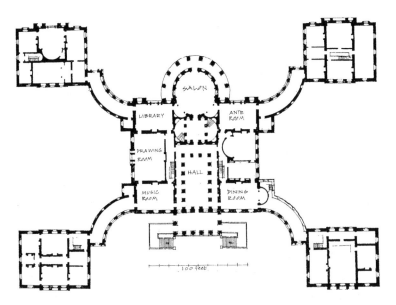

Figure 2.12 Plan of Kedleston Hall, Derbyshire, James Paine, 1761

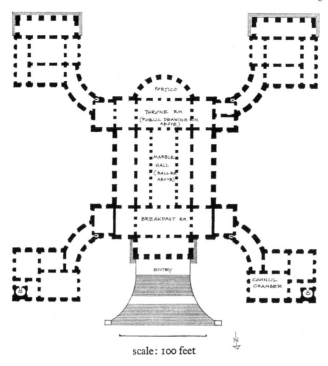

scale: 100 feet

Figure 2.13 Plan of Government House, Calcutta, Charles Wyatt, 1803

was taken up by the offices of the aides-de-camp and contained another dining room for use during summer. As in other buildings in Calcutta, every space was interconnected with adjacent spaces by numerous doorways. Even here, the main body of the mansion was elongated north–south, a peculiar decision only mitigated by the idea of double wings that extended to gather the view and breeze of the *maidan*. The council chamber occupied the first floor of the north-west wing, and the rest of the wing spaces contained the private apartments, a scheme similar to that of Kedleston, although differing in their individual layouts. The open plan of the main building was closed off by a wrought-iron railing and four imposing gateways delineating the premises of Government House. Significantly, all the ancillary offices, cook rooms, stables, and staff accommodation were located not only outside the building, but across the street on the north. This, however, did not imply that servants did not stay round the clock in the Governor's mansion; merely that there were no spaces within the main building specifically designed to accommodate them.

In Kedleston Hall the processional way into the state apartments was more tightly controlled. A single entry to the large central hall defined the route, then led into the grand stair hall and finally to the salon and its connected portico. From the central hall a set of doorways on the entrance side and another pair located on the opposite end of the room began the system of clearly articulated movement through the mansion into the dining room, music room, and library. Each of the main rooms was protected by a small vestibule or anteroom or a passage or stair. Unlike Government House, the careful disclosure of the rooms at Kedleston and their highly articulated walls created a separate identity for each room. They resembled a set of discrete figures brought together by a careful choice of connectors that emphasized the unique use of each room (Figures 2.14, 2.15, 2.16 and 2.17). The identities of the state apartments were accentuated by the skylit vaulted and domed ceilings. In its lack of equivalence in room definition, Kedleston was radically different from Government House (Figure 2.18). In Government House the main spatial organization retained the three-bay principle common in Calcutta, with adjunct spaces on the periphery. The domed salon of Paine's design for Kedleston broke the rectangular symmetry of the plan by being an integral part of the internal arrangement. In contrast, Government House's south portico, despite being surmounted by a dome, was a separate entity (albeit attached) next to the transverse hall; it did not disturb the integrity of the interior rectangular configuration. As if to emphasize the equivalent relationships of the spaces, the entire building was contained within the same roof. The only change in wall articulation was the difference in wall thickness, which increased on the exterior of the building. The concept of strategically placed stairs and passages in Kedleston Hall prescribing paths of movement, was absent in Government House. Here the private stairs were hidden within walls and moved to the extremities of the four wings to create a series of uninterrupted spaces. The stairs connecting the two main floors were located in the galleries next to the central spaces. But here the stairs did not direct traffic by closing off certain areas, and passages did not open to rooms selectively; and it was not for want of space. These formal differences in the articulation of walls, stairs, and passages, were critical. They did not simply represent a difference between Kedleston's baroqueness and the more static classical geometry of Government House. They did not proceed from purely aesthetic or symbolic considerations, nor were they solely due to climatic differences. The differences resided in the form of social life they were meant to accommodate.

The design of Government House anticipated a pattern of social interaction that flourished in other large Calcutta residences, although at a less grand scale. In his discussion of colonial houses in Calcutta, Sten Nilsson remarked that the large lots allowed for infinite variations in the planning of these large buildings.[78] On the contrary, eighteenth- and nineteenth-century houses were remarkably similar, and followed a predictable arrangement of rooms based on the three-bay or three-bays-and-one systems. What differed were the dimensions and the number of rooms one could afford to build.

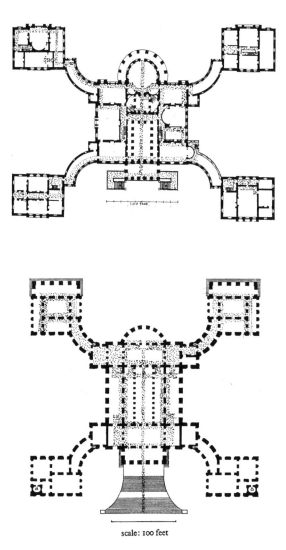

scale: 100 feet

Figure 2.14 Order of access in Kedleston Hall and Government House

The most significant difference between these colonial houses and the eighteenth- and nineteenth-century British contemporaries, of course, lies in the degree of openness allowed in the former and in the articulation of servant spaces. Seventeenth- and eighteenth-century plans of wealthy English households had already begun separating servant spaces from served ones, an idea that was elaborated and extended by Robert Kerr in his 1861 discussion of the "Gentleman's House."[79] If we take from

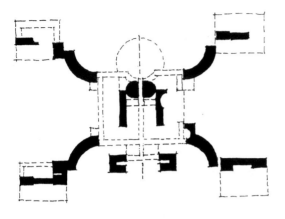

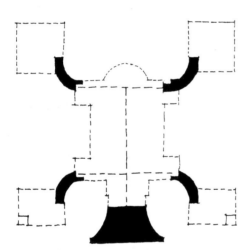

Figure 2.15 Connectors in Kedleston Hall and Government House

Robert Kerr's repertoire a mid-nineteenth-century example, we find an elaborate system of hallways, stairs, and passages delineating paths of movement, and providing each room with its own specific enclosure and identity (Figure 2.19). Kerr wrote at length about the classification of rooms based on such principles of privacy:

> It is the first principle with the better classes of English people that the Family Rooms shall be essentially private, and as much as possible Family Thoroughfares. It becomes the foremost of all maxims, there-

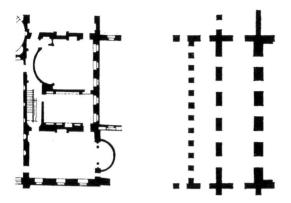

Figure 2.16 Wall articulation in Kedleston Hall and Government House

fore, however small the establishment, that the Servants' Department shall be separated from the Main House, so that what passes on either side of the boundary shall be both invisible and inaudible on the other. ... [t]hat most unrefined arrangement whereby at one sole entrance-door the visitors rub shoulders with the tradespeople, how objectionable it is we need scarcely say when a thin partition transmits the sounds of the Scullery or Coal-cellar to the Dining Room or Study. ...

[A]s we advance in scale in style of living, a separate Staircase becomes necessary for the servants' use; then the privacy of corridors and passages becomes a problem, and the lines of traffic of servants and family respectively have to be kept clear of each other by recognised precautions. ... In short in a small house or a large one, let the family have free passage-way without encountering the servants unexpectedly; and let the servants have access to all their duties without coming unexpectedly upon the family or visitors. On both sides this privacy is highly valued.

It is matter also for the architect's care that the outdoor work of the domestics shall not be visible from the house or grounds, or the windows of their Offices overlooked.[80]

In concluding his discussion on privacy, Kerr noted that the open central lines of thoroughfare in Italian plans favored publicity. Consequently, his suggested remedy was the "indirect routes of the Medieval arrangement" refined to suit nineteenth-century needs.

If nineteenth-century English houses attempted to provide each room with a zone of seclusion, why was not the same attempt made in Calcutta? The primary principle of Calcutta's nineteenth-century houses was the subordination of individual spaces to a larger unity generated by the large central hall(s) (Figure 2.20). In this arrangement, the halls provided the main path of circulation as well as living or dining space, and set up the

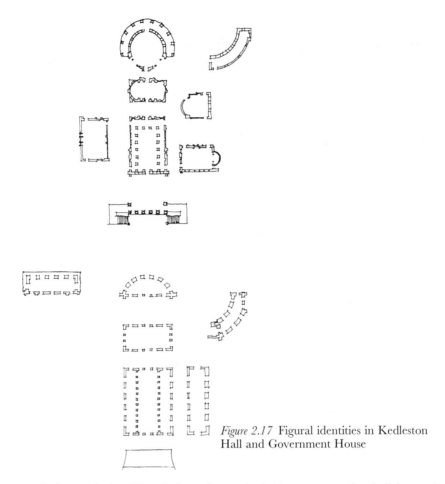

Figure 2.17 Figural identities in Kedleston Hall and Government House

equivalent relationship of the other principal rooms to the hall/central space by room-through circulation, ensuring multiple readings of the principal rooms: they could just as well be used for bedrooms, billiards rooms, or offices. Given the various models available to the builders, why did they decide on such an arrangement of rooms? Surely all of it cannot be attributed to changing market needs; Government House certainly was not built for speculation! For such a pattern to become acceptable, it must have fulfilled other needs.

"A long opera"

Most of the houses in the neighborhood of Middleton and Camac Streets discussed earlier were demolished in the first half of the twentieth century. No longer could the market afford the luxuries of 80 by 20-feet rooms.[81] The social life and social relations that such a plan embodied belonged to

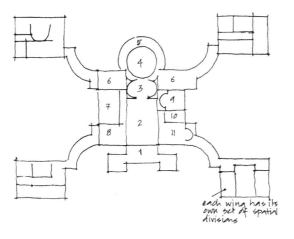

each wing has its own set of spatial divisions

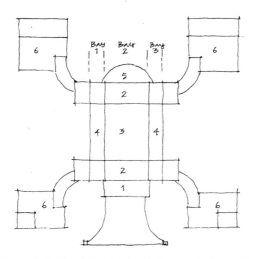

Figure 2.18 Spatial order in Kedleston Hall and Government House

a different era. It was a time when numerous tall windows and doors provided the maximum possible cross-ventilation in a house without a central courtyard. When the chief fear of disease was rising miasma, and heat was considered deadly in itself, tall ceilings and numerous air passages provided a sense of openness that soothed residents psychologically as well as physically. The articulation of private spaces by secondary channels of movement found in Gibbs's or Kerr's plans of English houses was a secondary concern, since it would invariably close some paths of air circulation. Instead of analyzing the colonial houses as inept copies of English

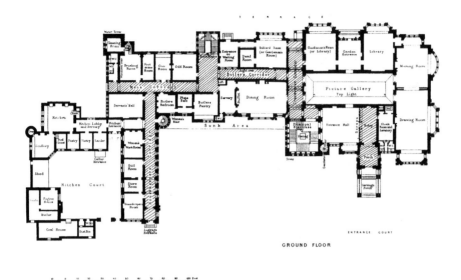

GROUND FLOOR

Figure 2.19 Ground floor plan of mansion in Bearwood, Berkshire, by Robert Kerr,
The Gentleman's House, 1862

residences, it may be more reasonable to see these buildings as accommodating the Indian model of the urban courtyard house (Figure 2.21). From
such a perspective, the colonial house design was an attempt to adapt the
principle of the Indian house of single-loaded passage around a courtyard
within the geometry of a single-roofed entity. In fact, the dimensions of the
central hall in some house plans explicitly suggest its use as the focal point
of gathering and as a source of access to individual rooms, much the same
way as a courtyard. It is not surprising that both the Little Russell Street
and Waterloo Street residences with courtyard-like halls were used as
boarding houses at one time. Centrally located shared spaces surrounded
by rooms that could be rented individually or as suites seemed as if they
had been planned with such a use in mind. Colesworthy Grant provided
another point of view for understanding these house plans.[82] He noted that
the arrangement of European residences was derived from the bungalow
plan of "middling classes of natives," which consisted of one or two rooms
surrounded by verandahs on all sides: "The European resident improving
upon this, encloses the verandah by erecting either a mat or brick wall, and
in like way, throwing partitions across the corners, converts the verandah
into little rooms for the convenience either of himself or visitor friends."[83]
The three-bay pattern with a large central room produced from such a line
of reasoning coincides remarkably well with the pattern derived from the

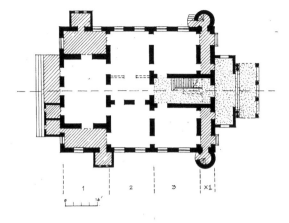

House on 3 Camac St.

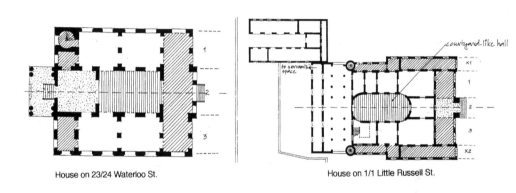

House on 23/24 Waterloo St.

House on 1/1 Little Russell St.

▨ Service spaces including bathrooms and servants' spaces

▥ Main central space

▦ Main entry

Figure 2.20 The pattern of nineteenth-century houses in Calcutta

courtyard houses, and perhaps together they explain the dominance of the three-bay pattern (Figure 2.22).

Much of the conformity of the European residences in this period was predicated on the need to accommodate large gatherings and so to make up for the scarceness of public places of accommodation and recreation. In the words of a resident, men of rank kept an "excellent table, those of

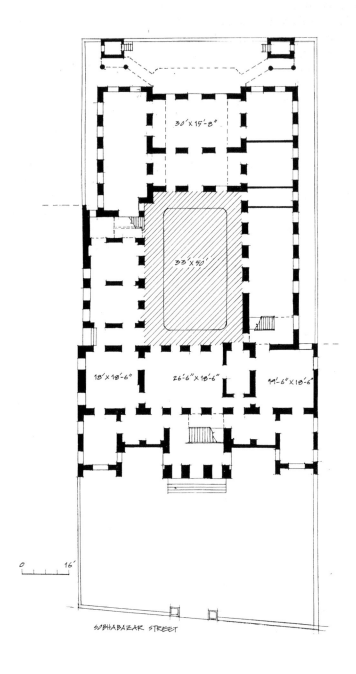

Figure 2.21 Plan of nineteenth-century house on 102 Sobhabazaar Street. Based on drawing in the collection of the Calcutta Municipal Corporation

small income a good one."[84] Breakfasts brought 15 people to the table and dinner, 25. Meals were conducted more in the style of medieval English houses and less like their nineteenth-century counterparts. Late nineteenth-century British visitors looked back wistfully to the days when up-country visitors and newcomers enjoyed the generous hospitality of the residents, with no need to resort to hotels. The large houses and their numerous servants could easily accommodate several guests, who often stayed for a while. Even for casual visits, each person was accompanied by his or her retinue of servants, adding to the numbers already present in the household.

Such a large space, busy with attending servants, recalls the painting of Lady Impey with her servants, attributed to Shaikh Zain-al-din (Figure 2.23).[85] Lady Impey was the wife of Elijah Impey, the Chief Justice of Calcutta. The picture, painted in 1780, shows Lady Impey sitting on a low stool in the center of a large room. The walls of the room are paneled, the venetianed French windows and doors are adorned with valences, and the scant furniture in the room is placed against the narrow wall spaces. A carpet large enough to cover the entire floor forms the field of action, its borders defining the edges of the room. One of the several

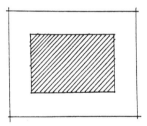

THE INDIAN BUNGALOW

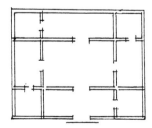

EUROPEAN INTERPRETATION OF ABOVE

Figure 2.22 The origin of the Anglo-Indian residence in Calcutta, by Colesworthy Grant, *c*.1860

doors in the room shows part of a bedroom. Seventeen Indian and one European staff are shown either waiting on the lady or engaged in their household work. The figures in the painting are so composed as to delineate a set of visually permeable spaces. The figures that are closest to the lady, such as the boy fanning, the *munshi* (interpreter), the tailor presenting a hat, and the European butler, constitute the center of the composition. The steward with a list of purchases, two embroiderers, tailors, and thread-twisters form the next circle, while the gardener, bearer, and a couple of *soontaburdars* and *chobdars* (standard-bearers/guards) define the outer edge of the event. The painter was not necessarily portraying all the actions that would take place in one room but, rather, all the actions taking place in closely interconnected layers of space that together formed one single event of household work in clear view of the lady of the house. Zain-al-din's painting bears this similarity with John Zoffany's 1784 depiction of the Auriol and Dashwood families in Calcutta (Figure 2.24). In Zoffany's painting the servants not only form the envelope of the composition, but

Figure 2.23 Lady Impey with her servants in Calcutta, Shaikh Zain-al-din, *c*.1780, from Jeremy Losty, *Calcutta* (London, 1990). Collection of Dr. Oliver Impey

their figures are inserted in the very center of the composition, where they serve at a tea-party. Without careful attention one could actually miss the black boy holding the plate with the teapot. As in Zain-al-din's painting, their proximity to the subject depended on the job they performed. It is this proximity of figures and virtually unimpeded visual access that were embodied in the plans of Calcutta's colonial houses. In other words, the service spaces were inextricably linked to the served spaces, constituting one fabric, even when the site plan showed physical separateness.

The connectedness of the spaces and the presence of numerous Indian subjects mirrored the habitation pattern of an extended Indian family, an idea that many British men had adopted in their cohabitation with Indian wives and mistresses in the eighteenth century. Such "unrestrained colonization" was increasingly seen as a problem among the British, and a deep distrust of miscegenation set in. This included sanctions against wearing Indianized clothes and Indian fabric and marrying Indian women. Between 1787 and 1793, in response to corruption among the East India Company's servants, Governor General Lord Cornwallis set in motion the process of Europeanizing the administrative structure, first by relegating Indians to minor roles in the administration and second by encouraging Company servants to distance themselves from natives and native lifestyle. Underlying this decision was the belief that Indian lifestyle was inherently

Figure 2.24 The Auriol and Dashwood families in Calcutta, John Zoffany. Collection of R. H. N. Dashwood

corrupting to morals, and that in order to secure individuals in the administration against moral degeneracy, strict social boundaries between rulers and ruled were necessary.[87] By the 1830s interracial domestic arrangements were frowned upon by the establishment and anxiously denounced by the increasing number of European women who came to India.[88] The sexual liaisons that bred "half castes" were one of the more detested and problematic aspects of Anglo-Indian life, particularly considering that the most light-skinned offsprings could pass as Europeans.[89] The presumption was that half-castes unable to overcome their flawed origins could be identified by their peculiarly Indian tastes and habits.

Consequently, wearing Indian fabric or smoking a *hookah* were considered severe breaches of etiquette among European women. These women felt the need, and were told by their male counterparts of the necessity, to cultivate a bourgeois interiority free from native influence. And this meant not simply what one read or how one communicated, but what one wore, ate, and how one organized residential space. Mrs. Fenton, as a newcomer to India, was told, for example, never to wear Indian fabric in case she was mistaken for a half-caste.[90] Such protocols could be maintained in fashioning dresses but not in other aspects of daily life.

The culture of interracial relations, however, did not disappear as Lord Cornwallis had envisioned. While interracial marriages became less frequent among the higher-ups in the administration, and all forms of racial mixing were designated as problematic, the "hybrid" culture did not and could not disappear until the spatial arrangement of colonial life was refigured.[91] The tensions inherent in a policy by which the British separated themselves from the natives on moral and administrative grounds while at the same time being dependent on them, was never more apparent than in the attitudes toward the sexual proclivities of European soldiers and the lower class of Europeans. Throughout the rule of the East India Company and the subsequent control by the British Crown, the policy of providing British soldiers with Indian prostitutes – which meant making room for Indian prostitutes specifically designated for British soldiers in cantonments and regimental bazaars – was retained even under severe criticism from many fronts.[92] And even for the upper crust of the administration in Calcutta, the spatial arrangement of domestic space would not be substantially refigured until the turn of the twentieth century. Consequently, although Mrs. Fenton despised the thought of her maid servant (the "black-faced thing") always at her elbows, she submitted to the prevailing domestic practices because in Calcutta, she told herself, one could not apply British rules of self-sufficiency.

In his treatise, Robert Kerr decried "speculative villas" that failed to separate different activities in the house and to provide separate domains for servants and residents. The builders of Calcutta's speculative villas worried little about arranging for the servants and spent most of the money on the construction of the main house. The servants' spaces were an after-thought. Kitchen and ancillary service spaces were never an integral part of colonial houses in India because of the differing perception of servants' needs in this context. The lack of articulation in the colonial context expressed a disinterest in spending any more than the bare minimum for the accommodation of servants. The distance between the house and the servants' rooms was expected to compensate for the lack of clearly artic-ulated territory, but it did not ensure visual privacy of the type found in British houses. And in the urban context, the distance between the house and the servants' quarters could not be great.

From her window, a newcomer to Calcutta in 1812, Lady Nugent, the wife of the Commander-in-Chief, could see her servants at work, since much of the preparations, including cooking, took place outdoors.[93] On her arrival she found a houseful of servants, "the inferiors arranging them-selves in the hall, the superiors attending us to the drawing room," and observed that "it seemed to be the duty of ten or twelve to remain on the staircase, and in the passage ... and we were both sadly annoyed with the number of salaams that are made, whenever we move from one room to another."[94] The house, she added, "is really full of these people." In 1835 Emma Roberts was "struck and rather scandalized by the strange position" occupied by servants:

> None of the inferior domestics keep themselves, as in England, in the background: the watercarrier alone confines his perambulations to the back staircases, all the others, down to the scullions, make their appear-ance in the state apartments, whenever they deem it expedient to do so; and in Bengal, where the lower order of palanquin bearers wear very little clothing, it is not very agreeable to a female stranger to see them walk into drawing rooms, and employ themselves in dusting books or occupations of the like nature.[95]

If the presence of servants is barely acknowledged in Zoffany's paint-ings despite their proximity, it was because being conscious of their presence was too uncomfortable. This was a time before electric fans replaced the *punkha*-pullers, who sat in an adjoining space and pulled the hand-drawn *punkhas* (fans) suspended from the ceiling in the room where the master or mistress contemplated sleep, work, leisure, or sex. In a society so acutely race-conscious, British residents had to conduct their most private conver-sations within the earshot of native servants, who were always present in an adjacent space in case they were needed. The small chambers and verandahs next to bedrooms and dining rooms were adjunct spaces that answered the needs of comfort. The spatial adjacency of servants and masters, the threat of sexual tensions, and the crucial role the servants played in raising European children combined to produce the specter of racial degeneracy.[96] Such proximity occasioned distrust, and the servants came to be regarded as a necessary nuisance. Amateur painters left impressions of the untrustworthiness of native servants who were privy to disputes between husband and wife (Figure 2.25) and more paranoid depictions such as that of an *ayah* (maid servant) stealing a child with the intent to offer her as a sacrifice (Figure 2.26).[97] Several attempts were made starting in the eighteenth century to control the salaries, duties, and activities of servants, but with little effect.

And yet no one suggested abolishing the system. During the age of the East India Company, the directors in London considered large retinues of servants excessive. Those in India ignored such rebukes as an inability on the part of the directors to understand the circumstances in a foreign land.[98] Even when they professed to detest the servility or habits of the Indian staff, the colonizers derived profound satisfaction from their presence. This was, after all, what ruling was all about. This was playing a part in the theater of empire. Many, such as the Eden sisters, in their descriptions of the pageantry of Calcutta life, could hardly contain their satisfaction and amusement. Emily Eden, who arrived in Calcutta in 1836 with her brother Lord Auckland, the new Governor General, felt "Robinson-Crusoeish," occupying a tiny island of civility:

Figure 2.25 The Bottle and Bed Scene in Calcutta, by James Moffat, *c.*1805, Oriental and India Office Collection, British Library, K80015. Notice servant watching from the doorway while master and mistress argue

*Figure 2.26 Ayah Stealing a Child, Confessions of an Oxonian, c.*1825, Oriental and India
  Office Collection, British Library, K88601.6

My particular attendant, who never loses sight of me, is an astonish-
ingly agreeable kitmatgar. . . . He and four others glide behind me
whenever I move from one room to another; besides these, there are
two bearers with a sedan at the bottom of the stairs, in case I am too
idle to walk . . .

  There is a sentry at my dressing room, who presents arms when I
go to fetch my keys. There is a tailor, with a magnificent long beard,
mending up some of my old habit shirts before they go to the wash,
and putting strings in my petticoat, &c., and there is the ayah to assist
Wright, and a very old woman, called a metranee, who is the lowest
servant of all. . . . George never stirs without a tail of fifteen joints
after him. William has reduced his to three, but leaves a large supply
at home; and Fanny has at present three outriders, and expects more;
but it is rather amusing when by an accident we all meet, with our
tails on.[99]

Describing a dinner in Calcutta, her sister Fanny made overt suggestions about the theatricality of the setting:

All the halls were lighted up; the steps of the portico leading to them
were covered with all the turbaned attendants in their white muslin
dresses, the native guards galloping before us, and this enormous building looking more like a real palace, a palace in the "Arabian Nights,"
than anything I have been able to dream on the subject. It is something

like what I expected, and yet not the least, at present, as far as externals go: it seems to me that we are acting a long opera.[100]

The brilliantly lit walls, the grand scale of the building, and the deployment of native servants transported Fanny to a world that seemed more like a dream or a theatrical performance than a real-life artifact. She was familiar with the formality of English country houses. This Calcutta house was, however, the "real palace," a reality that paradoxically only seemed to reside in fairy tales. Fanny was clearly unsure about how to describe her new-found fact of life that seemed to slip between real possibilities and unreal imaginings. Instead, she chose the analogy of the opera, which she thought would convey the blending of the real sensory experience with the make-believe stage set that demanded a certain suspension of disbelief. Only in such a world could the heterogeneous juxtaposition of figures and artifacts make sense – juxtapositions that dissolved the boundaries between that which was familiar and that which was foreign. The physical elements that enabled Fanny's long opera were the grand stairs and porticoes; the formal progression of connected spaces, creating a series of vistas; and the embellishment of the edges with servants and staff. But the interior of the residences was not an opera stage that calculated the separation between audience and performers and planned entries and exits by selective deployment of screens. The open-plan central-room design made it more like a theater-in-the-round. In the European model of the large house, all the spatial devices were garnered to accentuate a beginning-middle-end scenario of movement through the public apartments; one passed through a series of tightly bounded spaces with selective vistas. In the Calcutta houses, once beyond the front entrance, the interior space functioned not on the basis of a series of frontal planes but as a concentric arrangement that allowed multiple points of entrance and dispersal. The numerous doors and windows provided an almost uninterrupted view of the surroundings. In a very large building, such an arrangement could create the sense of endlessly repetitive spaces that one could only conjure in dreams. Such pleasures of imperialism were gained at the price of being watched by the servants. The same channels that extended one's view of the surrounds would permit the others' gaze to be turned inward:

> I am in my boudoir, very much the size of the Picture Gallery at Grosvenor House; three large glass doors on one side look over the city, three more at the end at the great gate and entrance: they are all venetianed up at present. . . . Emily and I are on opposite wings, far as the poles asunder, and at night when I set about making my way from her room to mine, I am in imminent peril of stepping upon bales of living white muslin that are sleeping about the galleries. . . .

> In this climate it is quite necessary to have every door open, but I am making a clever arrangement of screens to screen everybody out; though it seems to me that people push to extreme the arrangement to prevent having the slightest trouble, even of thought.[101]

Five decades later, Lady Dufferin refused to split up her family in separate wings to occupy this large mansion after established colonial patterns. In her journal she recorded the determination with which she set about generating a familiar ambiance of home in the unhomely "gigantic," house "with *no* room in it":

> I have thrown all conservative principles to the winds, have abandoned the rooms used by all previous Viceroys, and have moved into the visitors' wing. So that I have now a lovely boudoir looking on to the garden, instead of a dull room upstairs, without a balcony or a view, and a nice room next to it for the girls. . . . I am close to my own staircase, and nothing can be nicer. Having thus packed myself and my belongings into one of the elephant's paws . . . we are really comfortable.[102]

Lady Dufferin was doing her best to defy the spatial intentions embedded in the house plan to create a "private house," complete with a "homey" drawing room furnished with pink silk, little tables, screens, plants, photographs. Even the throne room was transformed into "our usual dining room" with carpets and curtains.[103] Lady Dufferin's attempt to re-form the house by transferring spatial conventions that promoted English ideas of "comfort" and "privacy" was mirroring an increased desire among her contemporaries to insist that home life in India be "English." And yet her desire for control was undermined by the large servant population at Government House. Instead of "one neat housemaid at work" she encountered "seven or eight men in various stages of dress" in her chamber.

For the elite British women, what had in the early nineteenth century seemed a luxury and nuisance, by the 1880s became the subject of the science of empire. Several housekeeping guides written by women, the most popular being Flora Annie Steel and Grace Gardiner's, *The Complete Indian Housekeeper and Cook*, emphasized taking control of the household and servants through rational planning, and by assuming an authority modeled on the public life of Anglo-Indian civil servants rather than the feminine norms of English domesticity.[104] The discomfort that lurked behind these calls for change in housekeeping was based on the recognition that the idea of constructing an "English" home in India was largely futile and fraught with the tension of dealing with potentially insubordinate servants.[105] Not only was the architecture of the houses different from those in England, preventing the creation of a private interiority – the space of the "intimate sphere," but the high cost of European furniture implied a difficulty in creating English interior arrangements. Few could afford the luxuries of Lady Dufferin. And none did away with the labor of Indian servants; Englishness in the colonies could only be formed by the mediation of Indian servants. Instead, the women resorted to imposing rules that asserted Englishness through the trope of empire. The task of housekeeping was now made equivalent to "maintaining empire."

The privilege of adopting the rhetoric of empire allowed British women to distinguish themselves not just from Indian women and those of "mixed-races," but also from lower-class European women. Authors such as Flora Annie Steel suggested that English women in India generate a new subjectivity to claim the responsibility of empire on equal terms with Englishmen. This self-presentation was directed less towards Indian women, and more towards the Indian men they came in daily contact with – the servants, who might underestimate the mistress's capacity to rule her household. But even when a physical separation from the public world was possible and the servants brought under control, Anglo-Indian homes in India could never be practically detached from the public sphere. All the rules, ceremonies, and hierarchies of colonial administration applied within the home. As mistresses of the household they recognized that no matter how carefully they designed menus and trained their servants, even within the confines of home life their sovereignty as mistress was only contingent on the company they happened to be entertaining – guests requested leave from the wife of the most senior official present and not from the hostess.

Changes in housekeeping went along with a slow change in the design of the houses themselves. It took the designers over 60 years from Robert Kerr's time, and about a century from the time of the Eden sisters' sojourn, to recognize that the more undefined the servant spaces, the more uncontrolled were their movements and spheres of action, an aspect that had been well understood and taken care of in contemporary English houses. Only in the early twentieth century did architects in Calcutta begin designing residential plans that emphasized the privacy of rooms, and minimized the role of the hall. In a 1921 house plan for 1 Camac Street, the hall had become primarily a passage and not a living space, and separate staircases for servants and family discretely cordoned off one domain from another (Figure 2.27).[106] More and more, bay windows and rounded verandahs would change the envelope of these buildings.

The situation of being surrounded by servants within the household was analogous to the organization of the larger urban context, which can be seen by highlighting the servants' spaces in a map (Figure 2.28). The practice of having servants' spaces next to the entrance and back walls created little islands, that could be interpreted as protected or besieged depending on one's point of view. Significantly, most of the residences did not even

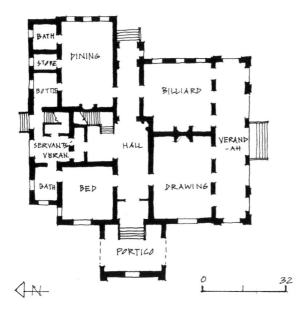

Figure 2.27 Plan of house on 1 Camac Street. Based on drawing in the collection of Mackintosh Burn Pvt. Ltd

face the public street to announce their grandeur, being satisfied with an abrupt demarcation between the private domain and the public space outside the walls. The open plans of the buildings were arrested by strictly defined compound walls. The buildings that set up a direct relationship with streets and articulated a transition space were shops and public buildings. Otherwise, neighbors shared nothing except the walls that separated them. Even in a locality where the residents were predominantly Europeans, the house next-door remained a relatively unknown entity. Neighbors were usually tenants who were there for a brief time. The high walls and ample intervening spaces resulted as much from suburban origins as from the uncertainty of market needs. The walls and the distance from the neighboring houses became tools for the owner to mitigate unknown challenges.

Although most British residents seemed to agree about the novelty of life in India and took pride in the pageantry that the colonial buildings afforded, few recognized or acknowledged the essentially heterogeneous nature of the spaces. The solid boundary walls, often designed so carefully after pattern books, provided privacy from the respectable natives but not from the laboring population. Attitudes toward the native population and the need of the real-estate market produced discrete containments where the colonizers could provisionally participate in the long opera.

Figure 2.28 Portion of "*sahibpara*" based on R. B. Smart's Survey of Calcutta, 1887–1909, with servants' spaces shown in black

The pleasures of imperialism did not simply necessitate native presence but were depended on and besieged by native practices in the very center of domestic life. British attempts to fix the signs of difference, in order to resist the effect of the hybrid, proved difficult, given the infrastructure of colonial dwelling. Colesworthy Grant, an astute observer, noted that few Europeans were willing to admit that they were products of a hybrid colonial culture. While the neo-classical architecture of the "native" town was understood as hybrid and dismissed as inauthentic, the colonizers refused to see how the houses they resided in were culturally-mixed concoctions that went beyond stylistic ambivalence. In other words, the problem did not lie in the proportion of the façade, the rhythm of the columns, or the dimensions of the entablature; it was something more fundamental, more immediately felt when using the space.

There were more similarities between the buildings in the so-called white and black towns than was commonly accepted. Having lived in these colonial houses, British residents were cognizant that hybridity did not simply reside in the foreign body and the native town; rather, it was that troubling presence in the formation of their own identity, an ambivalent space that they themselves occupied and whose impact they deeply felt. The difficulty resided in not only generating a "reality coincident with imperialist narrative."[107] As the British recognized, what was disturbing the "reality" effect was not a distant Other; the disturbance was the consequence of everyday practices that inflected their own behavior and their ability to sustain a narrative of superior difference. The open-endedness of spatial meaning unsettled dearly held ideas of public and private, self and Other, by denying colonizers a sense of safe confines within which to construct an imperial self. That is what made colonial cities like Calcutta problematic and necessitated the obsessive articulation of delimiting practices, even when they recognized that such territorial markings inhibited the colonial desire for a sovereign space and, in fact, the boundaries did little to prevent permeability.

3   Locating mythic selves

Public sphere and public space

In 1881 Henry Beverley submitted the following description of the census collection in Calcutta to the Government of Bengal:

> The hum of business was hushed earlier than usual and a great silence had fallen on the town. Streets that are ordinarily crowded with passengers were that evening totally deserted. . . . It was said that the street lamps were to be extinguished at that hour and that persons found outside their homes would get into trouble. . . . It has been requested that a night light be kept burning in each house until the enumerator had paid his visit. . . . As we drove along, we could see that a light was burning in each house, showing that the inmates were awake and still expecting the arrival of the enumerators. From time to time these officers were met with, accompanied in each case by a constable, and perhaps an assistant or two. Noiselessly the group flitted from one house to the next, the door was opened, and the head of the house was called; the names of the inmates were read out, corrections and additions made in the schedule, and the enumerator passed on.[1]

This description of Calcutta bears no similarity to the indecipherable "native" city described by British visitors. Here the din has been silenced, and the streets "teeming" with people have been cleared to make way for colonial authority. A transparent landscape where each house could be discretely identified and counted replaces the insidious network of houses and streets. It appears that the private domain is revealed and made accessible by erasing the public domain, signified by the extinguished street lamps. The collection of information also takes place "noiselessly" and efficiently, aiding the impression of authority. No resistance or argument disturbs the serenity of the operation, no words are wasted in the transaction, and no enunciatory difficulty troubles the gathering of knowledge. The apparent ease with which this spatial erasure is conducted suggests the absence of a legitimate and robust Indian public domain that might stand between the authority of the colonial state and Indian domestic sphere/space.

Beverley's eerie depiction raises three inter-related issues for our understanding of the "native" town. First is the practice of public space under colonial authority; second is the question of public sphere and its spatial correlates; and third is the problem of *translation* that we encounter in constructing the nineteenth-century public sphere in Calcutta. Beverley was recalling a scenario that was clearly different from everyday practice. The panoptic vision that surveyed the town and the nature of efficiency (invoking fear among the native population) that marked the process could only be possible when the town had been arrested out of its normal spatio-cultural mode. The presence of the police at the time of enumeration drives home both the basis of state authority, as well as the unease and difficulty that an undertaking such as the census entailed. By insisting on a controlled condition, Beverley not only suggested the existence of an undisciplined topography, but the impossibility of addressing it in the "normal" mode. Indian domestic space could be opened up to the inquiry of the colonial state only when the city's public space had been wrested from the indigenous population. There may be little doubt that the existing urban fabric was problematic to the functioning of colonial administration. Description of the urban fabric of the native city as irrational was not a new strategy, but Beverley's stunning claim that it could be understood, rationalized so easily, and erased at will, was new. Beverley's statement is also remarkable considering the date of the census. By the 1880s there was already a contentious debate between Bengali and British residents about the nature of the "public" in Calcutta, and over the rights to represent the public. Beverley's point of view turned census-taking into a mode of unchallenged authority – a confrontation between a modern state and the inhabitants of a pre-modern urban fabric, a rational mode of inquiry intervening in an irrational mode of cultural production. And it is precisely in such a vision that he betrayed a refusal to acknowledge the difficulty of ascertaining the spatial rules of recognition.

The confrontation between a modern state and a pre-modern urban fabric, of course, suggests a peculiar form of colonial anachronism. Here the development of a modern state is not presumed to be simultaneous with the development of modern private and public spheres. This modernization, in the form of authority and technology of the colonial state, is supposed to bear the burden of subjecting pre-modern Indian society to the discipline of modern life and to the regulations of the modern state. Such burden necessitates that Indian society be ideally turned into a colonial prison, an appropriate setting for interrogating the colonized. Once the spaces inhabited by the colonized could be translated into a gridded space of "experimentation," colonial knowledge entered its own sphere of epistemological dominance. Here, apparently, natives could be made to speak about their social practices – in Michel de Certeau's words,

the non-discursive could be translated into a discursive mode of experimentation and theory.[2] The struggle between the colonizer and colonized,
however, was not simply between discursive and non-discursive practices,
but the silent itineraries that operate in both texts and space, and the
performative strategies that complement the measured silences.

The emergence of a Bengali public sphere that challenged the assumption
of an exclusive colonial European public sphere was, from the early nineteenth century, dominated by the Hindu Bengali elite, and gave the spatial
politics of Calcutta its peculiar configuration. Much of the nineteenth-
century Bengali intellectual and political activity was directed towards erasing the hierarchical signification implied in the colonizer's view of public life.
The term, Bengali elite, in this context requires some clarification.

It is standard practice among historians of nineteenth-century Bengal to
refer to the Bengali *zamindars* (landholders) and middle class as the "indigenous elite." They formed the *comprador* class that had directly or indirectly
benefited from the quasi-feudal structure of revenue arrangement under
the East India Company – the 1793 Permanent Settlement of Bengal. The
Permanent Settlement "generated a wide gap between rent, which was
elastic, and revenue, that was fixed," and thus allowed the development of
a rentier class with a wide range of incomes.[3] Under a revenue system that
did not encourage improvement of the land, the relationship of these landholders to the land remained, for the most part, parasitic. The wealthiest
Bengali residents of the city invariably had very large landholdings in rural
areas, even if they were engaged in trade in the city. Those of middling
ranks increasingly came to reside in the city with the hope of supplementing
their modest income from the land with a professional income. They also
came to occupy minor offices in the East India Company's administration, the only ranks open to them after a series of administrative reforms
undertaken between 1787 and 1793 by Lord Cornwallis. By the end of
the nineteenth century most of the commerce of the city was in the hands
of Europeans, and Indians who could rely on a financial network in the
northern and western part of the country. As the ability to control trade and
the means of production became increasingly tenuous, Bengalis came to
dominate middle to low ranks of "white-collar" jobs in the city.

For the sake of analysis, I am making a distinction between the two groups
that formed this privileged class. That is, I am distinguishing between the
elite – the upper crust of the Bengali landed gentry residing in the city
that were routinely granted titles of *rajas* and *maharajas*, and the middling
class of professionals – teachers, lawyers, doctors, journalists, and those who
came to occupy middle to low ranks in the colonial services. In nineteenth-
century Bengali parlance the landed elite were referred to variously as *vishayi*
(propertied), *dhani* (wealthy), *abhijata* (aristocrats), *or baramanush* (literally,
"big" people), and the middling classes were referred to as *madhyabitta*
(middle income) or *grihastha* (householder). They, along with the "*daridra*

Respectable = freedom from manual labor

athacha bhadra" (poor yet respectable) constituted the respectable minority of the Bengali residents in the city – the *bhadralok*.[4] Freedom from manual labor (for the men) was the prime factor that designated these classes/castes as "respectable," a factor that distinguished them from the lower classes/castes or *chotolok*. The respectable strata typically consisted of the higher castes of Hindu society, and were connected socially through kinship and, increasingly in the later part of the century, through professional relations. They had access to and made use of English education, which by 1835 had been mandated by the colonial government. Considerable socio-economic and even caste mobility within the strata meant that the social distinctions between the middling classes and those I am calling the elite were not static, and increasingly became blurred as the very conditions and signs of Bengali respectability came under challenge in the last decades of the nineteenth century. And yet, to understand the production of urban space, we need to pay attention to the discrepant experience of the middling classes and the landed elite in terms of their ability to own and control space.

In the late eighteenth and early nineteenth centuries the northern part of the city was structured in great measure by the Bengali landed elite who bought vast tracts of land, settled tenants, and fostered a large number of dependents related by kinship and country connections. Most of these men had risen from a family status of small traders in a matter of two generations. Many of them made fortunes by trading in salt, silk, and opium, but their extensive investment in landed property both out-side and inside the city was the key to their rise to power. They took the opportunity of the yet to be established social order of late eighteenth-century Calcutta to move up in caste and status, and then set the profile of a social hierarchy in which they formed the apex with a large number of artisans, petty traders, and dependents soliciting elite patronage. Until the formation of a critical mass of middle-income residents in the mid-nineteenth century, there was a huge imbalance of power between the elite and the majority of the population. The elite formed the locus of social activity; the most significant events took place under their patron-age, and it was they who represented "native" opinion to the British authorities. In their large, self-contained mansions they acted as petty kings and generous hosts to both the Indian and European communi-ties and in the process gained political advantages they were otherwise denied. These mansions incorporated a range of "public spaces" that became key instruments for accumulating and demonstrating social power. The boundary between public and private was not so easily deciphered, however, even in the 1880s, as Henry Beverley would have us believe. One of the critical difficulties with the "undisciplined" topography of the native city resided in the indeterminate boundaries of "public space," an aspect that would also come to haunt the Bengali middle class, although with a different resolution. I discuss the latter problem in Chapters 4 and 5.

In problematizing the notion of "public space" I wish to trace a genealogy of Bengali spatial practice through which notions of publicness and
privacy, public and private space were articulated in the nineteenth century.
The discussion is anchored around salient concerns over presentation of
the (political) self in public. I place "political" in parentheses, to indicate the
Bengali elite's consistent attempt to bracket their political aspiration, given
that their right to have a "political" self was denied by the colonial authorities. This meant that the "political" was predominantly articulated through
the "cultural," a subterfuge that became evident to British authorities quite
early. A case in point is the British administration's requisition of an English
translation of Dinabandhu Mitra's play, *Nildarpan* (Mirror of Indigo). By
1861, John Peter Grant, the Lieutenant Governor of Bengal, decided that
the government should familiarize itself with the state of native opinion
regarding the agitation in the countryside over the forced cultivation of
indigo. His desire was to plumb the depths of native "feelings" that were
not outwardly expressed in the presence of Europeans.

The subsequent Anglo-Indian fury over the translation of this play, the
sentencing of James Long, who supervised the English translation, on the
charge of libel, and the collusion between the state and Anglo-Indian civil
society evidenced in the sentencing, blew open the "cultural" screen to
reveal the "political." Elite members of Bengali society made a public display of their support for James Long. Kaliprasanna Sinha paid Long's fine
in court, and at a public meeting held at the Nat-mandir of Radhakanta
Deb's mansion, the leaders of the Bengali community demanded a recall of
the judge from office for his "frequent and indiscriminate attacks on the
characters of the natives of the country with an intemperance . . . not compatible with the impartial administration of justice."[5] In later decades the
instruments of the Bengali cultural sphere, including the press and theater,
were heavily censored by the colonial state, in the very recognition of their
political power that Peter Grant had so clearly articulated.

According to Partha Chatterjee, the originality of Bengali nationalism
was to make a distinction between the "spiritual" or inner domain which
had to be protected against colonial intrusion, and the "material" or outer
domain of statecraft where European superiority had to be acknowledged,
carefully studied, and replicated. Chatterjee also makes the important point
that long before nationalism waged its struggle in the domain of the political, it began its self-definition in the inner domain of the cultural.[6] My
tentative distinction between the "cultural" and the "political" is in keeping
with Chatterjee's model. However, one of my objectives is to show how
the difference between the political/outer and cultural/inner domains
necessarily collapsed in response to the dynamics of Calcutta's public sphere
and public space.

My analysis of public space in Bengali society is extended over this
chapter and the next two. These are not meant to present an evolutionary
pattern of spatial change. Rather, they highlight how these concerns were

articulated by different constituents and by way of discrepant concepts of self, family, and community. In this chapter I discuss the elite landscape using three examples: *Kalikata Kamalalaya* (Calcutta, the Abode of Kamala or Lakshmi, the Goddess of prosperity), a didactic text written by Bhavanicharan Bandopadhyay and published in 1823; the "Nat-mandir" of the Sobhabazaar Rajbari of the Deb family built *c.*1840; and a painting, *The Hunchback of Fishbone*, by Abanindranath Tagore produced in 1930. All three artifacts were deeply embedded in the social world of the Bengali elite, and attempted to frame a set of "ideal" responses to the changing urban milieu. My plan is to read the symptoms of authority and anxiety that mark the external body of these three artifacts. While all three examples may be read textually, I also wish to point out the spatial dimensions that may not be fathomed by textual reading alone. I am interested in the gap between text and territory – it was here that social identities were mobilized to reap full political benefits within a structure of colonial dominance. Remaining in a position subordinate and beholden to the colonial state, elite men could "perform" what they could not "write." That which remained unsaid in text was re-turned through spatial practice.

In the early nineteenth century the Bengali elite pursued two modes of organizing the social landscape. The first consisted of the *dal* (group) and the second consisted of voluntary associations modeled after the European manner. By participating in the *dals* and voluntary organizations in tandem, the elite attempted to claim their own ground within the colonial order. The *dals* controlled the immediate socio-religious life of the community, while the voluntary associations imagined, in their desire to improve the condition of the "natives" and engage with the colonial government, a larger community whose boundaries went beyond the local.

For the elite, the public sphere was, however, a troubled territory. On the one hand, by participating in voluntary associations that debated policy issues of the colonial government they were claiming the political right they had been denied by the British. On the other hand, such activities occasioned meeting with Europeans, thus threatening socio-religious boundaries the respectable classes were expected to maintain. The elite leaders wanted to ensure that they did not fall out of favor with the colonial authorities whose policies they criticized. The double-speak that resulted from these contradictory impulses found articulation in contemporary texts and space.

Discursive strategies

In *Kalikata Kamalalaya* (hereafter referred to as KK) a stranger/country dweller and a city dweller discuss the decline of Hindu religious authority among Calcutta's Bengali residents. The text, in effect, is a conversation between these two archetypal characters about the emergence of a new Bengali society in Calcutta with norms radically different from that of the country. The main point of argument between the two is contamination, that is pollution of the sacred realm of the respectable Hindu household situated in the heterogeneous socio-economic framework of the colonial city. Men in the city spend long hours performing salaried work at the cost of neglecting religious duties prescribed for the Hindu householder, and their speech, clothing, reading and eating habits bear the influence of foreign material culture. The city dweller offers a defense of Calcutta's urbane life style, and constructs a "way-finding" map to navigate the potentially threatening landscape. As the conversation evolves we learn about the Bengali householder's duties and routines, about language contamination, about the institution of the *dal*, followed by activities of a reading public. In explaining the norms of Calcutta society to the stranger, the city dweller projects an "art of living" that does not need to compromise religious and ancestral duties to engage in the realm of, what I shall provisionally call, civil society. What KK insists upon is a superior urbanity and a committed engagement with the city and its community life.

The author, Bhavanicharan Bandopadhyay, was renowned as the editor of *Samachar Chandrika*, a news magazine that became the mouthpiece of the Dharmasabha. Bhavanicharan voiced one of the earliest concerns over new money in the urban colonial context of Calcutta, and its tendency to do away with old social distinctions. His text may be seen as a primer of social conduct and material culture practice that attempts to introduce new social boundaries around the self. In many ways it performs the ideological role of Bengali "housekeeping" guides in the later part of the century, and shares with these later texts many similar concerns about the sanctity of the domestic sphere. Unlike later guides, however, KK is entirely devoted to this "self" as male. The subject of the text is the upper-caste male householder, a description that would fit the author, an educated Brahmin. This construction of the self goes beyond the prescribed limits of the Hindu scriptures and invites questions of being in public, about the elite's public responsibilities in the nineteenth-century city.

People's external appearances in the city, Bhavanicharan argues, are unreliable indicators of their cultural and social pedigree. So at the outset he defines four categories among the respectable residents of the city, on the basis of income. KK concedes that there are "others" in the city – lower classes and foreigners, whose code of conduct is not within the debater's purview. The stranger's accusation may hold for these people, but such behavior is seldom seen among the (respectable) Hindus. A Hindu who neglected socio-religious duties "must be a Hindu only in appearance" (*Hindubeshdhari*).[7] KK's desire to understand/legitimize the actions of the respectable Bengalis is directed towards the goal of formulating a community in which individuals have learned to maintain appropriate socio-religious boundaries, that is, learned to be at home in a colonial-capitalist economy. The first three groups that constitute this community are engaged in some form of salaried employment: those who are "propertied" and hold high offices of *dewan* (financial stewards) and *mutsuddis* (commercial agents), the "middle-income" folks who are not rich but live comfortably, and the "poor but respectable" who hold petty offices.[8] In addition there is the category of the "extraordinarily fortunate": the extremely wealthy who live off the interest of their landed incomes. What distinguishes these groups is not simply their income level, but the degree of hardship they endure to make a living, and the number of hours they spend conducting salaried labor. While the extremely wealthy are capable of conducting religious duties without any impediment, men of the first three categories never spend any more time than is necessary at the place of work. The true Hindu, Bhavanicharan claimed, could maintain right conduct in the potentially polluting context of the city by scrupulously distinguishing between affairs of the world and religious affairs.

In KK foreign language or *javanik bhasa* (Muslim in the specific sense) becomes the master trope of contamination, demonstrating the importance of foreign language in constituting social distinctions in the urban colonial milieu. The English language, we must remember, was seen as the key to the "Western penetration" of Indian culture, on both sides of the colonial divide. British administrators and missionaries did not simply view English education for Indians as a necessity to create intermediaries between the administrators and the masses, but anticipated more far-reaching consequences of such education. For example, William Ward, the Baptist missionary working from Serampore, noted that British administrators must insist on English education for Indians, as it was the English *language* that would develop a "taste" for Western material goods among Indians, thus enabling England to enlarge the market for European merchandise in India.[9] Although middle-class Bengali men took up English education as a means of employment in the British administration, they were as convinced as Ward was of the language's impact on material culture. If Bengali women were given English education, the entire material and social apparatus of Bengali society would collapse, they insisted.[10] Those both for and against the introduction of English education assumed a fairly simple "structural" co-relation between language and other domains of material culture such as clothing, foodways, and household artifacts.[11] By the late nineteenth century an entire discourse had emerged in Bengali literature that concerned itself with the "language" of material culture itself, thus constructing a direct link between the use of language, gestures, material objects, use of space, and sensory pleasures. In KK we see a preliminary sketch of this discourse in the making.

Responding to accusations about the use of foreign language – English and Persian – instead of Bengali, the city dweller argues that such an accusation is misinformed. The study of Sanskrit and Sanskritized Bengali (*sadhu bhasa*) is common among respectable folks, and only after they have studied these do they learn English or Persian as an economic necessity. Here the city dweller offers a Sanskrit quote to remind the stranger that the use of foreign language in the domain of economy and affairs of the state is sanctioned by the scriptures. The stranger then suggests that Calcuttans use *javanik bhasa*, even when there are equivalent words available in Bengali. A long list of words in *javanik* and *sadhu bhasa* are produced to make his point. The city dweller reciprocates by citing another list consisting of words that have no equivalent in Bengali. The majority of words on this list are Persian and the rest are English words related to administration and justice.[12] The city dweller argues that foreign words introduced by alien rulers have to be accepted to conduct affairs of the state. And as long as these foreign words are not used when performing *daivakarma* (religious duties) and *pitrikarma* (duties related to ancestors and lineage), there is no threat of contamination. Such language is permissible in the domain of *vishaykarma* (duties related to wordly affairs and material well-being) and when used in light conversation. The two domains where contamination is allowed – the place of employment and the place of social and cultural gatherings, both involving meeting with "others," take up a large part of the householder's daily routine. The purpose of such meetings is also left quite open:

> Those engaged in important offices such as *diwani* and *mutsuddiship* wake up in the morning and after performing ablutions, meet with various people. . . . After their bath, they conduct religious rites, and then take their meal. Having rested a while, they . . . depart for the place of work. . . . Having stayed at work as long as they consider the work ought to take, they return home, change their clothes, touch Ganga water to purify themselves, proceed to perform evening prayers, and then after taking some refreshments, they again engage in *baithak* (meeting or assembly). Later many people assemble; some come with work-related matters, and some just to meet with them (*sakhhat karibar nimitto*), or sometimes they leave home to meet with others.[13]

Is it possible to think of these meetings as elements of an emergent Bengali public sphere? How are we to understand Bhavanicharan's diffidence in translating English words into Bengali? Does this indicate an abnegation of power in public life and affairs of the state? Dipesh Chakrabarty has argued that it would not have been possible for Bhavanicharan to accommodate his own actions in the fledgling public sphere within the tripartite division of *daivakarma-pitrikarma-vishaykarma* outlined in KK.[14] If the conceptual framework of KK falls short of explaining its author's practice in everyday life, we encounter a clear gap between rhetoric and practice. What conceptual strategy bridges/retains the gap?

These questions demand that we situate the tripartite framework suggested in KK in its context. Let us consider the translation of the word *vishaykarma* into English in pragmatic terms. If we translate *vishaykarma* as limited to those duties related to earning one's living, it is clear from KK that there are activities performed by the householder, and sanctioned by KK, that do not fall within the frame of *daivakarma-pitrikarma-vishaykarma-rajkarma*. This, however, does not imply that there was no pre-colonial conceptual category that could be appropriated to fit the "meetings" in which the nineteenth-century householder participated. All "meetings," in the paragraph from KK quoted above, are subsumed under the idea of *baithak*. And later in the text we encounter other terms, such as *sabha*, that designate formal meetings. *Baithak* and *sabha* were not novel concepts for the nineteenth-century Bengali elite. It is not unreasonable to surmise that the organizational activities of the middle class in the public sphere could be seen as conveniently subsumed under the form of the *baithak* and *sabha*. If we translate *vishaykarma* as duties related to worldly affairs in the broader sense – "worldly interests such as wealth, livelihood, fame, and secular power" – there is no evidence in KK that this domain has been unequivocally submitted to colonial authority.[15] Using this definition, and the openness of the purposes of assembly articulated in KK, *sabha* and *baithak* may be seen to belong under the category of *vishaykarma*. No matter which translation we choose to adopt we are left with a rather wide scope of secular engagement in this domain upheld in KK. In these intentionally open parameters of secular engagement we may discern the implicit desire for a capacity to rule, or rather, to dictate terms of such rule.

We cannot, however, conclude our discussion of the lack of desire to translate foreign words into one's own language in the context of KK so easily. If our understanding of Bhavanicharan's involvement in the public sphere hinges on the question – "which English translation of *vishaykarma* is more accurate?" – we have to deal with *translation* as a central problematic of colonial and post-colonial discourse. The practice of translation, as Tejaswini Niranjana has pointed out, has historically played an immense role in the British construction of India and Indians by producing "strategies of containment."[16] For the colonizer, translation functioned "as a transparent presentation of something that already exists, although the "original" is actually brought into being through translation."[17] This enabled the fixing of the culture of the colonized as something static. However, translation as a term that implies disruption, movement, and displacement, is open to other operational strategies as a tool of cultural and political intervention. In KK, translation is used to chart out a new way of being that quietly attempts to undo the colonizer's strategy of containment.

In wishing to know whether Bhavanicharan's text and actions may be organized in relation to the European idea of public sphere (here signified by the English word), we need to resist the temptation to see translation as a transparent transaction that simply substitutes one sign for another. "*Vishaykarma*" and "public sphere" circulate in two different conceptual economies. The meaning of *vishaykarma* in KK is dispersed over a large

and new territory, and refuses containment within the traditional limita-
tion of the Sanskrit word, or its English translation as "worldly affairs."
The public sphere in nineteenth-century Calcutta was not an accomplished
fact – a European blueprint transferred to a colonial territory. To borrow
a metaphor from Martin Heidegger, it was not being erected on a common
"ground" of understanding. The *ground* itself was under construction as
the edifice was being raised. What we have in KK is Bhavanicharan's
view of that ground under construction.

KK takes advantage of the scandal that inheres in the process of translation. The scandal of translation is not an unintended effect of the process,
a result of something that has been unwittingly misread, but a necessary
step for the transaction of ideas. By translation we mean the transporta-
tion of one idea or set of ideas from one language/concept/cultural milieu
to another. Translation produces a construct that neither belongs to the
language from which it is translated, nor to the one into which it is translated. It produces a space where one may knowingly disobey linguistic and
cultural rules, thereby inserting new meaning into the milieu. What makes
translation possible is the bringing forth of this "scandalous," improper,
space that strategically locates itself between two languages, two cultures,
two conceptual economies, while partaking in both. The most effective
translations are those in which this space is imaginatively carved out. This
improper construct when it locates itself in a cultural milieu – in the
context into which it has been translated – continues to effect changes in
the milieu's conceptual, linguistic, and spatial structures.

Bhavanicharan earned his living by serving as financial agent to
prominent English officials in India, and among the accomplishments that
recommended him was his proficiency in English, as well as Persian and
native Bengali – that is, his ability to move between languages. Bishop
Heber, one of his employers, remembered him merely as an "intelligent
servant," one of many "paraded" in front of him on his arrival in Calcutta.
Indeed, he noted that Bhavanicharan was the "editor of a Bengali newspaper," and knowledgeable about upcountry. Yet, it is evident from KK
and the manner in which its author was eulogized by his literary successors, that Bhavanicharan himself saw his role, as an agent, a "propertied
person," a seasoned traveler, a leader of the conservative section of the
Bengali community, and a luminary of the city's "public sphere," from a
more exalted perspective.[18]

In his professional and private life Bhavanicharan must have been
aware of such differences between Indian and British representations.
He must have encountered the difference that opens up between the
conceptual economies of the two languages at the moment of translation. For him the gap between the "original" (public life/sphere) and its
equivalent/"translation" (*vishaykarma*) is of strategic importance. Here, I
am intentionally posing the latter as the translated word (consistent with
the view that the idea and tools of the public sphere were of European

origin), as if Bhavanicharan was appropriating the "original" English idea
and situating it within his frame of reference and action. Seen from such
a perspective a drawbridge is constructed over the gap between the "translated" and the "original" to enable the author's provisional passage from
one conceptual terrain to another, so that *vishaykarma* may become the
translation as well as the original. This metaphoric drawbridge that
connects and separates the two conceptual economies is the "new" language
he uses in KK, and one with which he attempts to familiarize his readers
– a language that is insistently and scandalously heterogeneous and bears
the potential of translation as in travel. This new language lends to the
pre-colonial concept of *vishaykarma* a new "improper" valence; the impro-
priety of which then must be explained away with a myth of elite
responsibility towards caste. Bhavanicharan is presenting a language of
urban discourse that is fundamentally different from the English discourse
of the city.

KK contains two modes of translation – one that allows passage without
disruption of heterogeneity, and the other as linguistic appropriation. First
he defers the translation of English *into* Bengali (noting rather pathetically
that the language of the ruler has to be accepted in the affairs of the state).
Second, he exhibits a continual desire to translate verses from Sanskrit
scriptures into Bengali. The language of KK is, itself, freely punctuated
by Persian and English words. In refuting the country dweller's accusation of ignorance of Sanskrit and Sanskrit-informed Bengali, the city dweller
repeatedly demonstrates his command of these "pure" languages, by
moving back and forth between scriptural language and everyday language.
This allows Bhavanicharan to produce not only scriptural justification for
novel practices, but by bringing the "sacred" to reside in the "profane,"
so to speak, he changes the moral parameters of the everyday. His primary
concern is to demonstrate that acquaintance with, and even mastery of,
foreign languages, is no impediment to structuring one's changed life world
on the basis of sacred Hindu parameters. Once the sacred grounding has
been established, considerable risk of contamination may not only be
endured, but welcomed as a mode of secular power. Marks of heterogeneity in language and clothing to construct the new self are important
for Bhavanicharan as they enable his passage from the sacred to the secular,
from a private circle to the public arena.

To follow the city-dweller's passage from the sacred to the secular, it is
useful to pay attention to the structure of the text. We can decipher five
clear transitions in the main body of KK that divide it in six sections:
the introduction when the strangers establish their primary concerns, a
section where the householder's duties and routines are explained, a portion
devoted to language contamination, the next section devoted to the activities of the new social institution of *dal*, followed by activities of a reading
public, and the concluding section that deals with improper amusement
and the disingenuity of elite-centered social relations. KK does not seek

to escape the constraints of colonial civil society and seek refuge in the purer domain of the household concerned with *pitrikarma* and *daivakarma*. Rather, it charts a path that will escort the reader from the realm of the household to the realm of public life.

In the first section of the text the city dweller makes a long speech in which he questions the sincerity of the stranger's desire to learn about the ways of the city. This introduction anticipates the city dweller's frequent disparagement of the stranger as superstitious and ignorant country bum. He notes that people from the country are too eager to criticize urban residents and feel no social responsibility to benefit the city's people. Country folks undertake employment that would not be acceptable to the city's residents and, in the absence of close relatives in the city, country folks feel they need not fear a bad reputation. He makes a direct connection between economic labor – selling one's labor in an inappropriate manner – and ignorance of urban norms, a reason for social censure. The country folks' propensity to work longer hours for lower wages is harmful to the city's residents. If they somehow acquire wealth they always return to the village to undertake important social and religious functions, with the excuse that they have large landholdings in the country and it is the family's tradition to perform such functions at the village home. Besides, country folks claim that festivities in Calcutta can never be the real thing, as they devolve into material show and pomp.[19] KK's project is to inform its readers that Calcutta is not simply an economic resource, but it contains a respectable Bengali community that is committed to protecting *jati* (caste) and *dharma* (religion), and interested in intellectual pursuits as well.

We note twin desires in KK. First, to constitute Bengali society on its own terms of Hindu morality and, second, to engage with the modern instruments of power introduced by the colonizer. For the first case, we may consider the activities of the *dals* described later in the text, the essence of which was *samaj-sashan* or ruling society, by laws beyond the purview of the colonial state. A central precept of this Hindu morality was to retain the caste hierarchy and honor the ritual status of the Brahmins. For the second case, we can read the introduction of the activities of the School Book Society and the Hindu College in KK (here Bhavanicharan does not fail to mention that the regulations of the Hindu College are published in the *Samachar Chandrika*), as the willingness to characterize such activities in the public sphere as legitimate secular pursuits. In fact, Bhavanicharan introduces an implicit criticism of the Bengali community for not taking a sufficiently active role in the development of the public sphere. After praising the noble efforts of the missionaries in establishing Bengali schools, he is confronted with the question of whether affluent Bengalis have actively participated in establishing educational institutions. In response he mentions the names of the few men who had helped establish the Hindu College at the invitation of Justice Edward East. However, in response to the question of why more among this elite rank are not dedicated to improving this aspect of society, he prefers to remain silent. The answer, he notes, is open for speculation. His silence suggests an area of disagreement among the leaders of the community. It is important to note here that this reference to schools is about educational institutions after the European framework, and not the traditional schools or *tols* meant to dispense instruction of Sanskrit scriptures. The city dweller had already explained that many among the wealthy Bengali patrons support *tols*. While traditional forms of charity (involving gifts to Brahmins and the learned, food distribution among the indigent, establishment of temples and water tanks) are portrayed as a laudable practice among the elite, there is no equivalent emphasis on secular forms of charity.

Such silence is followed by the explicit criticism of the hangers-on who live parasitically on the elite. The only exception Bhavanicharan makes is the case of indigent Brahmins, who are included in this parasitic class. The following example illustrates such exception. Not knowing any trade, Brahmins find it difficult to make a living in the city. Their Sanskrit learning is relatively useless in a colonial economy. Two of them visit a *babu* (respectable Bengali gentleman) on a daily basis, but the ignorant *babu* fails to offer patronage to the Brahmins. The Brahmins plan an argument over scriptural interpretation and ask the *babu*, who is not versed in the scriptures, to act as an arbitrator. This indicates a reversal of the social order in which Brahmins are the ultimate judge of scriptural interpretation. The *babu*, who does not suspect their motives, is flattered at being considered superior, and proceeds to reward the Brahmins with money. KK suggests that such disingenuity on the part of the Brahmins cannot be deemed a fault as it is born of financial necessity.[20]

With this concluding example we are left with the impression that many faults (*dosha*) and contamination may be tolerated if they are required for economic necessity. While he insists on criticizing the pettiness of social envy caused by the discrepancy of wealth among the members of his community, he is willing to countenance ethical infringement and transgression of the scripturally and customarily prescribed social order if that is required for survival. The object of his criticism is the rich but ignorant gentlemen who refuse to confer on the Brahmins their traditional due. If we read this conclusion against his introductory criticism of the work ethics of newcomers to the city who submit too easily to the demands of the city's labor economy, we note a resistance to economic conditions that do not favor the mores of traditional socio-religious hierarchy. At the same time we must note that, while Bhavanicharan clearly applauds the establishment of *tols* in the city, he is equally clear-eyed about the limited usefulness of old-school Sanskrit education in the new socio-economic milieu. While discrepancies between ideal and practice must be explained away to secure the legitimacy of the class he represents, Bhavanicharan attempts to do so by problematizing questions of social labor within the context of the colonial economy.

For Bhavanicharan, the basis of a wholesome community resides in the exemplary performance of the elite. The elite-centered community described in KK, even though limited to the respectable folks, remains heterogeneous in its material relations. If KK does not present a "full-fledged" nationalist consciousness, it is not because it refuses to go beyond narrow self-interest. It is because Bhavanicharan does not wish to construe a community with a homogeneous material culture. Marks of heterogeneity in language and clothing to construct the new self are important for Bhavanicharan as they enable his passage from the sacred to the secular while retaining essential marks of difference. As he explains in relation to the use of foreign language – everyone cannot understand *sadhubhasa*. This accounts for the anxiousness with which Bhavanicharan sets his objective in the text, which is to explain why the city's cultural landscape is indecipherable to a stranger. What allows Bhavanicharan to keep up a balancing act between religious authenticity and corruption, ideal and practice, fixed order and change is precisely the large space he has at the outset given over to the domain of *vishaykarma* and *baithak*. As an early nineteenth-century text KK is particularly interesting in that it anticipates many of the traits (patriarchal, elitist, and obsessed with domestic practices) that came to characterize Bengali nationalist imaginings of the late nineteenth century.

The separation of the pure self from the polluting aspect of the material world dictated by colonial rule would become a familiar rhetoric in proto-nationalist and nationalist writings of the nineteenth century that were keen to explain the political and economic subservience of Indians to the British and how Indians could tolerate being ruled by a foreign people. In practice, however, the elite were seeking a sphere where they could transgress such boundaries with impunity. It was the in-between space where contamination could not only be allowed but celebrated and used as a form of resistance. If this had to be accomplished by retaining their elite status the rhetoric of loyalty to colonial rule and even powerlessness had to be professed from time to time to maintain routes of escape from colonial wrath. The elite, even when they criticized colonial rule, couched their statements in a characteristic rhetoric that claimed the privilege of loyal subjects.[21] In the eyes of the British, it was their explicit and expressive loyalty that gave these elite the authority to voice their disagreement. The case of Radhakanta Deb and the Sobhabazaar Rajbari exemplified the complicated, even contradictory, manner in which the elite used potentially contaminating European ideas for their own benefit to generate a public sphere in the early nineteenth-century city.

Translating architecture

A certain reticence towards the city's physical space sets KK apart from both Radhakanta Deb's Nat-mandir and Abanindranath Tagore's paintings of the *Arabian Nights* series. One of KK's salient characteristics is the absence of place names that describe the city as a lived matrix. Notwithstanding its deep concern with everyday life, KK's description of the city is contained within the overarching metaphor of the ocean. In the introduction to KK, Bhavanicharan noted his plan to write four "*tarangas*," although he completed only the first. *Taranga* or "wave" in Sanskrit, is a pre-colonial literary term to designate a chain of episodes (as in Kalhana's historical narrative *Rajatarangini*, literally "Waves of Kings"). By choosing the term *taranga* to refer to his first chapter, Bhavanicharan was connecting his urban discourse to an ancient literary frame of reference, in order to bypass literary forms introduced by the colonizers. The city's "originary" moment is, itself, marked by the metaphor of the churning of the ocean by Vishnu, which playfully does away with Job Charnock's "founding" act. By substituting a "myth" in place of "history," Bhavanicharan subverts the authoritative claim of imperial history, and generates a different narrative space that foregrounds his own concern as an elite resident. Radhakanta's Nat-mandir and Abanindranath's painting do something more than produce alternative narrative spaces, however. In their articulation of physical space, they present more powerful departures from the British imagination of the city. While KK resorts to a pre-colonial literary space to anchor the new myth that attempts to explain the elite self in the city, Radhakanta's Nat-mandir and Abanindranath's painting inaugurate mythic landscapes that are firmly anchored in their selves and their nineteenth-century mansions.

Eighteenth- and early nineteenth-century maps of Calcutta, which provided a very limited description of the native city emphasized the few Indian households that were considered significant in the social and political landscape. The most salient among these was the residence of the Debs of Sobhabazaar, which appeared in every map of Calcutta during that time. Nabakrishna Deb who established the family in Calcutta, moved from Govindapur to Sutanuti when the former had been appropriated by the East India Company for building Fort William. The Deb family house in Sobhabazaar, begun in 1764 and completed in 1780, was built by Nabakrishna on the courtyard pattern, the most preferred house form among the Indian population in eighteenth- and nineteenth-century Calcutta.

Nabakrishna started his career as a junior servant in the Mughal administration, and in 1756 became Warren Hastings's Persian instructor. He performed intelligence service for the Company during the military campaign against the Nawab of Bengal, supplied aid to the Company's army, and derived immense material benefits from the subsequent dissolution of power in Murshidabad. In 1775 the Mughal emperor granted him the status of *mansabdar* that allowed him certain ceremonial benefits, and in 1778 the East India Company transferred the *zamindari* rights of Sutanuti to Nabakrishna and his family in perpetuity in exchange for property outside Calcutta.[22] Several wealthy landowners in Sutanuti objected to this, since it effectively made the inhabitants of Sutanuti Nabakrishna's tenants.[23] The legal, economic, and social privileges of such a position could be formidable. His role in the Company's administration increased from that of a political *banian* to include the office of petitions, the treasury, the *diwani* and collectorate of 24-*parganas*, and the *jati-mala kachhari* (caste-court) for settling caste disputes, the work of which he conducted from several office spaces of his Sobhabazaar mansion.[24] Caste disputes in pre-colonial days were settled variously, by the caste-*panchayats* at the level of village governance, and by the "rajas" who presided over such disputes as *samajpatis* (society-heads) at the provincial/regional level. Consequently, the charge of the caste-*kachhari* was of symbolic significance. It gave Nabakrishna the status of *samajpati*.

Nabakrishna was fairly typical of the new generation of rich Indian merchants and *banians* who had collaborated with the British and profited from British ascendancy, settled in Calcutta in the second half of the eighteenth century, and cultivated appropriate social and political connections. Since the British were keen to foster ties with the Indian elite, whom they considered "natural leaders" of the population, it was extremely important on the part of the Indians that they be ranked high in the social scale, enabling and enabled by the continuous flow of princely titles and honors. In the uncertain political climate and early stage of the city's growth, social visibility became paramount. One had to keep up visibility through festive celebrations, charity, and by building large residences. In British eyes only a display of wealth at a princely scale that matched the stereotype of oriental splendor could earn those honors.

The British administration maintained elaborate lists to decipher the hierarchy of the native population. The British obsession with signs of difference, and the elite Indian desire to retain their status created a mutually supportive phenomenon of title-mongery. At the request of H. T. Prinsep, Radhakanta Deb, the grandson of Nabakrishna, drew up a list of high-ranking individuals – "the respectable and opulent natives" – of Calcutta society in 1822 and revised it in 1839.[25] The city was divided into 20 wards or *pallis* and the gentry were listed for each *palli*. Effectively, this meant the creation of a new set of kings and nobles to replace the ones deposed, with the hope that these newly selected nobles would be satisfied with ritual display and little political power. Only the largest landholders, whose families had settled in Calcutta in the eighteenth century and who were close allies of the British, preferably with pre-colonial princely ties, were considered worthy of inclusion. These were the *abhijatas* or aristocrats. Many families, including the Tagores, enlisted *ghataks* (matchmakers) who rewrote family histories and suitably gentrified them to be included in the coveted rank. In order to remain at the apex of society the elite had to convince each other and the British administration that they had strong constituencies among the native population. This, in turn, implied that the elite needed to impress on their adherents that they deserved the titles of rajas.

Early on, Nabakrishna Deb applied himself with a singleness of purpose to set the political and social barometers at the appropriate pressure. In addition to enhancing his caste, he outmaneuvered the Raja of Nadia to obtain the image of Krishna worshipped in the Raja's household and established the image as his own family deity.[26] Finally, he began a tradition of elaborately celebrating every religious and social festival. Thus, in his patronage of Brahmin pundits, poets, and folk singers, and in his settling of caste disputes Nabakrishna was seen as carrying on the tradition of the preceding Hindu rajas.

Although a devout Hindu, for formal recreation Nabakrishna Deb adopted the "high" style of the Mughal court, and he threw lavish parties in his expansive mansion to entertain his British acquaintances. Europeans were invited to the Durgapuja and Holi festivities as well as such occasions as the British victory at Plassey. A shrewd judge of the political climate, he recognized that the adoption of these various forms of sociability and social responsibility were critical for the maintenance of the privileged position in a society that was witnessing a changing of the guards. The eclecticism in sociability, architecture, and modes of consumption of these early *rajas* of Calcutta was not ideologically confused or a blind imitation of European manners, but an astute reading of local politics. In the social and political convictions and in the cultural choices of the late eighteenth- and early nineteenth-century elite was an attempt to shape a middle ground in which they retained power to ascribe meaning to their actions.

In the early nineteenth century Radhakanta Deb, Nabakrishna's grandson, became a leading member of the Hindu community. Learned in Persian and Sanskrit, and acquainted with English, Radhakanta assumed a conspicuous role in the public sphere.[27] He had the largest *dal*, and a powerful constellation of conservative members among the elite to emerge as a force that had to be reckoned with. The family's power and privilege that helped Radhakanta in his endeavor had been inaugurated two generations previously by his grandfather who gave vivid spatial manifestation to the privilege that had accrued over the years.

In pre-colonial days elite residences comprised of sprawling *mahals* (compartments), each *mahal* set apart for a different use and organized around a courtyard. Transferred to an urban context the residences were designed in a more compact form, with double-story wings accommodating different functions.[28] The courtyard as a generic form served several purposes: it created a suitable micro-climate in the courtyard, increased the perimeter of the house (which could facilitate better light and breeze), allowed more controlled interaction with the street, and increased the capacity of the rooms by providing a larger space into which various activities could spill out. At a time when spanning large spaces could be very expensive, a large open courtyard with surrounding rooms accommodated various uses, including large gatherings. The open court surrounded by a *ro'ak* (raised open-to-sky platform) led to a semi-enclosed *dalan* (porch) beyond which was built the single file of rooms. The size of the courtyard varied depending on its public or private function. The affluent houses in the city had multiple courtyards. The most formal of these contained the *thakur-dalan* (pavilion for the deity) on the north or east side, and a range of public rooms such as the *baithak-khana*, hall, *nachghar* (dance room), office, and library. In the late eighteenth and early nineteenth centuries, these courtyards and surrounding compartments comprising the *bahir-mahal* (outer-compartments) belonging to wealthy residences were an integral part of the network of the city's public spaces that included streets and markets. At particular times these spaces were open to the public to enable them to enjoy the festivities hosted by the elite. The outer rooms also functioned as *kachhari* (office) and were rented out or lent as a courtesy for meetings, theater rehearsals, and classes. Before the development of the professional theater in the late nineteenth century, public dramatic and musical performances were held in these courtyards and halls. Although the basic footprints of these mansions appear quite similar, there is, in fact, a great deal of variation resulting from site constraints, date of construction, and personal choices in site emplacement and architectural vocabulary.

Nabakrishna Deb built a range of mansions spanning an entire block on both sides of the street, which, inclusive of immediately adjacent tenanted land, covered 37 *beegahs*. The buildings on the north side of Raja Nabakrishna Street were inherited by his older, adopted son Gopimohun, and the buildings on the south side were inherited by his younger son Rajkrishna. Over the next century the respective branches of the family embellished their premises, and for the better part of the nineteenth century the mansions of Sobhabazaar remained one of the important sites of social power in the Bengali community. The street itself was built by Nabakrishna to facilitate connection between his mansion and the main arteries of the eighteenth-century city. Running east–west, the street stretched from Chitpur Road to the Circular Road and was soon named after the Raja himself. Such a connection not only facilitated movement of goods and people, it contributed to a selective network of arterial connections that enhanced the movement of ritual processions. The processions of the Bengali community in nineteenth-century Calcutta typically chose a route that incorporated Chitpur Road – the most important artery, and touched base with the major bazaars and famous households, thus bringing into relief the salient elements of the city's cultural landscape.

Along the north side of the street a range of small rooms formed a continuous edge and connected the house proper with the garden containing a large tank, the "summer house" and *nahabat-khana* (ceremonial music-pavilion) on the west (Figure 3.1). Two gates on either side of the tank

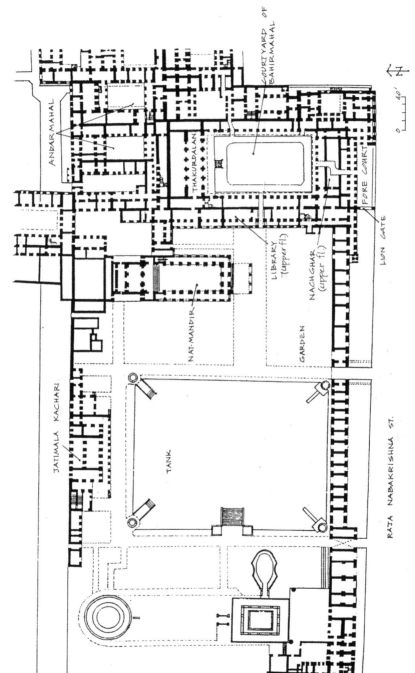

Figure 3.1 Plan of the north side of the Sobhabazaar Rajbari, mid-nineteenth century

controlled movement into the garden and provided access to the *jatimala-kachhari* and the Nat-mandir on the northern edge. The centerpiece of the north complex was the *bahir-mahal* (outer compartment) with its large public courtyard and surrounding apartments. On the north and east of the *bahir-mahal* a collection of apartments around several courtyards formed the *andar-mahal* (inner compartment), connected to the public courtyard with a series of corridors, galleries, and intervening courts. The imposing west-facing lion-gate to the *bahir-mahal* led to a small forecourt surrounded by the family's offices and the intervening *ro'ak*. A corridor in between the offices connected the forecourt to the main public courtyard. The main entrance to the court was centrally located, but approached axially to generate an impressive first view of the 107-foot by 66-foot enclosure. Another entrance connected the court from the garden on the west. The space for the deity, comprising of two adjacent *dalans*, stood on the north side on axis with the entrance. The *thakur-dalan* was raised four and a half feet and was promin-ently designated by six scalloped arches resting on clusters of composite columns (Figure 3.2). The arches were crowned with a bouquet motif and the composition finished with a solid parapet, decorated with terracotta plaques. A *ro'ak*, partially covered by a continuous running wooden balcony above, connected three sides of the court. Brick masonry columns and arches generated the primary spatial organization of *ro'ak-dalan-verandah-*rooms. The necessity of closely spaced columns created long slices of space 9 to 12 feet deep and spanned by wooden beams. These long spaces were

Figure 3.2 Thakur-dalan of Sobhabazaar Rajbari

further subdivided to accommodate cooking and storage facilities for ritual and ceremonial purposes and to make room for guests, priests, musicians, and servants. The *dalan* itself was used for a while as a classroom. Of the three staircases, two were located on the north-east and north-west sides of the courtyard, and the third on the south-west side connected the ground floor with the upper level public rooms. On the upper level the arcaded space was incorporated to form rooms with larger dimensions. The 75-foot-long room on the west became the library and the 55-foot-long one on the south became the *nachghar* (dance room). The form of the columns and the decoration of the *thakur-dalan* had no trace of European architecture. Instead, the design emulated the tradition of Mughal architecture. The Mughal influence was most clear in the design of the columns, the alcoves in the wall, and the floral stucco decoration of the *nachghar*. Decorated with care, the *nachghar* occupied a privileged position presiding over the best view of the courtyard.

Pre-colonial architecture emphasized the experience of the interior spaces and the many thresholds that connected the rooms with the interior open space, be it a courtyard or a garden. The eighteenth-century buildings of Calcutta designed for affluent Indians shared this tradition. They ignored a prominent street entrance, and lavished attention on the four interior faces of the courtyard.[29] The rooms were the least important of the spaces in the courtyard-*ro'ak-dalan*-room sequence, as most of the daily activities occurred in the open courtyard or the semi-enclosed spaces. Windows on the exterior face of the rooms were often small and the least articulated. In other words the envelope was de-emphasized to celebrate the interiority of domestic space. This focus on interiority would change in the nineteenth century for two reasons. One was the popularization of the European notion of a façade, and the second was the desire to *connect* with the increasingly busy street life, rather than withdrawing from it. The lion-gate at the main entrance of the Deb house, its south-facing verandah overlooking the forecourt and the street, and the circular arches on its ground floor were added at a later time to give the building a street-façade. This interest in generating a "front" was symptomatic of the new urge to outwardly *display* residences as symbols of wealth and status.

The *jati-mala kachhari* on the northern edge of the property had become defunct by the nineteenth century. But the complex was enhanced by the building of the Nat-mandir in 1840 by Radhakanta Deb (Figure 3.3). If, due to lack of space, the lion-gate of the *bahir-mahal* was placed perpendicular to the street, thus reducing its façade-effect, nothing would impede the expression of the neo-classical façade of the Nat-mandir. The garden in front of the Nat-mandir permitted an appreciation of the temple-front. The Nat-mandir was a combination of a temple form and a large enclosed public hall (Figure 3.4). The idea of the open courtyard for public gathering was abandoned here in favor of a double-height hall entered through a carriage port. The use of neo-classical motifs was not unusual in eighteenth- and

Figure 3.3 Nat-mandir of Sobhabazaar Rajbari seen from the upper corridor of the public courtyard. Only two of the nine-jeweled pinnacles at the back of the building remain

nineteenth-century temples in Bengal, neither was a large pavilion attached to the space for the deity exceptional in large temples, but nowhere had the use of a double-height space with overlooking balconies been attempted in a temple before. Clearly this temple was meant to accommodate a new set of uses and meanings. In the interior a series of columns created peripheral aisles that emphasized the central space and the raised dais. Two staircases on either side of the dais conveyed people to the balconies on the upper level arranged in the manner of a theater. Beyond the dais was the space for the family deity of Krishna, the roof of which was constructed after the *nava-ratna* (nine jewels or nine pinnacles) prototype. The *nava-ratna* temple symbolized wealth and piety.[30]

This temple, however, was not exclusively meant for religious gatherings. In Hindu temple architecture, a *nat-mandir* implied the patronage of a king, under whose auspices musicians and dancers performed in the temple pavilion as part of the ritual offering to the gods. Radhakanta's Nat-mandir accommodated both secular and religious gatherings. By calling the building Nat-mandir, Radhakanta was reaching for a spatial idea that transcended the common gathering of the village *chandimandap* (gathering space in front of a temple, roofed but open on the sides) for something more distinctly princely and classical. The Nat-mandir functioned as a "public hall" (substitute for the Town Hall) in which Radhakanta presided as the nominal raja. Conferring the name "Nat-mandir" to a building with a Palladian

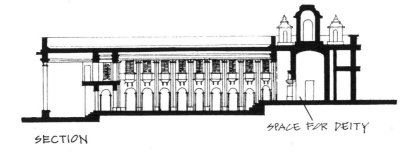

SECTION

SPACE FOR DEITY

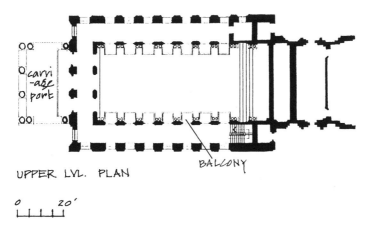

UPPER LVL. PLAN

carri-age port

BALCONY

0   20'

Figure 3.4 Upper floor plan and section of Nat-mandir of Sobhabazaar Rajbari

façade, Radhakanta set up a definitional challenge that was premised on his authority to impute meaning.

The hall was used not only for the meetings of the Dharmasabha, but for large public meetings as well. As I mentioned before, the public meeting to protest the conduct of the British judge in the *Nildarpan* affair was held in the Nat-mandir. He also used the space to host suppers and balls for the city's European elite. In the nineteenth century it was not unusual for the Indian elite to designate large halls as "ballrooms" and "billiard rooms" in their houses. That is not what Radhakanta chose to do. By adopting symbols from two different architectural cultures – Hindu temple architecture and Palladian classicism – Radhakanta literally set the stage for displaying his own position in the new political and cultural order and illustrated the capacity of an indigenous idea to accommodate new forms and encapsulate new uses. Such juxtapositions did not invariably give rise to a composite identity, but demanded attention to the relationship between the two entities.

Why did the Bengali elite so enthusiastically adopt neo-classical vocabulary? Critics have claimed that Indians lacked a "true" understanding of the classical order, and were "illiterate" in the grammar of the classical language.[31] In other words, if Indians deviated from the proportion and rhythm of the classical order, it indicated an inability on their part to grasp the rules and etiquette involved in using the new architectural language. One could argue that it was adopted because neo-classicism was fashionable at that time, that its scale had the possibility of creating grandeur, that it symbolized British rule and the elite were eager to follow their political superiors. The scale of neo-classical architecture clearly had the promise of generating an impressive façade, and such use is evident in the design of nineteenth-century Bengali residences. However, the scale was often diminished to suit the size of the building and the proportions adjusted to fit narrow lot conditions.[32] The freedom adopted in interpreting scale and proportion indicated that neo-classicism was used for its symbolic properties and not because the Bengali elite were interested in reproducing the "original" and got it wrong. The use of neo-classicism in the government offices and residences of the European population in Calcutta was connected to the Greek and Roman legacy of empire. In appropriating the vocabulary of empire the Bengali elite were not only adopting that which was novel, but that which enabled them to make a symbolic claim in the construction of that empire. By manipulating the proportions and through desirable juxtapositions they could create a different meaning, however, not one that attempted to recreate British intentions.

In analyzing the Nat-mandir we again encounter the problem of translation and attendant questions of representation, knowledge, and power. By invoking a literary concept in relation to architecture, I am also inviting a discussion of some problems we encounter when using such concepts to understand the production of space. The notion that architecture operates like a language, and that space may be read as a text finds subscribers from many disciplines and theoretical positions. It is, of course, in keeping with the practice of architects and architectural historians who have, for a long time, discussed architecture in terms of its vocabulary, grammar, and syntax. Since the 1960s the desire to apply theoretical insights of structuralism and post-structuralism to architectural discourse has made the idea of architecture as language even more secure. The theoretical implication of the intertwined lives of language and architecture, however, deserves attention as it may be traced back to colonial practices.

Evaluation of architecture in terms of what it "tells" about a people became increasingly critical in the establishment of European colonial authority, and was expressed in the need to document, categorize, and represent "native" architecture in the colonies. The visual and structural characteristics of native buildings were explained as a language, as colonizers attempted to gather the meaning of native building practices in comparison to their own, *without any native interlocuters*. A direct co-relation was made between architecture, language, and the state of civilization viewed in terms of racial characteristics. The representation of Indian architecture, for example, performed an important role in the British construction of India. Even before British surveyors and archaeologists began to systematically name different "styles" of architecture that one could find in India, there was a tacit assumption that like language, architecture could "speak" for and about India's past and present. This assumption aided the practice of Orientalist scholars who insisted on applying a comparative philological model to Greco-Roman and Indian literature and architecture so as to produce a history of Indian civilization.[33]

The central objective of British artists, surveyors, and archaeologists in representing Indian architecture was to produce India as a transparent entity. Knowledge of architecture promised a spatial visibility that remained beyond the reach of most Europeans in their encounters in Indian space. A watercolor painted around 1840 by William Prinsep, an amateur painter, exemplifies such a knowledge of architecture in the service of British construction of India. Prinsep's painting depicts a group of Europeans being entertained to a *nautch* (dance) during the Durgapuja festival in a mansion in Calcutta (Figure 3.5). Based on the date of the painting, Jeremy Losty has noted that this painting may be of Dwarakanath Tagore's mansion.[34] While Prinsep might have been representing such a visit, there is little in the remembering of the architectural details that would suggest a desire for replicating with fidelity the architectural details of the Tagore

Figure 3.5 Europeans being entertained to a nautch, by William Prinsep, *c*.1840, from Jeremy Losty, *Calcutta* (London, 1990)

mansion. The painting obeys Anglo-Indian artistic conventions rather than anything to be found in nineteenth-century Calcutta. It is a mistake to "read" this painting as a depiction of the Tagore mansion or any such building of the nineteenth-century Bengali elite. That does not, however, prevent the painting's authoritative claim to truth. The truth value of the representation is asserted by virtue of what I shall call a "linguistic" competence in more than one architectural language.

Prinsep's painting pieces together separate fragments of "native life," within a singular event of the Durgapuja. Here the painter is literally bracketing the brutality (dark side) of the heathen religion, signified by the goat about to be decapitated, to reveal the more commendable account of the encounter. The Europeans face away from the image of the goddess to see the dance performance. The elements to do with the Hindu religion are pushed to the periphery to focus on the well-lit space of the central performance. The peripheral events may not be erased though, as they help mark the native space of superstition that may not escape the view of the European. In the painting Prinsep translates the event into a language that privileges the vision of the European – as witness, painter, and viewer/voyeur. The visiting Europeans are witness to the curious phenomenon of the *nautch*, which in colonial discourse was coded in terms of debauchery. And yet the Europeans emerge as the subject of the painting because of their ability to narrate the proceedings, that is, translate the native performance to the painterly self. The painter brings his "knowledge of India," itself a product of Orientalist literature and art, to bear upon the painting, with the desire to visually supplement that which escapes the linguistic translation. The spatial incongruency as well as the sectional view depicted could not be supported in practice. From a pragmatic point of view, the ritual sacrifice would take place in front of the goddess and not out of her "sight," and the time of that event was unlikely to be simultaneous with the *nautch*. Yet, the space needed to be staged in a manner that facilitated the reading of the event in terms of colonial mastery. Finally, the viewer participates in the visual event by accepting it as a transparent translation. Through this chain of translations, the European representation of native India assumes authority, and their willing presence at heathen festivities takes on legitimacy. By creating the "original" event through translation, the painting demonstrates the European ability to see through native practices and native spaces.

The place of performance seem secured by tall "neo-classical" columns. The columns up front framing the event are askew with the performance space, to emphasize their difference in detail (that is their architectural signification) as well as their function as the viewer's frame (of reference) at a remove from the event. Similarly, the connection between the dark side-porch and the central space is fudged over to mask the painter's inability to present a coherent vision of the architecture. The painting contains the event between two architectural orders – European and Indian

[handwritten margin note: textual reading of painting]

classicism – which work as the two frames of reference, and presumes a dialectical reading between the architectural orders to bring out the significance of the event. One does not view the Indian architectural order through a frame of European classicism, however. One sees European classicism (and European civilization) "at work" in the spaces of native life from the privileged vantage of Indian history (signified by the Indian architectural order). Thus, by resorting to reading the space as a system of signs (a "textual" reading rather than spatial understanding) the English painter and viewer assume both vantages of Indian and European history. The event demonstrating the hospitality of the loyal Indian subject is worked into a coherent understanding of Indian history inaugurated by British presence.

The Indian elite, however, were able to construct a different representation of events such as these. The translation of European neo-classical vocabulary in the architecture of the Bengali elite necessarily entailed a *transformation* of meaning, and the creation of a space between what the architecture might "say," i.e. loyal subjects mimicking British material culture, and how such space "performed," enabling the production of shifting identities. This is what I have earlier referred to as the "scandalous" space of translation.

In Radhakanta's Nat-mandir, the neo-classical façade, and the *nava-ratna* temple form at the back, did not simply imply a relationship of front to back as a passage from profane to sacred, from outer domain of contamination (foreign vocabulary) to the purity of the inner domain (Indian classical vocabulary). That was just one possible reading. The theater-like space of the public hall, its use primarily for secular gatherings and its function as a public space in the public sphere of nineteenth-century Calcutta, provided opportunity for performances that did not rest on the plan or the building as a fixed script. The composition of the plan and the architectural assemblage were not attempting to fix a social order, but experimenting with models of "public" space that had yet to be liberated from its location in the domestic sphere. The multiple architectural references in Radhakanta's Nat-mandir meant that these references could be selectively called upon, made active through different forms of spatial practice during religious worship, political meetings, and secular engagements. It is in translation as in transport and transform that the possibility of architecture as a spatial strategy opens up to unpredictable possibilities challenging "strategies of containment."

To celebrate the British victory in the Sepoy Revolt and the subsequent assumption of imperial power by the Queen, Radhakanta hosted a lavish ball in the Nat-mandir and the adjacent gardens.[35] Three hundred guests were invited to a stand-up supper supplied by Messrs F. W. Browne and Company, and to enjoy fireworks in the "richly illuminated" garden. The English newspapers did not fail to remind their readers that this was after all the loyal family that celebrated the victory at Plassey on the same site. They were impressed with the hospitality and the magnificence of the decor of the "ball room" with its sumptuous carpets embroidered with gold, "the throne of gold on the top of a flight of steps at the northern end of the hall" surmounted with a crown and the royal standard of England.[36] Such an arrangement was strikingly similar to the manner in which the ballroom in Government House was decked out on similar occasions.[37] The garden and portico were lit by mottos of empire and the names of the hallowed grounds of Cawnpore, Delhi, and Lucknow – the bloodiest sites of the Sepoy Revolt. The colonial landscape of violence/victory was being recalled emblematically and reiterated by being placed dialogically with the everyday space of the mansion – both secular and religious. Radhakanta was creating a "mythical" landscape through spatial and temporal montage. Such emplacement invariably brought out the tension between the existing and the overlaid structures. The spaces in between the different elements of the montage prevented an impression of hybridity (ambivalence within a composite identity), while retaining a structure of heterogeneity advantageous to the host of the performance. It is too easy to read Radhakanta's choice of combining the vocabulary of a Nat-mandir and a ballroom or his simultaneous faith in *puja* and British loyalty as products of a desire to please the overlords, unless we recognize that it also spoke of an ability to appropriate colonial symbols and deploy them for a new set of purposes.

On the occasion of another Peace Celebration in 1860 the *Englishman* noted the "tasteful" decoration of the ballroom with the "usual groupings of banners and flowers," and not surprisingly invoked the *Arabian Nights*:

> With an excellent Band, beautiful fireworks, and tastefully lighted gardens, the Rajah's mansion was almost like a dream of the Arabian nights, and the large sheet of water, with its stone terraces and the lights gleaming on its surface, was as like the feast of Belshazaar as any thing that Martin has ever drawn.[38]

Nowhere in this description does one find the suggestion of "gaudy," fantastical decorations of tinsel ornaments, the "glaring display of lustres," the spraying of *attar*, or the dance of "abandoned females" that the Reverend Duff and other nineteenth-century English visitors recalled of *puja* celebrations in the houses of wealthy natives.[39] And there was no mention of the Hindu deity that resided in the Nat-mandir. Such a cultural assemblage signifying difference had been overwritten in the description of the Peace Celebration by a need to identify with the colonized. Instead of dealing with the specific contradictions of the Nat-mandir-turned-ballroom, the *Englishman* preferred to situate the experience in works that performed as metaphors of the Orient: *The Arabian Nights*, and the nineteenth-century biblical painting by John Martin in which the artist had gathered together Orientalist "knowledge" in a fantastic assemblage of "Indian," "Assyrian," and "Egyptian" architecture.

The *Englishman* was obviously willing to read the Peace Celebration within the parameters set by Radhakanta, and knew that such a celebration, although confined to the invitation of a few hundred, spoke to a larger audience about the Deb family's loyalty and proximity to the ruling class. Deb provided an excellent bit of public relations for the British government after the traumatic days of the Revolt. On Radhakanta's part, inviting *mlechhas* (outcastes) to share festivities in his temple-pavilion did not violate socio-religious boundaries, because such boundaries were symbolic, not physical, and the pollutive effects could be rectified by ritual cleansing. While religious festivities could be used to further his power in the domain of *vishaykarma*, the core of religious rituals could be isolated from the more secular rituals that *vishaykarma* demanded. The landscape, centered on his mansion, enabled Radhakanta to claim his own space and share in the empire.

Radhakanta Deb's success in maintaining the locus of power inherited from his grandfather was apparent in the surprising consensus of opinions expressed in the speeches given by the city's elite during a memorial service held in his honor.[40] One of the speakers, a Unitarian minister, the Reverend Charles Dall objected to Deb's being called an idolater.[41] Assuming the objective detachment of the third person he began describing his view of the position Radhakanta occupied under British rule:

> He saw there an extended procession of the councilors and governors of India, stretching through half a century . . . quickening as a flash of pure electric light, he saw the Rajah; the common link of all, bond of all. From Lord Bentinck (or before him) down to Canning and Elgin and Lawrence; from Heber down to Bishop Cotton, State and Church alike joined hands in him.

At this point the Reverend moved to the first person to authenticate his voice:

> The honored chairman had somewhat playfully called Radhakant an idolater. . . . I almost hear him now, saying, "Tell them all; let them know the truth; show them what was the religion which sustained me in all my work." That handsome temple of Krishna, which the Rajah built within his grounds not many years ago, is said to hold in its shrine an idol of the god, made of the nine most precious metals. I asked my venerated friend one day, "Rajah, do you worship that idol?" "No: – *men* never worship idols," was his reply: they are for our little ones." . . . "Then dear Raja, if you never worship idols, what do you worship?" – "My worship," he replied, "my religion, is *shalokkya*, to be always in the same place with god; *Shamippo* to be drawing nearer and nearer to god; *Shajugio* to be in conscious communion with god;

Neerban, to be lost on god, as a star in the morning light." This (I said) "This Rajah, is my religion: I was taught as a Christian child by a Christian mother . . . " Thus, friends, was it made clear to me that Radhakant was no idolater. . . . At the time of his magnificent celebration of Queen Victoria becoming Empress of India, the Rajah was particularly struck with one figure that occurred in a published notice of his loyalty . . . : "Out of an unknown antiquity there comes an unlooked-for wisdom in the fact that the gods, in the beginning, divided man into men, as the hand is divided into fingers, that it might be more helpful to itself." "That's it; that is the thing;" (said the Rajah to me) "you have it exactly!" And he went on to say something like a division of labor had clearly been ordained by God among all nations for the elaboration of true religion for the world.[42]

In his eagerness to speak *for* the Raja and bring the idolaters within the ambit of the "true religion" and the just empire, in his desire to believe that the "child idolaters" would one day become men free from such "base needs," the Reverend was unmindful of the double reading of the words he spoke for Radhakanta; he was not just demonstrating that Radhakanta agreed that the Christian colonizers possessed the truth, but that he could be using a Christian logic to justify caste divisions. Perhaps such an implication did not escape the Reverend; he hastily concluded that the Raja "went on to say something like a division of labor had been ordained by God." To avoid the implication of double-speak, the Reverend was relegating the idea of a "natural" division of labor as a mere extension of the main idea of a unitary God. In Radhakanta's view the central and peripheral ideas might have been reversed. Such reversal of meaning and the suggestion that every concept that Christian missionaries could suggest to justify conversion was already "preoccupied" by Hindu theology would have worried a more shrewd and paranoid observer such as Alexander Duff.[43] In his lavish display of loyalty to the East India Company and the British Crown, Deb, an orthodox Hindu, an idolater, had apparently not left the authoritative voice any room other than to disavow his idolatry. To include Radhakanta in the canon of empire (along with William Bentinck, whose reform policies Radhakanta had strenuously protested as offensive to the social and religious customs of Hindus), the colonizers were compelled to overlook the willful contradictions of the middle ground, the capacity of Radhakanta's mansion studded with reminders of "heathenism" to accommodate a celebration of the British victory in the Sepoy Revolt. The Reverend had to downplay Radhakanta's idolatry to the extent of obliterating it from public memory. In his premature eulogy which described the meeting of the Church and State in Radhakanta, the Reverend forgot that it was precisely the separation of religion and statecraft that was at the heart of Radhakanta's objection to the abolition of *sati* and widow remarriage. Radhakanta had mastered the politics of his day; his family could buy not only caste, but loyalty as well. Even when he could not control the meaning of the badges and titles he was honored with, he could create in his own domain a new set of spaces and a new set of symbols that resisted the fixation of meaning. The Nat-mandir with its theater-like balconies spoke vividly of a stage set; it invoked the possibility of performing new "acts," the possibility of becoming a different character, a native who had not been pre-defined by colonial authority. If the performance of empire required native presence, Radhakanta Deb could choose what that native presence would amount to.

The art of remembering

The theater-like space of the Nat-mandir with its potential for multiple acts would have generated Abanindranath Tagore's approval. Abanindranath's favored mode of describing his own childhood experience of the city was that of a performance in progress. In recollecting the nineteenth-century city in a series of written memoirs and paintings produced between 1927 and 1947 he repeatedly used the analogy of the *jatra* (a form of Bengali popular theater). Performance in public – informal social gathering of the *baithak-khana* or *adda*, the theater, and public speaking – had immense significance in nineteenth-century Bengali society. Between 1880 and 1930 Abanindranath, writer and painter, had invested much of his artistic talent in designing stage sets and performing in his uncle Rabindranath's plays. As heir to an illustrious family heritage, he was acutely conscious of the need to play the elite social role expected of him. His artistic production, particularly after 1930, was however attempting to fashion a self that did not comply with these public and even family expectations. This search for self took him into exploring the spaces of his childhood, to the nineteenth-century city and the realm of folklore.

In his description of the city as a performance space, he gave central importance to the household that he grew up in. To be more accurate, in recollecting his formative years in the house at 5 Dwarakanath Tagore Lane, he presumed to have described the city in all its lively complexity. For him his own residence and its companion house at 6 Dwarakanath Tagore Lane, if not a microcosm of the colonial city, was certainly the central site – the connecting link between two cultural worlds. He used the Bengali meaning of the word, Jorasanko – "double-bridge" – to develop this idea in the form of a mythical map of the city (Figure 3.6). The map, is indeed not of Calcutta, but an imaginary city, Halisahar, and is the central guide in a children's story *Putur Boi* (Putu's Book).[44] The nineteenth-century place names of Calcutta, however, appear on this map, thus suggesting we read this imaginary city with the colonial city as a frame of reference. The map uses the structure of a board game – *golokdham* – and shows a city divided along a main artery; on one side a

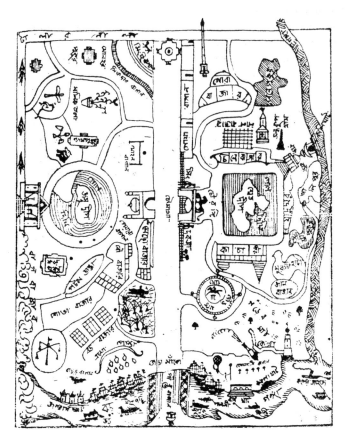

Figure 3.6 Map of Halishahar, *Putur Boi,* by Abanindranath Tagore, from *Abanindra Rachanabali* vol. 3 (Calcutta: Prakash Bhavan)

lion-gate leads to the Lal-Dighi in the middle of which is the "white island." Surrounding this water body are the colonial edifices of the Rajbari (Government House), the court-house, a church, the Black Hole monument, the race-course, and the Indian museum. On the lower right is the Fort Field with the Fort, and the in-between spaces are taken up by Jaanbazaar, Murgihata, Gorabazaar, Lal Bazaar, Benepukur, Alipore – neighborhoods that in the colonial city formed the edges of the "white town." On the other side of the street is the Gol-dighi, with the "black" island of "Jambudwip" in its center. Important place names of the native city compose this left-hand space, with Mechobazaar, Bowbazaar, Sobhabazaar, Patoldanga, Burrabazaar, Shyampukur, Maniktala receiving prominence. Connecting these two worlds, at the bottom of the map, is a small circle in the middle of a bridge, representing the Tagore household at Jorasanko. Most of this magical city disappears at the strike of nine at night, leaving behind fields, lakes, the Roy mansion, the Rajbari, and the three-story house at Jorasanko.

There is a certain literalness about this distinction between black and white spaces, both in the symbolic rendering of the places, as well as the associations they are meant to invoke. Here, however, the map does not claim to represent the "real" city. The power of naming and the authority of cartography are undermined by a semantic play on the place names. The map, as an accompaniment to the story, ceases to represent the physical city, and becomes the terrain itself. The myth of map-as-representation is fully explored by making only three elements in the landscape escape ephemeralness – the Roy mansion, the Rajbari, and the Tagore mansion of Jorasanko. The only firm anchoring is home – the author's own house. It takes the reader back to another mythical landscape and a "forgotten" moment, when only two edifices of power – one belonging to the Bengali raja and the other belonging to the British raja – invited the cultural mediation of the Tagore household. The existence of this originary moment and its anchoring in physical artifacts does not appeal to history for validation. Every night the return to a "lost" beginning presents a cyclical narrative space that refuses historicity. It presents the opportunity for fresh enactments, while ensuring a promise of return. There is no claim of representing the city as a historical artifact (that must enact and reveal the linear telos of capitalism). Here the city is re-turned as the productive site of self-imagination.

We need to remember two points when pursuing this strategy of inserting his own family dwelling in the cultural memory of the city. First, Abanindranath's recollection was augmented by the decay of the house as a physical artifact, and the possibility of it being sold off to developers. In other words, the remembrances were not simply reclaiming a lost time, but anticipating an absence. Second, the early phase in these writing and painting activities, between 1927 and 1931, perhaps the most productive five years in Abanindranath's life, was also one of the most public ones – he gave his Vageswari lectures at the Calcutta University during this time. This period also coincided with a volatile phase of nationalist agitation in the city. His response to these changes was to tell a different story of a city that used to be, one that still remained within the realm of imagination, and one that provided an alternate model to the nationalist self. The old city of his memoirs was part real, part imaginary, filled with the emancipatory romance of the *Arabian Nights*. The overlapping geographies of literature, city, house, and self, blurred the conventional understandings of private and public domains, *antar–bahir* (interior–exterior), painting and writing, to generate a new visual topography.

As an example let us follow Abanindranath's narrative as he recalled walking from the third floor through the "back alleys" of the house to the *thakurghar* (worship room):

Walking from the treasury room on the first floor along various narrow alleys, stairs, and courts we came upon a window with wooden shutters – beyond the window in a dark room a dark man was scooping water from a large vessel. Hearing the sound of footsteps, he looked up at me with his round eyes. Many years later I came to know that he was Kalibhandari – it was the *rotis* made by him that Ramalal fed me everyday. Kali was a nice person, but he had a terrifying look. When I read of the robbers and oil vessels in Alibaba's story, even today I can visualize that look of Kali, a shuttered room, and a large earthen vessel. After crossing the store room [came] a small red-tile lined courtyard, freshly washed. From there the north wall of the *thakurghar* on the terrace became visible, but it could not be reached easily. On the north side of the courtyard a few steps led to a room-wide staircase that led straight to the second floor. Next to this staircase was the room for the palanquin. After that a narrow alley – walled on one side, a wooden balustrade on the other. After crossing the alley (we) found a terrace and a narrow verandah. On one side of it a row of ovens – separate ones for boiling milk, frying bread, etc. At the end of this narrow verandah and narrow alley, a short flight of steps took you down to a dark and noise-filled room. I could feel the floor trembling under my feet. There a maid-servant, with plump arms, was grinding grain – a pile of *sonamug* next to her. Do I know then that it was this *dal* I ate with my *roti*?[45]

To him the walk is like the adventure of traversing an unknown city on a pilgrimage. This pilgrimage is different in that he begins in the public space of the house, and moves through a tortuous route into the unknown world of the "other" inside the house. This journey into the interior of the house also becomes a journey outward from the center of the self, from the space of confinement. Each vignette of the workings of the inside of the house represents a workshop, a storefront, a small space of labor that feeds the glittering city and keeps it going.

Abanindranath grew up in the house that used to be his great grandfather Dwarakanath Tagore's *baithak-khana bari* or salon. Dwarakanath, a prosperous landlord and partner in Carr Tagore & Co., built this mansion in 1823, next to the ancestral house established by his grandfather Nilmani in 1784. The *baithak-khana bari* was a completely separate structure that housed his offices and public life. The new mansion's footprint followed the contemporary pattern of detached colonial houses in the city. Designed on a three-bay pattern with a north carriageport and south verandah, the central space was occupied on the main floor by a large hall. Only on the third floor was a noteworthy deviation. The third-floor hall, designed as a banquet room, was distinctly set apart from the rest of the floor as a raised platform reached by short flights of stairs placed at intervals. The long sides of the hall were flanked by 12 pairs of columns, with railings in the spaces between the columns. In its openness the space simulated the covered deck of a ship, rather than a conventional "hall."

After Dwarakanath's death, when his older son Debendranath adopted the Bramho religion, Yogamaya, the widow of his younger brother, Girindranath, moved to the *baithak-khana bari*, taking with her the family deity. This *baithak-khana bari* had to be substantially reconfigured to make it habitable for a large extended family. New ways of configuring the *andar-mahal* were found, as were numerous additions in the second half of the century that gave the building a haphazard, a work-in-progress look. The ad-hoc strategies for connecting the different parts of the building, the narrow alleys, multiple levels, and hidden niches, the unfinished nature of the building had a lasting impact on the artist – the found places of the house seemed to be the most potent sources for generating images and stories.[46]

The *Arabian Nights* series of paintings, completed in 1931, was Abanin-dranath's way of exploring not simply the "deserted places of memory" of the nineteenth-century city, but through it he attempted to generate a visual space that deviated conspicuously from the British imagination of the city. Let us consider one example from this corpus: a watercolor titled *The Hunchback of Fishbone*, produced in 1930 (Figure 3.7). I have selected this because of the obvious reference to the Tagore family legacy – the white space on top right with a sign "Kerr Tagore & Co."

One thing is clear about the 37 paintings of Abanindranath's *Arabian Nights* series – they are not illustrations of the literary version – there are too many departures from the "original" stories, and sometimes the textual references in the paintings are slim at best. Rather, Abanindranath found the *Arabian Nights* a suitable vehicle for telling the stories he wanted to tell. Several aspects of the *Arabian Nights* made it a promising choice. The descriptions and references in the *Arabian Nights* to sea-faring commun-ities and cosmopolitan cities connected by long-distance trade made it ideal for thinking about the port city of nineteenth-century Calcutta as a place of cultural contact. The status of the *Arabian Nights* as the literary embodiment of the Orient also made it ideal for locating a competing response to nineteenth-century Orientalist discourse. Abanindranath's library contained Richard Burton's translation, the most authoritative colonial intervention, Ramananda Chattopadhyay's Bengali "domestic" edition, one Battala edition of *Thousand and one Nights*, as well as Urdu translations.[47] The cyclical narrative structure of the *Arabian Nights*, often containing stories nestled within stories, invited improvisation, and a possibility of inserting one's own story. Artfully narrated, one could see the stories as an infinite reservoir of stories yet to come, and "escapes to other texts and landscapes." Finally, the idea of story telling as a sub-versive move and a strategy for emancipation must have been at the core of this effort. Shaharzade was after all buying her freedom by telling the oppressive monarch stories. In the Bengali translation by Ramananda

Figure 3.7 The Hunchback of Fishbone, watercolor by Abanindranath Tagore,
Collection of Rabindra Bharati Society, Calcutta

Chattopadhyay we find Shaharzade telling her sister: "I hope to stop the
terrible wrongs being perpetrated in this kingdom through the strength of
stories."[48]

The painting itself is ostensibly about the first episode of the hunchback
story, in which the tailor and his wife invite an amusing hunchback to
supper. Unfortunately he chokes on a bite of fish and dies. Wishing to get
rid of the body, the tailor leaves it at the top of the stairs in the house of a
Jewish physician, who falls over the corpse. Assuming he killed the poor
man, the physician leaves it in the yard of a neighboring steward. The
steward in turn, mistaking the corpse for a thief, strikes it a heavy blow.
The corpse collapses, and the steward believing himself to be the killer,

drags it to the dark street. There a Christian broker, drunk after the night's celebration, starts to fight with the corpse. We find many of these characters and artifacts in Abanindranath's rendering, but they do not appear in the "original" form. They have been translated not only to the space and figures of nineteenth-century Calcutta, but in the process the valences have been reassigned. The clearest sign in the painting – "Kerr Tagore & Co." – may itself be read in two ways. The replacement of "Carr" by "Kerr," may be an Indianization of the English name Carr; Kar or in nineteenth-century Anglicized fashion, Kerr, was a common Bengali surname. Or it may simply be a replacement of one English last name with another, thus creating a distance between the original early nineteenth-century event and this painterly space in which another Tagore, the poet himself, presides. Insertion of industrial products (note the sewing machine and gaslight), English signage, and colonial artifacts and architectural spaces register the painted space as contemporary.

The Hunchback of Fishbone presents a collage of spaces – closely interconnected yet insulated from each other in terms of the activities occurring in them, a collection of sectional and elevational views that invite the viewer to see the goings-on of the city from a two-story high station point. The literary reference in the painting is located in the left central rectangular space – it shows the tailor and his wife trying to help the hunchback. Diagonally above it is a well-lit space showing a European gentleman and lady dining in a well appointed European-style room with their Indian host – the artist himself at the head of the table. The painting partially hidden by the hand-drawn fan is of Dwarakanath Tagore. The space of colonial encounter is marked most obviously by the sign Kerr Tagore & Co, forming a gateway to the house. Although the space of the Tagore house is presumably farther away, the diagonal relation between the space of literary reference and the space of familial intervention – as two overlapping rectangles – ensures that we interpolate them. All the frames taken together comprise a set of diagonal relations, which, if one chose to follow the story line, could be connected in a circular manner, starting from the middle left and ending with the top right. But the dominance of the two central spaces upsets any attempt to give equal emphasis to the four separate events – the four cases of misapprehension.

The spaces in the painting are dedicated to commerce and industry – heterogeneous, changing, and defying any sharp distinction between commercial and domestic space. While not every space is available to the viewer, the range of transparency and the staggered nature of the composition urge us to notice the thresholds and connecting spaces and the gaps between the frames. This enables the viewer to formulate a mobile vision. The interior spaces themselves are small and compressed – note the relation between the height of the figures and the height of the spaces – even the most generous one of the dining space is lower than it would be in the "real" house. Even if we assume that the painter is in no way trying to replicate the actual residence of the Tagores – the insertion of the actual railing design in the painting does not allow us to completely lose the familial point of reference, even when the story and imagination assume mobility. For example, the white gable roof was not reflecting the construction of Dwarakanath's *baithak-khana bari* – such masonry construction was extremely uncommon. Here the painter is fusing the idea of the *baithak-khana bari* as a residence and pleasure house grounded in the early nineteenth-century urban fabric with his vision of the house as an ocean-going vessel.

In the visual-narrative space that drew inspiration from the *Arabian Nights* he could insert the ancestral house and rescue it from disappearance. We may, however, approach this act of memorializing from another angle. The art of memory required a set of loci, and as the ancient Greeks would have it, preferably an architectural space in which to locate events.[49] Viewed thus, architecture becomes more than display, or a place of inhabitation, it becomes a mnemonic device. But for Abanindranath, such loci could not submit to the ordinary language of architecture. In *Apan Katha* (My Story), written some three years before he did this painting, Abanindranath noted:

> I became introduced with the outside world through houses and people I have not seen (*na dekha bari, na dekha manush*)! It was during this time I received, like a fragment of the *Arabian Nights*, the early story and early image of this third-floor room. ... When I was a child, the large hall was empty, but even at that early age I could imagine the hall all nicely decked. . .
>
> Calling the room a hall does not express it adequately – a *chandi-mandap* expresses even less – *baroduari* carries the sense somewhat, but to grasp its true meaning I have to imagine the deck of a huge ship – plucked from the ocean and placed here.[50]

Abanindranath went on to narrate how he could imagine the European architect standing next to Dwarakanath going over a plan of the house, and explaining to the architect the correct indigenous arrangement of *nachghar, baithak-khana, tawakhana,* etc. Clearly, this imagery of the client–architect meeting, and the use of Indian nomenclature for rooms, assured the prominence of the native voice, and the elite capacity to signify space. So, if Dwarakanath emerges as the authoritative past in this painting, the insertion of the painter himself as the narrator generates a newly privileged space – a space that is only accessible through the artist's "*antar-drishti*" – insight. This insight works in at least two senses. First, as the ability to see what is implicit, immanent, and not visible to the casual eye and, second, in the form of a gaze turned inwards, from the space of publicity to the domain of creativity.

The insight that enables him to imagine in meticulous detail the material environment in which the conversation between the European architect and the Indian merchant-prince took place, also aids the delineation of the spaces in these paintings, filled as they are with artifacts that generate the story's ambiance, and deliver the story's visual-narrative excess. He borrowed the compositional conventions of Mughal miniature and its love for delicately rendered artifactual detail, but applied these techniques in the service of a visuality that resisted the structure of imperial history and its demand for houses and artifacts as fixed anchors. Contemptuous of history's claim to veracity, objectivity, and painterly attempts to delineate the "real" world accurately, he rued the disinterest in telling stories – "no one knows how to tell stories any more," he noted, "all they write is history."[51] This is not simply contempt against fact-grinding, but a desire to play with the notion of historical time and space. And yet, here vision as *antar-drishti* does not constitute a transcendental move that seeks to overcome the mundane everyday materiality of city life by re-locating oneself in the eternal idyllic[52] – this vision allows the re-constitution of everyday materiality, lovingly, as so many sites of stories. This vision recites the tactility of everyday practices as a way of being at home in a human world inhabited by spirits, fairies, princesses, and animals that speak; it is assured by the transformative power of magic and myth.

R. Sivakumar has perceptively pointed out that "Abanindranath's self-reflexiveness" also contrasts with the "Orientalist-traveler-narrator's attempt to hide behind claims of scientific neutrality or scholarly objectivity and efface the colonial presence and thus time and historical change from his representation of the Orient."[53] For Abanindranath it was the realm of imagination, myth, and play that contributed to anything worth remembering, the material world that deserved posterity. The past then had to be rescued from the stranglehold of history and set afloat in the realm of imagination – the domain of storytelling:

> In the memory of dwelling resides the house. One day when its residents leave, the house dies a real death. Entering the realm of archaeology, it informs us whether it is built in an indigenous or foreign mode, in a Mughal or Buddhist style. Then one day the poet and the artist arrive. They generate new life into the house and its catalogued artifacts by rescuing it from the mortuary of history and archaeology.

Shortly afterwards, Abanindranath shifts to the first person: "It is through my remembrance – in painting, writing, and stories that there is any chance that the past will survive in the present."[54] The mention of archaeology is not a particularly obtuse reference to James Fergusson's method of writing the history of Indian architecture, and Fergusson's obsession with inventing stylistic categories. By disrupting any attempt to read in the fabric of the city marks of linear historical time, Abanindranath seeks to open up a new creative space filled with emancipatory possibilities.

The original space of creativity for him was the space of his childhood, with its spatial boundaries and restriction on movements, the same restrictions that applied more or less to the women of the house and to the servants. The formal space of the house – the first and second floors and the garden on the south – belonged to the masters of the house. The third floor and the sprawling addition on the south-west was the *andarmahal*. The north side that also formed the main entry to the house was the servants' domain. Strict rules of separation marked the boundaries between the *bahir-mahal* and *andar-mahal*. The shutters of the third-floor windows that overlooked the south garden remained closed until late at night – even looking at the men's space was considered poor etiquette for those not allowed entry into the privileged male space. Abanindranath suggests that precisely this restricted access allowed his imagination to be set free. When he sat on the ledge of the north window to look outside, the performance never became visible as a complete picture, but appeared in fragments, cut-up by the lines of the shutters that could be manipulated at will. The child could choose his frame and picture fragment, and make up the remainder with his imagination. He privileges a "pre-adult" vision not because of any claims to innocence or truth; he privileges the pre-adult ability to *see* beyond the obviously visible. This imagination brooks no boundaries between imagination as a subject-centered mentalist category and imagination as practice.[55]

In a different context, Abanindranath remarked that there are three levels of creative pursuit – the lower floor for services and craftsmen, the middle floor, the salon for the display and appreciation of art, and the top floor, the *andar-mahal/antar mahal* for creative inspiration. Such a remark produced the structure of his family residence as a model of creativity, but re-assigned the meaning traditionally attributed to these spaces. It is important to consider the original Bengali phrase he used to contemplate his first introduction to the ancestral house: "*na dekha bari, na dekha manush.*" "*Na dekha*" literally means "not-seen." The term when applied to people may mean people he never met, had never known. But it may as well mean those that remain invisible, those whom we forget to notice, those who perform their work behind the stage: the servants, the laboring class. His earliest memories were not of his parents, but of the servants who raised him – Padmadasi and Ramalal. In a touching anecdote, he recalled that suddenly one day, Padmadasi left after a quarrel with another servant. He remembered waiting expectantly for her return, not realizing that she had left for good. "Perhaps," he wrote:

> nowhere in this world anyone retains any memories of her (Padmadasi), except me. It may be why, having sat down to write my own story,

I can see the one who was the other, the distant – across the space of fifty five years, she sits pouring milk for me.[56]

Those assigned a peripheral place in the societal structure return to occupy the center of imagination, providing the essential everyday links with which to build one's edifice of longing.

In one sense, Abanindranath was introduced to his family through family lore recounted by the servants. The numerous servants who worked in the household also introduced him to the outside world. In his descriptions, they form the most entertaining part of the tableau of daily life. He makes them visible as an integral part of domestic economy and, by extrapolation in the painting, of the colonial economy. The big events are sutured and given meaning as a fabric by those serving the masters in small capacities. The tailor in the painting may very well be the bespectacled tailor of the Tagore household who lived in the room above the entry gate.[57]

While with one hand Abanindranath seems to naturalize existing hierarchies and boundaries, with the other hand he reverses the elite adult male privilege of being in the center of things, of having few boundaries. While he sets his characters to tell their own stories – of people and buildings that constitute his own identity, he relishes the authorial role of the master who sets the stage, establishes the connections, and edits where necessary.

What we have here are subtle subversions that illuminate a discomfort with one's location in the cultural and social milieu, and a not-so-subtle critique of the colonial city's public sphere. Cultural autonomy, for Abanindranath, however, did not reside in the *antahpur*, but at the threshold of domestic space, in the ability to re-envision connections with the outside world. Abanindranath's distaste for public performance (and public life of Calcutta in general) has been well recorded in his writings; he repeatedly criticized the modern colonial institutions – museums, universities, and art schools, and even modern forms of getting together in public – for their inability to produce creative thinking. He preferred the stationary vantage of the south verandah that he and his brothers had transformed into part salon, part stoop, part studio. It is from there that he wished to know the outside world, second hand, through stories told by visitors. He supposedly even refused to read the newspaper, but preferred being told about the news.[58] What he rejected in the need to occupy the city's public space, he reclaimed through a mobile imagination.

While the claiming of the city's public spaces through (violent) political agitation had been inaugurated by 1905 as part of the *swadeshi* (national self-sufficiency) movement, Abanindranath's repudiation of such strategies was premised on what he considered to be a distorted nationalist imagination that could either follow "western" dictates of the "public" or reach back to oppressive modes of a traditional Hindu community. The *Arabian Nights* series, and *The Hunchback of Fishbone* in particular, was the first attempt to *visualize* the city on radically different terms than that of the British and in so doing refused claims upon Western rationality, civil society, and progress as pre-requisites for becoming a nation. The nationalist construction of the self required redefining the space of the city through a much more complicated and subversive spatial imagination.

By discussing three different artifacts from three different moments of Calcutta's colonial history, I have attempted to trace some changes in notions of the public sphere and public space through which the city's Bengali Hindu elite attempted to work out their location in the city, and to contest prevalent British colonial visions of the "native." The difference between Bhavanicharan and Radhakanta/Abanindranath is significant. For Radhakanta and Abanindranath the construction of the self was explicitly tied to the materiality of city space, and spoke of their ability, as wealthy landowners, to perform in a manner different from not just Bhavanicharan, but the middle classes. The elite and middle-class claims to public space proceeded on different trajectories. The landed elite intervention in the public sphere was premised on their ability to own and control land, while the middle classes, in their limited capacity to own land, resorted to more subtle means of claiming space, and investing in the world of letters as a mode of power. The middle-class intervention in the city's physical space, as I shall explain in the next chapter, was powerfully mediated by literary imagination and practice. Literary space was not so much a compensatory space, but a realm in which spatial meaning was worked out to lend coherence to the physical configuration of dwelling and public space.

In their desire to present a competing cultural landscape as the basis of a nation, Bengali nationalists – both elite and middle classes – felt compelled to articulate other ways of describing the self and community that addressed, and at the same time bypassed, British visual knowledge. The latter stood for colonial paintings, maps, architecture, archaeology, census, and the whole range of modern techniques of governmentality that privileged the eye of the (European) observer. I have argued in Chapter 1 that British painters of colonial India, in their desire to establish spatial mastery, found it difficult to subsume the smell, noise, and tactility of the landscape within a modern visual regime. A modern Bengali visuality came to be informed by both a recognition of the power of these techniques, as well as a knowledge of sense perceptions that the Enlightenment had relegated to the realm of the primordial, or at best to a medieval worldview. The discursive, pictorial, and spatial strategies would engender a new politics of vision and the visible/invisible.

4   Telling stories

Dwelling in modernity

During my recent visits to Calcutta, I have often spent time in a book-store on College Street looking through books and chatting with the owner Mr. Dasgupta. In one of our conversations about old houses in Calcutta, he said, "You must see our old house, particularly the *thakurghar* (room for worship). It's a *thakurghar* of olden days – marvelous!"[1]

So, on a rainy Sunday morning I visited Mr. Dasgupta's old family home on Beniatola Street. For over 150 years several prominent business families have called this narrow street home. The house itself goes back to the early decades of the nineteenth century. It has been remodeled several times to incorporate new amenities such as piped gas, water, electricity, and the façade has been revamped, but the basic frame of the house has changed little. The ground floor of the two-plus story house has been rented out to a paper merchant for over 100 years, and their godown (storage) continues to occupy the courtyard on the ground floor. Two entrances – one from Beniatola Street and the other from the back alley – provided access to the Dasgupta family who resided in the house until 1967. Since then the house has been empty of people, most of its rooms locked up for storage purposes.

The rooms on the upper floor are connected by a narrow *dalan* (verandah) that runs along the three sides of the courtyard, and becomes wide on the south side, creating a generous living space. Beyond the south *dalan* three modest-sized rooms constituted the sleeping apartments. The west side was taken up by the *thakurghar*, the kitchen store, and another private apartment. On the north side, pride of place was given to the *jalkhabar-ghar* (refreshment room), and adjacent room for food preparation. This was also the kitchen for the women of the household; lunch and dinner were cooked by a salaried cook in a separate cook-room located on the third floor of the building. The rooms on the south and north sides were given different design accents to designate their relative import-ance and privacy – the ones on the north side have taller doorways with decorative fanlight and generous openings to the street.

This residence as it had begun to be used in the late nineteenth century, clearly did away with the usual spatial distinctions that designated the *bahir-mahal* (outer compartments) and *andar-mahal* (inner compartments) of Bengali households. This is, of course, not to say that distinctions between *andar–bahir* (inside–outside) had been entirely dissolved; rather the new spaces show a certain degree of manipulation of conventionally under- stood categories in its late nineteenth- and early twentieth-century usage. For all practical purposes the entire second floor was the domain of the *andar-mahal*, where the women and their work and leisure predominated. Memories of delicacies served in the *jalkhabar-ghar* remain inextricably linked to the stories and gatherings of the women. Etched on the floor of the *dalan*, in front of the door of the *jalkhabar-ghar*, is a plan of a board game – *baghbandikhela*. The deep impression of the cross-pattern perhaps carries the most tangible mark of their everyday lives. Fragments of their stories, a few photographs and paintings convey whiffs of the past.

We stood at the threshold of the *thakurghar*, and looked inside. I saw an empty room not larger than seven by nine feet; three framed pictures, and a floral engraving on the floor relieved the plainness of the room. I stood there while Mr. Dasgupta talked about his aunt who performed the household *puja*, fondly recalling the daily rituals . . . to him the place was full.

As we sipped tea, waiting for the rain to stop, we talked about the women in our families, about visiting ghosts, about the changing dynamics of Bengali spaces and Bengali patriarchy. Our conversation wove in and out of three modes of remembering – the public/published narrative of community in which men dominate; oral recollections of family life in which women take on a large though not exclusive role; and personal memories that enable us to make sense of the above, bridging the space between the printed and the spoken word, between the scene and the experience.

Several points struck me about this conversation. We were mostly talking about women's spaces and relying primarily on the latter two modes of remembrance. This conversation would not have taken place when the space was still in daily use. In the last 40 years women's access to the city's public spaces has changed enough for this conversation to be possible. And, ironically, the conversation could only take place when the interior spaces of houses such as these had been emptied of people and even contents. The emptiness of the house allowed for a discussion of women's spaces in ways that were not burdened by the demands of Bengali public discourse. The emptiness also foregrounded the ephemeral nature of the materials with which we are left to construct the stories of Bengali women. We were insistently drawing on passing sensations – tactile, aural, olfactory – much more so than the visual, to construct and communicate their stories. This insistence has been made necessary by the location of women in Bengali literature, and its characteristic contradictory concern with the visible aspects of material culture.

In late nineteenth- and early twentieth-century Bengali literature, the acclaimed site of Bengali modernity, we find only fleeting glimpses of the everyday experience of women, despite women being central objects of social discourse, and despite their occupying critical roles in novels and short stories. Their lifeworld is shrouded by a heavy mantel of social prescriptions and moral injunctions. The thick moralizing reveals a deep-seated anxiety about dwelling in a historical moment troubled by changes in social and spatial structures. The trope of "loss" – of a sense of family, community, domestic virtue, dominate this discourse, and gets addressed through the dichotomies of *andar–bahir*, *antarmukhi–bahirmukhi* – inside–outside, centripetal–centrifugal, spiritual–material.

We remember women, outside of such categories, only when we *speak* in private, absentmindedly almost. There is a hesitance about telling such stories in public – stories that spill over taxonomic norms. When women are included in public stories, a rhetorical space is set aside for them – anterior to narrative space and time – emphasizing the urge to retain the propriety of a spatial taxonomy.

This taxonomy was, itself, a product of nationalist response to the British image of the native community. Nationalist literature, by taking up the task of "remembering" the nation's history as a way of explicating the moral topography of community, became preoccupied with the visible aspects of material culture. The memory of the community was mobilized by asserting hegemony over non-visual ways of knowing, only to retain traces of an unreasoning modernity that took pleasure in the sound, smell, and tactility of everyday life. The latter constituted a delinquent domain that could only be spoken about, experienced, even cherished, within an *observable* regulatory framework. The visible markers, in what might seem an odd turn, became those that needed to be asserted but not trusted. The same nationalist discourse that produced the visible topography was underwritten by a deep distrust of the *merely* visible. This was exemplified in Abanindranath Tagore's paintings and writings (see Chapter 3). In the politics of the visible/ invisible, only some aspects of the emergent topography could be granted visual sovereignty. It is this contradiction, often surfacing as conceit, that marks the way Bengali literature continues to tell the city's stories.

It would not be an exaggeration to say that Bengali literature remains the lens through which we imagine the lifeworld of the nineteenth-century middle class. I would go farther and argue that it is through Bengali literature that the spatial imagery of Calcutta has been generated. Here the visible aspects of the physical artifact become markers of a gendered spatial economy, even as they offer frames to enter the domain where meanings gather depth in Bengali modernity. Without this recognition we cannot explain the deep disdain with which the visible city was treated in Bengali literature (and in some respects continues to be so treated) – Abanindranath Tagore was an exception – and the abiding affection of Bengalis for the city as a space of communal pleasure. Neither can we explain the perceptible gap between such literary representations that derided the city's visual culture and the concern with beauty expressed in the large majority of the late nineteenth-century elite and middle-class residences in the city. The extant physical fabric of Calcutta enables us to recognize the cultural contradiction of Bengali modernity.

If "dwelling" suggests at least two analytic possibilities – the existential question of one's being in the world, and the physical space of inhabitation – the relationship between the two, and between normative space and experience, between ideology and practice, however, is not entirely transparent in the production of Bengali modernity. The architecture as artifact – both physical and literary – merely alludes to possibilities, of strategies for refashioning a sense of self and community.

Nowhere is this spatial problematic more apparent than in the late twentieth-century literary discourse on *adda*, a modern Bengali form of sociality. Dipesh Chakrabarty describes *adda* as "the practice of friends getting together for long, informal, and unrigorous conversations."[2] It is a form of sociality that is considered predominantly, if not exclusively, male and middle class. Since at least the 1970s it has come to be recognized as a dying social practice, contributing to "an impressive amount of mourning and nostalgia." Chakrabarty views such mourning as an "unarticulated" yet anxious attempt to deal with the rapid changes in capitalist modernization, altering to a large extent "the individually distinct ambiences of modernism" that cities like Calcutta had built up in the first half of the twentieth century. "A history of *adda*," he suggests, "that is also a desire for *adda* may indeed be a requiem for a practice of urban modernism now overtaken by other pleasures and dangers of the city."[3]

Those of us who participated in and remember mixed-company *addas* in Calcutta in the late 1970s and early 1980s might have a different perception of the demise of *adda* per se as a social practice. It is entirely possible that by the 1970s, the early twentieth-century male *adda* had run its course. But keeping aside that point for the moment, let us consider what makes the early twentieth-century *adda* modern. The *adda* is, in part, derived from the rural *chandimandap*, in part from the pre-British *majlish* and the *baithak-khana*, and in part aspiring to the club and the salon and through all this contributing to a distinctly Bengali identity. Many of the well-known *addas* of the early twentieth century were high-brow intellectual assemblies. In fact, in Chakrabarty's view one of the attractions of the *adda* and its primary claim as a modern "institution" was its literary pleasure and contribution to Bengali literature. Modern Bengali literature, it would seem, was nurtured in the space of the *adda*.

The *adda* with its non-fixity of topic of discussion and even of space (not all *addas* had fixed space) may be seen as a critique of the more rational forms of "getting together," the *sabhas* and *samitis*, organizations that had a defined agenda for their meetings. The term *adda* only began to be used in this particular sense in the last decade of the nineteenth century. However, it is instructive to see, later on, the terms *adda*, *majlish*, and *baithaki adda* being used interchangeably.[4] As someone adept in *adda*, the Bengali writer, Sayyad Mujtaba Ali, described himself as the representative of all the *chandimandaps*, *zamindari-havelis*, and teashops in Bengal – heir to a long tradition of speech culture.[5] The time and space given over to the pleasure of communal speech connects the *chandimandap* with the *havelis* and teashops. The nature of orality changed, however, once the *adda* was removed from the bounds of the *baithak-khana* to the cafés of the early twentieth-century city. What was retained, even enhanced, in the process was the *affect* of communal speech; speech as passionate, multi-sensory experience, an occasion for heated discussion, its spontaneous and raucous nature far exceeding any yardstick of reasoned debate.

The communal pleasure of the *adda* and its male-centeredness are related in multiple ways. What is significant is that the physical presence of women in an *adda* has been invariably seen as antithetical to its mode of communal pleasure. The stories of women breaking up or attempting to dissolve the pleasure of *adda* are legion, and are guaranteed to make an *adda* laugh. The woman as an embodiment of domesticity is perceived as an intruding presence (particularly as a figure of male desire), and/or a figure of amusing disharmony in the city's public space and public sphere. This relation between gender and space deserves some attention, considering that a direct relationship is often made between the loss of urban space and the demise of the *adda*. Mujtaba Ali wrote in the early 1970s:

> It is incontrovertible that the genuine *adda* is dying. In how many of these new five-story, ten-story buildings cropping up in Calcutta would you find a *ro'ak* or a *baithak-khana*? The *ro'ak* is lost, the drawing room has replaced the *baithak-khana*. On one side a few snacks on a very fine porcelain plate placed on a small peg-table. On the other side a large Belgian-glass flower vase on a teapoy. You dare not lean comfortably against the sofa . . . .
>
> Not that conversations don't take place, but call it *soirée*, *matinée*, *conversazione*, whatever, might even call it a seminar, using today's language, but you cannot call it *adda*.[6]

A clear contempt for "modern" (he used the English word in the original text) Bengali architectural and urban choices resonates through Mujtaba's writings on *adda*. He was unambiguous about the need to create the *physical space* first: "Why is bathing in the Ganga on the decline, because religious-minded people are not building *ghats* . . . Why is the *adda* on the decline, because the moderns don't build *ro'aks* anymore."[7] But was he seeking a more "traditional" urban domain where the pleasures of communal gathering could flourish? Yes and no. While he mourned the loss of the *ro'ak* and *baithak-khana*, two of the fixtures of nineteenth- and early twentieth-century Bengali middle-class life, he also noted that the best *adda* took place only in cafés. What he appreciated most was the complete "freedom" of the café from domestic confines. *Adda* in a house destroyed its "democracy":

> Because the householder provides the *adda* with snacks, everyone seems eager to please him ... What is more, the lady of the house cannot either outright or indirectly through gestures suggest, "why don't these sordid men leave?"... You may sit in the café for hours, eat whatever you wish, the *adda* is in full strength, nobody urges you to go home, there is no fear that anyone's wife will pay a visit – what else do you want?[8]

In another essay he wrote sarcastically:

> What shall I do with a house? I was born in a hospital, did my studies from a hostel, made love in a taxi, got married at the registrar's office. I eat at the canteen, or wherever I can manage; the morning is taken up in the service of the bosses ... in the market and ration shop, the afternoon in the office, the evenings, sometimes, in the cinema. When I die I will be laid down at Nimtala (cremation ground) ... What I rather need is an exquisite *adda*.[9]

A deep antipathy towards salaried labor of the Bengali middle class, their entrapment in a modern institutional structure allied with the impossibility of enjoying a "home" in capitalist modernity runs through Mujtaba's writings. This impossibility of "home" is substituted by a longing for the all-male haven of the *adda*. For those familiar with the discourse on nineteenth-century Bengali modernity, the anatomy of this substitution will be transparent. The need to provide for a family drives middle-class Bengali men into salaried labor (*chakri*) under colonial rule, leaving no autonomous space, no room for creative pursuits.[10] Mujtaba borrowed an obscure poet's verse to describe the "plight" of the Bengali willing to sacrifice his life for *chakri* – "It is not advisable to run on a full stomach? Chewing food is good for health? Let me save my *chakri* first, brother, saving life comes later." To this Mujtaba appended a sarcastic note: "The food for which the Bengali engages in a clerical job, even that he cannot enjoy unhurriedly; you will not find such paradox, such selflessness outside of Bengal."[11]

In the instance of *adda*, the home and the colonial state (and later the post-colonial state) are not in opposition but connected by a chain of subservient labor and the desire for *kamini-kanchan* (women and gold). The space of the *adda* cannot be constructed out of a distinction between the inner domain of the spiritual/cultural (the domestic realm) that must be held autonomous against the imposition of the outer domain of the material (the political and economic domain). Neither is the *adda* a fragment of civil society positioned between the domestic and political. In a world where home and colonial service lie in a continuum of bondage, *adda* is a space that seeks to escape the domination of both home and salaried service, refusing the dictates of time, responsibility, reason, and progress, while simultaneously refusing narrowly held distinctions between traditional and modern. The mourning of an all-male, middle-class preoccupation as the passing of Bengali modernity, however, should give us pause. If *adda*, as Dipesh Chakrabarty suggests, is a thematic site for working out struggles about the location of gender in Bengali modernity, then why on this site do women only appear as objects of discourse?[12]

What I propose to do is look beyond the witty banishment of women from the privileged space of the *adda*. I have a perverse suggestion. The manner in which the *adda* has been written into Bengali cultural memory, and in extension into the production of Bengali urban space, is one of the most "successful" instances of cultural exclusion, of privileging a male, middle-class domain.[13] The absence of women from the *adda* was not simply a fall-out of contemporary practices about segregation of men's and women's spaces, rather *adda* as a social and literary practice extended the maintenance of these gender boundaries at a time when these boundaries were being breached. It was the male character that produced the "zone of comfort" in the first place. And when the maleness was erased, at least to a large degree, primarily with co-education in schools and colleges, it was for the mourners of *adda*, nothing less than the death of a beloved institution. If not the sole cause, the increased access of women into public spaces is certainly a potent reason behind the nostalgia for *adda* and a reign of "phallic solitude." In general, we should turn this idea around, and pose the following: the relative "absence" of women from the public space of the early twentieth-century city must be seen as the result of strategic erasure – a product of Bengali modern taxonomy. This legacy continues to shape the experience of the city today. My plan is to explore some of these strategies in this chapter and the next.

Turning from twentieth-century to late nineteenth-century practices of communal gathering in the *baithak-khana*, allows us to contemplate some of the problems in the idea of Bengali public space that run through the writings on *adda*. In nineteenth-century Bengali literature the *baithak-khana* anchors the spatial taxonomy of the city. It is a space of conversation, physically straddling the street and dwelling, public and domestic, and a space that has been profusely talked and written about. Its location, its "looks," as well as the social life it harbored were subjects of literary exploration, and consequently the *baithak-khana* holds promise for untangling some of the complicated relations between the formation of communal memory, space, and gender in Bengali modernity.

The rest of the chapter is organized in three sections. In the first section I discuss the characteristics of nineteenth-century speech culture that created a specific place for women and the "folk." In the second section I provide an analysis of the Bengali construct of the *para* (neighborhood), its male-centeredness, and the role of the *baithak-khana* in hosting different opportunities for social gatherings. Here, I rely primarily on architectural representations to map the physical relationship between the streets and buildings, and the implication of the building façade in defining Bengali modernity. In the concluding section I analyze the language of material culture of the *baithak-khana* and the importance of this visual language for enforcing a spatial taxonomy of male privilege.

The speech culture of the middle class

The remarkable growth of printing presses and the simultaneous growth of Bengali drama in the late nineteenth century enabled the creation of a public sphere that resorted not so much to reason as to the performative power of speech and the immediacy of the dramatic act.[14] Not surprisingly, the Bengali theater as well as the vernacular press were frequently censored by the colonial administration in recognition of their popularity and the extent of their impact on the public.[15] Many of the plays that were considered seditious relied on the subversive mode of humor. This was a long-standing attribute of folk culture, a means through which the lower classes had made their presence felt in the space controlled by the elite.

Folk music and plays were the most popular forms of entertainment and the mainstay of festivities in the eighteenth- and early nineteenth-century elite houses. In the milieu of Calcutta they received a distinctive urban stamp by improvising on older forms of composition to incorporate themes borrowed from the new urban environment, the emergent socio-economic structure and the culture of the *nouveaux riches*. Often they were ribald interpretations of mythological themes, filled with sexual allusions. The performances that became most popular were anecdotal in their content and took the form of a contest of songs or exchange of repartee. This gave the performers room to improvise extemporaneously depending on the mood of the audience and the nature of the reply. The *kobis* (poets), for example, most of whom came from the lower orders of society, dominated the popular entertainment scene with their distinctly urban *kobi-gan*.[16] A combination of music and poetry, the *kobi-gan*, was derived from the rural *tarja* and performed by one group competing against another in the *kobir larai* (verbal duel between poets) during festivities in the rich households. *Kobis* from all castes, including many women, were allowed into these performances. Despite elite patronage, they did not refrain from poking fun at their clients and at the elite in general.[17] Occasional insults during the festivities were tolerated, even encouraged, and the host was often expected to participate in these exchanges. Such deviation from daily norm acted as a safety valve in a society with huge

discrepancies in wealth and status. Giving the lower classes room for criticism also recognized them as part of the community. Social criticism was,
however, conducted strictly in the guise of humor. In a society that
remained closely linked by physical proximity, kinship, and patron–client,
tenant–landlord relations, humor was a convenient tool to dissipate the
animosity that might be at the root of such social critique. There was a
careful balance between respect and disrespect, assertion and deference,
self-critique and social critique.

By the mid-nineteenth century, the elite, who had simultaneously cultivated the classical Indian traditions of music and dance along with folk
performances, began to commission Bengali plays based on Sanskrit literary
tradition and European theatrical conventions. But such refined Sanskritized cultural forms with a liberal dose of British Romanticism could not
capture the imagination of the public, although they met the approval of
the British authorities. Soon Bengali authors were borrowing from the
repertoire of everyday speech to make the stories more "lifelike." In 1854
Peary Chand Mitra and Radhanath Sikdar launched a magazine called
Masik Patrika with the explicit objective of using everyday language which,
alone, they believed, could expand the readership of Bengali literature. "The magazine," they noted, "was meant for the ordinary reader,
particularly women."[18]

The effectiveness of folk speech and humor was not lost on the elite.
Kaliprasanna Sinha, a member of mid-nineteenth-century elite society
who, unlike the lower-class performers, had much at stake in the existing
societal order, adopted the spirit of folk humor in the best-known satire
in the Bengali language, *Hutom Penchar Naksha* (1861).[19] The satire became
an instant classic because of its successful use of colloquial Bengali. For
many, it signaled that Bengali had arrived as a modern language and was
not dependent on either Sanskrit or English literary forms to derive sustenance.[20] Writing in a period of intense soul-searching among the Bengali
community regarding social and cultural identity, Kaliprasanna celebrated
the city's public life and brutally criticized the new order in which clear
signs of distinction between the elite, middle, and lower classes seemed to
be disappearing. In the introduction of the book, however, he explained
his dilemma:

> There is nothing imaginary or baseless in this sketch – true, some may
> see their own faces . . . ; all I can say is that I have targeted everyone,
> and targeted no one, I haven't left out myself from the sketch either.
>
> I could have presented the sketch as a mirror; until recently we
> trusted that sensible people do not break the mirror if one's face
> appears ugly in it; rather tries to improve one's countenance. But
> seeing the trouble over *Nildarpan* I don't have the courage to hold a
> mirror to the face of dangerous animals. Consequently I had to opt
> for guise.[21]

Kaliprasanna's reference to the *Nildarpan* affair was undoubtedly a jab at the paranoia of the Anglo-Indian community and their willingness to bend the law for their own purposes. The use of pseudonyms, however, hardly prevented his readers from recognizing the characters he poked fun at. Adopting a disguise was not so much putting on a mask from behind which one could criticize others, but assuming a different image, presenting oneself imaginatively as a different character. This cultivation of a façade spoke of the mastery of a performer, rather than a face of protection from the outside world. This attitude towards public life, as we shall see later, would also give the street edge of Bengali neighborhoods its distinctive character.

Whether in paying the fine for James Long in the *Nildarpan* case, in having his satire published, or in translating the *Mahabharata* into Bengali, Kaliprasanna, a luminary of the city's public sphere, cultivated a self-conscious image. Such construction of the self, even by reaching for extremes, was intended to make him a "public" figure, a character whose stories would become part of popular culture. The cultural history of nineteenth-century Calcutta is replete with examples of individuals and groups, from the Derozians to the Baghbazaar Ganja Club, who invited notoriety by presenting extreme opinions to a society that remained for the most part conservative and closely knit. While such extreme efforts were disparaged, people recognized a certain aura in daring to go against the grain of prevailing social and political norms. Recalling mid-nineteenth-century Calcutta society, the actor and playwright Amritalal Basu lamented the passing of such great men. "These days, there are plenty of rich men," he noted, "but not many of them are great men. In those days the wealthy had generous temperaments; consequently wealth and greatness were synonymous."[22] In this context Amritalal remembered Kaliprasanna for his forthright criticism and his facility with speech. Kaliprasanna belonged to a nineteenth-century Calcutta speech culture that cultivated the spoken word, anointed the best speakers, the impromptu storytellers, a clever turn of phrase, the most sly and daring political and social critiques. But this speech culture was not simply about oratory. It was a communal, participatory process that demanded an exchange, craved a response. Kaliprasanna must have been pleased that a flurry of responses were published in retaliation to his sketch, and such sketches soon became the most popular form of social and political criticism. By becoming a character like Kaliprasanna Sinha, by cultivating the repartee, one could leave a mark in the "public" – in the *majlish*, in the *baithak-khana*, in the *sabha* (religious and political meetings) and in the law courts and Town Hall.

While the mass availability of printed books and the elite desire to cultivate a new literary sphere made a significant impact on the orality of urban folk culture, the category of "folk" also assumed a different meaning in the worldview of Bengali authors in the last three decades of the nineteenth century, one that was distinctly different from Kaliprasanna's.

In Kaliprasanna's sketch the elite and the lower classes speak the same language. That is, he feels no need to shift from colloquial Bengali to Sanskritized Bengali to claim the authenticity of the native voice, or when he wants to remind his readers of the necessity to sort through society in sync with the demands of a new urbanity. With Bankimchandra Chatto-padhyay and his followers this distinction between "elite" and "folk" became critical. The pleasure of folk speech would be hijacked in the service of new pleasures and pedagogical aims that were distinctly modern.

Rejecting the use of "coarse" Bengali for literary activities, Bankim, the foremost literary figure in nineteenth-century Bengal, opted for an ideal-ized location of the "folk" in his work. He opened up a new vista in Bengali imagination by excavating the "marginal" spaces of the folk that seemed destined to be consigned to the recesses of cultural memory by the logic of colonial progress. In an essay titled "Lokshiksha" (Mass Educa-tion), he complained that old forms of speech culture, such as *kathakata*, were fast disappearing because educated Bengali men, intoxicated by their threadbare knowledge of English, had failed to appreciate its merits.[23] The modern forms of communication that had sought to replace them – newspapers and public speeches – were inadequate in the context of Bengal. They were devoid of inspiration. Bankim gathered together a whole range of undesirability – the unrefined tastes of young men and their fondness for the prostitute-singers' latest musical performance, as well as those who wrote and spoke only in English with a European audience in mind – to drive home "the real point" that the public sphere of Calcutta demonstrated a lack of sympathy between the educated few and the illit-erate masses.

If community necessitates "communication" between its members, Bankim lamented the (impending) demise of the most promising model of communication, that of *kathakata*. Unlike later writers who laid the blame for the demise of *kathakata* on the changing tastes of educated women, he placed the responsibility squarely on the shoulders of the men. For Bankim it was the lack of the men's patronage, and their desire to distance them-selves from their rural roots that deserved criticism. Bankim viewed mass education necessarily as a trickle-down effect of elite education, and it is the latter's opinions and tastes that needed to be cultivated for the welfare of the masses. As for the masses, no amount of formal education in schools would be able to accommodate their needs, he argued. This was not simply a question of number, but what, in fact, needed to be taught. "Bookish instruction, grammar, literature, and geometry," could not be the ingred-ients of mass education, because the goal of the latter must be the cultural and moral rejuvenation of society – "inspiration and skill in one's own work."[24] The blueprint of mass education already existed in the popular oral tradition; it was only waiting proper emplacement. The "folk," for Bankim, retained a cultural purity lost to the English-educated urban middle class – it is from this culturally pure domain, conveying an unbroken spiritual tradition from antiquity, that moral lessons of the (Bengali) nation had to be unearthed. Bankim was not advocating that education of the masses be kept confined to religious scriptures. Instead he drew his readers' attention to the promise of folk speech and the spaces of folk gathering. Penned in 1878 we already hear a well-articulated formulation of national salvation through the cultivation of folk tradition.

For Bankim and his followers the "folk" was easily conflated with the category "woman," even though they had begun to construct the phenomenon of the educated Bengali woman as a separate subject quite distinct from her less refined, less educated sisters. For example, Sureshchandra Samajpati, in discussing Bankim's new literary language, drew a rather straightforward analogy between the everyday milieu (of women, children, friends, and servants) and popular language (*Prakrit*), as opposed to the elite literary language (*Sanskrit*) which he compared with the (male) "respected elders."[25] This analogy may not be dismissed as a quaint recitation of the nature/culture dichotomy, however. The informal/formal break along Bengali/Sanskrit is invoked to claim that the language that would reach the heart – the interior precinct of the community – is necessarily Bengali. The literary/nationalist desire here is not to confine women and the lower classes in their existing space, but to generate viable channels of communication between the agents of change (male educated middle class) and the subjects of their imagined community. This requires the emplacement of new spatial boundaries as well as (uni-)directional passage. It is important to note here that Sureshchandra's rhetoric does not make any specific room for the individual status of the subject on whose feelings the emotive power of language operates. The interiority of the individual subject is sublated into the interiority of the community, a construct over which there were already existing controls. The conflation of the categories of folk and women served the purpose of capturing this unreformed/reformable domain as an "interior," "domestic" space. Seen from this perspective Bankim's language acts as a medium that communicates with the internal cultural space where the heart of the nation must be won and fashioned according to superior ideals. Criticizing social reform pursued from a position of externality, far removed from the language of the masses, he noted that Rammohun and his followers had been trying to preach the Bramho religion for many years, but people had not taken to it. The closest successful historical reference he could produce as comparison was the dissemination of Vaishnavism in Bengal. Unlike Vaishnavism and its deeply emotive spirituality, the monotheistic Bramho religion had failed to capture the heart of the people. He attributed the failure not to the content of the message, but to the form of the message, to the means of communication.

Of course, the content of the message is not to be dismissed. Bankim's linking of English education and the loss of orality is not spurious. Capitalism and Enlightenment Reason necessitated the death of the spoken

[margin handwritten notes: "folk speech explicitly correlated w/ domestic & women's sphere"]

word in favor of the pristine, abstract space of the text. With Bankim, the oral invitations to the text do the double duty of resisting Christian pedagogy and instrumental reason. What at first might seem to be Bankim simply indicating the incompatibility of the European tools of the public sphere and the social condition in Bengal, soon turns out to be a fundamentally different quest for appropriate pedagogic content:

> Even those who work in the fields and in menial jobs, those who barely manage a subsistence would gather to (hear *kathakatha* and) learn that *dharma* is eternal and ordained by God, that self-fulfillment is not worthy of respect, that one's life must be dedicated to the welfare of others . . . that there is punishment for sin and reward for good deeds, that non-violence is the foremost *dharma*, that public welfare (*parahita*) is the greatest deed – where is that education now? Where has the *kathak* gone?[26]

The "lost" figure of the *kathak* allows Bankim to rework the preroga-tives of the European public sphere in a language that exceeds the limits and ideals of positivist thought with a flourish. The idea of public welfare – *parahita* (literally, "welfare of others") – is set within a conceptual frame of divine punishment and reward that insistently excavates those feelings that capitalism and the European public sphere had pronounced dead. The telling of stories (*katha*) – the new stories of the nation – from then on would be undertaken by authors like Bankim. That *kathakatha* is not purely "oral" but a performance based on written texts was no doubt extremely useful to Bankim. In his words, the *kathak* sat with the manu-script in front but with "no inclination to consult it."[27] The text remains the (silent) reminder of (spiritual) authority, a reference for descriptions, a fixity surpassed by the act of delivering the story.

In Bankim's novels the difference between textuality and orality is not obliterated but their relationship/priority reversed. He is imagining the text as oral practice. The wide popularity of Bankim's novels could be attributed to this factor that enabled its dissemination beyond the literate, and to the importance he ascribed to the domain of women, the depth of his female characters, and their "autonomous" language and spaces. His novels appealed to women. Rabindranath Tagore remembered the women in his family eagerly waiting for *Bangadarshan*, the literary magazine in which Bankim's novels were serialized. It was from this understanding of folk culture, imagined as an "interior" feminine space, presumably uncontaminated by Western reason and literary ideas, that modern Bengali would draw its sustenance in at least two, often contra-dictory, ways – as a (pure) site of cultural inspiration/appropriation, and as an arena of action/reform. It is possible to argue that this contradiction in Bankim's writing was mediated by the transformation of the literary language itself – by depending on the written language to create the deeply resonant spaces of the spoken word. This space is not a metaphor, but a socially produced place with an identifiable materiality.[28]

Bankim's familiarity with *kathakatha* went back to his childhood, when he had experienced the performance of *kathaks* in his ancestral house. *Kathakatha*, in brief, is a mode of narrating Puranic episodes.[29] The *kathak* rewrites the episode in his own words making it accessible to the specific audience, and improvises on the spot when necessary. While the *kathak* reads from his/her own manuscript, the art of *kathakatha* depends on extemporaneity, and effective use of exegesis and songs. The most captivating aspect of *kathakatha* appears to be the movement from narration to songs, and the lyrical descriptions that have the power to transport the reader to other landscapes and places. But no less important are the props and the body language of the *kathak* to lend the performance its affect, to make people laugh and cry, and carry them with the rhythm of the story. Equally, and perhaps the more important ingredient for a successful performance is an audience receptive to the feelings that structure such a performance.

My point in using Bankim as the exemplar of this mode of thinking about language and community, albeit reinvented, is that it would be incorrect to imagine the demise of oral culture with the arrival of the printed book. The rise of the novel in Bengal undoubtedly generated a certain domain of interiority that we have learned to identify with the European novel – the individual space of reading and imagination. But to understand the power of this literary form in Bengali culture we must situate it within a larger nexus of reading, speaking, and listening practices. Used to a long tradition of *panchali* and *kathakata*, of hearing the Ramayana and the Mahabharata being read aloud, all classes of people, women as well as men, enjoyed the news and even novels being read aloud. Gautam Bhadra has argued that *kathakatha*, in fact, reached the apex of popularity in the middle of the nineteenth century in both rural and urban Bengal.[30] Competing forms of speech performances and the availability of inexpensive religious texts necessitated that the *kathak* improvise to suit the taste of the audience. Similarly, the popularization of novels, rather than doing away with orality, indeed, helped energize the prevailing speech culture with a new exciting form. Authors reading out novels or poetry constituted an important part of the culture of the *baithak-khana*. If we stay with Bankim a little longer we can listen to this engaging description of the author reading aloud his first novel, *Durgeshnandini*, to a large gathering in his house in Kanthalpara, Naihati:

> Once, either during the holiday of Muharrum or Christmas, I don't remember which, a large number of *bhadralok* came (to our house). Among them were both literate and illiterate men. The pundits of Bhatpara were there as well. ... They sat listening in silence; the audience was annoyed if someone entered the room. ... Among the

audience were some men fond of opium, they frequently needed tobacco; they forgot to ask for it. An elderly gentleman, once in a while applauded loudly: "oh, what a delight, what a beautiful delivery." Thus it took two days to complete the story. Once it was completed, Bankimchandra asked the assembled Sanskrit pundits, "Have you noticed the grammatical problems?" Madhusudan Smritiratna replied, "we were so entranced by the story as well as the language, it was not possible to pay attention to the grammar." Famous pundit, Chandranath Vidyasagar remarked, "in some places I have noticed improper grammar, but it is exactly in those places the language has become sweeter."[31]

Worried about the improper application of grammar, Bankim had wanted the verdict of a community of listeners to ease his mind. The fact of *Durgeshnandini* being a novel, a literary form that came to epitomize the idea of the individual reader and his/her private space of imagination, did not deter this communal appreciation of the novel as spoken word. Even illiteracy was no deterrent to this form of participatory pleasure. What is more, it was the "delivery" of the story and its deviation from linguistic propriety that bestowed the novel's charm.

Bankim's power of description rested on his ability to utilize the deviations from linguistic propriety, to move effortlessly between everyday Bengali (*chalit bhasa*) and Sanskritized Bengali (*sadhu bhasa*), thereby casting a modern literary language that could convey the complexity of moods and settings. His use of the dialogic form and direct address to the reader, the heady mixture of sonorous Sanskrit words and folk songs that populate his novels, were conscious efforts to introduce dramatic conventions and cultivate the pleasures of Bengali speech culture.[32] Later in his life he is supposed to have told Sureshchandra Samajpati that he depended on his "ear" to determine the appropriateness of grammar – "if it sounds good to the ear I write it, I cannot be bothered with rules."[33] Bankim had no compunction about inventing rules. Reading Bankim meant cultivating a habit of listening to the new cadence of the literary language.

Bankim's primary audience were the educated middle-class men (and women). It was their "instruction" that Bankim deemed as defective, and which was at the heart of Bankim's search for literary pleasure. A new communal process of pleasure/pedagogy that wished to mark its distinction from older forms of "getting together," yet validated by certain older edifying practices also needed an appropriate physical structure for nourishment. The emergent middle class at mid-century who had limited capacity to own land, who did not control *dals* as a mode of exercising power, and did not have the wealth to spend on entertaining large gatherings, resorted to more subtle means of engaging in the city. The design gestures of individual buildings complied with each other to produce a recognizable sense of neighborhood or *para*.

On the edge of the street

Calcutta as a Bengali middle-class city gained its own spatial identity in the latter half of the nineteenth century. By 1856 the middle-class population of the city had increased appreciably. Engaged in the lower rungs of the colonial administration, employed as teachers, lawyers, and doctors, they began a lasting transformation of the urban form.[34] The changes did not occur overnight, but were tested against existing choices. A self-conscious creation of identity sought out a public presence both culturally and politically and in so doing rejected both the elite and lower-class cultures in their contemporary forms but retained some critical threads that tied these cultures as a community. In other words, the idea of community would be premised on rules that ensured the secure position of the middle class in the generation of a modern Bengali culture. For the purpose of the architectural historian these transformations are significant because they created physical changes in the urban fabric and invented new spatial rules to navigate the increasingly populous city. Soon the middle-class mode of living would set the pattern for the design of elite residences and not vice versa.

From Heysham's 1856 map of Calcutta and the Street Directories we know that even by the middle of the nineteenth century the neighborhood of the Sobhabazaar Rajbari remained fairly unencumbered. The imposing wall, arcade, and gates of the Sobhabazaar Rajbari conveyed a sense of grandeur but gave little glimpse of the generous "public" spaces inside. This lack of permeability stood in direct contrast to the mid-nineteenth-century mansions built in other parts of north Calcutta, which provided an option of direct contact with the street.

Some of the wealthiest households of the city were located within two blocks of Upper Chitpur Road in the locality called Jorasanko-Pathuriaghata (Figure 4.1). Here they occupied large properties next to small shops and residences and two large markets. Such a mixed-use urban fabric was typical of the main arteries, and an examination of the connection between the house and the street in this locality provides us with an idea of the permeability between inside and outside spaces. Most of these large houses followed the two-courtyard pattern, with the public court-yard located close to the street. The compartments around the public courtyard were generously connected to the street by a ceremonial flight of steps or a set of rooms that directly opened to the street arcade. Invariably these houses also had a separate, more controlled entrance to the public courtyard. The "Tagore Palace" was built right on the property line. The front façade consisted of a dominant set of Corinthian columns that held up a pediment sheltering the carriage port. The pediment itself was surmounted by an open verandah. The entrance portal led through a passage to an arcaded *dalan* around a large courtyard.

Between the Tagore Palace and Chitpur Road were situated several smaller houses, a few huts, a palanquin stand, and the large bazaar of Rajendra Lal Mullick. The Mullick Bazaar, called Notun Bazaar (New Market), had an imposing classical entrance, a vocabulary shared by the

A Tagore Castle
B Tagore Palace
C Notun Bazaar
D Mullick Mansion
E Seal Mansion
F Jorasanko Rajbati
G Lalubabu's Bazaar

Figure 4.1 Urban plan of portion of Upper Chitpur Road, from R. B. Smart's *Survey of Calcutta*, 1887–1909

mansions. On both sides of the bazaar grew a concentration of brass and bronze utensil shops, several doctors' offices, and pharmacies. These were interspersed with bookstores, printing presses, grocery stores, and warehouses.[35] These trades and professions occupied small lots, even tiny rooms, creating a very fine grain of urban occupation. Against this fine grain, the spacious mansions become all the more conspicuous. This desire to be close to "main street" (*baro rasta*) was illustrated by the large number of elite families who lived on this busy artery.

Opposite Pathuriaghata Street, two mansions owned at that time by the Seal and Mullick families had an almost identical spatial vocabulary. A wide flight of stairs leading from the street up to the main public entrance was marked by an imposing neo-classical façade. It was no accident that the grand design of this external stair shared a ceremonial desire with the formal entry to Government House. The conspicuous difference was, however, in the internal configuration, which in this case maintained a courtyard form. The grand entrance led to the first story of the public apartments raised above the basement. From this level, as well as from the large verandah above the entrance, one could have a full view of the street. A side entrance created space for carriages and connected directly to the outer ceremonial courtyard, which was subsequently connected to two more interior courts. Beyond the carriage entrance to the south, the back of the property, containing a tank, garden, and service buildings, was marked off by extending the walls of the outer mansion.[36]

One building down the street, the Jorasanko Rajbati occupied by the Roy family, made its side entrance the main public entrance marked clearly by a gate and an enclosing railing. There were no carriage ports. A large covered verandah extended the length of the building on the second floor of the south side of the public apartments (Figure 4.2). Similar to the verandahs in the houses in Chowringhee, these south-facing verandahs were extensions of living space. The pattern of north-facing carriage port was absent here. Another verandah on the east face made up for the lack of a prominent carriage entrance by accentuating the central portion of the three-part street façade. The central part projected over the sidewalk to create a street arcade as well as a partially covered sit-out connected to the second floor of the public apartments. The street-side apartments on the ground floor were designed to be rented out as shops.

The mansion on the opposite side, belonging to the Mullick family, was designed with a more complex resolution of the street façade (Figure 4.3). Like its counterpart, the Jorasanko Rajbati, the building's main entrance was through a gate on the southern edge of the lot, the main access then turning right into the public courtyard to pick up the north–south orientation of the building. A set of apartments along the west side of the public courtyard also opened directly onto the sidewalk. The street face of these apartments constituted the main façade. They were dressed with Corinthian columns, and crowned by a pediment surmounted by a clock to create a commanding presence on the street. It seemed to matter little that the

Figure 4.2 Street-side view of Jorasanko Rajbati, Upper Chitpur Road

Figure 4.3 Façade of Mullick Mansion, Upper Chitpur Road

pediment was not aligned on axis with the principal entry, which bypassed the street-level apartments, nor was it perfectly centered. The logic of the façade and the logic of the plan were independent of each other. The plans of these houses worked around the formal unity generated by the court-yards. The great talent of the masons and architects who designed these façades was their ability to treat the building as an assemblage of semi-independent fragments, as a way of responding to complex, often incom-patible demands of the building program. The street edge of the Mullick mansion was, in one sense, a pure façade. It formed a compositional code that rather than faithfully reflecting the organization of the inner spaces, stood as an independent entity responding to the street in a gesture of per-formance. The decorative wood doors of the lower-level rooms and the fine wrought-iron balconies of the upper-level rooms were incorporated in the façade as frames to watch the ongoing tableau of the busy street. In this sense it was more than an image; it was an event, a masquerade.

The pattern of renting out ground-floor rooms was followed in the smaller town houses (Figures 4.4, 4.5, and 4.6). The rooms on the street side were built in modules of 10 or 12 feet; together, the modules could form interconnected spaces of a larger commercial enterprise or residence or could be rented out individually. The service spaces were located either in the courtyard or in the back of the house. Typically the ground-floor rooms were used as shops and the upper-floor rooms were used for resi-dential purposes. The house plans of Chowringhee shared with these houses a built-in modular flexibility engendering the capacity to engage multiple uses. The main difference was the axiality of the house plans discussed in Chapter 2, which created a formal movement from a more public entry to a more private living space. In these townhouses, the axiality was absent or subdued. Direct opening from the house was eschewed in favor of an indirect path that shielded the interior of the house from the view of passers-by. A view to the street from the spaces adjoining the sidewalk was encouraged. The public life of nineteenth-century Calcutta spilled over from the streets to encompass the edges of the buildings that adorned them with elaborate arcades and verandahs (Figure 4.7). The private component of residences along the street edge was distinguished by a change in the composition of the façade. Verandahs of residences were often completely enclosed by a fine venetianed screen (sections of which could be opened as windows) to retain visual opacity from the street, while retaining a view towards the street. In fact, it may be more accurate to say that domestic and commercial space spilled from the interior spaces to the sidewalk and streets. In the words of Nirad C. Chaudhuri:

> [W]hatever public activity was on for the time being became visible to the eyes in the outward form of processions, open-air meetings, and other demonstrations, or could be detected in the behavior of con-courses on the thoroughfares of the Bengali quarters. . . . A mere glance at the pavement was enough to show whether something was on.[37]

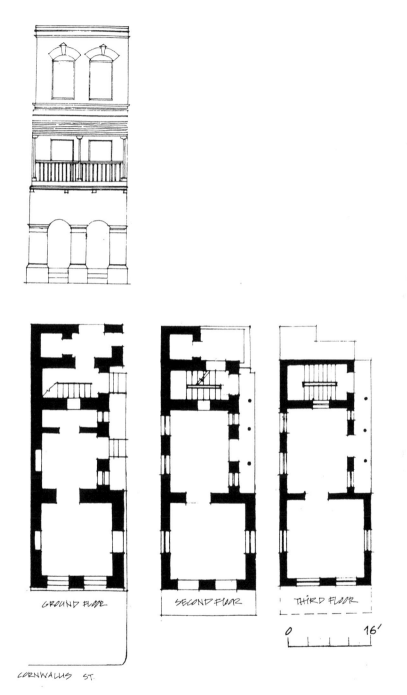

GROUND FLOOR

SECOND FLOOR

THIRD FLOOR

0   16'

CORNWALLIS ST.

Figure 4.4 Plan and elevation of townhouse on 68 Cornwallis Street. Based on drawing in the collection of the Calcutta Municipal Corporation

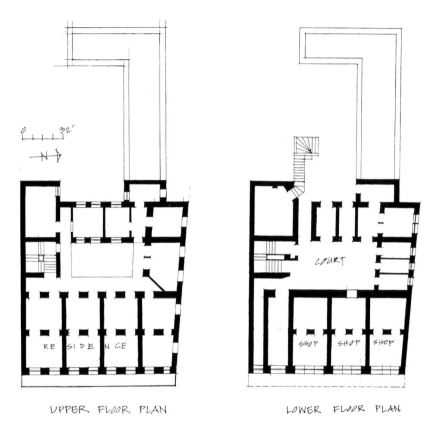

UPPER FLOOR PLAN   LOWER FLOOR PLAN

Figure 4.5 Plan of shops/residence on Upper Chitpur Road. Based on drawing in
the collection of the Calcutta Municipal Corporation

Chaudhuri was describing early twentieth-century Calcutta, where such
a pattern of interaction had become well established. Such a manner of
relating to the street was a product of mid-nineteenth-century Bengali
culture that recognized the self-conscious creation of the façade, encouraged numerous and highly articulated openings, and desired a robust
connection between interior and exterior public space. This was, after
all, no longer a town where status was easily recognized. Where land
and buildings had become commodities, one had to claim a presence by
displaying one's wealth, performing one's "culture." As in Radhakanta
Deb's Nat-mandir, the projecting second-level balconies and numerous
closely spaced doors and windows carefully designed with decorative
fanlights and opening to the garden and street announced a change of
attitude towards building practices. The intricate elevations of even smaller
houses were clearly meant to impress an image on the street. This change,
however, went beyond the aesthetics of the façade, and incorporated issues
about health and a modern life-style. Admitting a modern sensibility

Figure 4.6 View of shops/residences on Upper Chitpur Road

Figure 4.7 Verandah and *ro'ak* of middle-class residence on Jagadish Roy Lane

Radhakanta's Nat-mandir permitted light and breeze to enter directly from the outside, and not through the controlled micro-climate of the courtyard, reversing the sensory progression of moving from a well-lit open space to a dark enclosed space. In the mid-nineteenth-century residences, an amply fenestrated envelope was wedded to the idea of the courtyard to accommodate both the traditional social use of space and new ideas of well-lit and well-aired rooms.

Kanny Loll Dey, a Bengali surgeon, writing in 1861, noticed greater attention being paid to ventilation in the new houses.[38] Two decades later among the advice given to Bengali women with regard to interior arrangement, a clear emphasis was placed on the virtues of "modern" orientation of rooms. The best room in the house, with a sunny prospect and open to the direction of the wind must be the bedroom, announced one author. "The windows of the bedroom," she added, "must be very wide." Every morning windows of the house were to be thrown open to let out the "toxic" air and let in "pure" air.[39] This transformation of dwelling practices coincided with the new desire of the city's growing middle class to keep an open window to the happenings on the street.

By 1870 the large plots of land in the neighborhood around Sobhabazaar Rajbari were sold or rented out. The area became predominantly middle class, consisting of a collection of densely built smaller buildings on narrow lots (Figure 4.8). The traditional sequence of courtyard-*ro'ak-dalan*-rooms

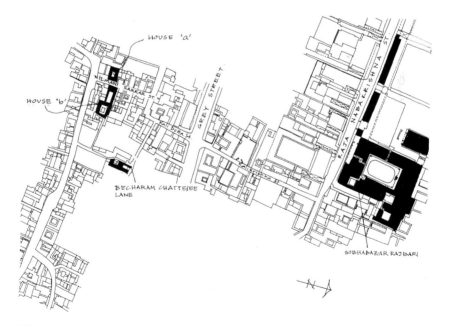

Figure 4.8 Street plan of the neighborhood of Sobhabazaar Rajbari, based on R. B. Smart's *Survey of Calcutta*, 1887–1909

was reduced in these smaller houses to its minimal form and adjusted to suit the density and heterogeneity of urban occupation (Figure 4.9). The size of the courtyards was diminished to 12 by 20 feet or variations thereof to fit 10- to 12-foot room modules, and the second courtyard was eliminated. When the second courtyard was eliminated the front row of rooms against the street formed a continuous edge in an attempt to ensure sufficient privacy to the only courtyard (Figure 4.10). The *ro'ak* then was frequently transferred to the outside to function as a stoop, in a sense to incorporate the open space of the street into the public space of the house. The 2½-foot *ro'ak* on the house on the west of Nilmani Sarkar Street was complemented on the upper levels by a continuous balcony. Opposite, a profusely decorated house belonging to an upper-middle-class family, abided by the norm of the double-courtyard prototype (Figure 4.11a). The two courtyards divided the house into front and back compartments. The

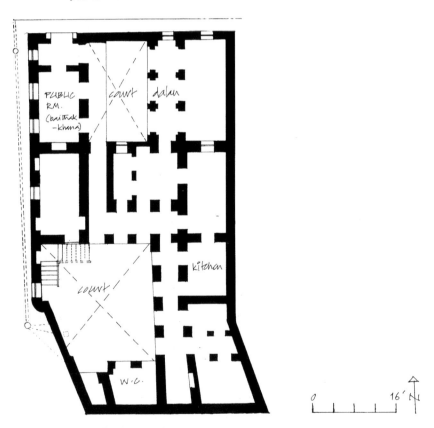

Figure 4.9 Plan of residence on Becharam Chatterjee Lane. Based on drawing in the collection of the Calcutta Municipal Corporation

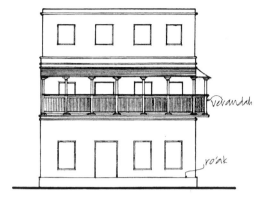

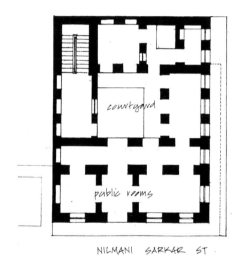

Figure 4.10 Plan of residence "a" on Nilmani Sarkar Street. Based on drawing in the collection of the Calcutta Municipal Corporation

private courtyard located in the rear housed the sleeping, eating, and cooking rooms, and was supposed to be the domain of the women. The public or outer compartments were the place for men's sociability. In the outer room or *baithak-khana* the men of the household entertained their friends. Like its more modest counterpart on the other side of the street the living space extended in the form of the *ro'ak* (Figure 4.11b). The width of these residential streets ranged from 10 to 15 feet, and even less in the lanes. The single- or, typically, double-story houses next to these narrow streets generated a volume of space that was well shaded on summer days,

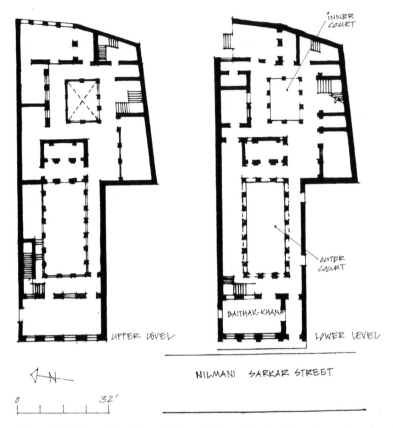

Figure 4.11a Plan of residence "b" on Nilmani Sarkar Street. Based on drawing in the collection of the Calcutta Municipal Corporation

and was conducive to face-to-face interaction. Men sat on the *ro'ak* and read the newspaper, shared stories and kept an eye on the happenings of the neighborhood. Here, the vagrants slept at night and peddlers set down their wares to rest. The thresholds eased the transition between the inside and outside and aided in creating a sense of community, albeit one that was male-dominated. In later years, this space of the *ro'ak* would generate a much valued place of *adda*.

A stoop or verandah extending out on the street has a long tradition in both rural and urban South Asia, and in mid-nineteenth-century Calcutta it found a suitable use in a society that cherished face-to-face interaction. In contrast to elite households which, in the early days, preferred physical containment rather than a permeable interface with the street, the *baithak-khana* of middle-class residences was small and could not accommodate the needs of several generations at the same time. It had to provide an alternate space in the *ro'aks* and verandahs. In other words,

Figure 4.11b Street view of residence "b" on Nilmani Sarkar Street

the self-contained spatial system of the elite mansions was stripped of its outer enclosing walls to create a more interactive spatial system. By giving over part of their property to a semi-public space, the owners traded the enlarged dimension of the interior room for an increased territorial claim on the neighborhood. Street noise and happenings filtered through the layers of spaces to create a continuum between the street and the dwelling.[40]

Under these conditions the façade in Bengali middle- and upper-class houses in the latter half of the nineteenth century came to perform a dual function. On the one hand it enabled the understanding and practice of public space as a strategic extension of domestic space. On the other hand, it is on the façade that distinctions between public and residential, men and women, respectable and non-respectable were articulated. Taking pleasure in the sound, smell, and activities of the street could be acknowledged and allowed once the façade and the interface between the house and street could work as an observable regulatory frame, defining one's social location.

The culture of the *baithak-khana*, essentially the pursuit of the *bhadralok*, was firmly rooted in the familiar network of the neighborhood. Here, young men were introduced to older "members," developed lasting friendships, and generated grand schemes of starting literary journals and dramatic groups. It was here, in Dipesh Chakrabarty's words, that they learned to "present themselves." Although a male domain within a house, the *baithak-khana*, occupied a position between domesticity and publicness. The *baithak-khana* consequently expressed this spatial idea vividly in the kinds of relationships and discussions one could generate within its confines.[41]

The promise and the limits of such *baithak-khana* culture are illustrated by an anecdote told by Amritalal Basu. In 1874 the Gaekwad of Baroda, Malhar Rao was accused of poisoning the British Resident Colonel Robert Phayre with a mixture of arsenic and diamond-dust in his drink. The Gaekwad was found guilty and exiled. The Indian community strongly supported the Gaekwad whom they considered to have been wrongly accused. Kristodas Pal, the spokesperson for the British Indian Association, however, wrote an obsequious editorial in the *Amrita Bazaar Patrika* supporting the action of the British government. Amritalal, who was then very young, wrote his first play, *Hirak Churna* (Diamond Dust), a farce based on the incident and Pal's denouncement of the Gaekwad. However, at one point he needed Pal's assistance and a common friend took Amritalal to meet Pal in his *baithak-khana*. Amritalal recalled this first meeting with Kristodas Pal:

> On hearing my name, a friend [of Pal's] said, "this is the guy who ridiculed you on stage." Leaning slightly back on the *takia* [cushion] Kristodas Pal said, "you are Amritalal Basu? Where do you live?" I replied politely, "in Kambulitola." He asked, "Kambulitola's Bose?

Is Kailashchandra related to you?" I replied, "I am his son." "You are his son?" He sat up: "You are his son? *I* am like a son to him. He was my teacher! So you are a brother to me." Having said this, he sat me down next to him and asked many questions with a great deal of affection.[42]

To locate Amritalal in the social landscape, Pal only needed to place him in a *para* (neighborhood), Kambulitola, and his credibility could be assessed by his family connections. Such connections went beyond the realm of immediate kinship to encompass relationships created in schools and workplaces. Despite their differences in political views Pal felt obliged to help Amritalal because they already shared a "relationship." The sense of communal obligation took precedence over political views expressed in the public sphere.

In Amritalal's youth the *baithak-khana* spoke of the presence of the patron, like Kristodas Pal presiding over the meeting, just as public entertainment rested on the patron's munificence. By the late nineteenth century the culture of the *baithak-khana* would be transformed into the new form of the *adda* that rejected the patronage of the *baithak-khana* to embrace the more egalitarian forms of getting together, even while retaining in its configuration and process traces of nostalgia for the *baithaki-adda*. If the pleasure of communal speech was retained in these new spaces, the notion of community was undergoing some important shifts from the scale of the locality to the scale of the city and the nation, shifts with which the likes of Amritalal Basu could not reconcile themselves.

Both the street-side *baithak-khana* and the *ro'ak* of middle-class households were distinctly nineteenth-century urban forms that embraced "togetherness." Nirad C. Chaudhuri, who disparaged both the *adda* and the native city, noted that the streets, although straight, never gave the impression of being straight, and "checked the growth of any impression of symmetry and harmony."[43] Symmetry in formal articulation was confined in the Bengali neighborhoods to local symmetry; symmetry of individual spaces, and not symmetry of the entire street. In contrast to what Chaudhuri seemed to recall, those who could afford to do so gave much attention to the street façade in their desire to appropriate the street. Instead of "standing back" to maintain a straight edge, however, the verandahs and *ro'aks* were enthusiastically made to encroach on the street to engage in building a range of spatial dimensions conducive to social interaction. Regularity of the street edge necessarily took a back seat in such a worldview. In the absence of regulatory setbacks the street edge changed continuously and was not predetermined, thus missing the mark of harmony in the eyes of Chaudhuri. There were no building codes until the1890s and the urban form was a result of experimentation with conventional building practices, always giving attention to pedestrian access ways and the structuring of communal spaces.

The creation of several thresholds that screened the interior spaces obviated the need for closed doors at the street level. However, it necessitated that the rules of spatial order – how the common spaces were to be used, who could enter where – were locally understood but not necessarily apparent to a stranger. It was this sense of local rules and familiar faces that generated the community of the *para* or *palli*, and not physical boundaries. Amritalal idealized such a community in his recollection of the good old days:

> During those days we Bengalis were small, we had not become great, we had not embraced India in our heart, we embraced the *palli*; consequently our *para*'s grocer was our grocer, the *para*'s *muriwala* (puffed-rice seller) was our *muriwala*, *para*'s timber peddler Sonaullah, our Sonaullah, *para*'s Oriya palanquin-bearer our Bhagwat Sardar; everyday the bearded man who sold *chanachur* (hot snack) was our *chanachurwala*, the women who used to come for alms crying Joy Radhakrishna was our Baishnabis, the pock-faced tall, blind man who came to our door at eight in the morning everyday for alms crying "Hey Dinanath, hey Madhusudan," (referring to God/householder), if he was not seen for a couple of days, I would ask (my grandfather), "Dada, is Dinanath unwell? haven't seen him for a couple of days." Thus the people we would see daily in the *palli* or in our houses, whether respectable or not, were our own people.[44]

In his desire to emphasize togetherness Amritalal repeated the word "our" (*amader*) nine times in one paragraph to refer to his own family and, in extension, the neighborhood. Significantly, all those with whom Amritalal claimed togetherness were the non-respectable people, the lower classes who served the community in various capacities or who were dependent on it for poor-relief. The respectable people were so obviously included in his framework of community that they did not need to be specifically identified. The non-respectable people belonged to a range of ethnicities, religions, and strata of social life. As a member of the *bhadralok* community he felt a kinship (*atmyiata*) with them which undoubtedly responded to the nationalist claim to unite the various ethnicities of the emergent nation. The *para* here became a microcosm of the nation, a community in which, Amritalal claimed, the problematic participation of a variety of ethnicities and religions had already been "solved." In his mind he could reconcile class, ethnic, and religious divisions by incorporating them within the shared framework of the *para*. No recourse to the category of "*jati*" (race/ clan/caste) or the abstract notion of the nation – "Bharatvarsha" – was necessary for Amritalal to describe the community that mattered most. This imagined community was willed into being through a language of familial intimacy that allowed it to be revealed as a product of everyday encounter.

Here, we are not provided with a sense of how the lower classes felt about this kinship. This assertion of togetherness is significant in the context of nineteenth-century politics of the city. The Anglo-Indian community claimed that men such as Amritalal who comprised the educated middle class were not in touch with the masses. Consequently, it became important for the middle-class men to assert that they shared a community with the less privileged, and thus could, indeed, represent the masses. One of the early occasions to display such solidarity was aroused by the Indigo Revolt and the subsequent publication of *Nildarpan* in 1860. James Long's prosecution following the translation of the play created a sensation in the Bengali community.

Amritalal, in recounting the rise of the modern Bengali theater, noted how the play had stirred Bengali society and described his theater group's intense desire to stage the play.[45] The first staging of *Nildarpan* was energized by a larger concern to "give expression to the pain suffered in the heart of the nation."[46] Dramatic performances suddenly took on a higher purpose. They held the hidden stories of the nation. Folk performances often adopted contemporary social issues for satire, but politics was left out of such humor. By inserting a political content in performances, the playwrights, theater organizers, and actors brought a different dimension to the public cultural sphere.

For most of the century rehearsals of dramatic performances were held in the outer compartment or hall of wealthy households and the plays took place in their public courtyards. The open courtyard form had easily accommodated the folk *jatra* that used the participatory format of the theater-in-the-round. In such a configuration the distinction between audience and performers was not paramount (although the performance arena was defined) and there was no designation of front and back. In 1835 the popular play *Vidya-Sundar* was held in the large mansion of Nabin Chandra Basu, in which several settings were designed and the performance shifted from one spot to another with the audience moving along with the performers.[47] Although the idea of a scene was used to create a desired ambiance, the participatory mode was retained and performers and audience were not yet separated as in a proscenium setting.[48]

When the Rajas of Paikpara built a permanent proscenium stage in their garden house in Belgachia in the northern suburbs of Calcutta, and other wealthy residents improvised on existing spaces to set up the first theaters in their residences, they were consciously rejecting the participatory mode of the folk performances. They were opting for a more polite form of entertainment where audience participation was limited to applause at particular moments of the performance. The clear distinction between audience and performers that a proscenium necessitated, however, suited the ambition of middle-class actors. These amateur actors could conceivably separate their own role of production and acting from the role of the audience who had not invested in the performance as they had. Now the responsibility – financial, social, and political – was split. The credit for a successful performance could now belong to the actors and producers, not

to the elite patrons. The spatial configuration of the proscenium was suitable for clarifying the actors' identities. Yet creating such a space with
limited economic means and claiming independence from older modes of
patronage was not easy.

Plays designed for a proscenium needed a stage and screens to be built
within the existing structure of the mansion. Painted scenes were used
to depict the setting of action and drop-screens were used to mark the
movement from one scene to another in a linear fashion.[49] Amritalal
recalled the first staging of the *Nildarpan* in the Sandeal mansion
(Madhusudan Sanyal's mansion, later the Mullick mansion) of Jorasanko
in 1872. The lower floor of the *bahir-mahal* was rented for 40 rupees and
a wooden stage was erected. Three kinds of tickets were sold: first-class
seats comprised of chairs rented for the purpose, second-class seats were
make-shift benches, and third-class seats were located on the stairs of the
dalan and the *ro'ak*. Even when tickets were sold and a proscenium stage
had to be erected to accommodate modern plays, the performances were
dependent on the willingness of the elite to share space. Basu vividly
recalled the elite presence in these plays:

> I was sitting on the stage dressed as Sairindhri. Looking up I saw some
> gentlemen, my elders, sitting in the front row. For a moment I was
> scared. I felt as if I had abandoned my *samaj* [society], my *jati* [caste
> community], my religion, and bearing this shame, I have appeared in
> front of my elders dressed up as a woman; as if excommunication was
> the only punishment for the shame I had brought upon my society and
> nation by selling tickets and acting on a public stage. You will not under-
> stand my thoughts at that moment. In those days there was the *samaj*,
> the bond of the *samaj*, and punishment for revolting against the *samaj*.[50]

The stage in the Sandeal mansion was close enough to the audience for
Amritalal to recognize the gentlemen in the front row. This spatial compres-
sion mirrored a society that was closely knit and whose members made it
their business to look into the affairs of others. Amritalal's fear was two-fold.
First, despite coming from a respectable family, he had chosen to act on the
public stage, which was not approved of in those days. Second, he and his
compatriots were attempting to create an independent theater group and a
public stage by selling tickets to pay for the preparations, which was, in
effect, a criticism of the elite order and a desire to reshape the public sphere.
While he praised elite patronage of dramatic performances in the first half
of the century, he noted that in such a format the host would determine the
guest list thus excluding those who were not appropriately connected. With
the sale of tickets, theater became a commercial enterprise; anyone who
could afford a ticket had access. This was distinctly different from the plays
held in elite houses, the purpose of which was to enhance a social or religious function, allowing the elite to parade their ranks. At the same time,

the majority of the actors insisted on expressing their amateur status. They were to be clearly set apart from the few men and all the actresses who were hired for the theater.

The initial workings of the new theater remained grounded in the familiar network of the *para*, in some cases helping to generate a new collectivity.[51] Elderly residents of the *para*, at first, were not impressed with the independent arrangements. When Amritalal's theater group was preparing for the performance, the elders criticized them for undertaking an endeavor beyond their means. As long as the plays were staged in the houses of elite residents, the elite retained power to censor the content of the play.[52] For the elite, there was some genuine concern in this regard. Since plays focused on contemporary social and political topics (sure to be a success with the audience) and were sometimes critical of British rule, the British government lost no time in applying a charge of sedition and imprisoning the organizers and playwrights. If such a play was taking place in one's own premises, the patron bore responsibility. The elite, typically wishing to be loyal to the colonial government, faced a dilemma. Either they had to appear irresponsible to their constituents and unmindful of their needs, or they had to be disloyal to the government. Consequently, when the first professional theaters were being built in the last two decades of the century, Amritalal rejoiced at the arrival of the "democratic" stage (he used the English word in his original Bengali text). No longer would theater organizers have to depend on the charity of the elite. The first professional theaters, such as the Great National Theater, did in fact, depend in large measure on the charity of the elite, but here the responsibility took the shape of monetary contribution rather than the form of personal responsibility for activities in public space. In this new configuration of public space the elite patron figure was decentered to make room for the ambition of middle-class actors and playwrights.

While Amritalal embraced the new Bengali stage, free as he considered it from elite influence, he could not quite reconcile the decentering of the elite patron. Several times in his memoirs he gratefully and affectionately remembered his compatriot Bhubanmohun Neogi, who came from an elite family and who had allowed the amateur actors to use his *baithak-khana bari*.[53] The rehearsals would take place in the large hall situated on the second floor of the house. The house was located on the banks of the Ganga (Hooghly) where the Neogi family had built a public *ghat* and a room for the dying (*sashan-jatri*).[54] The house and the attendant facilities were demolished when the Calcutta Port Commissioners decided to expand the Strand Road to facilitate trade. For Amritalal this was a demonstration of sheer greed on the part of the British authorities who understood only the price of land but could not comprehend the "sacred" significance of such a landmark. The disappearance of the Neogi *baithak-khana* in the face of modern demands was, for Amritalal, one of many examples that captured the larger picture of change that had swept away old memories and the old city. However, he placed the blame for such undesirable changes squarely on the shoulders of his own countrymen.

Amritalal's nationalist imaginings were repeatedly disrupted by a longing for the older order. When he implied that a concern with the nation as a community had adversely affected the sense of the Bengali community at the local, *para*, level, he meant it not so much as a criticism of nationalist aspirations per se, but the reshuffling of social and spatial norms that took place in the process. In his view, nationalism according to Western precepts invariably implied a loss of "feeling," an abstraction from the immediate, more pressing concerns of family and community. This is what made it antithetical to genuine social welfare.

Amritalal's memoirs of nineteenth-century Calcutta were written in the 1920s. One of the consistent themes of this remembrance is the distinction he made between the lost world of his youth and the Calcutta of his old age. The former was marked by simple needs, a sense of wholesome community alive to the sound, smell, and feeling of heterogeneous occupation, and memorable sacrifices for the cause of indigenous institutions, while the latter was marked by complex desires, a fractured sense of community, and a regressive acceptance of modern Western values:

> The truth is, the *bhadralok* have disappeared from the *bhadrashan* (the respectable household or place of respectability). Now the door of the *baithak-khana* is unlocked once in a while to seat the doctor on his visit. From every corner of the world the call for "women's independence" is being sounded, new articles are being written, new words are being coined to enhance the rights of women. But men, can you see how your own independence is being eclipsed?[55]

The humor and irony in the above quotation barely conceal Amritalal's anxiety regarding the changing ideals of domesticity and the implied disintegration of the extended family. He claimed that as soon as *baithaki-sahitya* (literature of the *baithak-khana*) was invaded by foreign ideas of domesticity and conjugal love, the secure world of the *baithak-khana* had made a retreat. The loss of the extended family necessitated that husbands keep their wives company. This, he claimed, had deprived the men of their "independence." That loss was symbolized in the disintegration of the *baithaki-adda*. Unlike in England, he noted, where the pleasure of male company brought working-class men to pubs and respectable ones to clubs, the latter option was not open to respectable Bengali men because they could not afford the cost. In the absence of respectable places of public entertainment they were confined to the household, captive to the demands of their wives.

If the *baithaki-adda* flourished as a site of literary and performative pleasures, it was not necessarily an exclusively male endeavor. The *majlish* held in the *baithak-khana*, even occasionally in upper-middle-class households,

invited female singers and dancers. The gender relationship in this case
was primarily that of client-performer. The necessity of hiring actresses
for the stage altered this relationship to a large degree. The actresses came
from the red-light areas of the city, and despite their considerable accomplishments, the stigma of being a "public" woman remained attached to
their acting careers, creating a grey area of cultural acceptance/refusal.
Amritalal wrote about his surprise when he recognized the actresses'
dedication to learning the craft of acting, only to conclude that the actresses
had repeatedly told him and the *bhadralok* theater organizers the ordeal
they had been spared given an opportunity for respectable livelihood:
"[E]ven under interrogation [we] were not able to make them say that
they pursued acting for the sake of glitter and fame."[56] The actresses are
given room in the respectable public imaginary of the city as those who
had been saved moral devastation by middle-class men like Amritalal.
While the distinction between paid actresses and amateur actors resulted
in a certain power dynamics that grated at notions of equality, long hours
spent rehearsing plays were based on mutual cooperation, and even allowed
room for friendship and camaraderie. Amritalal who only allowed two
brief references to these actresses in his memoirs, was not willing to acknowledge the depth of his relationship with the actresses, and the mutual
dependence between those who were salaried and those who were nomi-
nally amateurs. In describing the dedication of the actresses, however, he
allowed himself a small slip to describe them as friends and companions
of many days.[57] On another occasion he noted the pleasures of the mixed-
company of his theater companions:

> Gurudeb and I, such pals we were:
> At Bini's home, drinking beer.[58]

For the actresses, theater rehearsals were their closest experience of a
literary salon. The actress Binodini Dasi recalled the early days of the
theater:

> Numerous educated, respected gentlemen, would come – they were
> all excited about the theatre. The theatre in those days was a place
> for literary discussions. . . . I understood very little of it then, but I
> did realize that the theater was in those days a meeting ground for a
> distinguished group of *bhadraloks*.[59]

The asymmetry of access between the actresses and the actors and
bhadraloks frequenting the theater should be obvious. While Amritalal
had access to elite salons including those of the Tagores, where he was
sought out as an advisor for plays, the same did not apply to the actresses.
It was possible for Amritalal to move between Benodini's house and the
Tagore house without conflict, even though they resided within two separate
social frames. For Amritalal, friendship with the actresses and their large

contribution towards the public stage could not be rendered in the same light as that of the male actors and patrons of the theater. Located outside acceptable binaries of domestic/public, female/male these relationships had to be relegated to the margins, to the shadows of public memory. Only in a few households such as the Tagores of Jorasanko where, by the late nineteenth century, rehearsal *addas* involved mixed *bhadralok/bhadramahila* company, such opportunities for women of all classes remained rare.

The relegation of actresses to the margins of community memory was accomplished more blatantly by denying them any "public" space outside the domain of the theater. Actresses complained that they were not allowed to be present at a memorial meeting held in the Town Hall in honor of Girish Ghosh, actor and playwright, as it would presumably jeopardize the "respectability" of such an occasion.[60] Benodini Dasi in her auto-biography *Amar Katha* (My Story) spoke about being asked by her male compatriots to become a mistress of a patron on the promise that a new theater built with his money would be named after Benodini.[61] When the theater was built, her compatriots felt no obligation to keep their promise. Benodini's strategy of claiming space constituted of telling the story of the Bengali theater in a radically different form and from a radically different position than Amritalal's. Denied space in the public memory of the city, she charted a topography of Calcutta that threw into stark relief the labor of those, like her, who contributed to the making of the city's public sphere, while it questioned the hallowed constructs of domesticity and *atmyiata* that could only be asymmetrically applied to the respectable and non-respectable people.[62]

The language of material culture

Bengali visions of nineteenth-century Calcutta are so heavily dependent on literary imagination, that we often forget to question their status as representations. Discussing Calcutta's nineteenth-century and early twentieth-century material culture, Kalyani Dutta writes:

> Speaking of traditional household patterns, Bankimchandra's descriptions come easily to mind. If the three-parts of Nagendranath's mansion and garden in *Bishabriksha* could be reduced somewhat in length and breadth then it would easily fit the description of the Laha or Mullick houses.[63]

Not that these literary descriptions failed to match practices (even when they did not fit the specificities). Rather, to understand the full implication of these representations, it is more important to investigate the manner in which the meaning of domestic space and artifacts of domesticity were constructed through such literary works. Rameshchandra Dutta, for example, used the changing material culture of the *baithak-khana* to develop an entire progressive sociology of Calcutta society. What I am suggesting is that Bankim or Rameshchandra were not simply being faithful in their descriptions of contemporary material practices. Their invocation of material artifacts as external signs that spoke lucidly of inner consciousness of their characters was so skillful that these attributions of meaning grasped the Bengali imagination. Bengali literature gave coherence and meaning to contradictory spatial manifestations by placing them within a modern visual taxonomy. Visual attributes of material culture became markers that were expected to stabilize the new spatial dynamics of the city in which "respectability" had become a vexed issue.

Much of the significance of interior decor and spatial arrangement of Bengali households revolved around the introduction of Western artifacts. Such artifacts had been introduced in elite Bengali households from a much earlier era – from at least the mid-eighteenth century. This was a direct result of familiarity with European (primarily English and French) tastes in home furnishing. Wealthy Indian families such as the Burdwan Maharajas, the Debs of Sobhabazaar had become introduced to these practices, and had adopted them selectively. The most prominent among early introductions were European-style tables, chairs, couches, clocks, and paintings. Wills and probates conducted in the 1850s and 1860s inform us that these introductions had become a part of life among the professional class of English-educated Bengali men quite early on as well. But it was not until the 1870s, that is, not until the stalwarts of Bengali literature of that age – Bankim, Rameshchandra, and others – made the setting of domesticity an important aspect of their novels, that these artifacts began to gather particular kinds of meaning. "Western" furnishing was problematized in a new language of cultural encounter that underscored distinctions between desirable and undesirable spatial choices.

Rameshchandra Dutta's novel, *Samsaar* (Family Life) set in the closing decades of the nineteenth century begins in the setting of a Bengali village, where a widowed woman and her two young daughters are seen eking out a meager existence. The novel follows these two girls into early marriage and maturity. The early widowhood of the younger sister is central to the novel. This nine-year-old widow comes to reside with the older sister's family – her husband, Hemchandra, and two infant sons. The novel gathers momentum when this extended family moves to Calcutta in search of a better life. Once in the city, Hemchandra finds it difficult to secure a living, and visits a number of acquaintances in hopes of employment. It is during these visits that the reader is allowed glimpses of the house of the Bengali gentlefolk.

Rameshchandra describes the *baithak-khana* of three men in Calcutta, endeavoring to convey not simply the status and social life of these gentlemen, but their character mirrored in the interior decor of the *baithak-khana*. Debiprasanna Babu and Chandranath Babu are members of middle-class society of Bhowanipur, but they represent two approaches to material life. This difference is largely understood as a difference in education and

profession. While Debiprasanna Babu without the benefit of a good education has accumulated wealth by serving in a British agency house,
Chandranath Babu is a lawyer, his educational qualification enabling him
to remain professionally independent. The third gentleman, Dhananjay
Babu is an absentee *zamindar* (landlord), who has inherited an immense
amount of wealth ready for dissipation. His Calcutta mansion signifies everything that has gone awry in Bengali society under colonial rule, specifically
under the quasi-feudal system of the Permanent Settlement of Bengal.

Debiprasanna Babu had risen from a low position to that of head clerk
of an agency house, thanks to the generosity of the *sahibs*, and had amassed
a considerable wealth. This wealth went into improving the family house
in Bhowanipur in the suburbs of Calcutta, and adding a new *baithak-khana*:

> A clean mattress and sheets were laid out in the *baithak-khana*, a few
> plump pillows (strewn about), and a couple of light stands in the niches
> in the wall. The double wall shades were draped, and a number of
> pictures of both good and inferior quality were hanging on the walls.
> Some of these pictures were of Hindu gods and goddesses hung next
> to cheap German prints. In the (latter) pictures women were in different
> stages of disrobing, hair-dressing, bathing, and lying down. In addi-
> tion to these could be seen Caravaggio's "Magdalene," Titian's
> "Venus," and Landseer's "Deer," but the prints were so inferior that
> it was difficult to recognize them as such. Whatever was to be found
> in Bowbazaar or could be bought cheaply in an auction, and what-
> ever had suited the taste of Debi Babu or his *sarkar* – be it a print or
> an oleograph – had been gathered and hung on the walls.[64]

Although hospitable, Debiprasanna Babu's effort to claim respectability
by renovating his house had met with limited success. His salon was not
the product of a cultivated mind, his poor taste (itself a product of inadequate education and the society he kept) betrayed by the ill-chosen group
of pictures. It was not even certain that he had concerned himself with
the purchase of the pictures. Probably he had instructed his manager to
obtain prints as inexpensively as possible on the assumption one needs
pictures on the walls, and preferably some "European" ones, no matter
what their content. His taste was further compromised by the poor judgment demonstrated in hanging pictures of Hindu gods next to inferior
prints of European courtesans, epitomizing the proverbial imperfect assim-
ilation of Western and Indian ideas. Here the salon is a place of idle talk
with neighbors who, we are told, come around simply because the host
is well off, and allegedly could arrange for employment in a British firm.

Debiprasanna Babu's salon metamorphosed by an immense amount of
wealth constitutes the salon of the *zamindar*, Dhananjay Babu. On entering
it, Hemchandra stepped into another world. Nothing in rural Bengal had
prepared him for this extravaganza. The house was cordoned off from the

street by a high wall and overzealous guards. The floor of the *baithak-khana* was covered with a carpet in which birds mingled among rose vines. Hem was hesitant to place his dusty shoes on it. The carpet was complemented by a mahogany sofa with gold embossing, as well as ottomans, chairs, easy-chairs, a marble sideboard with a couple of gleaming cut-glass decanters and glasses, and a marble table. The sofa and chairs were trimmed with yellow silk. Marble statues and some expensive oil paintings on the walls completed the furnishing. It seemed to Hem as if the naked figures of Menoka and Rambha from Indra's court in heaven were laughing from the paintings. Hem felt bewildered by the beauty of this court on earth:

> From the street he had seen *punkhas* moving in the verandahs of Chowringhee mansions; he had seen the lion gate of Government House, he had even peeked inside English shops, but he never had the fortune of stepping inside such a beautifully decorated room. ... the gas light blazing in the crystal chandeliers lit up the room like daylight; shining through the window it illuminated the whole neighborhood.[65]

Unlike Debiprasanna Babu's *baithak-khana* the decor was in sync with prevailing custom, but its ostentation and glitter spoke of a lifestyle completely given over to bodily pleasures. All the lights of this "court" were ablaze, in contrast to Debiprasanna Babu's *baithak-khana* where the wall shades were draped, suggesting that in the latter they would be brought into use only on special occasions. Dhananjay Babu's salon did not require the actual physical presence of courtesans to remind the visitor of the sexually promiscuous lifestyle of the host – the courtesans smiling from the expensive (i.e., large) oil paintings attempted to recreate a heavenly immoral space.

In contrast, Chandranath Babu, a worthy, respectable Kayastha gentleman was widely regarded for his concern with public welfare. Barely over 30 years of age, Chandranath Babu was well educated, and had already become a well-known lawyer at the High Court. A respected member of the Suburban Municipality he had devoted much effort to the improvement of the suburbs. Accordingly, his house, although not large, was "clean, well built, and well maintained." Chandranath Babu's *baithak-khana* contained "a table, chairs, two shelves full of books, some tasteful pictures on the wall," and a couple of lamps on the table. The floor was matted and the room kept neat and clean: "One glimpse makes it clear that this is the clean orderly *workplace* of an accomplished, competent young man who enjoys his vocation"[66] (my emphasis).

Chandranath Babu's *baithak-khana* resembled not so much a drawing room after the European model, but a study or writing room. This space, however, was not simply given over to the luxury of one's personal contemplation. Here, the society of a few selected men was invited to improve one's mind and the cause of public welfare. Without attempting to imitate them lock, stock, and barrel, the host of this *baithak-khana* was not hesitant to adopt those elements of European material culture that appropriately reflected his educated tastes. The decor of this *baithak-khana* eschewed the undesirable aspects of both Bengali and European living rooms/salons. Chandranath Babu's *baithak-khana* did not contain the ubiquitous mattress covered with a white sheet (*farash*) to be found in the Bengali *baithak-khana*, where men lounged away their leisure hours in reclined positions smoking *hookah*. Replacing the mattress on the floor with simple straight-backed chairs – not easy chairs – implied a change in the habit of resting one's body against furniture. To maintain a sense of dignity, one is expected to sit upright in a chair with feet planted on the floor, as opposed to the ease with which one would be tempted to adopt a reclining pose on a mattress on the floor. Obviously, one could sit upright on the floor as well, but the author is keen to banish all reminders of lassitude associated with the Bengali gentleman's *baithak-khana*. Chandranath Babu's *baithak-khana* is neither a space where one whiled away time, nor is it a stage for the display of material wealth. The space that is meant to reflect the refined character and noble values of a young progressive Bengali gentleman is conspicuously plain, refraining from all decorative effects, except for the few unidentified pictures. The "tastefulness" of the pictures presumably constituted an absence of immoral femininity. It is in this new kind of austere masculine space devised by Chandranath Babu that Rameshchandra saw the possibility of an improved society. Later in the story we learn that Chandranath Babu was supportive of many progressive causes such as widow remarriage.

While these all-male spaces of the *baithak-khana* represented the gentleman householder, they each implied a corresponding inner compartment of domestic life. As the story progresses we learn that the salon of Dhananjay Babu and the lifestyle it harbored had been wrought at the cost of conjugal life. The glitter of the salon and its "centrifugal" life given over to women and wine hid a bleak inner compartment where the lonely bride withered away in neglect. The ability to afford any material comfort had erased Dhananjay Babu's boundaries of desire, without which one could not cultivate a blissful domestic life. The ambiguity in the material indicators of taste depicted in Debiprasanna Babu's *baithak-khana* actually confirmed that his domestic life had not been completely ruined, despite a custom-entrenched household and a self-indulgent lady of the house. The gods and goddesses, after all, had not disappeared from his scheme of representation, but were awkwardly juxtaposed with foreign artifacts that spoke of ill-understood received values. Instead of crafting his own opinion about the merits of European culture he was satisfied to follow vaguely understood norms – good or bad. His household maintained the traditions of worship and piety expected of a Bengali gentleman. Remaining tethered to traditional practices also kept him within certain known confines and saved him the domestic tragedy that befell Dhananjay Babu's household. What is interesting, perhaps, is the absence of any description of the *andar-mahal* of Chandranath Babu's house. Rameshchandra was unwilling to risk the description of the female counterpart of Chandranath Babu – the educated urban Bengali woman. Reconciling the conception of a modern Bengali woman and Western artifacts was a troubling endeavor given the prevailing images of such women. Consequently, the feminine counterpart of this progressive domain must only be conveyed through the attributes of men. Rameshchandra's novel brings out the significance he bestowed upon the visible attributes of material culture with a deep concern about the power of images to convey and cast a moral topography. At the end he chose to refrain from describing too much, seeking rather to rely on a common understanding of what might be "tasteful" in the urban milieu. The modern Bengali woman could not be described without raising the specter of improper visibility.

European-style furniture was prized in Bengali households for its novelty and as a marker of social status. In somewhat affluent families, European chairs were placed next to indigenous modes of seating. The 1859 probate of a Bengali lawyer residing in the suburbs indicates a somewhat similar range of seating arrangements. One of the rooms in the house meant for entertaining guests contained the following: two couches, three easy chairs, an invalid chair, one wooden chair, a couple of marble-top teapoys, two footstools, and a pier glass with *saloo* cover, as well as a *guddy* (mattress) on the floor with *takeas* (large cushions), a large *jajeem* or sheet.[67] In houses of more modest means, chairs were few and, not surprisingly, were used to mark out a distinctive space or use. As a raised seat, it invariably generated the sense of an honorific place in relation to the floor seating common in such houses, a characteristic that could be used to designate separateness. But their European provenance also contributed to certain informal restrictions regarding their use. What is more, the same artifacts that spoke of an enlightened outlook in the *baithak-khana* – European-style chairs, writing tables, newspapers, books – produced a space of censure for women.

When Abanindranath Tagore needed to indicate the *baithak-khana* of the Roy family in his map of Halisahar (see Chapter 3), he used two elements – a European-style chair and a *hookah*. These two motifs captured the idea of the *baithak-khana* as a space of conversation and leisure, in which the juxtaposition of Western and Indian artifacts had become naturalized. The same two motifs, however, would be used a few decades earlier, in popular paintings and prints – Kalighat paintings and Battala woodcuts – in the context of depicting a prostitute.

In Kalighat paintings city space was constructed not through a rendition of the streetscape or building interiors, but by a spare assemblage of artifacts that worked metonymically to signify a larger physical setting. The event was to be understood relationally between the meanings attributed to the artifacts and the gestures of the figures in the paintings. A frequently used signifier of "public space" (or domestic space losing its respectability) in Kalighat paintings was the chair. The paintings were typically titled, "Nayika," or "Bibi." Were these representations of prostitutes, actresses, or upper-class foppish women? Perhaps all three. What connects them is the loss of the halo of middle-class domesticity – once the upper-class woman begins wearing shoes, sits on a chair, uncovers her head, and plays musical instruments, she partakes in the activities associated with public spaces of entertainment, thus crossing the line of respectability to become indistinguishable from the "public woman." No "respectable" woman would be caught sitting on a chair smoking a *hookah*, while being attended by a male barber (Figure 4.12). If indeed such a figure is of a middle-class woman, the message is her availability to men from outside the family. The pictures contain a certain overlapping of public and private space, and rather than destabilizing the attributes of the public woman, these representations make them legible markers of a sexual economy. While the artifacts mark the space as public, the gestures allude to a personal space of the body that invites the male viewer's gaze. Their capacity to return the viewer's gaze, and their leisurely "private" posture – perched on a chair with one leg raised on the seat (as one often sat on the floor), or sitting with feet slightly splayed – hint at the possibilities of sexual access.

The only way to overwrite these artifactual connotations was to reinscribe the attitudes "respectable" women were allowed in the public space of the *baithak-khana*. In Prabhat Mukhopadhyay's story *Gahanar Baksha* (The Jewelry Case), for example, a twelve-year-old prospective bride arrives in the *baithak-khana* and sits on the only chair while the matchmakers, all men, occupy the low *taktaposh* (divan).[68] Here, the girl is being put on display, while ensuring that her space may be understood as sacrosanct – distinctively set apart from the male space within the *baithak-khana* – even while she needs to make herself available to male gaze. The sari draped over her head, her downcast eyes, and soft speech help generate the required signifiers of feminine gentility and reinforce the spatial barrier that needs to exist between her and the three yet-to-be-related men. Needless to say, such demands on respectability in the form of a newly regimented seclusion for women were antithetical to their participation in any form of literary gathering in which men were present.

The *baithak-khana*, however, was used not just for the leisurely gathering of men, but also for social and legal arbitration, and increasingly came to be used as an integral part of a nexus of "public" spaces for political discourse. The limitations placed on women's access to this space produced larger socio-economic as well as political ramifications amid the increasingly politicized space of the city as a nationalist setting. The spatial taxonomy of material and spiritual, inner and outer domains with which Bengali ideas of public sphere and public space were constructed was far more critical in asserting social control over women and the lower classes, than for addressing British political adversaries. The more strident these rhetorical distinctions, however, more pathetically they showed up the

Figure 4.12 Barber cleaning a woman's ear, Kalighat painting, late nineteenth
century. Herwitz Collection, Peabody Essex Museum, E302188

impossibility of confining the experience of the city in terms of these categories. The carefully articulated edge of the street acted both as a visual marker of a ritualized taxonomy and as a permeable interface that allowed noise, smell, and delinquent sight to cut across the normative visible intents. The façade itself continued to be adorned as part of a celebratory ritual of belonging to the city well into the mid-twentieth century – a ritual that one practices but ceases to believe in. In the next chapter I pursue the problem of making public space a legible device for ascertaining social relations, and the difficulties experienced in enforcing the visible gendered spatial taxonomy.

5 Death in public

The story of the mythic Sati. . . . a transaction between great male gods fulfills the destruction of the female body and thus inscribes the earth as sacred geography. . . . . There is no space from which the sexed subaltern subject can speak.

Gayatri Chakravorty Spivak[1]

Women in public

My mother has told me this story many times:

The year was 1888 or 1889. Suradhuni had been married at the tender age of six. Soon after the marriage, her husband went back to Assam, where he worked as a school teacher. Suradhuni was left behind with her in-laws. A few months had passed since the marriage. She was lonely and homesick and wanted to visit her parents who lived across the river in Nabadwip. But her in-laws would not hear of it. One day she slipped out of the house, went to the river *ghat* and asked one of the boatmen to give her a ride across the river to her parent's house. The boatman recognized the unchaperoned girl, and advised her to go back. She pleaded with him, and against his better judgement he escorted Suradhuni to her parents' house. When Suradhuni's parents learned that she had come without her in-laws' permission, they sent her back. But her in-laws would not take her in. Having left the house without permission, Suradhuni had left her *kula*.[2] Her parents were afraid of the social repercussions of taking back a girl who had received such opprobrium; they had two more daughters to marry off. By taking in a *kulatyagi* daughter they did not want to imperil the chances of marriage for the other daughters. So Suradhuni's father took the little girl to Calcutta and abandoned her there.

My mother had heard the story from her father-in-law, my grandfather. In all probability my grandfather learnt of this from his father. Suradhuni was my great grandfather's first wife.

This story of criminal abandonment has been handed down in our family with considerable regret not simply as a bit of family lore, but also in the context of remembering the family lineage. During the annual Hindu rituals of *pindadan* and *kalsi utsarga*, in which ancestors are given offerings of food and water to ease their travails in afterlife, one has to recite the names of all the deceased members of the extended family. My grandfather, no doubt prompted by a sense of guilt, decided to include Suradhuni's name among the names of the deceased family members to be recalled on this occasion. Suradhuni, who was accused of leaving her *kula*, was thus re-inserted in the *kula* and thus into family memory by a belated sleight of hand. In the "official" family tree of the Chattopadhyay clan she finds a presence as well. Against her name is a terse note: "dead, without child."[3]

There are several important issues in this remembrance of domestic cruelty. First, when this event occurred, the public debate concerning socially abandoned Hindu girls and women, who had left their *kula* willingly or unwillingly because of the strictures of Bengali Hindu society, had already been in place for several decades. The movement for the remarriage of widows had been inaugurated in the 1850s. By the 1870s there was already a civil marriage law, and attempts to abolish child marriage and to give women the right of divorce had been launched. And the Age of Consent debate in 1890 had created a mass agitation.

Second, what had in the family been considered a social "necessity" even in the late 1880s, after one generation, had come to be seen as a lamentable act of social cruelty. Yet the idea of the village home as a spiritual site opposed to the profane city had not entirely disappeared by my grandfather's time. In other words, the abandoned Hindu woman as a nineteenth-century modern subject had been grafted into the specifics of this family's memory by the early twentieth century, bringing with it a vague but palpable sense of Calcutta as the "other" space. But the city as "other" space could never be entirely torn out of family memory of the village home – they had been already connected not just by economic relations, but through social acts.

This brings me to the third issue, and the one I consider to be the most remarkable aspect of my family anecdote: the value and function accorded to the city of Calcutta by those who lived just about 50 miles away from it. In the anecdote, Calcutta performs as the place of death to the extent that leaving one's *kula* was equivalent to dying. The *kulatyagi* was treated as dead to the family. The city as a place of death also accumulated other meanings in its being situated in opposition to the home in the country. Here a clear distinction was made between the village home, the sacred site of the *kula*, and the profane world outside. In this outside domain, Calcutta occupied a conveniently close yet distant space – its unfamiliarity arising from unfamiliality (no close relative lived in Calcutta) rendered it distant, even immoral. Suradhuni was abandoned in this immoral space because she would not be taken back into the family. Calcutta, perceived as a place of transgression, was seen as appropriate for someone who had transgressed social boundaries, even if she was a child. The city was deemed morally pernicious and a threat to Hindu caste rules not simply as a site of foreign administration and trade as in Bhavanicharan Bandopadhyay's *Kalikata Kamalalaya,* or by being perceived as a vast bazaar, a nexus of economic relations unsuitable for respectable women, but also as a site that was profaned by the presence of women in public.

[margin note: why city is profane]

What then concerns me here is the location of women in the city's public space. In examining the representations of women in the nineteenth-century public sphere and public space, I argue for a gendered connection between literary imagination and spatial practice that contributed to the understanding of Calcutta as a modern artifact. And here I wish to make a substantial leap from my family's way of remembering to the literary memory of Bengali culture. In the two previous chapters I have already suggested that literary narrative is perhaps the most significant device through which Bengali male identities in the nineteenth-century public sphere were constructed. In this chapter I expand on the parameters within which women were located in this narrative-spatial imaginary of the public. And here, I would again emphasize what I have rehearsed in the previous chapters – that there was no pre-defined "public space" in the nineteenth-century city for the Bengalis to step into. The term "public space" does not simply refer to residual space outside home, but to this "outside" as a carefully meditated physical and social construction. Calcutta's public spaces were produced at the cross-section of several discourses and social practices that brought together in conflictual relationship questions of the immediate community and the imagined community of the nation. One could make an inventory of such spaces – bazaars, streets, *ghats*, parks, theaters, temples and places of worship, libraries, educational institutions, cafés, teashops, the Town Hall – and study the manner in which these were accessible to different groups of inhabitants. That is, however, not the primary task I take up in this chapter. While I shall discuss some of these sites and their refiguration during the nineteenth century, I am attempting to explain what the idea of *being in public* meant in nineteenth- and early twentieth-century Calcutta. The Bengali words used to denote "public" are *prakashye* (in public), *prakashya sthan* (public place), and *janasadharan* or *sarbasadharan* (the public – as a collectivity). The terms *janasadharan* and *sarbasadharan* were nineteenth-century inventions to accommodate the notion of a political public. I will address one aspect of this larger problem that has to do with women and the public sphere of Calcutta, and the refiguration of the city as public space. It is the question of women in public that produced the most anxious social commentaries in the city – in both English and Bengali – and was the *central* problematic of the Bengali discourse on modernity. The idea of being exposed to public view (*prakashye*) attained significance in this discourse, suggesting the limitations within which women could be represented in the late nineteenth- and turn of the twentieth-century Bengali imagination of family and community. I pursue this aspect of Calcutta's modernity produced at the crossroads of colonialism and nationalism through the themes of death (of women), sexuality, and spatial control. What ultimately rendered Calcutta as a modern space in Bengali sensibility was the question of women's access to public spaces dominated by the presence of men.

Anyone familiar with nineteenth- and even early twentieth-century Bengali literature would notice that women in novels and plays die at an alarming rate. These women seem to die from several causes: childbirth and improper medical attention, by contracting a sudden disease, due to mistreatment at the hands of family members, by committing suicide, or by being murdered. In addition, they suffer the ritual death meted out to Suradhuni – cast out of her *kula*, and immersed in the life of a *kulata* – prostitute, who by virtue of her profession is deemed an outcaste. Or, as widows they await death through an incessant routine of household labor under the most draconian dietary and social restrictions, and by eking out an existence at one of the pilgrimage sites in north India. Modern Bengali literature also has a history of connecting death with women appearing in public space. Appearance in public space causes their real death or ritual death through widowhood and/or prostitution.

In his autobiography *Mahasthabira Jataka*, Premankur Atarthi cites this case of a widow who was hacked to death on the street:

> A woman was murdered in front of the Sadharan Bramho Samaj on Cornwallis Street. Several Bramho families lived on the narrow lane next to the Samaj. Girls from these families either attended the Bethune School or Miss Neal's School. . . .
>
> Miss Neal was about to depart for England and on that occasion there was a gathering at her school. . . . At night, the school bus was dropping off the girls at home . . . when assailants came and murdered one of the girls. The girl was a Hindu widow, living in the house of Debiprasanna Chowdhury, the editor of the journal *Nababharat*. . . . The assailants fled from the scene, the girl was left groaning on the sidewalk. They had given the unfortunate girl twenty four strokes with a large assault knife.[4]

Atarthi went on to narrate the heroic story of his father's attempt to rescue the girl with the consequence that he himself suffered deadly blows, and subsequently received accolades from the community. The story of the assailants and the motive for murdering the girl belongs to a different history, he noted. Atarthi, who in his autobiography narrated with great sympathy the stories of women mistreated by family and acquaintances, felt the need to consign the history of the unnamed murdered woman outside the realm of his family memoir. That unfinished story of violence, however, allows us to build upon a possible set of issues and meanings that such an event encompassed.

In her discussion of nineteenth-century women's education and access to the public sphere and public space that education necessitated, Tanika Sarkar has made the perceptive argument that two dyads – educated woman and widow, and the educated woman and the immoral woman (prostitute) – run into each other to generate a single triangulated structure. The widow and the immoral woman may be merged together to form the apex term, the educated woman, who comes to occupy both the states of widowhood and immoral woman. Not defined by the presence of the husband, all three sustain an inherent immorality:

> The educated woman shares with the immoral one an extramarital desire. It makes no difference that in her case it is a desire for learning – she is not supposed to possess a desire for anything that does not come through, or is not related to her husband. ... Education is a double repudiation of the husband. It is both immorality and non-conjugality.[5]

We may draw a parallel structure of woman-death-public space to Tanika Sarkar's model of widow-educated woman-immoral woman to recognize the full import of Sarkar's model. Rather than being the agent of her husband's death, in the relationship I suggest, women bring death upon themselves by being out in public.

To explain the connections between these two models, I will draw upon three distinct realms of representation that informed each other: first, the popular Kalighat paintings of the Mohant–Elokeshi affair produced in the mid-1870s; second, Bengali "high" literature represented by the works of Bankimchandra Chattopadhyay and Rabindranath Tagore, focusing on Bankim's novel *Bishabriksha* (Poison Tree, 1872) and Rabindranath's short story *Strir Patra* (Letter from the Wife, 1914); and third, the realm of the prescriptive/legislative: Bengali "housekeeping" guides and government reports on prostitution produced in the second half of the nineteenth century. Notwithstanding the divergence of opinions, the predominantly male nationalist thought struggled with what it saw as the fundamental contradiction between the city as public space and the hallowed imagination of the space of the nation. The nation's women and the city needed to be separated by new conceptual and physical boundaries.

Representing sexual transgression

In 1873 the death of a Bengali woman at the hands of her husband made the headlines. This was the well-known Mohant–Elokeshi affair that scandalized Bengali society, resulting in a well-publicized trial, and numerous paintings and plays. The *mohant* (head-priest) of the temple at Tarakeswar, near Calcutta, was accused of seducing and raping a sixteen-year-old housewife, Elokeshi, from a nearby village, on the pretext of giving her medication for childbirth. When her husband Nabin, who resided in Calcutta, came to know of the affair, he murdered Elokeshi in a fit of rage. Nabin received life in prison while the Mohant received three years of rigorous imprisonment.

Numerous popular prints – Kalighat paintings and Battala woodcuts – of the salacious affair, murder, and trial were produced in the following decade, borrowing their themes and motifs from the plays written on the subject. At least 19 plays were based on the affair, and the actor and playwright Amritalal Basu recalled how the incident had brought life to the Bengali stage – it became the big money maker.[6] As the titles of most of these plays suggest, the main crime here was deemed to be the priest's inappropriate conduct, and not the murder by Nabin.[7] The priest was the chief instigator of a chain of events in which Elokeshi's death was the inevitable conclusion. The wife/object of desire had to be killed to restore the husband's honor. The relation between paintings and plays is important in this case. The immense popularity of the plays, the immediacy of the theatrical act, and the rhetoric of sin and morality, inspired the painters to capture the spirit of the tragedy as spectacle. Depicted as a series, the important scenes were painted on separate sheets, namely the meeting of the Mohant and Elokeshi, the seduction, Elokeshi seeking Nabin's forgiveness, three stages of the murder itself, followed by the courtroom scene, and the Mohant doing time in prison.

All of the paintings attempted to portray the sensational nature of the events by relying on compositions that are dynamic and animated with clear gestures of physical force and refusal. In at least one representation of the Mohant and Elokeshi together, Elokeshi is shown resisting the advance of the Mohant (Figure 5.1). She is sitting on a chair moving away her upper body and pulling her sari over her face, while the Mohant has grabbed her right hand. In his other hand he holds a glass of alcohol or drug. In the depiction of the "first blow" the end of her sari is flying while she adopts a defensive position trying to avoid the blow of the fish knife (Figure 5.2). At the moment of decapitation her body appears limp, collapsing under its own weight, while Nabin, recognizing the degree of injury, seems surprised (Figure 5.3). His right arm raised to his face suggests a person about to repent his actions. The drawing technique used in Kalighat paintings, its use of bold lines and volume, allowed the violence of the story to be conveyed forcefully. The stock of motifs used in such paintings was adequate for representing the meeting of the Mohant and Elokeshi and the murder itself. For example, the presence of European-style chairs in the scene of the meeting between the priest and Elokeshi opens it up to suggestions of infidelity.[8] The depiction of the trial, however, invited some spatial imagination (Figure 5.4). The painting of the court scene, with the murdered female

Figure 5.1 Elokeshi resisting the advances of the Mohant, Kalighat painting, mid-
1870s, Collection of the Victoria and Albert Museum, I.S. 111-1965

Figure 5.2 The first blow, Kalighat painting, mid-1870s, Collection of the Victoria and Albert Museum, I.M. 140-1914

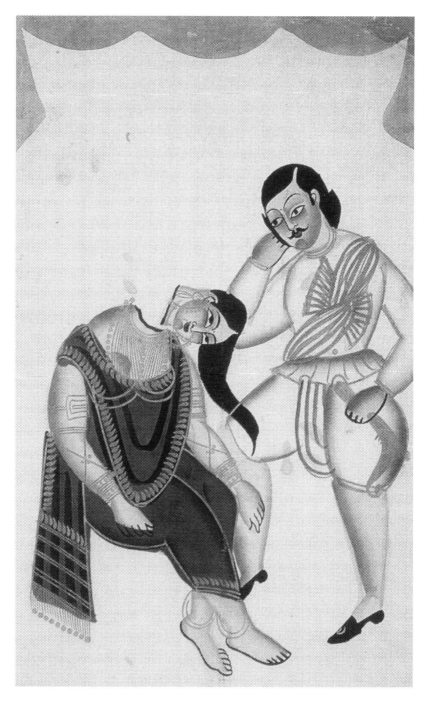

Figure 5.3 Nabin murders Elokeshi, Kalighat painting, mid-1870s, Collection of the
Victoria and Albert Museum, I.S. 240-1961

Figure 5.4 The trial of the Mohant of Tarakeswar, Kalighat painting, mid-1870s, Collection of the Victoria and Albert Museum, I.S. 38-197

figure lying in court while the trial is seemingly in progress, is also the most potent of the lot in terms of signification.

The courtroom as a colonial public space is clearly designated by the European furnishing and the presence of the European judge. The judge receives the most prominent location in a circular composition, impassively listening to the descriptions of the case from the legal counselors, while on the bottom left Nabin, escorted by a guard, looks at the figure of the Mohant in the dock, standing in a gesture of supplication. The decapitated body and the murder instrument occupy the center of the composition and present a unique example of a female body in public space. Needless to say, the body of the woman could not have been present at the trial. Its graphic presence, however, is key to the narrative space of the painting. The deceased body "appears" as evidence of several transgressions. It is through the constant reference to these bodily transgressions that the legal proceedings can continue.

The initial transgression occurred at the temple precinct where Elokeshi was introduced to the priest. The relationship between a male priest and a female worshipper was among the few allowed between a young woman and an unrelated man. Even then Elokeshi went to the temple with a chaperone. The second transgression occurred when the priest decided to seduce her, and the third transgression ensued when Elokeshi was willingly or unwillingly (pressured by her family or the priest's followers) seduced, resulting in several trips to the priest's house. The nature of the transgression is significant because two moral codes are being violated – the trust bestowed on a priest and the trust bestowed on a housewife. The sacred sites of home and temple are both contaminated by illegitimate sex. Elokeshi's exposure to the world outside the home brings about sexual misconduct – stepping on a thin line that separated "being in public" from being a "public woman." Her repentance and desire for forgiveness could have brought her again within the moral circuit of domesticity, but it does not happen. She dies a violent death at her husband's hands. Instead of a ritual death of being cast out of her *kula*, she is actually killed. But she cannot escape the further transgression of appearing in court as a deceased presence, as the focus of a lurid discourse.

Elokeshi's head separated from her body is exposed in the painting; using a nineteenth-century cultural code, she is bereft of *lajja* (shame or modesty) – a mark of an *asati* (unchaste woman). In the painting, her body – the upper part being uncovered – is literally exposed to the scrutiny of the lawyers, the European judge, and the public. The painting fixes the image and imagination of a violated female body in space. More tragic and spectacular than her death, the viewer is reminded, is this exposure to public scrutiny – the posthumous appearance in "public space" and the public sphere. It mattered little that she could not have been present in the court. What we witness here is public space as a construct in nineteenth-century Bengali culture where Bengali/Indian women took up only certain roles. This production of space, centered on Elokeshi as a violated figure, affirms the relationship of woman-death-public space. The violence of Elokeshi's death was not simply justified in the public eye that found sympathy with Nabin, but even for those who found sympathy with Elokeshi, her death was naturalized as a price of transgression, even if she might not have been "at fault."

The violated figure of Elokeshi, using another nineteenth-century cultural code that imagined the nation as a feminine figure, stands for the violated social fabric of Bengali society and, in extension, the nation. Her exposure to public scrutiny and colonial interrogation exposes the failings of the inner workings of the Bengali household that she was supposed to embody in its more perfect incarnation of the *grihalakshmi* (goddess of the household). Here the village home as the sacred site of the *kula* is torn between two spaces that were meant to sustain it – the temple site that failed as the moral center of the community, and the colonial city where Nabin was employed. In the first, women were allowed a space, no matter how contingent; in the latter women were superfluous or dangerous. The job in the city that necessitated Nabin's prolonged absence from home was the first act in the tragedy, as this meant not only lack of communication and conjugality between husband and wife, but the danger of her being outside the husband's sight and protection. Nabin's killing of Elokeshi – his "inability" to take her to the city with him – only plays out the inevitability of the notion that a woman's presence in the city is premised on an impossibility. The paintings and plays, all products of a colonial cosmopolitanism, incessantly refer to a troubled culture that had lost its traditional, local moorings – any sense of real place. It cannot then come as a surprise that the penultimate sequence of the tragedy is played out in a colonial courtroom, a surreal space where a whole set of confrontations – between two sections of the community, represented by the two counselors, between the priest and the salaried *bhadralok*, between the colonial state and the nationalist community, between the home and the city, between the colonizer and the colonized – are played out over the body of a dead woman. In the troubled relation between home–city–holy site, the colonial courtroom can intervene only imperfectly. The courtroom signifies that which Bengalis understood as another kind of violence; the intervention of the colonial state, embodied by the figure of the *sahib*, in matters internal to the community. The unimpassioned *sahib*, removed from the domestic tragedy and the moral code of the community, is the ultimate deliverer of justice.

What made the Mohant–Elokeshi affair so spectacular? After all, women from respectable families having sexual relationships outside of marriage could not have been that uncommon. If the scores of social tracts and light pornography are even to be remotely believed then liaisons between respectable women and male relatives were not that rare, and even male servants were not left out of the possibilities of sexual desire. Liminality of the pilgrimage site, a place where everyday moral codes could be flouted, was acknowledged as well. Earlier in the century, Bhavanicharan Bandopadhyay wrote an entire work in verse, *Dutibilas*, on the mechanics of the extra-marital affair in a titillating language and graphic detail.[9] Even in the more "reformed" worldview of the 1870s, acts of transgression were common themes of novels and plays. The Mohant–Elokeshi case, indeed, contained several ingredients for tragedy as melodrama: a Brahmin family, an absent husband, a young (and presumably lonely) wife, a sexual relationship with a priest, the possibility of an "illegitimate" child, village gossip, the wife's confession and possible reconciliation between husband and wife, and the death in one sudden fell swoop. But it was the violent nature of the murder itself that was key in allowing the representation and imagination to take flight.

The assault on the body in the painting is not simply about changing the syntax of the feminine body as represented in Kalighat paintings, but about framing it with a host of male figures that govern the rules of public space. In Kalighat paintings women were often depicted with paramours or in dallying poses. This Mohant–Elokeshi series plays out the dark possibility embedded in those representations. A private pleasure turns into a public violence to narrate the morality tale in its entirety, so to speak. Elokeshi's death could not close the moral circuit; it left a gaping wound in the moral imagination of late nineteenth-century Bengali culture that fed on visions of women in transgression. The theme of city-village home-holy site was enacted over and over in Bengali literature, and like any repetition bespoke a nervousness and uncertainty about one's proclaimed itinerary.

The figure of Elokeshi as a deceased body in public space, the object of male gaze shared by both colonizer and colonized, may be seen as part of an emergent pictorial and literary tradition that sought to control Bengali/Indian women's sexuality through the act of representing desirable and undesirable forms of femininity. A whole series of ideological apparatuses would be invented during the heyday of anti-colonial nationalism (between 1870 and 1950) to manage female sexuality as a necessary condition for a new nation.

Desire and devotion in nationalist imagination

> I can die, but would that help Suryamukhi live? No, Nagendra. Suryamukhi won't survive if you die, but it would have been better for you to die.[10]

Neither of the two characters, Nagendra and Suryamukhi, in Bankimchandra Chattopadhyay's *Bishabriksha* died in the literal sense of the term. Rather, Bankim felt compelled to sacrifice three other characters: Kunda and Debendra died, while Heera went insane. The female characters in Bankim's novels died so frequently, that their deaths became the subject of much public discussion. When he killed off the character of Rohini in

[margin handwritten notes:] managing female sexuality necessary as a condition for nationalism

the novel *Krishnakanter Will* there was a public outcry. In Bankim's novels social transgression had clear, pre-defined spatial coordinates. The inevitable end for women involved in such socio-spatial transgression was death. While the male characters often initiated these transgressive acts, not all of them died as invariably as the female characters caught in the transgressive web. It is through the death of the woman caught in transgression that the moral climate of the novel was restored, a morality that was centered within carefully delineated spaces for men and women in the household.

Bankim's novels had a complexity not completely addressed by this characterization, however; a complexity produced by his own struggle to articulate the "woman's question" within what he considered an appropriate Bengali/Indian frame of reference. Since the start of the debates over the abolition of *sati* in the early nineteenth century, questions of moral agency and the death of women continued to be visited by Bengali authors. It was Bankim, however, who for the first time gave this problem a spatiality by inscribing it within a specific agenda of the nation. The principal site of discourse became the Bengali household, and its moral environment the authors' central preoccupation.[11] For Bankim's illustrious successor, Rabindranath Tagore, this problem became the touchstone that enabled him to work out a series of shifting positions over the course of his writing career. Both Bankim and Rabindranath changed their stance on women's appropriate location in society by the end of their lives (allegedly Bankim became more conservative and Rabindranath became more liberal), but neither was willing to move beyond the household as an ideal discursive locale. This is what I would like to address by seeking out a few texts in which these concerns appear salient, rather than try to do justice to their oeuvres.

The frame within which notions of the Bengali self and moral community were located changed vastly between the early and late nineteenth century. If we look at Bengali literature for guidance, the difference between Bhavanicharan and Bankimchandra, and between Bankimchandra and Rabindranath is striking. For Bhavanicharan Bandopadhyay, the moral geography of the city is grounded in the exemplary performance of individuals who respect the caste structure of Hindu society and are capable of recognizing the distinction between acceptable and non-acceptable sources of ritual contamination. In other words, morality is understood as a code that prescribes the difference between sacred and profane actions. Physical space takes a back seat in this scheme of things. Many aspects of *daivakarma* (religious duties) and *pitrikarma* (duties towards ancestors) after all, were conducted outside the household, in temples and places of pilgrimage, and sometimes *vishaykarma* (worldly duties) was conducted at home. Thus, the line of demarcation between sacred and profane was not drawn around the public/private or world/home division. In fact, such boundaries were often not physical markers, but symbolic ones. One symbolic separation between the two domains was the changing of clothes and ritual ablution on returning home from daily business with foreigners; the symbolic marker is crucial for understanding the physical configuration of nineteenth-century Bengali households.[12]

At the same time Bhavanicharan was quite permissive in his descriptions of sexual transgression, accepting it as a reality of contemporary society, even if at the conclusion of his texts he felt the need to moralize about such transgressions. We must note that he wrote *Dutibilas* both to fill a "paucity" of erotic literature in Bengali, and to demonstrate the limits of extra-marital sex. In his scheme, sexual morality and *dharma* of the householder are only related because of the need to maintain the purity of the lineage. Its parameters defined by caste rules, morality resides in the individual capacity to uphold religious prescriptions and attend to the sanctioned relationship between husband and wife. His advice to his male readers (he simply assumed that his reader was male) was to turn their sexual energies towards satisfying the sexual needs of their wives, which if not met would look for a different source of satisfaction. He did not cite the scriptures, like Bhudev Mukhopadhyay, to suggest that sex between husband and wife should only occur for procreative purposes, and ideally cease after the birth of the first son.[13] For Bhavanicharan, it is the male desire to look for sex outside of marriage that ultimately sets the house-wife off-course, leading to the loss of *kula* and the purity of lineage. Moral agency, therefore, resides with the men given the charge of satisfying their wives' sexual desires and channeling women's sexuality into socially approved reproduction.

For Bhavanicharan, the extant caste structure and scriptural limits were adequate for this task. Not so with his successors 50 years later. Faced with trenchant British criticism of the inadequacy of all aspects of Hindu society, and the specific characterization of Bengali men as effeminate – lacking physical strength, courage, and leadership qualities – the central task of Bengali nationalist thought became the identification of a male subjectivity by reviewing and transforming Hindu religious and social practices. Morality came to occupy a larger ideological terrain, exceeding the limits of one's personal spiritual quest, purity of lineage, and responsibility towards the caste system. The physical "lack" seen in the light of Hindu spirituality was turned into a moral plenitude.

By the 1870s space as a designator of morality became central to Bengali literature, and its chief expositor was Bankim. No doubt, the thick description of a setting as demanded by the form of the novel had much to do with this. But it also had to do with the desire to depict society in accordance with the new moral order of the nation. If literature had to carry the burden of revealing the potential of the nation, then, for Bankim, it seemed only natural that beauty and art had to be located spatially in the moral imagination and reframed within a new quest for cultural truth. Bankim's quest began with a search for the nation's history and culminated in the articulation of a moral philosophy that took as its vantage the Hindu religion and as its touchstone the moral attributes of Krishna.

In making the moral order in literature an aesthetic problem, Bankim was able to reach a broader space of moral action. He claimed literature to be the first step towards a moral self in the pursuance of *dharma*. The objective of both literature and *dharma* is the realization of truth, the sole source of joy in life.[14] But the aim of literature is not to preach. Its objective is the purification of the heart through the creation of the highest form of beauty. The source of this beauty resides in nature, but the author's creation must exceed the imitation of nature if it is to leave a deep impression on the mind.[15] The aim must be to link *antahprakriti* (internal nature) and *bahiprakriti* (external nature). It is this tracing of the shadow of one on the other that would enable the poet to transcend the gross sensory facts and arrive at the domain of the pure (*pabitra*). This movement towards the pure constitutes the subject of art. If empiricism entailed a faithful description of the external world, Bankim suggested that it is only when the "reality" of the natural world is seen in the light of inner spirituality that a work becomes truthful, becomes art.

Well-versed in eighteenth- and nineteenth-century Western philosophy, Bankim had imbibed from it a deep faith in empiricism and positivist modes of enquiry. The emphasis Bankim placed on history as a mode of knowledge resided in this faith. "Krishnacharitra" (1892), Bankim's exegesis on the life of Krishna, is a case in point.[16] The objective of his strenuous exercise in analyzing the character of Krishna was the need to establish Krishna as *the* ideal male persona (*adarsha purush*), the perfect role model as the incarnation of god on earth, the ultimate example of both morality and beauty. A reinterpretation of the life of Krishna as it was found in the Bhagavadgita was meant to demonstrate the purity of his character, and to overwrite the falsity of the twelfth-century poet Jayadeva's preoccupation with the sensuousness of Krishna.[17]

The tricky task of managing Krishna's sexuality and the pleasures of playful, sexual imagination (both being direct responses to Orientalist constructions of India), necessitated the working out of the concept of *bhakti* (devotion) (he saw love and charity to be subsumed under devotion), that would mediate between opposing forces: internal nature and external nature. For Bankim this conflict was primordial, and required a multidimensional approach of resolution. In other words, reason alone was not adequate to the task. *Bhakti* articulated as a complete, multi-pronged approach to humanity, was not inimical to reason. Rather, it provided the Western idea of reason with a corrective touch of love and charity. It was, after all, to reason, without the corrective touch of devotion, love, and charity, that he attributed the power as well as the ills of Western society.[18]

In making room for one's inner (Hindu) spirituality in the projection of truth, Bankim made a strategic clearing for a new male subjectivity and moral topography, one that could be positioned as different and superior to the British subject's knowledge of Bengal/India.

The core of this new moral topography became the family and the house-hold.[19] The practice of *dharma* mandated a domestic life because it was here that the natural emotions were most strongly experienced. These emotions had to be restrained and channeled from the self to the community. The keystone to the integrity of the household and community was *bhakti* towards elders – devotion of students towards teachers, of children towards parents, of the wife towards the husband. Here Bankim saw fit to add that *bhakti* of the husband towards the wife was also desirable, even if the Hindu scrip-tures sent mixed messages in this regard. So he preferred to insert Auguste Comte's ideas about conjugality in which devotion must be reciprocal, as "more deserving of respect."[20] *Bhakti*, he was perfectly aware, worked asym-metrically, as devotion towards "elders." Consequently, in his scheme, devo-tion of the wife towards the husband and the husband towards the wife could not be equivalent. So the task was to designate for the woman a role that would earn her "respect" precisely because of her (loving) subjection to her husband. A moral household required such a devoted woman, and conversely she could only earn true respect within the normative space of home. Bankim's idealization of femininity within the bounds of conjugality (and its threatening obverse) found its most clear delineation in *Bishabriksha*.

Bishabriksha is a story about the blissful marriage of a young couple, Nagendra and Suryamukhi, ruptured by sexual/spatial transgressions.[21] Nagendra is a wealthy landlord. The story begins with Nagendra's acci-dental encounter with a beautiful, orphaned girl, Kunda. He becomes enamoured with her looks, and brings her home, whereupon she is married off to Suryamukhi's adopted brother. Soon after the marriage, Kunda becomes a widow and returns to live in Nagendra's house. She now becomes the love object of two men, Nagendra and Debendra, another landlord. The only person who knows of these liaisons is Heera, a maidservant engaged in Nagendra's household. She, herself, falls in love with Debendra, thus beginning a chain of unfortunate events. The story itself is stretched over a large territory that includes Nagendra's mansion in the Bengal countryside, Calcutta, and Benaras, the socio-spatial connectivity of these three locations reiterated by journeys taken between them by boat, on foot, and horseback.

Bishabriksha contains an abundance of detailed spatial descriptions. Each setting conveys certain moral attributes, and enables the author to bring out the emotional struggles of his characters. All the settings signify some variety of domestic insufficiency. The problem of Nagendra's vast mansion is that there are too many spaces not under the immediate vigilance of the lady of the house. Nagendra's house is first described when Kunda looks upon it with awed eyes. The mansion is beyond Kunda's childish comprehension – a space she would never master. So the narrator steps in and picks up the slack in spatial mastery, and provides a laboriously detailed description of the mansion.

The house consists of a simple but elaborate rectangular spatial grid consisting of three outer apartments (*mahals*) and three inner apartments. Suryamukhi's bedroom at the center of the new *andar-mahal* (inner compartment) occupies the most private and quiet location. Nagendra's property stands for his wealth and fortune, but it is also a symbol of Suryamukhi's able housekeeping (it precipitously falls apart when Suryamukhi leaves the household).[22] The old *andar-mahal* with its low and dirty rooms harbor the tradition of an extended family and dependents – signifying the continuation of a past practice even if imperfect. The new *andar-mahal* with its novel architecture represents the wholesome form of conjugality between Nagendra and Suryamukhi. It is not free from transgression however – it is the presence of Kunda in the house that becomes unbearable for Nagendra, ultimately leading him to profess his love for Kunda.

In Bankim's novels women bear the responsibility of the moral climate, in the capacity of both ruining it and conserving it. Suryamukhi is no doubt the model of femininity. Because she cannot reconcile her husband's love for Kunda, she leaves home. At the end she is overcome with the desire to see her husband, presumably recognizing that she has a higher duty that must transcend her own sense of self. This is where she wins where Heera and even Kunda, finally awakened to the depth of her feelings for Nagendra, cannot bear the burden of love's asymmetry. Kunda takes poison because she recognizes that Nagendra's love for her never transcended the physical. Heera goes insane because she cannot overcome the betrayal by Debendra, who used her in the hope of getting Kunda.

Bankim represents the love of all three women as far more complete and capable of sacrifice than that of the two male characters. Neither man has control over his physical desires. Debendra and Nagendra here represent two sides of the same person, demonstrating the difference domestic circumstances and conjugal love make. Nagendra is saved because of Suryamukhi, but there is no redemption for Debendra and Heera, while Kunda's only redemption is death. When Kunda dies at Nagendra's feet, Suryamukhi exclaims, "You fortunate one! I wish to have your pleasant fate!"[23] It is Kunda's "fortunate" death that enables the return of normalcy in the family.[24] While she was contemplating death, Nagendra and Suryamukhi were finding solace in each others' arms in Suryamukhi's room, with its suitably edifying decor.

Suryamukhi's bedroom is described as large, with a tall ceiling and marble-lined floor. The furnishings consist of an expensive wood bed decorated with ivory, large mirrors, and sofas covered in colorful fabric. Six paintings hang on the walls, depicting scenes from Sanskrit literature, all proclaiming the superior position of the husband to the wife, and the loving submission of the wife to the husband. Suryamukhi and Nagendra had selected the themes of "ideal" conjugality and had them painted by an Indian painter, tutored in the European tradition.[25] Lying in the room, awash with grief, Nagendra seemed to see Suryamukhi represented in all these pictures. He read the words Suryamukhi had herself inscribed on the wall: "In the year 1853, for the establishment of my lord, my husband, this temple has been built by his servant Suryamukhi."[26] Suryamukhi inscribes her own name in the intimacy of her bedroom only to acknowledge her complete submission to her husband. Her authorial signature can only appear within a regulatory frame of subjection and sacrifice. Her redemption is her return into this sanctified space to serve her husband, while Nagendra's redemption is in his acknowledgement of Suryamukhi's devotion. Even the space she "designs" and supervises is not to be claimed by her. She also expresses no interest in supervising her husband's estate when he mismanages it.

The character that generates the story line of *Bishabriksha* is, however, Heera. She is both a marginal figure and the most complex, as well as dangerous, character in the novel. Even though a person of lowly status she is the central figure of conflict. Heera represents every kind of inequity offered by Bengali society. She is a child widow, brought up in impoverished circumstances, and destined to a life of servitude. Beautiful and not easily susceptible to sexual advances, Heera owns a small, neatly maintained house, and attempts to retain a dignified life. It is this spatial mastery that allows her to control the story line. But this privilege in a woman also becomes the cause of tragedy. The house, subject only to her supervision, becomes a site of illegitimate encounters.

In Bankim's view Heera's sin is her self-centeredness, a love that has not learned the value of self-sacrifice and unattachment in the face of sensory pleasure. The defect in her character is not inherent, but produced by circumstances. She has never had the privilege of patriarchal protection – a sense of happy belonging – where she could imbibe these qualities. For someone who had not enjoyed the bliss of love, self-sacrifice was impossible. In *Bishabriksha* tragedy resides as much in social inequity as human frailty – the inability to reconcile the tension between desire and sacrifice, external and internal nature. Bankim is not questioning the necessity of moral codes; he rather demands them.[27] He is reflecting on the inadequacy of codes, the ineffectiveness of the regulatory frame of conjugality that can neither prohibit nor subsume the complexity of the human heart. Heera occupies the outer margins of this regulatory frame and poses a threat to the normalcy within. And yet by the end of Bankim's novels, the moral space of the respectable Bengali home, once disturbed through social transgression, is returned to its sanctity.

The detailed renditions of space in *Bishabriksha* should not be hastily read as Bankim's subscription to their moral stature. The separate spheres of *andar* and *bahir* cannot become perfect constructs for Bankim unless the women themselves subscribe to their need, and find fulfillment in them.

But, more significantly, a spatial order untested by the litmus of spiritual love cannot claim invincibility. Even the most idealized space of the novel – Suryamukhi's bedroom and the devotion that went into its decor – was inadequate to prevent the love triangle. An important function of these spatial descriptions is not just to reflect the inner struggle of the characters, but to delineate the limits of their idealization. Bankim's strong female characters discover their selves and strengths in the face of unprecedented odds in the outside world, of course only to return to the fold of domesticity. For Bankim, what makes Heera's character tragic is that she is bereft of the possibility of returning home – her insanity leads her into wandering aimlessly, a homeless destitute. In refusing the "satisfaction" of Bengali spatial itinerary, by mis-reading service as bondage, Heera submits herself to an irreconcilable internal conflict.

Then, to make women understand their socio-spatial role in the project of the nation became the hegemonic task of Indian nationalism. To that extent, one had to talk about women's problems, address them directly, and work out their interiority in the public sphere. This is the task Bankim carried out in novels such as *Indira*, *Krishnakanter Will*, and *Debi Chowdhurani*, in all of which the strong women characters find ultimate fulfillment in submission to the husband and the household.

If in his later novels Bankim empowered women with the moral agency to demonstrate and criticize the failings of society guided by men, in his essays, he transferred this agency back to the men. Bankim had been deeply influenced by John Stuart Mill's philosophy of social equality. In several essays he openly acknowledged his debt to Mill. His reading of Mill against the grain of nineteenth-century Bengali society, however, produced results quite different from Mill's. The fifth section of his essay "Samya" (Equality) is about the social inequity between men and women in Bengali society.[28] Written in 1879 it was perhaps the most radical critique voiced in nineteenth-century Bengal about women's rights.

At the outset he proposed that inherent differences in physical strength cannot be assumed as a basis for discrimination. If physical difference alone, including courage and the capacity to work hard, is considered a basis of rights, then "why do we scream at the unequal rights between the British and the Bengali?" he observed.[29] Similarly, inherent differences between Bengali men and women cannot be constituted as a basis for withholding privileges from women. These privileges included education, the right to marry after the loss of a spouse, access to public space, property rights, and the right to earn a living. The question of chastity, however, assumed central importance:

> If you die, your wife must remain a widow, and that would make her more loving. By the same logic if you become a widower why don't you remain chaste and show your love? . . . Why the rule would not apply to you? . . . Because *you* make the rules. . . .

Of all the inequities between men and women nothing is more pernicious and unjust than locking up women like caged animals in the house. . . . Everyone acknowledges the unfairness and ill-effects of this practice, but no one attempts to disobey it. The reason: fear of disrespect. Another will be able to lay his eyes on my wife and daughter. What a shame! And there is no shame in locking up your wife and daughter in cages like animals? No disrespect in that? If you feel no disrespect attaches to that, then I die in shame at your impaired sense of self-respect.

Let me ask, what right have you to oppress them just to save your vanity? Were they born to demonstrate your prestige, to be counted among your goods and chattels? . . . The women need to be caged for the protection of religion? . . . why bother with such religion? Uproot its anchors and start a new foundation.[30]

The essay was addressed to his male readers, but here he abandoned the self-irony he typically reserved for his unsparing criticism of Bengali men. This part of the essay was also different in its rhetoric from the parts concerned with class and caste, where he employed a rather standard positivist mode of reasoning. The periodic insertion of accusatory invectives that addressed the reader directly sustained the language of persuasion. This same rhetorical excess, however, suavely turned from women's rights to the rights of men – the laxity of moral injunctions on their behavior. On the issue of *sattitwa* (chastity), he argued not against setting such moral standards for women, but not setting them as stringently for men, as well.[31] There were scores of examples in the scriptures that condemn such behavior among men, he noted, but society was unwilling to enforce them, because those who controlled society were men. The problem, then, resided not with the Hindu moral code, but rather with its practice in contemporary society. Enforcing norms to save one's vanity and self-interest was not simply unjust, but an immoral act (*adharma*), an insurmountable obstacle in the construction of the nation. Vehemently against social reform by judicial mandate, he sought the personal approach of addressing the male reader directly, an appeal to his subjectivity to see his own life as a colonized subject reflected in the tragedy and ideals of the life of Bengali women.

Bengali women, he suggested in another essay, needed the protection of the men for the nation's survival.[32] What then of women's rights and feminine agency? In his essay on the theory of religion, Bankim made a distinction between *anushilan* – as practice that enhanced one's natural abilities, and *abhyash* – as practice that worked against the natural flow of one's abilities.[33] Women in the outer world were working against their natural strength (he used horse riding and techniques of self-defense as his "extreme" examples). He was not against having equal rights, in theory ("let men breast-feed if they can"), but the building of a nation required the *anushilan* of one's natural powers.[34] Bankim seemed to be doing two things at once. By pointing out the unjust treatment of the "weaker sex," he was suggesting that the subordination of women be seen in a similar light as the subjection of Bengali men to the British colonizer. At the same time, he was addressing the dominant British criticism of Bengali men as undeserving of equal treatment – "see how they treat their women" – by arguing for a change in the treatment of Bengali women, if Bengali men were not to capitulate to British racism.

Women, although positionally inferior to the men in the household, were singled out by Bankim as historically capable of the most supreme devotion. This practice of devotion was born out of the fact that scriptural knowledge had been traditionally denied to women. Unable to access God through the sacred word, they contemplated the beauty of God and made His beauty and that of His natural surroundings the object of their love. In women, an exercise of feelings substitutes the intellectual path to religion. But the sexual desire of the *gopis* (cowmaidens) for Krishna in *rasalila*, in Bankim's interpretation became only a metaphor for the most earnest desire to be one with God. This capacity to experience pleasure without getting engrossed in sexuality, the ability to transcend external beauty in search of inner purity, seemed to have been lost to contemporary Bengali society, and needed to be revived through practice. Bankim made a distinction between feminine and masculine forms of devotion only to neutralize this distinction through a secondary metaphorization – feminine devotion becoming a metaphor for the highest form of devotion – enabling men to access the more superior state.

In an essay, "Striloker Rup" (Women's Beauty), he elaborated on this idea by taking women's appearance as the point of departure. Many women, he claimed, consider their beauty to be powerful enough to wreak havoc in the minds of men – "the edifice of their manly duties, their common sense, their morality are torn asunder when hit by the gale of feminine beauty."[36] And men, in composing love poetry, have only abetted this idea. The root of women's degradation is the excessive concern for their *rup* (external form/appearance). Women get the object of their desire only in exchange for their beauty. This notion of exchange had created the institution of prostitution. In beauty lies the root of women's domestic slavery. "I do not wish to hear," he proclaimed, "that impermanent beauty is the only possession of women to navigate in this world."[37] The clamor over feminine beauty has overshadowed the real greatness of women – their capacity for love, devotion, and self-sacrifice. He ended this essay with a paragraph waxing on the beauty of a woman committing *sati*:

When I contemplate the greatness of women, I see in my mind the image of a woman committing *sati*. I see the pyre aflame, the woman sits there clasping her husband's feet. Slowly the flame spreads, it burns one limb and reaches another. The wife, engulfed in flames, contemplates the husband's feet, once in a while asking or gesturing to the people to utter the name of Hari. There is no expression of bodily fatigue. Her face is joyous. The flame increases, her life departs, her body is reduced to ashes. Praised be forbearance! Praised be love! Praised be devotion!

When I think that until recently the weaker sex in our country, in spite of their tender bodies, could die like this, then I get a new lease of hope. Then I begin to believe that the seed of that greatness is buried in us as well. Would we not be able to demonstrate this greatness in the future?[38]

Bankim's slow-panning over the image of the *sati's* burning body, simultaneously reiterates the architecture of sexual desire, and dismisses it in proclaiming the triumph of the spirit over the body. It is this modern imagination of *sati* as self-sacrifice, the ability to represent the *sati* of the past that allowed Bankim to locate his hope for the future of the nation. For whose benefit – the community or family – was this sacrifice necessary? Nothing that Bankim wrote about the practice of *bhakti*, the central premise of which was service to the family, community, and society, would provide an answer. The answer resided in the need for a regulatory frame to control the sexuality of women. If representation is itself an act of regulation, then the image of the burning woman as *sati*, became in Bengali nationalism the regulatory frame *par excellence*. One of the few instances when the woman was to be viewed in public in an intimate proximity with her husband, and made the object of the gaze of the community, was at the threshold of her death. The rituals that governed the condition under which she could be allowed this privilege of public appearance, including a cleansing bath for which a menstruating woman would have to wait publicly until the fourth day, ensured that her sexual impurity would not threaten the regulated space of the ritualized spectacle.

Bengali nationalist patriarchy (that is the authority of the male figure) was not, as Dipesh Chakrabarty has accurately recognized, premised on the concept of the death of the father.[39] It was, I argue, based on the death of the unhomely figure – the sexually threatening woman, marginalized beyond socially approved reproductivity. Only with the destruction of this woman's body could manliness and patriarchy be renewed. How could the seed of *sati* as greatness, practiced only by women, get transferred to Bengali men?[40] Bankim would argue that it could be transplanted because the seed remained buried in the moral fabric of Hindu society, and not with women per se. That only women had to practice *sati* becomes a historical contingency, which could be resuscitated and denied at will. The mediating attributes of Hindu love and devotion enable an agile transference of moral will from the female to the male. The subjectivity of women is not Bankim's quest here, but the subjectivity of the colonized male who is forced to contemplate himself as the weaker sex in relation to the colonizer. Only through the control of Bengali women's sexuality, both as a metaphor and as materiality, could Bengali men rewrite their own sexual history, the sexual history of the nation. Bankim's advocation to abjure one's sexual impulses (beyond the reproduction of the first son) only enabled the placement of sexuality at the center of the nation's discursive space. His successors built on this theme with a similar anxiousness.

Displacement

In a discussion of Bengali women's subjectivity, Dipesh Chakrabarty has traced a technique of interiority that three Bengali authors, Bankimchandra Chattapadhyay, Rabindranath Tagore, and Saratchandra Chattopadhyay, used to make a distinction between external and inner beauty.[41] While Bankim's women (and men) had to struggle with the tension between the love of the eye, and the love of the mind, in Rabindranath's and Saratchandra's novels women's beauty was dismissed as a non-issue. Articulating the inner attributes of Bengali women, idealized as *pabitra prem* (pure love), the latter two invested them with a unique modern subjectivity. Chakrabarty makes this argument in the context of analyzing the Bengali widow as a modern subject. Let me quote at length from Chakrabarty's essay here:

> The novels thus established the idea of a disembodied, private, but communicable sphere of interiority – something critical to the category of the modern subject in European thought. Bengali literary thought acknowledged lust as animal passion residing in the body. To this it opposed the idea of *prem* or love. *Prem* came to mark the autonomy of the individual in the widow by seeing the achievement of purity or *pabitrata* in love as the act of separating the self from the body. Society could indeed oppress the individual – in this case, the widow – but it could not take away her individuality. Fiction thus shone a light by which to see (and archive) the widow as an individual endowed with interiority. . . .
>
> The body remains the unresolved problem in these novels. It is either completely marginalized as the seat of lust that *pabitra prem* (true/pure love) conquers, or it comes back (as in Bankim) in the problem of *rup* (form, appearance), as fate that teases the human's internal nature (*antahprakriti*). In either case, there is nothing like the Freudian category of "sexuality" mediating between the body and the interior space of the subject. . . .
>
> It was the respectability of the extended family, not just the loving couple – that was at issue. The pursuit of *pabitrata* . . . sustained a particularly Bengali family romance.[42]

This removal of the Bengali male gaze from the female body to the interior of the female subject constitutes a peculiar violence to the materiality of women's lives by constructing an impossible position of subjectivity for women. It needs to be pointed out here that this attribute of *pabitra prem* was asymmetrically applied to women, and arose out of the specific problem of the sexed body of the young widow.

The marginalization of the sexed body could only produce a disembodied female subject with no claims upon any space, including the space of her own body. It was by removing the female *body* as a sexual signifier from the discursive domain that the priests of "high" literature constructed the autonomy of nationalist patriarchy – coming to occupy positions of authority in regard to both the female body and spirit, the former as a site of cultural practice, and the latter as a site of enunciation. It is a two-step maneuver: the ruse of endowing women with subjectivity (using a Western liberal tradition) differentiates between the body as property and the interior psychological sphere, producing a gap, a necessary distance between subject and object; then the body is violently "removed" from view and female occupation (only to "posthumously" appear as occupied by male desire), thus collapsing the dialectic into the hollowness of an abstract female interiority.[43] The absence of a category such as "sexuality," mediating between the psychological and physical passions, retains the mark of difference from European thought only by denying Bengali women a subjective *space*. Female subjectivity, as a spatial problematic, was articulated by both Bankim and Rabindranath in ways that were troubled by their "inability" to regulate the threatening sexuality of women. Both imagined conjugality within an extended family to be the appropriate containment, and yet their texts strain at the edges of the regulatory frame.

If in Bankim's novels the home ultimately retains moral authority, in the work of his successors the Bengali home is a far more contested site. Frequently, the home, particularly the restriction-bound urban home, was portrayed as an immoral space from which women needed to escape to retain their sense of self-worth, even if that escape was at the cost of life. In Rabindranath Tagore's short story *Strir Patra*, the death of one woman causes another to question the value of her own life and consequently to leave the confines of the traditional household.[44] The short story is structured in the form of a letter that Mrinal, the Mejobou (wife of the second son), writes to her husband after she has left the house of her in-laws in Calcutta and traveled to the pilgrimage site of Puri. Rabindranath portrays the author of the letter, Mrinal, as an empathetic woman who follows her innate sense of morality and justice, and defies her family by refusing to abandon an orphaned girl, Bindu, whom she has sheltered from hardship. When Bindu is married off to an insane man and ultimately commits suicide, Mrinal leaves the family.

The story brings together several clearly recognizable signs of modernity in the character of Mrinal, articulated through the chosen literary form, through the critique she voices, and in defining the space she occupies in this world. The form of the letter, itself a mode of personal communication, functions to disclose the intimate world of contemplation about the domestic sphere to a public audience. Saliently absent in this modern form of communication in *Strir Patra* is that factor on which such communication is presumed to be based: intimacy of feelings and, in this case, conjugal intimacy. The form of the letter and its personal address sharpens the absence of shared feelings between husband and wife, and holds up for the reader the uneven social cost that women bear in this absence. Since the intimate sphere of the family cannot support a moral foundation based on empathy, this intimate communication seeks from the reader of the novel in the public sphere that which the domestic sphere cannot provide. The letter delivers the outpourings of Mrinal's heart in a suitable literary form to the modern reader, seeking his/her empathy to substitute for that of the husband's. Women in Mrinal's position need a space outside the household to fathom their full potential, and the proof of this newly emerged self is the ability to construct an extended critique of existing conditions. It is through the literary act of writing the letter, and finding the *space* to write the letter (made impossible and unnecessary within the household), that Mrinal constructs her new subjectivity. The original Bengali word that Rabindranath used in this case – *phank* – which I have translated above as space, literally means "gap," and stands for both space (that is empty) and time (that is unoccupied – *abasar*). It is the control of both space and time that is crucial for this new subjectivity to come into being, and in Mrinal's case that control could only be exercised outside the domain of the household. Writing, she tells the reader, is not new to her: she had secretly written poetry even in the most unpoetic setting of the household – "even if [the poetry] was rubbish, the walls of the *andarmahal* had not circumvented it; that was my freedom, only there I could be myself." The only space of creativity she could conjure within the household was literary, by brief escapes into the world of letters. And yet, as in many of Rabindranath's novels and plays (e.g. *Ghare-Baire*), the woman gains self-recognition once she physically steps out of the confines of the household into the outer world. This is akin to Bankim's conceptualization of women, but from here on the difference between Bankim and Rabindranath is noteworthy. At the very beginning of the letter Mrinal writes:

> I am the Mejobou of your family. After fifteen years, standing at the edge of this ocean, I have recognized that I have another relation with the world and its God [*jagadiswar*]. That is why I have found the courage to write this letter. This is not a letter from the Mejobou of your family . . . I am writing this letter to clearly explain that I will not die.[45]

Through this defiant articulation of the woman's self outside the material bounds of home, Rabindranath outlines a moral geography that is far removed from that of Bankim's narratives, and distanced from his earlier preoccupation with women and space in novels such as *Ghare-Baire*, and *Gora*. This moral geography is given depth by being articulated through the happenings of Mrinal's own life. The letter, written in an autobiographical form, serves the purpose of delivering both contemplative distance and the immediacy of the sensory world.

The letter recalls the salient moments of Mrinal's passage from childhood as she was made aware of being just a girl – the daughter that survived when the son did not, the 12-year-old girl who was burdened by the terror of an entire neighborhood as the matchmakers came to examine her good looks, and then the daughter-in-law who had to be discreet about showing affection to those for whom she cared the most, namely, the domestic animals in the household, her activist brother whom she rarely invited out of fear of disapproval, and of course, the orphaned Bindu. The autobiography that evaluates her own life builds on a dialectical relationship with her critique of the household. When towards the end of her recollection she notes, "I do not wish to register a complaint," she launches her strongest critique – she refuses to re-enter the conjugal relation within the extended family.[46]

In effect, the short story points out that social critique and the emancipation of women from the *old* patriarchy cannot begin at home, crippled as it is by the dominant cowardice of men and the insecurity and unquestioning servitude of women. The unequal burden of the absence of conjugal intimacy and familial empathy is brought out in one of the most evocative denunciations of the architecture of domestic arrangement:

> There is a small garden attached to the outside apartments of the house, and those rooms lack nothing in terms of furnishing and decor. But the inside apartments are like the reverse side of an embroidered silk; there is no modesty, no beauty, or state of dress. Here the light burns dimly, breeze enters stealthily, the garbage in the courtyard remains unmoved.[47]

The asymmetry of the dual system of *sadar-andar* (outside-inside) is brought to bear its full (colonial) force by being seen through the eyes of an English doctor who visits Mrinal at the time of her labor. The doctor, Mrinal recalls, was surprised by the *andar-mahal*, and annoyed by the condition of the birthing room. The doctor presumed that these physical lacks caused the women daily hardship, but he was mistaken: "when self-respect is lowered, being uncared for does not seem unfair."[48] Mrinal's infant daughter died, but she survived.

Here, Rabindranath suggests a fairly direct correlation between the home as material artifact and the space of unethical practice that together produce domestic slavery. The critique of the domestic sphere takes the form of a critique of code-based morality in need of replacement by an ethic-based morality. A domestic sphere based on ethical practice, therefore, required a literate, intelligent woman capable of recognizing justice in everyday life and thus re-forming the space of domestic arrangement. Mrinal notes that dying is so common among Bengali women, she is "ashamed to die":

> People of the entire country got angry (at Bindu's death). They said, "it has become a fashion among women to die by placing their saris on fire." All of you said, "this is all play-acting (*natak*)." Perhaps. However, why the theatrical amusement is always performed over the *saris* of Bengali women and not the *konchas* of the brave Bengali men, requires some thinking as well.[49]

The specific context in which Rabindranath wrote *Strir Patra* was the controversy aroused by the suicide of a 16-year-old Bengali girl, who burnt herself to death two weeks before her marriage.[50] The excessive dowry demanded by the prospective in-laws would have financially ruined her parents. The reference to theatrical performance here has another implication. One of the most common criticisms of Bengali women reading novels and watching modern dramatic performances was that these provided women with unsuitable role models and inspired them to think of their own selves in romantic terms.[51] It is such a sense of self that enabled a woman to claim her own life as a way of claiming her own body. Both reading novels and attending the public theater, of course, implied the possibility of women having their own space – a privilege that was customary only for men. In the short story, *Manbhanjan* (1905) Rabindranath had explored the problem of this unequal access.[52]

The young, beautiful Giribala, housewife in an upper-class family in Calcutta spends her time in the sole company of a maid-servant, while her husband spends his nights outside the house with an actress. One day Giribala visits the theater to judge the attraction for herself, and is transfixed by the play. Soon after, her husband abuses her and leaves the house for the actress. Giribala then announces that she is leaving for her family home. But instead she joins the theater and becomes a successful actress. Her husband, curious about this new actress, shows up at the theater. He is furious upon recognizing the actress on stage as his wife and attempts to disrupt the play. He is thrown out of the theater, while "all of Calcutta filled their eyes with Giribala's performance."[53]

From Rabindranath's carving out a space outside the home for Mrinal and Giribala we cannot, of course, presume that he approved of this "extra-marital" space. For him the tragedy resides in women having to occupy this space outside home, and yet it is only through this move into the outside world that they achieve self-worth. Even when Rabindranath waxed eloquent on the figure of the *grihalakshmi* (housewife/goddess of the household) as the harbinger of beauty and poetry (in opposition to the colonial office where men slave away in a dismal environment), he did not extend that poetics to the "home," per se. Just as in *Bishabriksha* Bankim was insistently demonstrating the well-regulated domestic space as refuge, straining against the strength of his story line, in short stories written in the first two decades of the twentieth century Rabindranath continually exposed the deficiencies and limitations of such hallowed imagination.

We must, however, note the difference between Mrinal's and Giribala's "emancipatory" moves. Mrinal's defiant statement, "I am writing this letter to clearly explain that I will not die," acquires a twist. Stepping outside the household she would have died a ritual death, that is, if she did not suffer real death from murder or suicide. Mrinal turns this notion upside down. She refuses to sacrifice her life within the conjugal bonds of such a household, seeking release in a spiritual world where she can finally begin to live. No despair can claim her life now. Mrinal leaves home and travels to Puri, a pilgrimage site that carries a deep spiritual and literary resonance for Bengalis. Standing on the sea shore at Puri, she attains her true consciousness through a communion with God/Nature. This consciousness is the attainment of *bhakti*. By realizing God's love she has been able to discard her identity as "Mejobou" – "He is looking upon me with loving eyes, He finds this unappreciated self (*rup*) in me beautiful. Mejobou has died at last."[54] Rabindranath is playing on the semantics of the Bengali word *"moreche"* (died) to refer to both "falling in love" as well as to a transformation of socially ascribed identity.

In the background of Mrinal's enlightenment is the story of the Bengali medieval Vaishnav saint Chaitanya who spent his last days in Puri. In devotional literature Chaitanya's suicide is portrayed as attainment of God; in a state of spiritual ecstasy he walked into the blue ocean imagining it to be the embodiment of the dark-skinned Krishna.

By the time Rabindranath wrote *Strir Patra*, Vaishnav *bhakti* had become a channel through which many women authors found ways to claim an autonomous space within the patriarchal bounds of nineteenth-century Bengali society.[55] Vaishnavis (female practitioners of Vaishnavism) were almost the only women who were well educated. They had inherited a literate tradition and were employed as teachers for women in wealthy households.[56] Consequently, Vaishnav *bhakti* was a logical choice for Rabindranath to indicate an autonomous space of imagination and action for his fictional female characters.

And yet how different is this space from the space that Giribala came to occupy on stage. Giribala's loss of home is substituted by a life on stage where she is exposed to the eyes of the entire city. The concluding scene of *Manbhanjan* is also the concluding scene of the play "Monorama" in which the actress Giribala enters the stage/bedroom as the newly wed beautiful woman to the surprise of her own husband. When Giribala acts out the intimacy of conjugality on stage, seducing her stage-husband and the audience, the revelation is that of her physical beauty. At that moment Giribala, the neglected housewife recognizes her power as the woman who is physically beautiful. Such awareness is appropriate in the space of the theater, where domesticity is performed as make-believe, and seeks resolution through the revelation of the physical self. The domestic performance with which Giribala could not gain her own husband's attention, assumes "reality" on stage. Her "domestic" performance on stage becomes credible to her audience. Here, the woman (without husband) reigns in popularity, if not respectability. When the respectability of marriage and life within domestic confines proves to be a sham, she claims in public a finite recognition of a different sort.

Mrinal's revelation, her recognition of the insignificance of marital bonds, socially approved domestic conduct, and her inner self, however, moves beyond the physical and touches the infinite resources and calm of the spiritual. It is only in a natural setting suffused with the strains of Vaishnav *bhakti*, that Rabindranath could find a space for Mrinal to inhabit in public. He falls back on the broad contours of the city/pilgrimage site, material/spiritual to articulate a much-nuanced modern subjectivity. His spatial imagination of Calcutta could not admit of any such space of spiritual release for women within the city. His insistence on finding a place for women in Bengali literary imagination works out as their displacement from the city's public space. Had his character been male, this spatial transference would not have been necessary. It may be relevant to mention here, that Rabindranath himself recalled having felt his own spiritual transformation while watching sunrise from a house on Sudder Street in Calcutta.[57]

The trouble with their bodies

Actresses in the nineteenth century inhabited not only a problematic space in Bengali literary modernity, but as colonial subjects they could be subject to an entirely different set of rules. As modern subjects, the significance of the actress/prostitute and the "respectable woman" (*bhadramahila*) resided in the interface of two types of discourse: national (literary) and colonial (legislative). In this section I will examine the normative spatial imagination that animates these discourses of granting and refusing women space in the city.

Popular literature, missionary tracts, government reports, and newspapers all attest to the existence of well-established brothels along every major street in Calcutta, immediately adjacent to middle-class and wealthy houses and educational institutions.[58] "The Annual Report of the State of the Police of the Town of Calcutta for 1852–53" claimed a "frightful amount of prostitution in the city," with 12,419 women of ill-fame occupying 4,049 homes, and "a large number . . . whose habits are less openly abandoned."[59] The Contagious Diseases Act of 1868 (CDA) was intended to extend the reach of the 1864 Cantonment Act devised to protect European soldiers from venereal disease. While the Cantonment Act regulated a small population of Indian prostitutes meant to serve British soldiers, the CDA brought within its jurisdiction the common prostitutes. The CDA was applied to Calcutta in 1869, and was the first concerted effort to negotiate prostitution in the city. Much has been written about the ideological and political significance of the CDA that made some blatant assumptions about race, class, and the rights of European men vis-à-vis Indian women.[60] Here, I want to analyze the application of the law in Calcutta in order to foreground two aspects of this larger debate. The first has to do with the classificatory goals of the CDA, and the second with the difficulty of regulating prostitution in large cities such as Calcutta.

The objective of the CDA was to define the population among Indian prostitutes who consorted with British soldiers, and to keep them free of disease so that the soldiers would not contract venereal disease from them. Two key assumptions went into its formulation. First, one could not expect soldiers to control their sexual appetites, and a pool of prostitutes was the only alternative to the absent wives. Second, venereal disease emanated from the body of the woman. Consequently, it was this location of the disease that had to be contained before one could gain from monitoring the health of the soldiers. Prostitutes were required to register themselves with the local police, indicating a willingness to pursue the trade, and periodically subject themselves to medical examination and compulsory treatment if they were found to have contracted a disease. If they failed to report for examinations they were subject to imprisonment.

A report of 1868 arguing for the enactment of the CDA submitted this description of Calcutta:

> there is not a single street in the Native town where these unfortunate creatures are not found in numbers, or a *bustee*, a quarter of the female population of which does not consist of single and unprotected women without any ostensible means of earning a livelihood . . . Sobha Bazar and Durmahata Streets are infested by them. Chitpore Road from north to south, is swarming with these women, so are Cornwallis Street and College Streets, the centres of educational establishment for the young Hindoo population. The three-fourths of the female population of Goa-Bagan are prostitutes. This class of women are to be found everywhere in Calcutta – in the three-storied house, of Sobha Bazar as well as the most dilapidated and miserable hut of the filthiest *bustee*.[61]

The same report classified the prostitute population among seven groups, using a curious admixture of class, caste, race, and location in the city: Hindoo women of "high caste who live a retired life, and who are kept and supported by rich natives"; Hindoo women of "good caste, who being possessed of small means, live by themselves, receiving a limited number of visitors of their own, or of a superior caste"; "Hindoo women living under a Barreewallah, either male or female . . . and receiv(ing) visitors without distinction of caste"; "dancing women, Hindu or Mussalman, living singly, or forming a kind of chummery, under the apparent protection of some man, but practicing prostitution publicly, and receiving visitors without distinction of creed or caste"; Mussalman public prostitutes; low caste Hindoos and low Christian prostitutes; and European prostitutes.

The problem of applying the CDA began with a difficulty of recognition. The breathless condemnation of these reports, punctuated by classificatory efforts, demonstrated both a desire to believe that description and classification would somehow contain the corrupt bodies in space and map out a system for deciphering the immoral landscape, and at the same time brought home the impossibility of containing the population. The overwhelming visibility of the prostitutes in the city, instead of producing a transparency only seemed to proliferate an indeterminacy, thwarting any possibility of enumerating the population accurately.

In reading the administration's predicament, we must remember that the goal was not to eradicate prostitution from the city. Rather, a population of prostitutes was deemed necessary for the functioning of the colonial army. The attempt was to contain the *visibility* of prostitutes in the landscape. However, in extending the jurisdiction of the CDA to the city, one had to deal with the local municipality and ensure its support. The well-being of the soldiers had to appear congruent with the well-being of the residents of the city at large. The government, for example, expected the Calcutta Municipality to pay for the cost of Lock hospitals, and consequently it repeatedly appealed to the "moral" and "scientific" sensibilities of the Justices (later Commissioners) – "it is a measure of public hygiene in the true sense of the word. . . . It is a moral and public duty the Justices have to perform." In fact, the Municipality owed it to the soldiers:

> Calcutta owes its prosperity, and the inhabitants their security and wealth, to a class who, until recently, seemed to have been totally forgotten by us, – to those men whom Dr. Chevers in his lectures calls, with just pride, the intrepid sons of Great Britain.[62]

Proponents of the CDA brought to bear on this problem a rhetorical repertoire that had been developed by the colonial medical profession in the description of the colonial landscape as a diseased entity needing European supervision. Both the prostitute's body and the space of the colonial city were deemed to require the same techniques of sanitary regulation. By treating the bodies of prostitutes in an instrumental manner as sites of medical inspection and action, one could hope to act upon the conditions of visibility of women in public space. Colonial medical practice that had launched itself by claiming a mastery of the environment found itself ideologically well geared to launch an enthusiastic campaign for identifying and inspecting prostitutes.[63]

Cataloging and mapping, and thus determining a population of prostitutes, however, turned out to be a formidable project. Sanitation reports spoke of the existence of a class of women who practiced prostitution in a clandestine or irregular manner. By 1872 it came to be recognized that "a large number of women evaded the law . . . with impunity."[64] Since the burden of proof lay with the police, a woman could not simply be arrested because her life was "disorderly." The police also had to prove that she had received money by plying her trade. Many were married women, "who, in not a few cases, with the connivance of their husbands, added in this manner to their small means of subsistence."[65]

As the CDA became a vehicle for apprehending prostitution at large, irrespective of clientele, the difficulties of controlling prostitution touched on the larger issue of arousing disaffection among the native community. A stricter and wider application of the law would, it was feared, only target "chiefly those of the higher classes who are mostly inaccessible to Europeans." It was generally acknowledged that prostitution, in nineteenth-century Calcutta, was intimately linked with the economic and social interests of the city's landed gentry. Any legislation that attempted to deal with the city's prostitution at large had to encounter this fact. For British administrators the recognition of different classes of prostitutes was important precisely to distinguish the domains of two important constituencies – European soldiers and the native landed gentry. The administrators could not devise any satisfactory criteria by which to isolate this class from the larger population of the city. In 1871 the Sanitary Commissioner indicated that there was little or no relation between the proportion of women on the register and the actual number of prostitutes in the city, and that "considerable diversity of practice obtains in this matter of registration."[66]

Bengali commissioners of the Calcutta Municipality who saw the wider application of the CDA as infringements upon "their" community, protested attempts to give the local police extra powers to arrest offenders on an allegation of prostitution. What would be considered sufficient to arouse such suspicion, they asked. What if a "respectable" woman was accosted merely on the charge of speaking to a man, someone she knew? The Bengali commissioners, in fact, tried to turn the table on the European gentry of the city by suggesting that Anglo-Indian shop-girls and those women who frequented the drives in the evening be looked upon as possible sexual offenders as well.[67] Presumably there were no external signs that marked the prostitute from that of a "respectable" woman. Early legislative measures had assumed that classification of prostitutes would bypass this problem, and the population would present itself in terms of the classi-fication. As the reports indicated, this did not work. The grey areas of respectability were utilized to evade the law, and to both speak for and against legislative measures.

Even the accommodation of patients under the CDA became a bone of contention. Many in the administration considered the building of Lock hospitals in central locations or even in the southern suburbs unaccept-able.[68] Prostitutes could not be admitted to the female ward of the General Hospital, because "women decent in their modes of life . . . would regard the admission of the class indicated as a degradation and an insult." The Surgeon-Major of the General Hospital conceded that in the past some "syphilitic cases" had been admitted in the female ward, but then they had not been received as *"declared as prostitutes suffering from syphilis"* (original emphasis).[69] A legislation that received impetus from an eagerness to protect European soldiers by monitoring the bodies and spaces of a certain class of prostitutes, soon turned out to be a problem of deciphering the avowed from clandestine practitioners, of distinguishing between respectable women in public and public women.

In 1881 the government decided to retract from its earlier proposition to curb prostitution in the city at large, and instead concentrated on executing a "sanitary cordon." In colonial urbanism, a sanitary cordon referred to the band of space – often a green belt – that separated black and white towns, the *cordonne sanitaire* supposedly acting as a disease barrier for the protection of white residents. In Calcutta this idea was adapted quite differently. The Commissioner of Police in Calcutta designated certain areas "in which women who are visited by soldiers reside,"[70] and instituted a sanitary cordon around these areas. The core of this regula-tory space were the neighborhoods adjoining Fort William, and from there it extended to enclose an area between the river to the west and the Circular Road to the east, and from Colootola Road to the north and Garden Reach Road to the south.[71] Prostitutes residing in this area were not allowed to go elsewhere to pursue their profession, and soldiers and non-commissioned officers were under orders not to go beyond the "sani-tary cordon." Faced with trenchant opposition from many sections of the press and the Indian community, the CDA was abandoned in 1886. It had become clear to the administrators that the CDA had little impact on the problem of venereal disease among the soldiers.

If the CDA, faced with the impossibility of controlling the visibility of prostitutes in the landscape, took upon the task of sanitizing the site of sexual encounter, that is, the bodies of the prostitutes, then the nationalist literature produced by Bengali men set itself the project of occluding the woman's body from the landscape on the belief that the body could not be "sanitized," so to speak.

The obsession with respectable women's access to public space in Bengali literature touched on various social issues. But in the shadow of all such debates worked the figure of the prostitute – as a constant even if sometimes silent referent. The literary elite's attempt to separate the body and mind of the modern female subject to allay the threat that her sexuality otherwise might pose, exposed its ideological trappings most clearly when it crossed paths with the more prosaic domain of popular literature and "housekeeping guides." It is the latter genre in Bengali – and here I am referring to a wide range of social tracts and guides under this appellation – that produced the perceived trouble over women's bodies most unabashedly. Most of these from the late nineteenth century were written by men, and differed from those of the female authors, particularly those that were published in the 1910s and 1920s. Since my purpose is to locate the form of male anxiety, I will concentrate primarily on the former.

By mid-century the visibility of women in public space had found a place in Bengali literature. Kaliprasanna Sinha's satire *Hutom Penchar Naksha* is replete with images of women in the city's public places – in the bazaars and market places, selling flowers and vegetables, haggling with customers, partaking in public performances, and gazing at the bustling street life. By evening the red-light areas of the city – Mechobazaar, Harihata, the corner of Chorebagan, Poddar's shop in Jorasanko, Notun Bazaar, Battala, the lanes of Sonagachi, and the crossing of Ahiritola – swarmed with people.[72] The density of experience was formed as much by the crowd and the number of activities as by the permeability of the urban fabric that allowed sounds and sights to infiltrate the buildings that lined the streets. The shops and dwellings that lined the main streets had the most privileged seats to watch the ongoing drama on the street. The physical artifacts that made that connection possible were the proliferating thresholds and transition spaces: the verandahs, *ro'aks*, terraces, windows, and doorways that opened directly on to the street, making the presence of women an integral part of street life. Describing a Durga Puja procession Kaliprasanna Sinha wrote:

> The wide road of Chitpur was filled with people. The prostitutes watched the *tamasha* from the roof tops and verandahs while enjoying their silver decorated hookahs; the people on the streets were caught between seeing the moving image of Durga and the standing images of the prostitutes.[73]

While Kaliprasanna would go on to rue the blurring of distinctions between *bhadralok* and *chotolok*, the respectable classes and the lower classes, Kaliprasanna's description of the city was based on an intimate familiarity with the milieu. It also implied a pleasurable complicity on the part of the native residents with the "disorderly" public life of prostitutes. From time to time, the educated Bengali middle-class men joined hands with European missionaries to condemn the public visibility of prostitutes – the favorite suggestion, once made by Kaliprasanna himself, being to remove the red-light districts to the outskirts of the city, as one would a polluting factory.[74] The suggestion was never taken up seriously, as the native gentry had too much at stake in the existing urban fabric.

For the Bengali middle class, Calcutta's heterogeneous landscape meant that there was always an imminent threat of being influenced by the lower classes, or worse, being mistaken for one of them. In dime novels we find the "modern" man speaking against the traditional outings of respectable women in the city – going to the Ganga for bathing, and visiting the temple at Kalighat – on the premise that these were sites frequented by the lower classes and prostitutes; it was increasingly becoming difficult to decipher class distinctions in such places. His preferred alternative – an evening drive to the esplanade – is refused by the "ideal" modest female character in the novel as too "westernized" a habit for women.[75]

The traditional proponents of seclusion emphasized that the women not be seen or heard, but in a dense city like Calcutta, it was far more difficult to control what the women heard from the streets and the outer compartments, and what they saw from within their confines. For the new middle class, however, it became equally important that, at least within the household, the information that reached women in the form of sight and sound be censored. Respectable women would be influenced by the innumerable prostitutes in the city and become attracted to their loose morals and freedom, they argued. The densely linked urban form had become too easy for the lower-class culture to infiltrate through the many interstices of the urban fabric. In a landscape that physically resisted the isolation of different groups and refused to be polarized, fresh attempts were made to construct the space of the respectable woman so as to distinguish her from the public woman or prostitute.

The prescriptions of housekeeping manuals all concerned "respectable" women, and were premised on three basic ideas: that Bengali households demonstrated a lack of the modern virtues of cleanliness, health, and beauty; that middle-class women needed to be told about the ideals and duties of a good housewife, and that they needed to learn new modes of housekeeping in the interest of the nation. In short they prescribed household reform as a service to the husband, family, and the nation. Few actually concerned themselves with the house as a physical artifact, even while speaking of the desire to prescribe domestic space and the language of material culture. They were written within a growing sensibility about the porosity of the household envelope, and set their objectives in terms of abstract ideals. The pressing concern of these authors was the education, sexual behavior, social labor of women, and their desire to step out of the bounds of domesticity.

In setting their ideal of the good woman, the housekeeping guides insisted upon retaining the first principle of the Bengali household – a distinction between *andar-mahal* and *bahir-mahal*. Two inter-related precepts were to guide the conduct of women: *lajjashilata* (modesty) and *satitwa* (chastity).

In explaining the quality of *lajja*, Satishchandra Chakrabarty noted: "*Lajja* in women is like a beautiful ornament. . . . Another great benefit of *lajja* is that it does not allow a woman to take the wrong path."[76]

Bhudhev Mukhopadhyay in his authoritative work *Paribarik Prabandha* (Essay on Domesticity) banished any idea that women could attain these qualities of modesty without the husband's instruction. In his essays addressed to a male audience, he placed the responsibility of the woman's work, education, and moral character squarely on the shoulders of the husband.[77] He was to adopt an active educative and advisory role to his wife, who in return was to submit completely to his tutelage. The instilling of appropriate conduct in the woman, with due attention to *lajjashilata* rested on the husband.[78] This was contrary to traditional practice in which the task of teaching housewifely duties to a young bride resided with the mother-in-law and the senior women in the household. What Bhudev essentially did was to set up a new conjugal space in which other relations, particularly those of the women in the family, receded in comparison to the husband as teacher.

For Bhudev, the central fallacy was any presumption of equality between men and women. Hindu marriage, he reminded, was not a contract, but a *samskaar* (belief, sacrament) that made for the coming together of the man and woman completely as one, with the precondition that the wife submit to the husband's wishes unquestioningly.[79] In such a relationship *samsaardharma* (household duties) constituted a single phenomenon, that could not be split without the husband relinquishing his sole authority. The woman, in Bhudev's world, could not aspire to any form of subjectivity, any kind of existence that was somehow unrelated to the will of her master. Her entire social and reproductive labor, even her deportment and respect in society could only gather significance if her husband chose to grant her so.[80] Praising the inseparability of religion and daily life in the "Arya system," he pronounced that in European society the wife is a partner and companion, in Arya society she is a goddess – a goddess who nevertheless needs to imbibe spiritual traits from the husband. Herein lies the critical difference between Bhudev's and Bankim's rhetoric about woman's agency. Bankim's women "choose" to submit to the new patriarchy because they come to understand the well-being of the primary unit of community – the home – better than the men. Bhudev had no need for this subterfuge.

The concept of *grihalaksmi*, that is the secularization of the idea of the goddess of prosperity and fecundity, could be brought to bear its full meaning in defining the status of the desirable housewife, once her total submission to the husband was mandated. For Bhudev, the expression of *sattitwa* was the constant desire to *see* one's husband – "as soon as the husband is out of sight her world is empty . . . any work that does not involve the worship of the husband does not even occur to the *sati*."[81] Her vision engaged completely in her husband, it was unnecessary to pay attention to the spaces that remained unoccupied by his presence, including that of her own body. The woman's figure in Bhudev's idealized imagination was empty, waiting the husband's fulfillment.

That emptiness, in the eyes of most authors, could be masked by the metaphor of the goddess or by the metaphor of the whore with equal ease. The inextricable connection between *lajja* and *satitwa* generated a visual economy that constructed the woman's body as irreducibly sexed, one that needed to be placed under wraps to sustain the moral order of the community:

> Women are by nature irresolute and desirous, and if they are allowed to travel at will, then will it not bring forth bad fruit? . . . "If the woman does not get the place, the opportunity, and the intermediary, then over time she might per chance become a *sati*."[82]

Since *satitwa* in the language of these male authors was not a natural attribute of a woman, one that needed cultivation against every natural urge of the woman herself, she had to be watched incessantly, and denied every possibility of having her own private space (*nirjane*) in which to contemplate and converse. For women, certain forms of orality and access to public space were meant to be read as transgressions that invariably translated into a slide from respectability to prostitution.

In this spatial arrangement, public education for women became controversial. Women's education was perceived as a threat to the traditional extended family, where girls married at a very young age and were expected to obey the rules of the household. Consequently, when social reformers attempted to establish schools for girls in the city, the conservative section of Bengali society did not take such efforts kindly.[83] Deterrents to small girls traveling to school included the threat of physical violence and rape, publicly announced in contemporary journals. Caricatures of the educated woman lasted well into the twentieth century. Nineteenth-century Kalighat paintings of the woman trampling on her husband, gave way to Jatin Sen's depiction of a women sitting on a chair reading a book and smoking an oversized cigar. What we find in these housekeeping guides is an anxiety about gender ambiguity being articulated in the language of sexual promiscuity – the ambiguity between the respectable woman and the prostitute.

The equation of formal education and sexual liberties was closely tied to the fear that labor in the household was about to change if women were to devote part of the day to studies. Right into the twentieth century, the household remained a primary site of production. In this respect there was little difference between the rural and urban household. A massive amount of labor went into different stages of food production, from husking grain, making dairy products, grinding spice, cooking, and serving. The heavy work of washing dishes and grinding spices was done by servants in most middle-class homes. That still left the "respectable" women with a packed routine. Women were also meant to perform the daily religious rituals of the household that the men increasingly could not find time to perform. Even in wealthy households, women were expected to do a very large share of the housework.[84]

Leisure for women was considered debilitating. Household advice to even small girls drilled in the need to labor in the pretext of "getting exercise." While young boys were to learn swimming, engage in sports, girls of comparable age were expected to play a little but concentrate on those physical activities that were productive – husking grain, sweeping floors, laundering clothes, and doing dishes.[85] Such exercise was meant to ensure that the woman would be healthy to bear children, while at the same time leaving her no idle time for immoral acquaintance. Bhudev chided the men for allowing their wives to neglect housework under the influence of received notions of social equality and the false impression that Englishwomen did not labor in the household.[86] Issues of household economy and women's education were carefully tied to the moral and physical well-being of the family and, in extension, the nation, for both liberals and conservatives like Bhudev.[87]

The ground of argument for and against women's education was the same on both sides of the divide. Throughout the nineteenth century Bengali reformers argued for female education not for the sake of the women themselves, but to fulfill a higher cause of building a better nation.[88] More importantly the environment of these schools had to mimic the Bengali household. Radhakanta Deb had set this precedent in 1848. A few days after the Hindu Female School was established with the blessings of the government and on the pledge of admitting only Hindu students, Radhakanta Deb started a school for girls in his own house. Deb argued that girls in respectable families were given a basic education until they were married and these families would not condescend to send their daughters to public schools. Within the private confines of his own mansion, however, he could control the course content and behavior of these women, thus alleviating the threat public education posed to their respectability. Such communal education, he could argue to his conservative constituents, was still domesticated, and there was no threat that the women would be inculcated with unsuitable ideas propagated in missionary schools. For the women, one of the rewards of school education was precisely the ability to go out of their households, see things that they had been denied, and converse with people they never had an opportunity to know. But only if the woman carried with herself the envelope of domesticity itself could this move to the outside world be legitimated.

Several decades later, while Kailashbasini Gupta vehemently denounced the Bengali home as a dark site of ignorance and oppression, she could only produce a guarded vision of public schools. She argued that although proper education for women was necessary, girls' schools had to cultivate a domestic environment before girls could be allowed to attend.[89] These spaces needed to be modeled after "Hindu *antahpurs*" if they were to be suitable. In other words, if public places had to be suitable for women, they had to be designed as domestic space. I would like to suggest an interesting reversal occurring here. After all, for Kailashbasini, the model could not be the contemporary Bengali home, which she did not see as the possible site of improvement. For her this was not the autonomous space of Bankim's imagination where women loved, played, and ruled as queens of the household, with the loving consent of their husbands. Only properly designed public schools could become the enlightened *antahpur*, where women could develop their selves in a surrogate domesticity free from the intervention of men.

Almost every form of public space for women carried with it the model of an ideal domestic space. But in each case the importation of this model into public space was different. What might seem as Kailashbasini's capitulating to the demands of patriarchy may actually be underwritten by the deep desire to reinvent "women's space" itself.

The problem was also viewed from the other side of the lens. Abanindranath Tagore recalled a "creative" effort to construct an appropriate space for women in public. The Tagore family put up their own show on public stage, and since the women of the household could not attend an event in public space, for one day the theater was reserved for the family alone. It was not enough, however, to control the access of outsiders. The men in the family felt it necessary to get rid of the usual furnishing of the theater, and redecorate it as if it were a residential space.[90] If women had to attend a theater, the reminders of "publicness" had to be removed. The space was denuded of any references to "being in public," thus allowing respectable women entry.

The conceptual model of woman-death-public space, with which I began this chapter, operated in the above example, as much as it did in Bhudev's or Bankim's writings. Even as the different strands of nationalist thought produced areas of disagreement, they informed each other to produce an entire set of symbols, spaces, and behavioral codes that came to be understood as distinctly Bengali, modern, and respectable. The symbols included a different way of wearing the sari, a manner of speech, and bodily comportment. Appropriate clothes for women, in particular, proved to be a controversial issue. Some of the suggestions for wearing a blouse, jacket, and shoes not only smacked of the *memsahib*, but the idea of jackets and shoes too closely resembled the attire of men. To add to the concern, prostitutes were also donning these articles of clothing. To distinguish between the respectable woman and prostitute, the former was expected to put on a wrapper over the sari when she stepped out of the house. The dress that ultimately became accepted was the *bramhika* sari, complete with a jacket and petticoat. It was clearly set apart from the ordinary way the lower classes wore the sari, without a blouse or petticoat. The elite who prescribed these dress codes emphasized that the saris should not be made of transparent muslin, but of stouter, opaque fabric. The bounds of seclusion and privacy inside the household, characterized by various degrees of opacity, were translated to the public domain in the form of the individual personal space of every *bhadramahila* or "respectable" Bengali woman.

If we must think of the experience of the city in terms of a public/domestic distinction, in the late nineteenth century that distinction became drawn around the figure of the *bhadramahila*. On this figure was located all the symbols of a new privacy, symbols that were emphatically opposed to those associated with the public domain inhabited by the lower classes and prostitutes. Within the boundaries cast by middle-class Bengali society, her bearing, dress, speech, and access, were insistently interiorized, and she could only vicariously inhabit the public domain. The woman was placed in the position of *visible inaccessibility* that was predicated on already available male access. After all, control over the bodies of women was not to protect the women, but to protect the freedom of the men to move between the two worlds of the prostitute and the *bhadramahila* without conflict.

In examining the location of women in the Bengali public sphere, one is made aware of the stakes involved in the gendered marking of public space. The successful functioning of the public sphere increasingly came to depend on the ability to imagine, configure, and control admission into public spaces. Reshaped according to middle-class male hegemonic aspirations, it was the practice of public space and its understanding as a strategic extension of domestic space that continued to haunt Bengali imagination of the possible "modern."

Mapping domesticity

I have been studying the dominant male discourse produced by both the colonizer and the colonized at the risk of reifying a certain form of textual authority. In conclusion, I wish to complicate the implications of this form by posing the following questions: are there ways of thinking about the experience of nineteenth-century Bengali women other than as ciphers that stand for ideological structures, or as categorical sites where they become the arena for ideological warfare? If nineteenth-century novels and housekeeping guides reinforce the taxonomy of *andar-sadar*, *ghare-baire*, did these constructs retain the same meanings when they touched the physical correlates of space? How did these distinctions operate in practice?

The evidence on prostitution and the anxiety over women's space – personal, public, and institutional – expressed in housekeeping guides, I have argued, suggests an unmanageable porosity between taxonomic boundaries. Any effort at representing the woman in the public sphere threatened to assault the boundaries between that which was domestic and that which was public. The central paradox of devising a new domesticity congruent with the middle-class male desire to confine women to their "natural" sphere (the home) was that it could only be materialized through a passage in the public sphere and public space. Sometimes this meant literally the need to drag out the women from confinement to have them attest to the extent and effectiveness of seclusion. At other times, the authorial access into the inner workings of domestic space and the female characters of the novel, was itself viewed as a form of transgression. Sashisekhar Basu recounted an anecdote of a romantic novel being read aloud to a domestic audience of an extended family, *c.*1875.[91] Among the questions asked by the audience was the troubling issue of whether such romantic relationships actually took place in respectable households – how did the author know of these dalliances? Had the author bothered to enter a middle-class home to know how things actually were? The questions from the female audience were more critical as the author was, presumably, a man. What did men know of how a household was run? Apart from questioning men's knowledge of the household, these questions contain the problem of how appropriate was it to write about, to represent, the inner workings of a respectable family, making it available to a public?

The problem of "representing" the *bhadramahila* in the nineteenth century involved not simply finding her appropriate place within the normative categories of *andar/bahir*, but also the troubling question of "exposing" the female figure and her normative space of the *andar-mahal* to the public gaze. It is in the troubled territory between domesticity and publicness, at precisely the moments when their "respectability" became challenged that Bengali women found it possible to make room for their own claims to space and subjectivity.

The *andar-mahal*, the conduct of women, and the practice of *purdah* (seclusion) in Bengali social discourse had everything to do with the family's claim to respectability. As a cultural construct, *purdah* conveyed protection from unwanted physical, aural, but most significantly, visual contact. Amritalal Basu, in fact, suggested that the new conditions of seclusion not be understood as *purdah*.[92] What we see in Amritalal's writing is the nationalist desire to move the language of social construction of the household away from the old categories that could not be rescued from the taint of (Muslim) oppression and hidden from legislative intervention of the colonial government.

In British colonial discourse the *andar-mahal* or the *zenana* carried certain connotations not necessarily compatible with Bengali notions of domesticity and the status of women. As a space removed from male gaze, unless related to the family, the *zenana* and the status of Hindu (as well as Muslim) women attracted intense curious speculation among British circles, much of which was nurtured by Orientalist visions of sexual promiscuity and/or enslaved brown women deprived of monogamous domestic bliss.

The practice of *purdah*, among both upper-class Hindu and Muslim families, designed to shield women from the outsider's gaze had an important legal implication. The *purdanashin* (woman behind the *purdah*) was granted certain protections under colonial jurisprudence on the assumption of her vulnerability against unscrupulous family members and strangers. This vulnerability was a product of the *purdanashin*'s lack of knowledge of the outside world, a lack of education that would qualify her to make informed choice in legal matters, as well as the practice of seclusion that provided barriers to her free movement. It was the colonial equivalent of protecting the "weak, ignorant, and infirm" under the law in England. The establishment of the criteria, however, was complicated; at the end of the nineteenth century not all women of Bengali Hindu households would qualify for this protection. The 1898 legal suit brought by Nistarini Dasee, a 37-year-old widow from an upper-class Bengali family, against her brothers-in-law (husband's brothers), Nandalal Basu and Pashupati Basu, illustrated this problem.[93] The latter two, it may be relevant to mention, are remembered in the city's history for their contribution to the Bengali community and, in particular, to the nationalist cause. Nistarini's name is virtually forgotten.

Nistarini Dasee was married at the age of 11 to a man almost 30 years older. She became a widow two years later, and since that time resided in her in-laws' house. She was never told by her in-laws that her husband had willed a third of the family property in her name, but she heard it from her grandfather. She shared a room with her widowed sister-in-law (husband's sister), Kadambini, and performed the range of chores and religious duties expected of a widow in the household. In addition she took care of her bed-ridden mother-in-law. When the two brothers, Nandalal and Pashupati, divided the house into two properties they did not consider it necessary to give Nistarini her own separate space. When they divided the silver utensils and the gold and precious jewelry between themselves, Nistarini's share in these was simply overlooked. Only upon specifically and repeatedly asking for a monthly remittance was she given the paltry sum of 25 rupees.

In her suit Nistarini Dasee claimed that her deceased husband's younger brothers had refused her the share in family property that her late husband had willed in her name. In the course of the legal proceedings it also became clear that Nistarini's husband had only willed the landed property in three parts, between his wife and his two brothers. But nothing was mentioned in the will about the moveable property. In other words, technically speaking, all moveable property in the household could be considered to be Nistarini's. The suit itself resulted when Nistarini's brothers-in-law had a dispute about family property, and Nandalal pressured Nistarini to join his side in the legal wrangle. She was upset when served with an attorney's letter. She wanted to be left out of the dispute. Nandalal refused to comply, fully cognizant that as someone who had a legal right to the family property (although she had been deprived of that

right by deception), her support was critical. When everyday modes of
social pressure did not work, he tried intimidation. One day he arrived
in the *andar-mahal* with the *kulaguru* (religious advisor to the family),
Upendranath Thakur, to meet Nistarini. This is how Nistarini described
their arrival and what followed:

> I was in the *dallan* (verandah) of the inner apartment of the house and
> as soon as I saw him coming I ran into the adjoining room. . . . Nundo
> Baboo came and stood in the *dallan* (verandah) where I had been and
> asked Kadambini as to where I was. She pointed out the room into
> which I was. He came into this room. Nundo Baboo did with the
> Thakur Mohasoy. I gave the Thakur Mohasoy a carpet to sit on. The
> Thakur Mohasoy took his seat on the carpet and Nundo Baboo closed
> the door of the room and sat against the door with his back to the door
> and asked me to sit down and I did so. He said that he got me married
> and had brought me after the marriage to the house and ever since
> I had been living with him and all along doing as he wished me to
> do. That he was quite sure that I would do as he wished me to do;
> that I had done all along whatever he told me to do; that he had never
> had to find any fault with me; that every one was satisfied with my good
> conduct, and that my good conduct was a source of pride to the family
> and that he always boasted about it to outsiders. That he all along
> respected and esteemed me, that he had never knowingly done me
> wrong. . . . When this conversation was going on Pashupati Baboo
> came to the *dallan* (verandah). On hearing his voice Nundo Baboo bolted
> the door which had been closed before. Pashupati Baboo then went to
> the eastern verandah and stood near that door of the room which opens
> out to the verandah. Nundo Baboo got up and went to the door to bolt
> it, and on seeing Pashupati Baboo said, "who is there? Is it you Pashu?"
> You had better go to the outer apartments for a short time, we have a
> private conversation with Boro Bow (meaning me) and in fact we are
> having that conversation. Upon that Pashupati said that it was not at
> all proper to have conversation with the Thakur Mohasoy in my pres-
> ence after bolting the door of the room at night. He, Pashupati, furthur
> said that he (Nundo Lall) might carry on litigation as he was doing, but
> it was not a proper thing to have a private conversation in a room after
> bolting the doors. He (Nundo Lall) could not do these two things at the
> same time. It was not consistent. Thereupon the Thakur Mohasoy said
> "Oh is it you Pashupati? Come in, come into the room." . . . Thakur
> Mohasoy said, Why should I carry on litigation? It was not the proper
> thing to do so. Nundo Baboo was willing to pay all and every expense
> that I might incur performing religious and pious acts. . . . Thakur
> Mohasoy also said that Nundo Baboo would not put any cash in my
> hands, but he would pay all expenses in respect of religious and pious
> acts I might perform.[94]

Several years prior to the suit Nistarini had wanted money from Nandalal to build a *chandni* (covering) at Neogi's Ghat on the Ganga as an act of religious merit, but was refused by Nandalal. The *kulaguru* on that day, however, emphasized the merit of religious deeds undertaken by a widow. In Bengali society, this could be construed more as a threat than a charity on the part of the family. Widows were often expected to spend their lives at pilgrimage sites out of the sight and protection of their households.

When Nistarini refused her support even after the religious advisor's intervention, Nandalal threatened her with a summons. This meant she would have to appear in a public court. Nistarini, who had made little of the property rights she had been refused by her husband's brothers until then, was incensed at this provocation. To her, the attorney's letter and the summons were artifacts of the public world that she had never partaken in, and which she saw as infringements on her self. Getting involved in the dispute between the brothers implied a sudden change of rules imposed on her conduct. At her husband's death Nistarini was given no space to claim as her own; she had complied with rules set by those with power in the household. However, she refused to accept this new directive that was purely geared to the convenience of the men in the household. She left her in-laws' house, and with the help of her brother, a lawyer, brought a suit against the two brothers, although it was evident that Nandalal Basu was the main defendant. If she, indeed, had to negotiate public space and the instruments of the public sphere, she would do so in her own self-interest, and on her conditions of privacy.

In the interrogation by lawyers that followed, many details of her relation with the men and women of the household, as well as with male acquaintances were brought under scrutiny. Nistarini's legal deposition was taken in her in-laws' house. As a mark of her *purdanashin* status she sat during the entire proceedings in a room adjoining the *baithak-khana*, and behind a screen to answer the counsels' questions. There, she was accompanied by a representative of the defendant, Nandalal's son, Benode, whom she had once considered a trusted member of the family. The two other female members of the Basu family, Nistarini's sister-in-law Kadambini, and Nandalal's daughter-in-law, Elokeshi, gave their deposition in support of Nandalal, but they did not sit behind *purdah*.

Nistarini's status as a *purdanashin* hinged on the question of her ability to read and write, as well as to understand the contents and implications of legal documents. She argued that her education was rudimentary, consisting of the ability to read two Bengali primers, sign her name, and to decipher a manuscript in Bengali only if it was written in clear letters. She had never had the privilege of a school education. Kadambini and Elokeshi gave counter evidence, insisting that Nistarini could read Bengali fluently, and was used to reading religious texts, newspapers, novels, letters, and adept at keeping household accounts. Their evidence tried to establish her as an "educated" woman, who consequently understood the implications of her earlier assent to the distribution of family property. The court did not accept their version, satisfied with Nistarini's plea that she had all along trusted her brothers-in-law without any knowledge that she might have been signing documents that adversely intervened in her own property rights.

The entrée of the women of the household in court to testify in matters of the *andar-mahal* meant exposing the inner workings of an extended household to public scrutiny. Critical in this respect was Nistarini's claim that she had not attended any arbitration hosted by the two brothers to resolve their disagreement about the partition of property. This arbitration was supposed to have been held in Pashupati's *baithak-khana* located close to the *andar-mahal* (Figure 5.5). The defendants claimed that Nistarini attended the arbitration by sitting in the verandah next to Pashupati's *baithak-khana*, and from time to time she was shown legal documents to evince her approval. This contention gave rise to a whole set of questions that foregrounded the conditions of women's seclusion.

The plan of the house, crucial to determining the viability of incidents and events, was submitted as an exhibit in the case. The cross-examination demonstrated that more than the separation of the apartments into *andar* and *bahir*, more than the importance of the rooms per se, the necessary ingredient for setting up spatial relations with all their subtlety were the spaces in-between, the connectors between rooms. The passages, partition screens, ante-rooms, verandahs, *dalan*, stair halls were the spaces that held the secret stories of the Bengali household. The status of adjoining spaces here is not very different from those in Anglo-Indian households (see Chapter 2), but here it is imbued with a different set of meanings concerned not just with servants, but the women of the household. The circular pattern of arrangement of the rooms around a courtyard that seemed to do away with hierarchy, and therefore with a spatial indication of degrees of privacy and/or importance, was overwritten by a principle of primacy that privileged the senior men in the household. Privacy and publicness of a room was not fixed in any determinate way, but was entirely contingent on the presence or absence of those with power in the household. In Nistarini's case, her "private" space of the bedroom became "public" when Nandalal and the Thakur Mohasoy visited to negotiate terms. She was no longer in a position to dictate who entered or did not enter the room – Pashupati, we may remember, entered the room at the invitation of the Thakur Mohasoy and not Nistarini. Consequently, rather than seeing the plan of the house as a determinate representation of social order, it is far more productive to recognize it as a set of contingencies.

The practice of seclusion in Bengali households – the proscriptions against speaking with strangers, and between certain close relations, for example between a married woman and her husband's older brothers – were rather easily circumvented in practice through an interlocuter or in the absence of the interlocuter by any moveable object that could substitute for a screen. Here, *purdah* became a pure formality – a mode

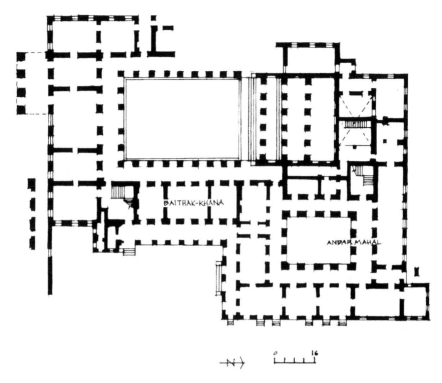

Figure 5.5 Plan of the Basu family house in Baghbazaar, Calcutta. Based on drawing by Shivashis Bose in the collection of the Calcutta Municipal Corporation

of attending to social rules and transgressing them with impunity. Thus, spatial boundaries in the household between *andar* and *bahir* could become rather inconsequential as a practice of segregation of the sexes. It is useful to think of these physical distinctions as props – just like the moveable screen or curtain – around which social relations could be idealized.

The examination of the witnesses also brought out in glaring terms the flexibility of the notion of *purdah*. Not all members were subject to the same rules – many could choose conditions of seclusion – to a great extent it was Nistarini's "choice," an old habit and a legal strategy that she adopted the status of the *purdanashin*. While earlier in life she maintained *purdah* in front of both her brothers-in-law, by the time she brought the suit against them, she had started appearing in front of Pashupati, whose children she raised, and with whom she was on more amicable terms in comparison to Nandalal. And yet, the force of Nistarini's statement and the judgment delivered in her favor clearly assumed that both the architecture of the house as well as the social practices that guarded or facilitated relationships between male and female family members were to be understood in absolute terms.

Once having granted Nistarini the status of a *purdanashin*, the officiating English judge refused to deviate from the concept of the *purdanashin* as anything other than fixed – you could either be a *purdanashin* or not.

What we see here is the British colonial concept of a *purdanashin* coming up against practical tests of authenticity, and the changing dynamics of the *andar* as a social space. The legal protection accorded to the *purdanashin* was based on a clear-cut notion of her dependence on others to navigate in the outside world. *Purdah* signified an abrogation of rights – withholding access to knowledge, speech, spaces, and one's labor; in other words, it was seen as a form of social bondage. The state needed to intervene on behalf of the subject to restore these rights that had been alienated from her. The question of Nistarini's uncompensated labor in the household entered the discussion, as did a detailed mapping of the space that she inhabited. She was repeatedly asked about the degree of seclusion she entertained when dealing with the men of the household and with male family friends, including her legal counselors. Clearly, her own conduct of seclusion changed during her lifetime. For the judge, *purdah* represented a colonial problematic, a phenomenon to be investigated and compensated. The status of the *purdanashin* was independent of any "fiduciary" relationship with the family – the question of family trust did not arise in the designation.

The suit brought in conflict Bengali ideals of the family and *atmyiata* (kinship) and Nistarini's experience of these constructs, as it highlighted the state's ability to ignore any claims of familial and community trust to engage with the *purdanashin* as a modern subject with certain fundamental rights. In one sense the state could extricate the legal subject from the confines of family and community and re-position her in another institutional domain where the state was sovereign. The events leading up to the suit had led Nistarini to make some difficult legal, financial, personal, and spatial choices based on the discrepancy between familial and kinship responsibilities on the one hand, and her rights as an individual legal subject on the other. The testimonies made it clear that a large number of her kinfolk had deceived her. It was the familial threat of dispossession by violating her "privacy" – the personal space of her body – by forcing her to appear in a public space, however, that prompted her to turn definitions of *purdah*, of a Bengali widow, and of a woman, to her advantage. She refused to submit to the threat to her "respectability" posed by her family and community – the death in public – by exploiting the definitional rigidity maintained in both the familial and judicial discourses. She chose to remain within the confines of the family and community that had betrayed her by demonstrating her ability to negotiate the gap between these two forms of control. Nistarini garnered this capacity to re-map her self and her domestic arrangement, not through any easy access to the public sphere, but on the basis of her legal right to property in the city. This bitterly contested spatial claim enabled Nistarini to demonstrate that the hallowed respectability of the Bengali household could be challenged both at the edges and at the center of the household.

Nistarini reminds us that if we wish to hear the voices of women challenging patriarchal norms we must look at the interface between familial and legislative/judicial discourses. It was precisely because public space was understood as a problematic but necessary extension of domestic space in Bengali imagination, that mapping nineteenth-century domestic space implies charting a range of practices that take us from the household to the public spaces of the city, from the domestic to the public archive.

Conclusion

The politics of representation

> For Space has rules they cannot hope to learn
> Time speaks a language they will never master.
> We live here. We lie in the Present's unopened
> Sorrow; its limits are what we are.
>
> W. H. Auden[1]

In the previous chapters I have discussed the dominant modes of representation used by the British and the Bengalis to lay claim to the city, and the ways in which these representations were destabilized both from within and without. The British encoded the city's space through modern techniques of representation in their bid for spatial mastery – here we have an entire history of mapping, surveying, depicting, and writing that came to be used for governing the city. Such representations mediated between the British Subject of history and the city as the Object of history, generating a necessary distance – of both space and time. A city that could only be gathered in fragments was projected as a (British) composition with clearly defined boundaries, discrete monuments, and clearly distinguished dark and lit spaces. The distance between Subject and Object held the present of the physical city, the colonial uncanny at bay, and enabled Calcutta's colonial masters to speak of the city's future as probable representations of other spaces – European cities to which it must aspire, must ceaselessly be compared, but never become that city, that nation. It is in that impossibility of becoming – the perpetual deferral of modernity actualized – that the British imperialists inserted themselves as spokespersons of the city. This anachronism of imperialism was produced through these representations and not the other way around.

The very modes of representation that claimed to produce transparency, however, were underscored by a deep anxiety about the opaqueness of the object of inquiry. This paradox of vision in British imperial representations was greeted by Bengali writers, painters, and politicians by producing myths of a different sort – myths of the everyday that both took the challenge of modern representations seriously and re-encoded these modes by grounding them in the semiotics of immediate community. The most powerful departures from British modes of representation were not geared towards illuminating the opaqueness that could not be accessed through Western modes of representation, but to strategically redistribute the opaqueness over a larger area. This opaqueness is produced by sedimentation of meaning, is embodied in gestures, and practiced as everyday rituals. The redistribution was guided by rules of recognition that bestowed new meaning upon artifacts of domesticity, upon ideas of public and private, upon the construction of the self. While the British and the Bengali representations shared an acknowledgement of the power of vision, the British anxiety of not being able to see through spaces was paralleled in Bengali discourse by a deep distrust of the merely visible. This was a conflict of two very different modes of vision, description, and spatial practice. In drawing this book to a close I want to cite two examples that bring us to the juncture where the British and the Bengali discourses crossed paths. Both were Bengali attempts to claim the city as its own, yet produced from two very different positions of address. The first is Durgacharan Ray's travel narrative *Debganer Martye Agaman* (The God's Visit Earth, 1880), and the second is Amritalal Basu's farce *Sabash Athash* (Bravo Twenty Eight, 1900).

Ray entices the imagination by describing a revelatory journey. In 1880 Brahma, the Creator, he tells us, took a train to Calcutta with his fellow gods to see for himself the effects of British rule.[2] Brahma had been persuaded by Indra (Lord of Thunder, King of Gods) and Barun (the Rain God) that the most ominous power had been unleashed on earth in the form of British rule. British technology had tamed thunder and steam, built the railways, and lit the streets with electricity. Although heaven itself was safe from British occupation, Barun ruminated that this was only because the British had not yet found the way.

Stepping on Indian soil they confronted the new world order. They were asked by the coachman to pay in currency with the "Queen's" stamp on it, and while they recognized the convenience of "paper currency," "match-boxes," and "post-cards," they also realized that they were barred from entering the "waiting room for gentlemen" in the railway station; only the British qualified as gentlemen. When the gods arrived in Calcutta they were struck by the sight of the river Ganga teeming with vessels. Surveying the shoreline they saw a vast stretch of buildings and huge chimneys belching smoke in the air. Brahma was reunited with her daughter, Ganga, who complained of her wretched condition:

> see how they have gagged me ... my fate is such that the king who is supposed to protect his subjects, has himself taken the initiative to torture this helpless woman. He binds me with bridges wherever he chooses, and has broken my back by forcing me to carry heavy ships like a slave.

Ganga, of course, did not fail to chronicle the social upheavals that had accompanied such a rule when reverence for the sacred Ganga had been lost.

Despite Ganga's bleak depiction and their own reservations about fast-moving carriages and the moral dimension of city life plagued by cheats, drunks, and prostitutes, the gods were impressed with cosmopolitan Calcutta, its large mansions and brisk business. On their daily tour they visited a large number of commercial establishments and government offices, in order, we presume, to learn about modern institutions and modern trade. In the government offices and shipping houses they were chagrined to find legions of Bengali *keranis* (clerks). These clerks slaved in low-paying jobs all day only to be harassed by prostitutes and petty shop-keepers in the streets. The gods refused to shoulder the blame for the degraded state of Bengali *keranis*, believing that the clerks' lack of personal initiative was at the root of the problem.

In touring the city, the gods mapped a parallel topography of commerce and social power where the *keranis* could seek the answer to their problems. Pictures of colonial inequity and class conflict embodied in the Bengali *kerani* were interspersed with giddy consumerism and the immense opportunities that awaited enterprising individuals, the narrative being studded with vignettes of illustrious careers. At the High Court the gods were introduced to prominent Bengali judges and barristers. On entering one room they saw a Bengali and a British judge on the bench and a Bengali pleader presenting his case in English. Barun introduced the two Bengalis for the gods' conveni-ence: "the judge is Rameshchandra Mitra, and the one delivering the English speech is Hemchandra Bandopadhyay." "Hembabu," he added, "is considered a talented Bengali poet." On Bramha's request, Barun then proceeded to chronicle the life and achievements of these individuals. Similarly, the most significant fact they learned about the Town Hall was that Surendranath Banerjee was scheduled to give a speech that very after-noon. At this point the gods were provided with a sketch of Surendranath's life, ending with a note that he was sentenced to three months in prison for writing an editorial criticizing Judge Norris. As the gods traversed the city, what emerged was a map of conspicuous Bengali achievement superim-posed on a geography of imperial power anchored by such institutions as the Geological Survey Office, Museum of the Asiatic Society, Government House, Bengal Bank, the Lal Bazaar Police Station, and Presidency Jail.

Durgacharan Ray was clearly not writing an ordinary tourist guide. The moral and material lesson of Ray's narrative had to be imbibed by following the gods in their spatial exploration, sharing with them the dangers of walking in a modern city, their ability to enter prominent buildings, and their being shut out from others. Written from a position of conservative nationalism, the travel guide charted a territory of Bengali socio-economic and political power that was not confined to the native town and whole-sale markets, but operated in the heart of British power – in the High

Court, Town Hall, and Government House. The gods were portrayed as provincial visitors. Such a province was connected to Calcutta by economic relations and yet was perceived to maintain the sovereignty of the traditional order, as opposed to Calcutta, where class and caste distinctions, the linchpins of the traditional hierarchy, seemed irretrievably blurred. The gods hardly seemed to notice that their speech was invaded by a host of English words. Neither were they averse to modern conveniences such as piped water and electricity. In fact, they were thrilled to purchase the latest fashion, and wished to build a museum and a High Court in heaven. Such transference of ideas, goods, and spaces, however, was to be conducted on their terms.

Ray's narrative exhorted Bengalis to become economically self-sufficient, and was a sly political criticism of British rule at a time when Bengali publications were scrutinized by British authorities for sedition. Consequently, his complex urban portrait significantly differed from the imperial history of a dual-city – the glory of the white town and the sprawling appendage of the black town. Ray's richly detailed narrative produced a finely grained socio-economic landscape of Calcutta, in which the Bengali middle class was determined to claim its share of political and economic power.

Ray's mythic travel narrative was part of an emergent Bengali sensitivity to modes of narration, representation, and the Bengali public sphere. We need only to remind ourselves of the political climate in the last quarter of the nineteenth century to assess the urgency for alternative modes that had not submitted to colonial authority. In 1876 a Municipal Act was passed to make the Calcutta Municipality a representative body, in which Bengali commissioners established a majority; in 1875 the Dramatic Performances Bill was enacted to curb the criticism of unpopular government measures on stage; in 1878 the Vernacular Press Act was passed to control the seditious tone of Indian-language newspapers; the controversy over the Ilbert Bill erupted in 1883–84; and in 1884 the Bengal Government initiated an investigation into the sanitation of Calcutta, convinced that the native commissioners of the Municipality were not up to the task of evaluating the health of a British city. Calcutta and its native Bengalis were deeply implicated in these policy issues. The image of the city became enmeshed in the rhetoric of representation, self-representation, and misrepresentation.

Durgacharan Ray's optimism about the Bengali public sphere, however, received a setback in 1896. A plague scare prompted the Chamber of Commerce to mobilize Anglo-Indian opinion to ask the Government to revamp the representative structure of the Municipal Corporation. The Lieutenant-Governor, Alexander Mackenzie, proposed a Bill to allow British residents, particularly British commercial interests, a majority. This was to offset the effect of the large number of Bengali commissioners who had been elected to the Corporation. Mackenzie claimed that the Corporation had become "an armoury of talk and an arsenal of delay." This was inevitable in a Corporation constituted not of merchants and bankers, but lawyers and doctors, who were not "practical men of business," having little stake in the city, and representing only a variety of heterogeneous interests. What was needed was a "silent sensible vote" and not a "long speech or acrimonious debate."[3] Private interests, he claimed, were working to the detriment of the public weal:

> Private owners cannot be permitted to maintain death-traps, cholera and plague nurseries, for the destruction of their fellow citizens. . . . The only remedy was to drive broad roads through these quarters, and to replace these horrid pig-sties (where indeed no normally constituted pig could live) by respectable well-sanitized dwellings. . . . The Government must, for its own credit and the sake of the commerce of Bengal, see that these reforms are carried out.[4]

Mackenzie went so far as to claim that the Act was designed to provide representation to the poor and the Muslims who would have no voice were it not for the Government. Bengali newspapers asked how many "poor" residents had the Government nominated and would it consider expanding the franchise by giving the small rate-payers a voice in the election?[5] No one, Surendranath Banerjee urged, had a deeper stake in the city than the native Bengalis:

> Calcutta is the city of our birth . . . it is destined to be the city of our children's children. We have a far more permanent and abiding interest in its sanitary well-being than any other section of the community could possibly have. We would welcome any rational scheme of sanitation which would bring to our people an accession of health and all the blessings which the possession of health implies. . . . It is money and not change in the constitution of the Municipality that is required for the sanitation of Calcutta . . . greatly as we value sanitation, we are not prepared to sacrifice our civic freedom for its sake, especially when such sacrifice is unnecessary and uncalled for, and when it will be disastrous to the fortunes of our people in other higher and nobler directions.[6]

The protest against the Bill, Surendranath reminded the government, "emanates from the voice of a united community." "It is repeated in every newspaper," he continued, "it is represented in every vernacular journal, it is the talk of every bazaar in the Indian part of the town, it is the staple of conversation of every Indian home, and it has at last been reproduced on the Indian stage."[7] Surendranath's rhetoric of rationality, civic freedom, and sanitary science suggested that the colonial state was coming up short by these self-proclaimed standards. And yet if he must choose between civic freedom and sanitary improvement he knew his option. For Surendranath, self-governance was the only means to assure civic freedom, to speak for and represent the community.

Notwithstanding resistance from virtually every section of the Indian community, Mackenzie's Bill was passed in 1899. In an unusual display of solidarity, 28 Indian commissioners resigned in a united body.[8] Commemorating this political solidarity Amritalal Basu wrote a farce, *Sabash Athash*, in which he rendered the relation between the two meanings of representation – as depiction and as political representation – with much more clarity than Surendranath. If Surendranath pointed out the limits of modernization for the nationalist cause, Amritalal drew attention to the power and limits of representation itself.

Amritalal's play begins with a conversation between husband and wife:

Hara: What can I say? With the new rules if you want to build a house you will have to submit a plan to the Municipality. Soon they will have us draw a map of Bharatvarsha (India).

Shyama: Why, what relation are they to us?

Hara: What do you mean?

Shyama: Those people you mentioned – Bharatvarsha or whatever – what is our relation with them?

Hara: . . . Never mind that; listen while I explain – we will have to submit a plan of the area over which the smell of frying fish will carry from our newly built house – we have to produce a plan that is in keeping with houses that are located in the range of sight or smell.[9]

This is a rare example relating power, modes of representation, and different scales of community – household, neighborhood, and nation. Amritalal used the standardized architectural plan demanded by the Municipality to assure adherence to the new Building Act as a way of speaking about the need to resist Western modes of representation. The municipal plan as form of representation was, itself, a technique of colonial governance. As noted in Chapter 1, for at least three decades medical officers of the Municipality had emphasized the need for "accurate plans" of every neighborhood and *bustee* to confront the city's ill-health. Conformity with Municipal regulations suggested a kind of civic consciousness and a form of community in which Amritalal saw little merit, however. Amritalal accurately recognized that these new regulations about house construction meant an overhauling of norms by which houses were, until then, conceptualized and built, thus allowing the state to intervene in the domestic realm.

Such plans also demanded a type of visual literary that had not become normalized in the city even at the turn of the twentieth century. Amritalal's farce is a reminder of our recent acquiescence to this mode of thinking about space and community. Amritalal suggested that the only problem in the Municipal debacle is not the colonial state failing to live up to self-proclaimed liberal formulations of civic right, representative government, and progress, but the Indian nationalists yielding to the rhetoric of Western liberalism and instruments of modernization. Nationalist sensibility must reside in the mode of representation, if Indian nationalists were not to submit unequivocally to the dictates of the colonial government. Representations of the self and the community must be performed by rethinking modes of depiction and narration. Without the ability to imagine alternate modes of description, political representation in a colonial regime would inevitably be a farce. Thus, in Amritalal's explanation the plan as a visual artifact is understood in terms of that which defies the limits of vision – the more powerful sense of smell – in particular, the smell of frying fish that is deeply rooted in everyday Bengali sensibility. The idea is made available to someone not tutored in modern systems of representation in a language that cuts through its mode of dominance. The abstract representations of the nation and "civic" community recede to make room for ways of asserting control over space that are characteristically "un-modern," of ways of being that are scandalous in their refusal to accept that space and time have only one set of rules.

The thrust of Amritalal's argument would engage serious attention from Bengali nationalists and would be used during the Swadeshi Movement against the 1905 Partition of Bengal to chart a new politics of space. Bengali spatial hegemony would re-make itself by cynically co-opting the "un-modern." And yet, Amritalal, as well as Abanindranath, Benodini, and Nistarini, through their widely different and conflictual strategies remind us of possible practices that would not submit easily to the dominant discourses of space and time. Calcutta bears traces of their defiance against overwhelming odds.

Notes

Introduction: the city in historical imagination

1 Janet L. Abu-Lughod, *Rabat: Urban Apartheid in Morocco* (Princeton: Princeton University Press, 1980), 257.
2 For a quick summary of these images see Gaston Roberge, "Images of Calcutta: From the Black Hole to the Black Box," in Jean Racine (ed.) *Calcutta 1981: the City, its Crisis, and the Debate on Urban Planning and Development* (New Delhi: Concept Publishing Company, 1986).
3 Frederick C. Thomas, *Calcutta Poor: Elegies on a City Above Pretense* (Armonk, NY: M. E. Sharpe, 1997), 7.
4 Abu-Lughod, *Rabat*, 257.
5 For example, in Peter Hall's massive work titled, *Cities in Civilization* (New York: Pantheon, 1998) a place of creative honor is accorded to both Paris and Vienna as seen in a chain of creativity in the Western world running from Athens, Greece to Los Angeles, US. He emphasizes that these were the results of internal cultural dynamism.
6 Marshall Berman, *All That is Solid Melts into Air* (New York: Viking Penguin, 1988).
7 Ibid., 232; also see 235–236, as well as his comparison between Paris and Petersburg.
8 Ibid., 175.
9 Ibid., 15.
10 Paul Gilroy, *The Black Atlantic: Modernity and Double Consciousness* (Cambridge: Harvard University Press, 1993), 46.
11 Berman, *All That is Solid*, 13.
12 See Partha Chatterjee, *The Nation and its Fragments: Colonial and Postcolonial Histories* (Princeton: Princeton University Press, 1993) for the importance of nationalist practices in the domain of the "cultural" long before addressing the explicitly "political" realm of statecraft. For the political exercise in municipal debates see, Rajat Kanta Ray, *Urban Roots of Indian Nationalism: Pressure Groups and Conflict of Interests in Calcutta City Politics, 1875–1939* (New Delhi: Vikas, 1979).
13 For a discussion of the city vs. country in nationalist imagination see Dipesh Chakrabarty, "Nation and Imagination," in *Provincializing Europe: Postcolonial Thought and Historical Difference* (Princeton: Princeton University Press, 2000).
14 Edward Said, *Culture and Imperialism* (New York: Alfred Knopf, 1993). In Said's words: "I am talking about the way in which structures of location and geographic reference appear in the cultural language of literature, history, or ethnography, sometimes allusive, and sometimes carefully plotted, across several individual works that are not otherwise connected to one another or to an official ideology of empire" (52). Here Said was expanding on Raymond Williams' idea of a "structure of feelings" by suggesting the need to recognize the territorial significance of empire.

15   Walter Mignolo, *The Darker Side of the Renaissance: Literacy, Territoriality, and Coloniza-tion* (Ann Arbor: University of Michigan Press, 1995), 15.

16   The colonial history of the city by British authors includes the nineteenth-century work of H. E. Busteed, *Echoes from Old Calcutta: Being Chiefly Reminiscences of the Days of Warren Hastings, Francis and Impey* (Calcutta: Thacker, Spink & Co., 1905), and two in the early twentieth century: Kathleen Blechynden, *Calcutta: Past and Present* (Calcutta: Thacker, Spink & Co., 1905); and H. E. A. Cotton, *Calcutta: Old and New: A Historical and Descriptive Handbook of the City* (1907; reprint, Calcutta: General Publishers, 1980). These were, in their turn, influenced by the earlier work of Robert Orme, *A History of the Military Transactions of the British Nation in Indostan from the year MDCCXLV* (London: J. Nourse, 1775–78), and several chron-icles and correspondence of early merchants, travelers, and administrators such as Alexander Hamilton, John Z. Holwell, William Hickey, Warren Hastings, Eliza Fay, Viscount Valentia, and Emily Eden. The earliest urban history of Calcutta written in the twentieth century, authored by A. K. Ray, is entitled *A Short History of Calcutta* (1901; reprint, Calcutta: Riddhi, 1982). This was soon followed by Raja Benoy Krishna Deb, *The Early History and Growth of Calcutta* (Calcutta: Romesh Ghosh, 1905). Later studies include P. C. Bagchi, *Calcutta: Past and Present* (Calcutta: Calcutta University Press, 1939); Nemi Bose, *Calcutta: People and Empire* (Calcutta: India Book Exchange, 1975); Pradip Sinha, *Calcutta in Urban History* (Calcutta: Firma KLM, 1978); S. N. Mukherjee, *Calcutta: Myth and History* (Calcutta: Subornorekha, 1977); and *Calcutta: Essays in Urban History* (Calcutta: Subornorekha, 1993).

17   See, for example, Philip Davies, *Splendours of the Raj: British Architecture of India* (London: John Murray, 1985); Norma Evenson, *The Indian Metropolis: A View Toward the West* (New Haven: Yale University Press, 1989).

18   I owe this insight to Gauri Vishwanathan's study of the introduction of English education in India: *Masks of Conquest: Literary Study and British Rule in India* (New York: Columbia University Press, 1989), 15–18.

19   This summary is from P. J. Marshall, *Bengal: The British Bridgehead* (Cambridge: Cambridge University Press, 1987).

20   See Sunil K. Munshi, "Genesis of the Metropolis," in Jean Racine (ed.) *Calcutta 1981: The City, its Crisis, and the Debate on Urban Planning and Development* (New Delhi: Concept Publishing Company). Munshi calls the founding act of Job Charnock the "rebirth" of Calcutta as a colonial city.

21   P. J. Marshall, *Bengal*, 66. This point is also emphasized by Rajat Kanta Ray, "Asian Capital in the Age of European Domination: The Rise of the Bazaar," *Modern Asian Studies* 29, no. 3 (July 1995): 449–554.

22   In 1765 the Mughal emperor appointed the British East India Company his Diwan for the provinces of Bengal, Bihar, and Orissa. The company was given the responsibility of financial administration of the provinces in return for a fixed tribute of Rs. 2,600,000. The Nawab of Bengal retained the responsibility for law and order, defense, and the administration of justice, and was granted a fixed allowance for his court expenses. The rest of the revenues of Bengal were at the disposal of the East India Company.

23   For example, John Z. Holwell, *A Genuine Narrative of the Deplorable Deaths of the English Gentlemen and Others who were Suffocated in the Black Hole* (London: A Millar, 1758).

24   Busteed wrote in *Echoes from Old Calcutta*:

> By 1756 Calcutta had reached such a stage of industrial progress, that its trade is stated to have exceeded one million sterling yearly, and that some fifty vessels or more annually visited its port. . . . The houses of the English inhabitants were scattered in large enclosures for about half a mile to the

north and to the south of the fort, and for a quarter of a mile to the east of it. Beyond the English houses were closely clustered the habitations and huts of the natives; the better classes of them, including the "Black Merchants," dwelt to the north; the lower classes to the east and south. . . .

To these insanitary surroundings were added the near vicinity of a dense jungle, of unsavoury marshes to windward and an inundating river. . . . Modern Calcutta can scarcely realise the appalling insalubrity amidst which those poor pioneers had to maintain a struggle for existence.

(4–5)

25 Dell Upton, "Architectural History or Landscape History," *Journal of Architectural Education* 44, no. 4 (1991): 195–199.

26 Some of the most erudite scholars on colonial urbanism take it for granted that the colonizers' ideas were the ones that really mattered. See for example, Paul Rabinow, *French Modern: Norms and Forms of Social Environment* (Berkeley: University of California Press, 1989). For critiques of Immanuel Wallerstein's notion that the pre-colonial South Asian economy did not have a strong enough network of independent origin and consequently had little to contribute to world capitalism, see Ray, "Asian Capital in the Age of European Domination"; Shreeram Krishnaswami, "Colonial Foundations of Western Capitalism," *Economic and Political Weekly* (July 25, 1992): PE 81–89; and David Washbrook, "South Asia, the World System, and World Capitalism," *The Journal of Asian Studies* 49, no. 3 (August 1990): 479–508.

27 W. J. T. Mitchell, *Landscape and Power* (Chicago: University of Chicago Press, 1994), 1–2.

28 Swati Chattopadhyay, "Nineteenth-century British attitudes towards Calcutta and Bombay," in S. J. Neary, M. S. Symes, and F. E. Brown (eds) *The Urban Experience* (London: E&FN SPON, 1994): 455–467.

29 In *The Road to Botany Bay* (Chicago: University of Chicago Press, 1987), Paul Carter notes:

Hence, imperial history's defensive appeal to the logic of cause and effect: by its nature, such a logic demonstrates the emergence of order from chaos. Hence, too, its preference for detachable facts, for actual houses, visible clearings and boats at anchor . . . Orphaned from their unique spatial and temporal context, such objects, such historical facts, can be fitted with new paternities.

(xvi)

30 For an overview of British attitudes towards India during colonial rule, see Francis G. Hutchins, *The Illusion of Permanence: British Imperialism in India* (Princeton: Princeton University Press, 1967); and George Bearce, *British Attitudes Towards India, 1784–1858* (London: Oxford University Press, 1961).

31 Denis Cosgrove and Stephen Daniels, *The Iconography of Landscape* (Cambridge: Cambridge University Press, 1988). For a similar approach see Dell Upton, "The City as Material Culture," in A. E. Yentsch and M. C. Beaudry (eds) *The Art and Mystery of Historical Archaeology: Essays in Honor of James Deetz* (Boca Raton: CRC Press, 1992), 51–74.

32 Chatterjee, *The Nation and Its Fragments*, 7.

33 Jurgen Habermas, *The Structural Transformation of the Public Sphere: An Inquiry into a Category of Bourgeois Society*, translated by Frederick Burger and Thomas Lawrence (Cambridge: MIT Press, 1989).

34 Rajat Sanyal, *Voluntary Associations and the Urban Public Life in Bengal* (Calcutta: Riddhi, 1980), 14.

35 Chatterjee, *The Nation and Its Fragments*, 6.

36 Ibid.
37 Habermas, *The Structural Transformation of the Public Sphere*, 45.
38 Ibid., 157.
39 Kevin Hetherington, *The Badlands of Modernity: Heterotopia and Social Ordering* (London: Routledge, 1997), 81–82.
40 Nancy Fraser, "Rethinking the Public Sphere: A Contribution to the Critique of Actually Existing Democracy," in Craig Calhoun (ed.) *Habermas and the Public Sphere* (Cambridge: MIT Press, 1992), 126.
41 Ibid. Also see Mary Ryan, "Gender and Public Access: Women's Politics in Nineteenth-century America," in Craig Calhoun (ed.) *Habermas and the Public Sphere* (Cambridge: MIT Press, 1992). Also in Calhoun's book see Habermas's response to criticism by Ryan and other scholars, and his willingness to reconsider some aspects of the model he had presented in *The Structural Transformation of the Public Sphere*.
42 See Mary Ryan, *Women in Public: Between Banners and Ballots, 1825–1880* (Baltimore: Johns Hopkins University Press, 1989).
43 The "women's question" of course is not a new concern in the history of nineteenth-century Bengali culture. For two earlier texts see Ghulam Murshid, *Reluctant Debutante: Response of Bengali Women to Modernization* (Rajshahi: Rajshahi University Press, 1983); Meredith Borthwick, *The Changing Role of Women in Bengal 1849–1905* (Princeton: Princeton University Press, 1984).
44 Chatterjee, *The Nation and Its Fragments*, 133; Chakrabarty, *Provincializing Europe*, 216.
45 Chakrabarty, *Provincializing Europe*, 218.
46 Ibid., 211.
47 Henri Lefebvre, *The Production of Space*, translated by Donald Nicholson-Smith (Oxford: Blackwell, 1991), 300–309.

1 The colonial uncanny

1 Elisabeth was married to Captain Neil Campbell of the 13th Light Infantry, who died within a year of Elisabeth's arrival in India. In 1828 she married Captain Michael Fenton, and the couple eventually immigrated to Australia.
2 Elisabeth Fenton, *A Narrative of Her Life in India, the Isle of France (Mauritius), and Tasmania During the Years 1826–1830* (London: Edward Arnold, 1901), 8. *Dandi* is a Bengali word for oarsman.
3 Ibid., 10.
4 See Martin Jay's discussion of ocularcentricity of knowledge in the early modern era in *Downcast Eyes: The Denigration of Vision in the Twentieth-Century French Thought* (Berkeley: University of California Press, 1994), 69. By the time Elisabeth Campbell arrived in India there were dissenting voices challenging the assumption of ocularcentricity. But the force of empirical knowledge refigured in the nineteenth-century mold continued to hold its sway, and travelers and administrators rarely failed to point out their authoritative vantage point in their descriptions of India.
5 For discussion of travelogues authored by women see Sara Mills, *Discourses of Difference* (London: Routledge, 1991), and Dea Birkett, *Spinsters Abroad, Victorian Lady Explorers* (Oxford: Basil Blackwell, 1989).
6 In *The Birth of the Clinic*, Michel Foucault noted the "two great mythical experiences on which the philosophy of the eighteenth century wished to base its beginning: the foreign spectator in an unknown country, and the man born blind restored to light." Translated from the French by A. M. Sheridan Smith (New York: Pantheon, 1973), 65.

7 See David Spurr's discussion of Johann Fabian's idea of "visualism" and Pierre Bourdieu's concept of "objectivism." *Rhetoric of Empire: Colonial Discourse in Journalism, Travel Writing, and Imperial Administration* (Durham: Duke University Press, 1993), 25–26.

8 Gyan Prakash, "Science Gone Native in Colonial India," *Representations* 40 (Fall 1992): 153–178.

9 G. W. F. Hegel, *The Philosophy of History* (New York: Dover, 1956), 141.

10 Ibid., 162.

11 Ibid., 101.

12 Mrs. Mary (Martha) Sherwood, *Life of Mrs. Sherwood with Extracts from Mr. Sherwood's Journal During his Imprisonment in France and Residence in India* (London: Darton, 1857), 246–247.

13 In the nineteenth century this was the established format for women writers. See Dianne Harris, "Cultivating Power: The Language of Feminism in Women's Garden Literature, 1870–1920," *Landscape Journal* (1992): 113–123.

14 Sherwood, *The Life of Mrs. Sherwood*, 247; Ibid., 243.

15 Ibid., 244.

16 Stephen Greenblatt, *Marvelous Possessions: The Wonder of the New World* (Chicago: University of Chicago Press, 1991), 88.

17 Ibid., 247.

18 See Birkett, *Spinsters Abroad*, 159.

19 Fenton, *A Narrative*, 44. For similar analogies see Sherwood, *The Life of Mrs. Sherwood*, 243, 250.

20 Maria Graham, *Journal of Residence in India* (Edinburgh: Archibald Constable & Co., 1812), 132. For similar descriptions see Sherwood, *The Life of Mrs. Sherwood*, 254, 360–361; Lady Maria Nugent, *A Journal from the Year 1811 Till the Year 1815, Including a Voyage to and Residence in India, with a Tour to the Northwestern Part of the British Possessions in that Country, under the Bengal Government* (London, 1839), 75–77; Lord Viscount George Valentia, *Voyages and Travels to India, Ceylon, the Red Sea, Abyssinia, and Egypt, in the Years 1802–1806*, vol. I (London: William Miller, 1809), 59; Bishop Reginald Heber, *Narrative of a Journey Through the Upper Provinces of India, from Calcutta to Bombay, 1824–1825* (London: John Murray, 1828), 7; and William Huggins, *Sketches of India, Treatise on Subjects Connected with the Government; Civil and Military Establishments; Characters of the European, and Customs of the Native Inhabitants* (London: John Letts, 1824), 3–4. The temple that Mrs. Graham referred to was not a temple of Kali, but dedicated to the sage Kapil. The reference to Kali enabled the creation of a more horrific imagery.

21 Bishop Heber, *The Narrative of a Journey Through the Upper Provinces of India* (London: John Murray, 1828), 7.

22 Sherwood, *The Life of Mrs. Sherwood*, 361.

23 For analysis of colonial rhetoric as applied to the Sunderbans see Paul Greenough's "Hunter's Drowned Land: An Environmental Fantasy of the Victorian Sunderbans," in Richard Grove, Vinita Damodaran, Satpal Sangwan (eds), *Nature and the Orient: The Environmental History of South and Southeast Asia* (Delhi: Oxford University Press, 1998). Although Hunter included the Sagar Island in the 24 Parganas and dealt with the Sunderbans separately, I am suggesting that Hunter's "invented" vision of the Sunderbans as a fearful place was analogous to the late eighteenth-century and early nineteenth-century British descriptions of the Sagar Island. Hunter was extending this popular rhetoric to the Sunderbans and using it for similar purposes.

24 For analysis of Burke's conceptualization of India as the sublime, see Sara Suleri, *The Rhetoric of English India* (Chicago: University of Chicago Press, 1992), 24–48.

25 Thomas Metcalf, *An Imperial Vision* (Berkeley: University of California Press, 1989).

26 Graham, *Journal*, 132–133. For similar descriptions of the enchanting city see Fenton, *A Narrative*, 13.

27 Anonymous London Missionary, *Travels in India* (MDCCCLII; reproduced in Nair (ed.) *Calcutta in the Nineteenth Century*, Calcutta: Firma KLM, 1989), 917.

28 Ibid., 917.

29 Ann Bermingham, *Landscape and Ideology, the English Rustic Tradition, 1740–1860* (Berkeley: University of California Press, 1986), 11–14.

30 See, for example, Uvedale Price, *Essays on the Picturesque*, vols. I–III (London: J. Mawman, 1810).

31 See Christopher Hussey, *Picturesque Studies in a Point of View* (London: J. P. Putnam & Sons, 1927), 86.

32 Bermingham, *Landscape and Ideology*; and John Barrell, *The Dark Side of the Landscape* (Cambridge: Cambridge University Press, 1980).

33 David Arnold, *Colonizing the Body: State Medicine and Epidemic Disease in Nineteenth-Century India* (Berkeley: University of California Press, 1993), 32.

34 Fenton, *A Narrative*, 12.

35 Anthony Vidler, *The Architectural Uncanny* (Cambridge: MIT Press, 1994), 18.

36 Ibid, 27.

37 Ibid.

38 Fenton, *A Narrative*, 49.

39 Sigmund Freud, "The 'Uncanny'," *Writings on Art and Literature* (Stanford: Stanford University Press, 1997), 217.

40 The Indian picturesque has been viewed as an internal phenomenon of British culture, divorced from the issues of imperialism. This reading is particularly emphasized in G. H. R. Tillotson's essay "The Indian Picturesque," in C. A. Bayly (ed.) *The Raj: India and the British 1600–1947* (London: National Portrait Gallery, 1990).

41 On December 1, 1784, Thomas Daniell obtained permission from the East India Company to go to India as an engraver, and a few days later the permission was extended to his nephew William (Sir William Foster, "British Artists in India, 1760–1820," *The Walpole Society*, Annual Volume, XIX, 1931, 20–23). Foster records no less than 60 European artists who visited India between 1760 and 1820.

42 For more information on the Daniells' stay in India, and William Daniells' Journal see, India Office Library Mss. Eur. 268.

43 Foster, "British Artists in India."

44 Mildred Archer, *India and British Portraiture: 1770–1825* (London: Sotheby Parke Bernet, 1979).

45 William Hodges, a pupil of Richard Wilson, was appointed draftsman for Captain Cook's second expedition to the Pacific in 1772. On his return in 1775 his drawings were used to illustrate an account of the expedition. He went to Madras in 1780, traveled up-country as far as Agra, and left India in 1783. Three years later he published his *Select Views of India*, consisting of 48 aquatints, and in 1793 he published an account of his journey entitled *Travels in India During the Years 1780, 1781, 1782, 1783* (London: J. Edwards). See Sir William Foster, "William Hodges, R. A. in India," *Bengal Past and Present*, vol. XXX, July–Sept 1925, 1–8, and "British Artists in India, 1760–1820," *The Walpole Society*, v. XIX, 1931, 40–42.

46 William Hodges, *Travels in India*, iii–iv.

47 Ibid., iv.

48 For a similar argument consult W. J. T. Mitchell's "Imperial Landscape," and David Bunn's "'Our Wattled Cot': Mercantile and Domestic Space in Thomas

Pringle's African Landscapes," in W. J. T. Mitchell (ed.) *Landscape and Power* (Chicago: Chicago University Press, 1994).

49 Thomas Daniell, *A Picturesque Voyage to India by the Way of China*, (London: Longman, Hurst, Rees, Orme, 1810), i–ii.

50 In *Ungoverned Imaginings: James Mill's History of British India and Orientalism* (Oxford: Clarendon Press, 1992) Javed Majeed notes that the imagery of Jones' writing on the subject of translation "suggests a breaking into sacred precincts, or unlocking of hitherto unopened riches" (20).

51 Jones and the Daniells knew each other. Jones had communicated with Thomas Daniell about an illustration he wanted prepared for his book. Letters to Samuel Davis, 5 April 1789, and 6 Jan 1791, in Garland Cannon (ed.) *The Letters of Sir William Jones* (Oxford: Clarendon Press, 1970), 830–831, 879.

52 The painting is titled, "Captain Antoine Polier and his friends Claud Martin, John Wombwell, and the artist," Lucknow, 1786 or 1787. See, Archer, *India and British Portraiture*.

53 The second series of *Oriental Scenery* was published between 1797 and 1798, the third series in 1803, and a 12-set of views was published as *Antiquities of India* in 1799. See Mildred Archer, *Early Views of India: The Picturesque Journeys of Thomas and William Daniell, 1786–1794* (New York: Thames & Hudson, 1980), 219–225.

54 See Nicholas B. Dirks, "Guiltless Spoliations: Picturesque Beauty, Colonial Knowledge, and Colin Mackenzie's Survey of India," in Catherine Asher and Thomas R. Metcalf (eds) *Perceptions of South Asia's Visual Past* (New Delhi: Oxford and IBH Publishing Co., 1994).

55 See Mathew Edney's discussion of the absence of representations of British surveyors in the field in India in *Mapping an Empire: The Geographical Construction of British India* (Chicago: University of Chicago Press, 1997), 74–75.

56 The paintings that came out of the Mysore Wars in the last decade of the eighteenth century, particularly those by Arthur William Davis and David Wilkie, contributed significantly to an authoritative vision in the late eighteenth century.

57 Holwell, *A Genuine Narrative*. Holwell's chronicle described how 146 people were crammed into an 18-feet-square space overnight, and 123 people died by the next morning. Holwell's *Genuine Narrative* appealed to the British audience and was frequently reprinted.

58 For a discussion of the portrait of Mr. and Mrs. Andrews see John Berger, *Ways of Seeing* (Harmondsworth: Penguin, 1972); Bermingham, *Landscape and Ideology*.

59 For example "The Auriol and Dashwood Families" by John Zoffany, 1783–87.

60 For an analysis of the picturesque in the context of North America see the work of Ian S. Maclaren, "The Limits of the Picturesque in British N. America," *Journal of Garden History* 1, no. 5: 97–111.

61 William Daniell's Journal, Mss. Eur. 268, British Library.

62 Jonathan Crary, *Techniques of the Observer* (Cambridge: MIT Press, 1994).

63 Excerpts from William Daniell's journal in M. Hardie and Muriel Clayton, "Thomas and William Daniell: Their Life and Work," *Walkers Quarterly* 35: 6.

64 Archer, *Early Views of India* (New York: Thames & Hudson, 1980), 6–7.

65 The number of travelogues are too numerous to cite, but I mention several in this chapter among other references. Two history books were critical in shaping knowledge of India – Robert Orme's *A History of the Military Transactions of the British Nation in Indostan*, and James Mill's *History of India* (London: J. Madden, 1848).

66 In 1817 James Mill published the *History of India* without ever having seen the country, and in it he disclaimed the necessity of firsthand knowledge of Indian culture or the need to learn Indian languages. He turned the prevailing model of acquiring knowledge about India, exemplified by William Jones and H. T. Colebrooke, on its head by suggesting that it was indeed their close

acquaintance with India – their ocular participation in Indian culture – that had prejudiced their interpretation of its culture.

67 Hodges, *Travels in India*, 30–33.

68 Richard Temple, *A Bird's Eye View of Picturesque India* (London: Chatto & Windus, 1898), 84–86.

69 For such associations see Hodges, *Travels in India*, (25), where he compares the country around Colgong with English parks. Mrs. Fenton who visited the same spot about 50 years later invoked similar associations on seeing the hills. See Fenton, *A Narrative*, 46–49.

70 Here I am disagreeing with Mathew Edney's suggestion that the "emotive elements of the Picturesque slowly disappeared as the British reconfigured India to be naturally Picturesque" (see Edney, *Mapping an Empire*, 74). My reading of the Daniells' paintings does not suggest an emotional emptiness through naturalization, but the displacement of values about the English countryside with a set of values and emotions that worked to naturalize India for the colonizers.

71 Conspicuously missing from these drawings and narratives were depictions of contemporary Indian urban centers, reflecting the denial in these colonial representations of contemporary viable Indian urban patterns. Where Indian cities were depicted they were always surveyed and drawn from a distance.

72 For a historical survey of the buildings of Calcutta painted by British artists see Jeremy P. Losty, *Calcutta, City of Palaces: A Survey of the City in the Days of the East India Company, 1690–1858* (London: British Library and Arnold, 1990).

73 Losty, *Calcutta*, 48.

74 Raymond Betts, "The Allusion to Rome in British Imperialist Thought of the Late Nineteenth and Early Twentieth Centuries," *Victorian Studies* (Dec. 1971): 149–159.

75 Malcolm Campbell and The Arthur Ross Foundation, *Piranesi: Rome Recorded* (Philadelphia: Smith-Edwards-Dunlap Company, 1990).

76 One reason for this distorted enlargement of the distance between the station point and the buildings is the use of a camera obscura to make the initial drawing (Losty, *Calcutta*).

77 Archer, *Early Views of India*.

78 For an early example see Mrs. Kindersley's long list of servants in *Letters from the Islands of Teneriff, Brazil, the Cape of Good Hope, and East Indies* (London: J. Hourse, 1777).

79 James Baillie Fraser arrived in Calcutta in 1814 with the intention of engaging in the eastern trade, but became more engrossed in drawing the city. His "Views of Calcutta and its Environs" consists of 24 colored aquatints that were published in London between 1824–1826.

80 Cited in Mildred Archer and Toby Falk, *India Revealed: the Art and Adventure of James Baillie Fraser* (London: Cassell, 1989), 40.

81 Charles D'Oyly, an amateur painter, was Collector of Dacca (1808–1818) and later an opium agent in Patna. He made several drawings of Calcutta, which were reproduced in 1848 as a set of colored lithographs entitled *Views of Calcutta and its Environs* (London, 1848).

82 Losty, *Calcutta*, 48.

83 Such depictions of fragmented, spatially ill-organized bazaars are consonant with traditional historical readings of Indian trade. For the growth and nature of bazaars in Asia see Ray, "Asian Capital in the Age of European Domination." Ray makes a persuasive argument against previously held notions of the bazaar as a "debased, fragmented and marginal sector absorbed and peripheralized within the capitalist world economy of the west."

84 Losty, *Calcutta*, 48.

85 John Falconer, "Ethnographical Photography in India, 1850–1900," *The Photographic Collector* 5, no. 1, 1984. Also see Falconer's essay, "Photography in Nineteenth-Century India," in C. A. Bayly (ed.) *The Raj*.

86 In *An Essay on the Diseases Incidental to Europeans in Hot Climates with the Method of Preventing their Fatal Consequences* (Philadelphia: William Duane, 1811), James Lind noted:

> [I]f purchasing of negroes on the coast of Guinea can be justified, it must be from the absolute necessity of employing them in such services as this is. It does not seem consistent with British humanity, to assign such employments to a regiment of gallant soldiers, or to a company of brave seamen.
> (105–106)

87 Arnold, *Colonizing the Body*.

88 James Johnson, *The Influence on Tropical Climates, More Especially the Climate of India, on European Constitutions* (London: J. J. Stockdale, 1813), 108.

89 Ibid., 58.

90 Ibid., 95.

91 Ibid., 108–109.

92 Ibid., 39.

93 Mark Harrison, "Tropical Medicine in Nineteenth Century India," *The British Journal for the History of Science* 25 (1992): 299–318.

94 Martin, *Notes on the Medical Topography*; *Report of the Committee Appointed by the Right Honorable the Governor of Bengal for the Establishment of a Fever Hospital and for Inquiry into Local Management and Taxation in Calcutta* (Calcutta: Bishop College Press, 1840), 14–15; hereafter *Fever Hospital Committee Report*.

95 Ibid., 15.

96 Ibid., 45.

97 Ibid., 45.

98 Ibid., 49.

99 Ibid., 51.

100 Ibid., 18.

101 Ibid., 24.

102 Ibid., 24.

103 Rev. James Long, "Calcutta and Bombay in their Social Aspects." Read before the Bengal Social Science Association (Calcutta: City Press, 1870), 8.

104 Harrison, "Tropical Medicine."

105 Johnson, *The Influence of Tropical Climate*, 71.

106 Ibid., 60.

107 Fenton, *A Narrative*, 242.

108 Ibid., 253–254.

109 Lord Viscount Valentia criticized Alexander Hamilton for writing about imaginary minarets in the native town. Fanny Parks was an exception in considering the architectural similarity pretty.

110 William Ward, *A View of the History, Literature and Mythology of the Hindoos* (Serampore: Mission Press, 1818).

111 At about the same time James Mill suggested that the very absence of fixed signs was indicative of rude civilizations such as India.

112 See H. J. Dyos and Michael Wolff (eds) *The Victorian City: Images and Realities* (London: Routledge & Kegan Paul, 1973); and Judith Walkowitz, *Prostitution and Victorian Society: Women, Class, and the State* (New York: Cambridge University Press, 1980) and *City of Dreadful Delight: Narratives of Sexual Danger in Late Victorian London* (Chicago: University of Chicago Press, 1992).

113 Ward, *A View of the History*, 209.

114 "Resolution on the 1889–90 Calcutta Municipality Administration Report," *Municipal Proceedings* Nov. 1890, File M 1R/2, 15–18.
115 Memo from Edward Goodeve, Esq., M.D. to the Secretary, Sanitary Department, India Office, dated 24 June, 1868, *General/Sanitation Department Proceedings #3*, Jan 1869.
116 See R. J. Morris, *Cholera 1832: A Social Response to an Epidemic* (New York: Holmes and Meir Publishers, 1976); Charles Rosenberg, *The Cholera Years: The United States in 1832, 1849, and 1866* (Chicago: University of Chicago Press, 1962).
117 Arnold, *Colonizing the Body*.
118 Ibid.
119 Cited in Arnold, *Colonizing the Body*, 189.
120 Memorandum of the Army Sanitary Commission on the Administration Report of the Calcutta Municipality for 1880.
121 *Fever Hospital Committee Report*, 1840.
122 Ibid.
123 Ibid., 3.
124 "Report of the Health Officer," in the *Calcutta Municipality Administration Report*, 1872.
125 Ibid., 5.
126 Ibid., 6.
127 Ibid., 7.
128 Ibid., 7.
129 See C. Macnamara, *A History of Asiatic Cholera* (London: Macmillan and Co., 1876). Also see the discussion of cholera in Arnold, *Colonizing the Body*.
130 *Calcutta Municipality Administration Report*, 1876.
131 "Report of the Health Officer," 1872, 10.
132 *Report on Sanitary Measures in India*, 1878. Also see Arnold, *Colonizing the Body*.
133 See, for example, the "Reports of C. Fabre-Tonnerre, Health Officer of Calcutta to S. S. Hogg, Chairman of the Justices of the Peace," March 1874, and March 1875; "Report on Sanitary Measures in India," *British Parliamentary Papers*, vol. LIX, 1878; and *Calcutta Municipal Proceedings*, March 1884, Coll 2–9. The Cholera Commission of 1887, headed by Dr. George Gaffky and assisted by Dr. Robert Koch, determined environmental causes and habits of natives, particularly of the Hindus, to be largely responsible for the disease (Calcutta Municipality Administration Report, 1887–88).
134 Baron Dowlean, "Calcutta in 1860"; reproduced in N. Bose (ed.) *Calcutta: People and Empire* (Calcutta: India Book Exchange, 1975), 9.
135 Memo from A. Mackenzie, Secretary to the Government of India to the Secretary of the Government of Bengal, Municipal Department, Coll 2–78, 1885.
136 W. J. T. Mitchell, "Imperial Landscapes," 19.

2 The limits of "white town"

1 In the case of India see Norma Evenson, *The Indian Metropolis: A View Towards the West* (New Haven: Yale University Press, 1989); Anthony D. King, *Colonial Urban Development: Culture, Social Power, and Environment* (London: Routledge, 1977); Sten Nilsson, *European Architecture in India, 1750–1850* (New York: Taplinger Publishing Company, 1969); Pradip Sinha, *Calcutta in Urban History* (Calcutta: Firma KLM Pvt. Ltd., 1978).
2 In cantonment towns in India the separation between rulers and ruled was more of a possibility than in the presidency towns where the European community

was a minority within a large Indian population (See King's *Colonial Urban Development*). But even in cantonment towns the physical separation was not always adequate, as Kenneth Ballhatchet's discussion of prostitution and the Contagious Diseases Act demonstrates (*Race, Sex and Class under the Raj: Imperial Attitudes and Policies and their Critics, 1793–1905* (New York: Saint Martin's Press, 1980)).

3 For example, see Evenson, *Indian Metropolis*, 48–51. For a reading of the "unsuccessful" adoption of neo-classicism in Indian architecture see G. H. R. Tillotson, *The Tradition of Indian Architecture: Controversy, Continuity and Change* (New Haven: Yale University Press, 1989), 12.

4 Few scholars have done justice to the complex conditions that result in hybrid forms when building ideas are carried from one region of the world to another. For an exception see John Michael Vlach, "The Brazilian House in Nigeria: The Emergence of a Twentieth-century Vernacular House Type," *Journal of American Folklore*, 97, no. 383 (1984), 3–23.

5 See Philip Davis, *Splendours of the Raj: British Architecture in India* (London: John Murray, 1985); Evenson, *Indian Metropolis*; Nilsson, *European Architecture in India*; Sinha, *Calcutta in Urban History*.

6 In 1822 Lieutenant Robert Grenville observed in *Fifteen Years in India: Or Sketches of a Soldier's Life* (London: Longman) that "Chowringhee, Park Street, Dhuromtola, the Jaun Bazaar and Esplanade now form the European part of the town" (65). Two decades later Leopold von Orlich (*Travels in India Including Sinde and Punjab* (London: Longman, 1845), 45) and Edward Thornton (*The Gazetteer of the Territories under the Government of the East India Company and the Native States on the Continent of India*, reproduced in P. T. Nair (ed.) *Calcutta in the Nineteenth Century* (Calcutta: Firma KLM, 1989, 986), seemed convinced that the city was divided into two distinct parts formed by a line from Beebee Ross Ghat eastward. Orlich and Thornton were probably both quoting the *Bengal and Agra Guide* of 1841. Thornton, however, pointed out that a considerable part of the "European division" was inhabited by natives, "chiefly Mussalmans and the lower caste Hindoos, while very few Christians have their abode in the native quarter." William Baillie's 1792 map indicated the area around Tank Square (between Beebee Ross Ghat and Esplanade Row), the strips along Bytaconnah/Bowbazaar Street, Dhurmtola Street, and the Chowringhee area as inhabited by Europeans.

7 Emma Roberts, *Scenes and Characteristics of Hindoostan* (London: W. H. Allen, 1837), 9.

8 For the full details of the proclamation see Ray, *A Short History of Calcutta* (1901; reprint, Calcutta: Riddhi, 1982), 116–119.

9 Proceedings of the Calcutta Committee of Revenue, Oct. 24, 1774, cited in Sinha, *Calcutta in Urban History*, 18.

10 The census data of the time are not reliable, but the available figures indicate the following changes in the population of the city:

1821	179,917
1822	230,552
1831	187,081
1837	229,714
1850	361,369
1866	358,362
1872	428,458
1876	409,039
1881	401,671
1891	470,835
1901	542,686

11 See the details of wills in Sinha, *Calcutta in Urban History*. This trend continued later. In my own sampling of wills and probates of Bengali residents between 1840 and 1895 I found extensive owning and/or letting out of landed property.

12 W. S. Seton-Kerr, *Selections from Calcutta Gazettes* (Calcutta: Military Orphan Press, 1864), vol. 3, 567. Similarly, an advertisement for Belvedere House noted that it would be appropriate "for a gentleman of distinction." Although Company services were disciplined along race lines under Lord Cornwallis, it would take longer for such attitudes to be entrenched as a mode of real-estate practice. One *bigha* (or *beegah*) is about one-third of an acre, and equivalent to 1,600 square yards, one *catha* (or *cotta*) is 80 square yards; and one *chattack* (or *chittack*) is 5 square yards.

13 Sinha, *Calcutta in Urban History*, 149–152.

14 See discussion in Chapters 3 and 4.

15 R. H. Phillimore, *Historical Records of the Survey of the Eighteenth Century*, vol. 1 (Dehradun: Survey of India, 1945), 52.

16 Ibid., 53.

17 Ibid., 53.

18 Sinha, *Calcutta in Urban History*.

19 See Radharaman Mitra, "Gangar Ghat," *Aitihashik* (Jan. 1977): 49–108, for historical information on the large number of *ghats* in Calcutta.

20 Seton-Kerr, *Selections*, vol. 1, 56–57.

21 I. H. T. Roberdeau, "A Young Civilian in Bengal in 1805," reproduced in P. T. Nair (ed.) *Calcutta in the Nineteenth Century*, 46–47.

22 *Calcutta Gazette*, April 7, 1785.

23 In advertisements the taverns emphasized the respectablity of their establishments. Announcing the opening of the Anchor Hotel and British Coffee House in 1807, the owner William Dougherty noted that "he pledges himself to strain every nerve to conduct the business in every department with strict propriety." Seton-Kerr, *Selections*, vol. 4, 425.

24 In 1801 the *Calcutta Gazette* contained the following advertisement: "A neat small lower-roomed house, situate in Crooked Lane, near Cossitola, admirably adapted for the accommodation of a native family; it has undergone a thorough repair, has seldom been unoccupied, and never let for less than Rs. 40 per month." Seton-Kerr, *Selections*, vol. 3, 553.

25 Seton-Kerr, *Selections*, vol. 1, 69.

26 A. Wilson, watchmaker's shop was on Council House Street; Carriages and horses were available from several stables on Cossitola Street and Dhurumtola Street; Joseph Dickson, cabinet- and coachmaker and undertaker, operated from 41 Cossitola Street. James Palmer, who started his undertaker's business in 1784 from Cossitola Street, next to Mr. Oliphant's the coachmaker, ironically, was doing so well in a few years that he expanded his business and started operating from 39 Radhabazaar Street, one block away from Europe, China, and European Warehouse. Seton-Kerr, *Selections*, vol. 1, 48, 285; vol. 2, 524, 532, 536.

27 Keya Dasgupta, "A City Away from Home: The Mapping of Calcutta," in Partha Chatterjee (ed.) *Texts of Power: Emerging Disciplines in Colonial Bengal* (Minneapolis: University of Minnesota Press, 1995).

28 Arunkumar Mitra (ed.), *Amritalal Basur Smriti O Atmasmriti* (Calcutta: Sahityalok, 1982), 92. For a description of the markets and social life of Calcutta in the second half of the century refer to this autobiography.

29 Cited in S. W. Goode, *Municipal Calcutta: Its Institutions in their Origin and Growth* (Edinburgh: T. A. Constable, 1916), 237.

30 *Lottery Committee Report* cited in Keshab Chowdhuri, *Calcutta: Story of Its Government* (Calcutta: Orient Longman, 1973), 30.

31 Cited in Samita Gupta, "Theory and Practice of Town Planning in Calcutta, 1817–1912: An Appraisal," *Indian Economic and Social History Review* 30, no. 1 (January–March 1993): 29–55.

32 Quoted in Gupta, "Theory and Practice of Town Planning in Calcutta," 44.

33 Goode, *Municipal Calcutta*, 238.

34 I will address the Indian point of view in Chapters 3 and 4.

35 Describing the life in the *para* in the fin-de-siècle city the Bengali novelist Premankur Atarthi wrote that "every person had an 'obligatory' good relation with every body else in the *para*," (*Mahasthabira Jataka*, vol. 1, Calcutta: Ranjan Publishing House, 1943), 152.

36 Dasgupta, "A City Away from Home."

37 As early as 1790 we see these lots being filled. The "large house on the corner of Old Court House Street, opposite the Governor General's stables, containing thirteen pieces above stairs" was "improved" by adding 211 feet of space for 15 godowns and shops. Seton-Kerr, *Selections*, vol. 2, 517.

38 Lord Viscount George Valentia, *Voyages and Travels to India, Ceylon, the Red Sea, Abyssinia, and Egypt, in the Years 1802–1806*, vol. I (London: William Miller, 1809).

39 The Notice from the Governor of Fort William stated:

> It having been represented to the Most Noble the Governor of Fort William that considerable inconvenience is experienced by the European part of the community who resort to the Respondentia, from the Crowds of Native Workmen and Coolies who make a thoroughfare of the Walk.
>
> His Lordship is pleased to direct that Natives shall not in future be allowed to pass the Sluice Bridge (but such as are entering or leaving the Fort), between the hours 5 and 8 in the Morning, and 5 to 8 in the Evening.
>
> Seton-Kerr, *Selections*, vol. 5, 76

40 Sir Charles D'Oyly, *Views of Calcutta and Its Environs* (London, 1835). Also see Jeremy P. Losty, *Calcutta: City of Palaces, A Survey of the City in the Days of the East India Company 1690–1858* (London: Arnold, 1990).

41 Elisabeth Fenton, *A Narrative*, 14–15.

42 James Ranald Martin, *Notes on the Medical Topography of Calcutta* (Calcutta: Military Orphan Press, 1836), 63.

43 "Plan of Calcutta and its Environs surveyed by the Late Major J. A. Schalch for the use of the Lottery Committee and containing all their improvements with addition from the Surveyor General's Office and from recent surveys made by Captain T. Prinsep," 1825–32, reproduced in Anil K. Kundu and Prithvish Nag (eds) *Atlas of the City of Calcutta and Its Environs* (Calcutta: National Atlas and Thematic Mapping Organisation, Government of India, 1990).

44 Seton-Kerr, *Selections*, vol. 3, 550. Eight *sicca* rupees were worth 1 Pound Sterling.

45 Ibid., 547; also, vol. 5, 117.

46 Ibid., 557.

47 Ibid., 567.

48 For example, see an 1805 advertisement in Seton-Kerr, *Selections*, vol. 3, 581–582.

49 Seton-Kerr, *Selections*, vol. 1. James Palmer, an undertaker attempting to diversify his business notified the Ladies and Gentlemen of the Settlement that he had procured a large assortment of marble slabs due to "the practice universally adopted among the genteel families of the Settlement, of having baths in their houses, lined, or only floored with marble slabs, likewise Halls and other Apartments" (285).

50 Seton-Kerr, *Selections*, vol. 2, 543. *Abdarkhanna* means wine-cellar.

51 Seton-Kerr, *Selections*, vol. 1, 34. The same notice contained an advertisement of a smaller single-story house on the east of China Bazaar, "highly raised from

the ground" and containing a hall, two bedrooms, a verandah, a *bottle-khannah*, cook room, and necessary house, standing on 5 *cottahs*, and yielding 100 *sicca* rupees in rent. A *bottlekhana* refers to a pantry/storage.

52 For example, the following advertisement appeared in 1786:

> A commodious and elegant House formerly occupied by the late Edward Wheeler, Esq. and at present tenanted by the Hon'ble Charles Stuart, at the monthly rent of Sicca Rupees 900, consisting of 2 halls, 8 large chambers, with 4 open verandahs, a grand staircase, and backstairs, closets, &c., all highly furnished, and in complete repair. The first floor raised 7 feet from the ground, and has under it eight excellent godowns. The premises occupy three beeghas, fourteen cottahs, and six chittacks of ground. The detached offices are extensive and convenient, fit to accommodate a large family, and all pucka built.
>
> Seton-Kerr, *Selections*, vol. 1, 167

53 Seton-Kerr, *Selections*, vol. 2, 501–502.
54 Seton-Kerr, *Selections*, vol. 3, 533.
55 Seton-Kerr, *Selections*, vol. 4, 432–433.
56 One of the houses, located adjacent to Tiretta's bazaar, contained "pucka sheds 200 ft long and 32 feet wide." Seton-Kerr, *Selections*, vol. 1, 292. Also vol. 2, 517.
57 Colesworthy Grant, *Anglo-Indian Domestic Sketch* (Calcutta: Thacker and Spink, 1862).
58 Ibid., 8.
59 Ibid., 11.
60 Ibid.
61 Ibid., 9.
62 Robin Evans, "Figures, Doors, and Passages," *Architectural Design* 48, no. 4 (1978): 267–278.
63 All three are initially indicated in the Schalch Plan, 1825–32.
64 Building drawings from the archives of Mackintosh Burn Pvt. Ltd, Index no. 2087, dated 1911. Blueprints of this building and others discussed in this essay were all prepared in the first and second decades of the twentieth century to seek municipal permission to add bathrooms and make other alterations. Consequently, they contain traces of previous changes made in the buildings. My discussion is based on the changes indicated in these drawings.
65 The urge to have such large spaces unimpeded by columns caused structural problems. The dance floor of the Town Hall had to be reinforced with extra beams, while the London Tavern's large ballroom was rumored to be unstable, an accusation that caused the proprietors to bring out an advertisement vouching for its safety.
66 The house is indicated in Schalch's 1825 map. In an 1808 advertisement in the *Calcutta Gazette* there is reference of "two newly built" houses on the north side of Middleton Street. Since there were only three buildings on the north side of Middleton Street including this one, this house was likely built in 1807/1808. Building drawings from Mackintosh Burn Pvt. Ltd, dated 1905. The Schalch plan indicates that the house address was 8 Middleton Street.
67 *Thacker's Street Directories*, 1852 to 1892.
68 Ibid.
69 An entry to Camac Street is shown in a Map of Calcutta prepared by W. Heysham in 1856, reproduced in *Atlas of the City of Calcutta*.
70 Site Plan from Mackintosh Burn Pvt. Ltd, Index no. 2087, dated 1911.
71 Drawings from the archive of the Calcutta Municipal Corporation. The drawing dated 1925 was submitted to the municipality for approval of changes made

in the building. The simplicity of the elevation suggests that this was an early nineteenth-century building. It is not present in the Schalch map of 1825, however. That part of Chowringhee Road was not completely built up in 1825. The house appears in Heysham's 1856 map without the shops on the right, leading me to conclude that it was built in the 1830s.

72 The address is 54 Free School Street. Drawings from the archive of Mackintosh Burn Pvt. Ltd, Index no. 2332, dated 1914.

73 Drawings from the archive of Mackintosh Burn Pvt. Ltd: Building on 1/1 Little Russell Street, Index no. 2345, dated 1907.

74 James Gibbs, *Book of Architecture: Containing Designs of Buildings and Ornaments* (London: W. Innys and R. Manby, 1739).

75 Mark Girouard, *Life in the English Country House* (New Haven: Yale University Press, 1978).

76 Nilsson, *European Architecture*.

77 Seton-Kerr, *Selections*, vol. 3, 563–564.

78 Nilsson, *European Architecture*.

79 Robert Kerr, *The Gentleman's House* (1864; reprint, New York: Johnson Reprint, 1972).

80 Ibid., 67–68.

81 H. E. A. Cotton, *Calcutta Old and New* (1907; reprint, Calcutta: General Publishers, 1980), 121.

82 Grant, *Anglo-Indian Domestic Sketch*.

83 Ibid., 6.

84 William Huggins, *Sketches in India: Treatise on Subjects Connected with the Government; Civil and Military Establishments; Characters of the European, and the Customs of the Native Inhabitants* (London: John Letts, 1824), 110.

85 Elijah Impey and his family lived in a large house on Middleton Row, now occupied by the Loretto Convent. I am grateful to Dr. Oliver Impey for informing me that the painting is attributed to Zain-al-din, but there is no hard evidence to prove that he was the painter.

86 See Ballhatchet, *Race, Sex and Class*.

87 For an account of the East India Company's policy on dress codes that prohibited Company's servants from wearing Indian clothing, see Bernard S. Cohn, *Colonialism and its Forms of Knowledge: The British in India* (Princeton: Princeton University Press, 1996).

88 See, for example, Lady Maria Nugent, *A Journal from the Year 1811 Till the Year 1815* (London, 1839), 123.

89 See, for example, Lord Viscount Valentia, *Voyages and Travels*, vol. 1, 242.

90 Fenton, *A Narrative*, 82.

91 For example, the 1879 will of Magnus J. Stone directed that after selling off as much property as was necessary to clear his debts, the rest of his financial assets would go to Moti Bibee, "my faithful friend of nearly twenty years" (23), India Office Library Collection: L/AG/34/29/122.

92 Ballhatchet, *Race, Sex and Class*.

93 Nugent, *A Journal*, 112.

94 Ibid., 85.

95 Emma Roberts, *Scenes and Characteristics of Hindoostan*, 7.

96 Laura Ann Stoler, *Race and the Education of Desire* (Durham: Duke University Press, 1995), 157–164.

97 It is also likely that this image pokes fun at such paranoia about servants.

98 Cotton, *Calcutta*, 76–80.

99 Emily Eden, *Letters from India* (London: Richard Bentley, 1872), 84–85.

100 Ibid., 91.

101   Ibid., 91–92.
102   Marchioness of Dufferin & Ava, *Our Viceregal Life in India: Selections from My Journal 1884–1888* (New York: Scribner and Welford, 1890), 8–9.
103   Ibid., 10.
104   Flora Annie Steel and Grace Gardiner, *The Complete Indian Housekeeper and Cook* (London: William Heineman, 1909, 7th edn).
105   For a more detailed exploration of the model of Anglo-Indian domesticity see my article "Goods, Chattels, and Sundry Items: Constructing Nineteenth-century Anglo-Indian Domestic Life," *Journal of Material Culture* 7. No. 3, (Fall 2002), 243–271.
106   Drawings from the archive of Mackintosh Burn Pvt. Ltd 1921. Index no. missing.
107   Homi Bhaba, "Signs Taken for Wonders," *The Location of Culture* (London: Routledge, 1994), 115.

3   Locating mythic selves

1   *Report on the Census of the Town and Suburb of Calcutta taken on 17th February, 1881, by Henry Beverley*, 9–10.
2   Michel de Certeau, *The Practice of Everyday Life*, translated by Steven Rendall (Berkeley: University of California Press, 1988), 61.
3   Tanika Sarkar, *Words to Win: The Making of Amar Jiban: A Modern Autobiography* (New Delhi: Kali for Women, 1999), 21–22. For a more detailed analysis of the Permanent Settlement see, Ranajit Guha, *The Rule of Property in Bengal: An Essay on the Idea of Permanent Settlement* (original pub. 1963; Durham: Duke University Press, 1996).
4   For this distinction among the respectable classes see Bhabanicharan Bandopadhyay, *Kalikata Kamalalaya* (1823; reprint, Bishnu Basu (ed.) Calcutta: Pratibhas, 1986), 117–118.
5   Partha Chatterjee, *The Nation and its Fragments* (Princeton: Princeton University Press, 1993), 23.
6   Ibid., 5–6.
7   Bandopadhyay, *Kalikata Kamalalaya*, 117.
8   Ibid., 117–118.
9   William Ward, *A View of the History, Literature and Mythology of the Hindoos* (Serampore: Mission Press, 1818).
10   Partha Mitter, *Art and Nationalism in India 1850–1922 Occidental Orientations* (Cambridge University Press, 1994), 171, 173; Tanika Sarkar, *Words to Win*, 109–110.
11   Here I am using the term, material culture, to refer to a range of practices involved in the production and use of cultural artifacts, including language.
12   Bandopadhyay, *Kalikata Kamalalaya*, 121–127.
13   Ibid., 117.
14   See Dipesh Chakrabarty, *Provincializing Europe* (Princeton: Princeton University Press, 2000), 221–224. My point is that Chakrabarty's argument that in KK civil society and the state are considered to be external constraints and therefore less important than the ritually pure domains of *pitrikarma* and *daivakarma* misses the central argument of KK.
15   This is the definition used by Chakrabarty in *Provincializing Europe*.
16   Tejaswini Niranjana, *Siting Translation: History, Post-structuralism and the Colonial Context* (Berkeley: University of California Press, 1992), 3.
17   Ibid.
18   *Sahitya Sadhak Charitmala*, vol. 1 (Calcutta: Bangiya Sahitya Parishad, 1976).

19 Bandopadhyay, *Kalikata Kamalalaya*, 114–115.

20 Ibid., 151–152.

21 See, for example, Ramchandra Palit (ed.), *Speeches by Babu Surendranath Banerjee* (Calcutta: S. K. Lahiri & Co., 1890–91), and *A Nation in the Making: Being the Reminiscences of Fifty Years of Public Life*, New York: Oxford University Press, 1925).

22 "Grant of the Talookdarry of Sootalooty &c., The Honorable East India Company to Rajah Nobkissen, Dated 28th April 1778," Copy of Grant in the collection of the Deb family.

23 Loknath Ghosh, *Kolkatar Babubrittanta* (1881; reprint, Calcutta: Ayan, 1983).

24 Ghosh, *Kolkatar Babubrittanta*; Beepin Beharry Mittra, *Life of Maharaja Nava Krishna Deva Bahadoor* (Calcutta: Stanhope Press, 1879).

25 S. N. Mukherjee, *Calcutta: Aspects of Urban History* (Calcutta: Subornorekha, 1993), 127.

26 Mittra, *Life of Maharaja Nava Krishna*.

27 Radhakanta had an international reputation as a Sanskrit scholar, and was the leading member of the Dharmasabha and the British Indian Association, a member of the Board of Hindu College, and the Secretary of the School Book Society and Sanskrit College. See Ghosh, *Kolkatar Babubrittanta*, 78–80.

28 See Dhriti Kanta Lahiri Chowdhuri, "Trends in Calcutta Architecture, 1690–1903," in Sukanta Chowdhury (ed.) *Calcutta: A Living City* (Oxford: Oxford University Press, 1990).

29 One of the oldest surviving examples of this eighteenth-century tradition is the house of Gobindaram Mitra in Kumartuli, Calcutta. See Lahiri Chowdhury's description of the house in "Trends in Calcutta Architecture."

30 George Mitchell (ed.), *Brick Temples of Bengal* (Princeton: Princeton University Press, 1983).

31 G. H. R. Tillotson, *The Tradition of Indian Architecture: Continuity, Controversy and Change since 1850* (New Haven: Yale University Press, 1989).

32 The house of Govindaram Mitra is one of the earliest examples showing this adjustment.

33 Bernard Cohn, *Colonialism and its Forms of Knowledge* (Princeton: Princeton University Press, 1996), 54–55.

34 Jeremy P. Losty, *Calcutta: City of Palaces* (London: British Library).

35 Rajah Rajendra Narayan Deb Bahadur, *Rajah Sir Radhakant Deb Bahadur: A Brief Account of His Life and Character* (Calcutta: Indian Daily News Press, 1880).

36 Ibid., 14.

37 See Charles D'Oyly's aquatint "Tom Raw's Misfortune at the Ball," *c.*1820, in his *Tom Raw Griffin* (London: Ackerman, 1828).

38 Deb, *Rajah Sir Radhakanta Deb*, 1.

39 Alexander Duff, *India and Indian Missions* (Edinburgh: J. Johnstone, 1839), 253.

40 Deb, *Rajah Sir Radhakant Deb*.

41 Charles Henry Appleton Dall was a missionary of the American Unitarian Association, who came to Calcutta in 1841 and spent the rest of his life in the city. While having empathy for Indians, Dall was convinced of the need to fundamentally restructure Hindu society according to Christian principles.

42 Ibid., 58.

43 See Homi Bhaba's analysis of Alexander Duff's writings in *The Location of Culture* (London: Routledge, 1994).

44 Abanindranath Tagore, *Putur Boi*, in *Abanindra Rachanabali*, vol. 3 (Calcutta: Prakash Bhavan, 1985). I am grateful to Keya Dasgupta for bringing this map to my attention, and to Arun Nag for helping me locate it.

45 Tagore, *Apan Katha*, in *Abanindra Rachanabli*, vol. 1 (Calcutta: Prakash Bhavan, 1985), 51–52.

46 Ibid., 51–54.

47 Mohanlal Gangopadhyay, *Dakshiner Baranda* (Calcutta: Viswabharati, 1980), 50.
48 Ramananda Chattopadhyay, *Arabya Upanyas*, vol. 1 (Calcutta: Prabasi, 1921).
49 Frances Yates, *The Art of Memory* (London: Routledge, 1966), 3.
50 Tagore, *Apan Katha*, 30. "*Baroduari*" literally means a 12-door room.
51 Tagore, *Abanindra Rachanabali*, vol. 1, 61–62.
52 This is the argument that Dipesh Chakrabarty has made in a discussion of Rabindranth Tagore's poetry in "Nation and Imagination," *Provincializing Europe*.
53 R. Sivakumar, "Abanindranath's Arabian Nights: Native Flanerie and Anti-colonial Narration," *Nandan*, Essays in Honor of K. G. Subramanyan (No. XIX, 1999), 167.
54 Tagore, *Apan Katha*, 57.
55 See Chakrabarty, *Provincializing Europe*, 172–179.
56 Ibid., 6.
57 Purnima Debi, *Thakurbarir Gaganthakur* (Calcutta: Punascha, 1999), 44.
58 Gangopadhyay, *Dakshiner Baranda*, 105.

4 Telling stories

 1 I am grateful to Aurobindo Dasgupta for taking time to show me around the Dasgupta family home and for conversation on the subject.
 2 Dipesh Chakrabarty, *Provincializing Europe* (Princeton: Princeton University Press, 2000), 180.
 3 Ibid., 181–182.
 4 Pramatha Bishi, "Katharasik Sayyad Mujtaba Ali," *Mujtaba Rachanabali*, vol. 1 (Calcutta: Mitra & Ghosh, 1990); also see Gajendrakumar Mitra, "Introduction," in the same volume.
 5 Sayyad Mujtaba Ali, "Adda," *Rachanabali*, vol. 1, 83.
 6 Mujtaba Ali, "Adda," *Rachanabali*, vol. 3, 318–319.
 7 Mujtaba Ali, "Adda," *Rachanabali*, vol. 3, 319.
 8 Mujtaba Ali, "Adda," *Rachanabali*, vol. 1, 82.
 9 Mujtaba Ali, "Adda," *Rachanabali*, vol. 3, 317. The adjective he used to describe his ideal *adda* in the original Bengali is "atyutkrishna," which I have quite inadequately translated as "exquisite" because I don't quite have the courage to attempt translation of the pun he implied in his invention of the Bengali word.
10 For more elaborate discussion of this issue, see Partha Chatterjee, *The Nation and Its Fragments*.
11 Mujtaba Ali, "Kisher Sandhane," *Rachanabali*, vol. 1, 42.
12 Chakrabarty, *Provincializing Europe*, 212.
13 It is important to mention here that *addas* in the *baithak-khana*, café, and *ro'ak* carry different social valences in the popular imaginary, with the *adda* in the *baithak-khana* considered the most elite and the *adda* in the café the most intellectual.
14 Partha Chatterjee, *The Nation and Its Fragments* (Princeton: Princeton University Press, 1993), 55.
15 The Vernacular Press Act was passed in 1878 to curb the seditious native opinion propagated through the print media, and The Dramatic Performances Act was passed in 1876 to ostensibly prevent obscene performances, but mainly to stop the criticism of Anglo-Indian society on the public stage. See Pramila Pandhe, *Suppression of Drama in Nineteenth-Century India* (Calcutta: India Book Exchange, 1978).
16 Sumanta Banerjee, *The Parlour and the Streets* (Calcutta: Seagull, 1989).
17 Ibid., 102.
18 S. N. Mukherjee, "Introduction," *The Poison Tree*, translated by Marian Maddern and S. N. Mukherjee, (New Dehli: Penguin, 1996), xxviii.

19 Arun Nag, *Satik Hutom Penchar Naksha* (Calcutta: Subarnorekha, 1990).

20 Pyarichand Mitra's *Alaler Ghare Dulal* published two years before *Hutom Penchar Naksha*, was also hailed for its success in colloquial Bengali. Mitra noted in his introduction that his book was meant to be read by women, and not designed for the pundits.

21 Nag, *Satik Hutom*, 21.

22 Arun Kumar Mitra, *Amritalal Basur Smriti O Atmasmriti* (Calcutta: Sahityalok, 1982), 139.

23 Bankimchandra Chattopadhyay, "Lokshiksha," *Bankim Rachanabali*, vol. 2, 323–325.

24 Ibid., 324.

25 Sureshchandra Samajpati, "Bankimchandra," in *Bankim Prasanga* (Calcutta: Mukherjee Bose and Company, n.d.), 140.

26 *Bankim Rachanabali*, vol. 2, 323.

27 Ibid., 324.

28 For reasons of space I cannot elaborate on this point here. For some indications see Abanindranath Tagore, *Apan Katha*, and Gautam Bhadra's article cited below.

29 See Gautam Bhadra (ed.), *Yogasutra* (Oct.–Dec., 1993).

30 Bhadra, "Kathakathar Nanan Katha," in *Yogasutra* (Oct.–Dec., 1993), 169–278.

31 Purnachandra Chattopadhyay, "Bankim Prasanga," cited in Jogeschandra Bagal, "Upanyas Prasanga," in *Bankim Rachanabali*, vol. 1, 28.

32 For a discussion of the impact of music in Bankim's work see Shyamali Chakrabarty, *Bankimchandrer Shilpa O Sangiter Jagat* (Calcutta: Aruna Prakashani, 1990).

33 Samajpati, "Bankimchandra," 329.

34 The 1866 Calcutta census shows the following under the Hindu male population of the "Professional Class": 1,365 engaged in offices of the government, 2,075 clergymen, ministers, priests, 394 lawyers or law stamp dealers, 583 physicians and druggists, 260 authors and literary persons, 644 teachers. In addition, 20,357 males were shown to be engaged in banking, various kinds of buying and selling, and general dealership. *The Census of Calcutta*, 1866.

35 See *Thacker's Street Directory of Calcutta* for the 1880s and 1890s.

36 One of these mansions was demolished and the other now serves as a hospital.

37 Nirad C. Chaudhuri, *The Autobiography of an Unknown Indian*, (1951; reprint, Reading: Addison Wesley, 1989), 381.

38 Kanny Loll Dey, "Hindu Social Laws and Habits Viewed in Relation to Health," An address delivered at the 3rd Anniversary of the Bengal Branch of the British Medical Association on the 15th March, 1886 (Calcutta: R. C. Lepage & Co., 1886), 4–5.

39 "Ramanir Kartabya," *Bamabodhini Patrika*, no. 265 (Feb. 1887), 303.

40 Mitra, *Amritalal Basur Smriti*, 94. Also see Kaliprasanna Sinha's description of the bustling street life in Nag, *Satik Hutom*, 34.

41 Chakrabarty provides an excellent example from the writing of Rajshekhar Basu to demonstrate the limits of the *adda*. See, *Provincializing Europe*, 192–193.

42 Mitra, *Amritalal Basur Smriti*, 28–29.

43 Chaudhuri, *The Autobiography of an Unknown Indian*, 267.

44 Ibid., 97–98.

45 Ibid., 54.

46 Ibid.

47 Banerjee, *The Parlour and the Streets*.

48 For a similar nineteenth-century format that is used to the present day see Richard Schechner's discussion of the *Ramlila* in Ramnagar, India, in *Between Theater and Anthropology*, (Philadelphia: University of Pennsylvania Press, 1985).

49 Banerjee, *The Parlour and the Streets*.

50 Ibid., 56–57.
51 Mitra, *Amritalal Basur Smriti*, 54.
52 Banerjee, *The Parlour and the Streets*, 182.
53 Mitra, *Amritalal Basur Smriti*, 183–186.
54 In Hindu society dying on the banks of the Ganga was considered meritorious. A room was sometimes built for the dying so that they did not suffer from the elements during the last moments of their lives.
55 Ibid., 119.
56 Ibid., 198.
57 Cited in Sumanta Banerjee, *Dangerous Outcast: Prostitutes in Nineteenth-century Bengal* (Calcutta: Seagull, 2000), 134.
58 Rimli Bhattacharyya, *Binodini Dasi: My Story and My Life as an Actress* (New Delhi: Kali, 1998), 206.
59 Ibid., 149.
60 Cited in Banerjee, *Dangerous Outcast*, 122.
61 Benodini Dasi, *Amar Katha O Ananya Rachana* (Calcutta: Subarnorekha, 1987).
62 For a very good analysis of Benodini's text see Bhattacharyya, *Benodini Dasi*.
63 Kalyani Dutta, *Thor, Bari, Khara* (Calcutta: Thema, 1992), 15.
64 Rameshchandra Dutta, *Samsaar, Granthabali*, vol. 1 (Calcutta: Basumati, 1894), 88–89.
65 Ibid., 115–116.
66 Ibid., 118–119.
67 Bengal Inventory of Deceased Estates, L/AG/34/27 series, India Office Library Collection. The artifacts and pattern of furnishing in Bonnerjee's probate is fairly representative of upper-class nineteenth-century Bengali households, and this pattern did not change substantially until the early twentieth century.
68 Prabhat Mukhopadhyay, "Gahanar Baksha," *Prabhat Rachanabali* (Calcutta, n.d.).

5 Death in public

 1 Gayatri Chakaravorty Spivak, "Can the Subaltern Speak?" in Cary Nelson and Lawrence Grossberg (eds) *Marxism and the Interpretation of Culture* (Chicago: University of Illinois Press, 1988).
 2 *Kula* refers to a clan or lineage. *Kulatyagi* is one who has abandoned his/her family or clan.
 3 "Chattopadhyay Bangsher Ekadesh Karika," (Calcutta: Banimandir Prachar Bibhag, 1961).
 4 Premankur Atarthi, *Mahasthabira Jataka* (Calcutta: Indian Associated Publishing Co. Ltd, 1955), 55–57.
 5 Tanika Sarkar, *Words to Win* (New Delhi: Kali for Women, 1999) 77.
 6 Arun Kumar Mitra, *Amritalal Basur Smriti O Atmasmriti* (Calcutta: Ranjan Publishing House 1943), 56–58.
 7 The following are some examples of the titles of plays: "Mohanter ei ki Kaaj" (Is this the Conduct of a Mohant?), "Mohanter ki Durdasha" (Mohant's Punishment), "Bhanda Tapaswi" (The Fraud Sage).
 8 I discuss this aspect of material culture in some detail in Chapter 4.
 9 Bhavanicharan Bandopadhyay, *Dutibilas*, in *Rasarachanasamagra* (Calcutta: Nabapatra Prakashan, 1987).
10 Bankimchandra Chattopadhyay, *Bishabriksha*, in *Bankim Rachanabali*, vol. 1 (Calcutta: Sahitya Samsad, 1994), 299.
11 Bankim, in fact, inaugurated the idea of a Bengali "landscape." I treat this subject of spatial mastery in more depth in a forthcoming article: "Envisioning History: Bankimchandra Chattopadhyay and the invention of a Bengali landscape."

12 It was a common practice in large houses to have a "dressing room" for men, located between the outer and inner compartments, for changing clothes before they entered the inner compartments.

13 Bhudev Mukhopadhyay, *Achar Prabandha* (Hooghly, 1893; original publication 1882), 132–134.

14 Bankimchandra Chattopadhyay, "Dharma ebong Sahitya," *Bankim Rachanabali*, vol. 2, 225.

15 Bankimchandra Chattopadhyay, "Uttarcharit," *Bankim Rachanabali*, vol. 2, 161.

16 Bankimchandra Chattopadhyay, "Krishnacharitra," *Bankim Rachanabali*, vol. 2, 353–524. The first part of Krishnacharitra was published in 1886, and in 1892 it was published in its entirety.

17 Ibid., 408.

18 Bankimchandra Chattopadhyay, "Dharmatatwa," *Bankim Rachanabali*, vol. 2, 558–559.

19 Ibid., 555.

20 Ibid.

21 Bankimchandra Chattopadhyay, *Bishabriksha*.

22 Ibid., 238.

23 Ibid., 247.

24 Ibid.

25 Ibid., 240–242.

26 Ibid., 242.

27 See the somewhat different argument offered by Sudipta Kaviraj, "A Taste for Transgression: Liminality in the novels of Bankimchandra Chattopadhyay," *Occasional Papers on History and Society* (New Delhi: Nehru Memorial Library, 1987), 40–65. For more elaborate discussion of Bankim's literature see his *Unhappy Consciousness: Bankimchandra Chattopadhyay and the Formation of Indian Nationalist Discourse* (New Delhi: Oxford University Press, 1995).

28 Bankimchandra Chattopadhyay, "Samya," *Bankim Rachanabali* vol. 2, 348.

29 Ibid., 345.

30 Ibid., 346–348.

31 Ibid., 350.

32 Ibid., 595.

33 Ibid., 596.

34 Ibid.

35 Ibid., 605–606.

36 Bankimchandra Chattopadhyay, "Striloker Rup," in "Kamalakanta," *Bankim Rachanabali*, vol. 2, 63.

37 Ibid., 65.

38 Ibid., 65–66.

39 Dipesh Chakrabarty, *Provincializing Europe* (Princeton: Princeton University Press, 2000) 231.

40 For discussions of the absent female subject in the discourse on *sati* see Gayatri Chakravorty Spivak in "Can the Subaltern Speak?"; and Lata Mani in "Contentious Traditions," in Kumkum Sangari and Sudesh Vaid (eds) *Recasting Women: Essays in Indian Colonial History* (Rutgers: Rutgers University Press, 1990). My analysis takes a different angle to this absence by foregrounding the impossibility of a female space in public.

41 Chakrabarty, "Domestic Cruelty and the Birth of a Subject," *Provincializing Europe*.

42 Ibid., 140–141.

43 Here I am trying to point out the strategy of disembodiment that is different from that allowed in Western contract theory. Most useful here is Carol Pateman's discussion in *The Sexual Contract* (Stanford: Stanford University Press, 1988); in particular see her discussion of the "dispension" of the body in Chapter 3.

44 Rabindranath Tagore, *Strir Patra*, in *Rabindra Rachanabali*, vol. 12 (Calcutta: Viswabharati, 1995).
45 Ibid., 329.
46 Ibid., 337.
47 Ibid., 331.
48 Ibid.
49 Ibid., 337.
50 Sumit Sarkar, "Nationalism and Stri-swadhinata," *Beyond Nationalist Frames: Relocating Postmodernism, Hindutva, History* (New Delhi: Permanent Black, 2002). See Sarkar's discussion of *Strir Patra* in the context of Rabindranath's other novels and short stories during that period.
51 For example, "Strishikshar Sutrapat," *Bamabodhini Patrika* (Phalgun-Chaitra, 1908), 248.
52 Rabindranath Tagore, *Manbhanjan*, in *Rabindra Rachanabali*, vol. 10.
53 Ibid., 349.
54 Rabindranath Tagore, *Strir Patra*, 338.
55 Rassundari Dasi, *Amar Jiban* (1876; reprint Calcutta: De Book Store, 1987). For a nuanced discussion of Rassundari's autobiography see Tanika Sarkar, *Words to Win*. Vaishnav *bhakti* is a form of devotional discourse and practice that establishes a direct emotional connection between Vishnu, in his incarnation as Krishna, and the devotee or *bhakta*. The cult of Vaishnavism had a mass following in Bengal and had generated a large volume of devotional literature, recited and performed in the elite households as well as among the lower classes. Vaishnavism promised salvation to the poor, outcastes, women, all those who resided beyond and beneath Brahmanical deliverance. In glorifying the *lila* (play) of Krishna's illicit love with Radha and her cowmaidens, Vaishnavism provided an unusually large role for women. Vaishnav texts primarily used the voice of women, personifying Radha, to express the love of God and the trials of attaining divine presence. *Chaitanyalila*, one of the key texts of Vaishnav literature, narrated the life of Chaitanya, the medieval Bengali saint, who forsook society and worldly desires for the love of Krishna.
56 One of the reasons for the immense success of the Bengali press in the early years was the demand for Vaishnav literature. See Sukumar Sen, *Battalar Chaapa o Chabi* (Calcutta: Ananda Publishers, 1989), 14–16.
57 Rabindranath Tagore, *Jibansmriti*, in *Rabindra Rachanabali*, vol. 9 (Calcutta: Viswabharati, 1994), 492.
58 To cite a few examples: The 1870 Annual Police Report, for example, noted a theft in the house of a "woman of the town" in Masjidbari Street, located in the the middle-class residential neighborhood. The Bengali newspapers frequently complained about prostitution in "respectable quarters" of the town, and particularly along College Street (Report on Newspapers, week ending February 7, 1885, 878; Report on Native Newspapers, Week ending June 27, 1887, 653; Report on Native Newspapers week ending December 12, 1891, 1271).
59 According to missionary reports these figures had risen considerably; see *Social Evil of Calcutta, Its Strengths, Its Haunts, Its Causes, Its Consequence with Suggestion for Hindering Its Growth and Rescuing Its Victim* (Calcutta: Thomas S. Smith, City Press, 1871). The same report also indicated the location of these brothels that were scattered all over the city.
60 See Kenneth Ballhatchet, *Race, Sex, and Class* (New York, 1980); Mark Harrison, *Public Health in British India: Anglo-Indian Preventive Medicine, 1859–1914* (Cambridge: Cambridge University Press, 1994); and Sumanta Banerjee, *Dangerous Outcast: the Prostitute in Nineteenth-century Bengal* (Calcutta: Seagull, 2000).
61 "Sanitary Administration of Military Cantonments under the Bengal Government," *Proceedings* for June 1868.

62 Ibid.
63 Ibid.
64 "Working of the Contagious Diseases Act," *Sanitation Proceedings* 3–5, General Department, August 1872, p. 5.
65 Ibid.
66 "On the Working of Measures for the Prevention of Venereal Diseases," *Sanitation Proceedings* 3–5, General Department, August 1872, p. 5.
67 "Extracts from an Abstract of the Proceedings of a Meeting of the Council of the Lieutenant-Governor of Bengal, for the purpose of making Laws and Regulations held on Saturday, the 23rd March, 1895," *Judicial and Public Proceedings*, 1895.
68 For example, "Memo from Arthur Howell, Officiating Secretary to the Government of India, Home Department to the Secretary to the Bengal Government of Bengal (no. 5039 dated Dec. 30, 1868), *Sanitation Proceedings* 42–45, General Department, April 1869.
69 Memo of Norman Chevers, Principal Medical College to G. Saunders, Deputy Inspector-General of Hospitals, Presidency Circle (no. 23, dated April 14, 1869), *Sanitation Proceedings* 42–45, General Department, April 1869.
70 Cited in Banerjee, *Dangerous Outcast*, 158.
71 Ibid., 158–160.
72 Arun Nag, *Satik Hutom Penchar Naksha* (Calcutta: Subarnorekha, 1990), 35–36.
73 Ibid., 117. In his descriptions Sinha specifically delineates the places well known for prostitution.
74 "Kaliprasanna Sinha," Brajendranath Bandopadhyay (ed.), *Sahitya Sadhak Charitmala*, vol. 1 (Calcutta: Bangiya Sahitya Parishad, 1986), 20–23.
75 Jogendranath Chattopadhyay, *Khurima ba Prayaschitta*, (Calcutta, 1906), 83–85.
76 Satishchandra Chakrabarty, *Lalana Suhrid* (Calcutta, 1924; first publication 1889), 16.
77 Bhudev Mukhopadhyay, *Paribarik Prabandha* (Calcutta: Bhudev Publishing House, 1921), 15–17.
78 Ibid., 37–38.
79 Mukhopadhyay, *Achar Prabandha*, 172–173.
80 Mukhopadhyay, *Paribarik Prabandha*, 46–47, 91, and passim.
81 Ibid., 21.
82 Dr. Ajij Ahmed, *Lalana Suhrid (Gahrastha Niti)* (Chakbere: Amiya Prakashan, n.d.), 83.
83 See Uma Chakrabarty, *Condition of Women in the Second-Half of the Nineteenth Century* (Calcutta, 1963); Ghulam Murshid, *Reluctant Debutante: Response of Bengali Women to Modernization 1849–1905* (Rajshahi: Rajshahi University Press, 1983); Meredith Borthwick, *The Changing Role of Women in Bengal 1849–1905* (Princeton: Princeton University Press, 1984); Malavika Karlekar, *Voices from Within: Early Personal Narratives of Bengali Women* (Delhi: Oxford University Press, 1993).
84 For detailed description of such housework in an upper-class household see Purnima Devi, *Thakurbarir Gaganthakur* (Calcutta: Punascha, 1999).
85 Mukhopadhyay, *Paribarik Prabandha*, 233.
86 Ibid., 187–190.
87 Ibid., 190.
88 Kailash Basini Gupta, *Hindu Abalakuler Bidyabhyash* (Calcutta, 1872), 2.
89 Ibid., 38.
90 Abanindranath Tagore, *Gharoa*, in *Abanindra Rachanabali*, vol. 1 (Calcutta: Prakash Bhavan, 1985), 127.
91 Arun Nag, *Chitrita Padme* (Calcutta: Subarnorekha, 1999), 90–92.
92 Mitra, *Amritala Basur Smriti*, 120.

93 "Deposition of Sm. Nistarini Dassee. In the Privy Council On Appeal from the High Court of Judicature at Fort William in Bengal Between Rai Nundo Lall Bose One of the Defendents Appellant and Sreemutty Nistarini Dassi & Other Plaintiffs and Other Defendents Respondents." Record of Proceedings, Suit No. 311 of 1898. I am indebted to Debashis Basu for loaning this document to me. In this regard also see Gautam Bhadra, "Ekti Paribarer Nathipatra," *Aitihashik* 6, no. 1 (June 1998), 83–125.
94 Deposition of Nistarini Dassee, 533.

Conclusion: the politics of representation

1 W. H. Auden, *Selected Poems*, Edward Mendelson (ed.) (New York: Vintage, 1979), 74.
2 Durgacharan Ray, *Debganer Martye Agaman* (1880; reprint, Calcutta: Dey's Publication, 1984).
3 *Municipal Proceedings*, January–April 1897. File M 1-C/1.1.
4 Ibid.
5 Ibid.
6 Speech delivered at the Bengal Legislative Council, March 19, 1898. Ramchandra Palit (ed.), *Speeches of Babu Surendranath Banerjee*, vol. 6 (Calcutta: S. K. Lahiri & Co., 1890–91), 445.
7 Speech delivered at the Bengal Legislative Council, September 27, 1899. Ibid., 448.
8 *Calcutta Municipality Administration Report*, 1889.
9 Amritalal Basu, *Sabash Athash*, in *Amrita Granthabali*, vol. 2 (Calcutta, n.d.), 4.

Index

Printed in the USA/Agawam, MA
June 22, 2012

566894.032